Region Building
in the Pacific

Pergamon Titles of Related Interest

Dolman   GLOBAL PLANNING & RESOURCE MANAGEMENT:
  Toward International Decision-Making in a Divided World
Feld   WESTERN EUROPE'S GLOBAL REACH: Regional
  Cooperation & Worldwide Aspiration
Feld/Boyd   COMPARATIVE REGIONAL SYSTEMS
Laszlo   RCDC (Regional Cooperation Among Developing Countries)
Nicol   REGIONALISM AND THE NEW INTERNATIONAL
  ECONOMIC ORDER
Tasca   U.S.- JAPANESE ECONOMIC RELATIONS

Related Journals*

BUILDING AND ENVIRONMENT
GEOFORUM
LONG RANGE PLANNING
SOCIO-ECONOMIC PLANNING SCIENCES

*Free specimen copies available upon request.

PERGAMON
POLICY
STUDIES

ON INTERNATIONAL POLITICS

Region Building
in the Pacific

Edited by
Gavin Boyd

Pergamon Press

NEW YORK • OXFORD • TORONTO • SYDNEY • PARIS • FRANKFURT

Pergamon Press Offices:

U.S.A.	Pergamon Press Inc., Maxwell House, Fairview Park, Elmsford, New York 10523, U.S.A.
U.K.	Pergamon Press Ltd., Headington Hill Hall, Oxford OX3 0BW, England
CANADA	Pergamon Press Canada Ltd., Suite 104, 150 Consumers Road, Willowdale, Ontario M2J 1P9, Canada
AUSTRALIA	Pergamon Press (Aust.) Pty. Ltd., P.O. Box 544, Potts Point, NSW 2011, Australia
FRANCE	Pergamon Press SARL, 24 rue des Ecoles, 75240 Paris, Cedex 05, France
FEDERAL REPUBLIC OF GERMANY	Pergamon Press GmbH, Hammerweg 6 6242 Kronberg/Taunus, Federal Republic of Germany

Library of Congress Cataloging in Publication Data
Main entry under title:

Region building in the Pacific

(Pergamon policy studies on international politics)
Includes index.
Contents: TransPacific politics / Gavin Boyd --
Problems of regional development, East Asia /
Gavin Boyd -- Japan's regional policies / Sueo
Sekiguchi -- [etc.]
1. Pacific area--Economic integration--Addresses,
essays, lectures. 2. Pacific area--Foreign
economic relations--Addresses, essays, lectures.
I. Boyd, Gavin. II. Series.
HC681.R43   1981   337.9   81-13844
ISBN 0-08-025985-5   AACR2

Printed in the United States of America

Contents

Preface and Acknowledgements   vii

Chapter

  1   TRANSPACIFIC POLITICS
         Gavin Boyd   1

  2   PROBLEMS OF REGIONAL DEVELOPMENT:
         EAST ASIA
         Gavin Boyd   17

  3   JAPAN'S REGIONAL POLICIES
         Sueo Sekiguchi   53

  4   ASEAN REGIONAL POLICIES
         Gavin Boyd   78

  5   TRANSPACIFIC INTERDEPENDENCIES
         Martin H. Sours   103

X 6   PROBLEMS OF REGIONAL DEVELOPMENT:
         NORTH AMERICA
         Gavin Boyd   143

  7   U.S. AND CANADIAN PACIFIC PERSPECTIVES
         Charles Doran   162

✝ 8   MEXICO'S NORTH AMERICAN AND PACIFIC RELATIONS
         Yale H. Ferguson and Sang-June Shim   184

  9   PACIFIC REGION BUILDING
         Gavin Boyd   234

Index   277

About the Contributors   281

Preface and Acknowledgments

This volume is addressed to political leaders, government officials, managers of national and international firms, and academics, in both East Asia and North America. All are urged to agree that there should be wide-ranging cooperation between the open market economies bordering the Pacific, and principally between Japan, the United States, the members of the Association of Southeast Asian Nations (ASEAN), Mexico, and Canada. To make such cooperation possible, concerned individuals are encouraged to support the work of associations dedicated to the promotion of policy harmonization between Pacific governments. The largest and most active of these associations is the Pacific Basin Economic Council, whose top figures in Japan and the United States are providing excellent leadership for transPacific business and government collaboration.

East Asian-North American policy coordination, it is hoped, will contribute to the evolution of a Pacific Community. A case for the formation of such a community is presented, with reference to Japanese, U.S., ASEAN, Mexican, and Canadian interests, as seen in the context of economic and strategic forecasts for the regional groupings on each side of the Pacific. The contributions to this volume reflect differences of view and approach, but these should not obscure the logic of the common theme, namely, that Pacific cooperation must be fostered by nongovernmental groups. This line of strategy holds possibilities for integrative activity at a more advanced level than was possible at first in the European Community.

The preparation of this book was made possible with generous support from the Center for Asian Studies at Arizona State University, Tempe, Arizona, where I was a Visiting Professor for the 1980/81 academic year. I profited greatly from stimulating discussions with the Director, Sheldon Simon; with associates of the Center, especially Robert Youngblood; and with Patrick McGowan, Chairman of the Political Science Department.

Gavin Boyd

1 TransPacific Politics

Gavin Boyd

In the contemporary literature on international politics the most important theme is the imperative to manage the complex interdependencies between the industrialized democracies more effectively and in the general interest. The open political economies of these states are becoming more closely linked, with the growth of transnational production and international trade, and the functional connections between their domestic and foreign economic policies are becoming tighter. Their current degrees of cooperation in trade, investment, and monetary policies, however, result from bargaining that does not sufficiently engage with issues of common interest. Mixes of liberal and neomercantilist international behavior are producing an international political economy in which unequal gains from trade and transnational investment are increasing disparities between the more vigorous, more integrated national economies and the weaker ones.

The most significant collective endeavors to manage interdependencies are occurring in the European Community. Policy integration in this group of states is substantial and is increasing, although incrementally and disjointedly. The Community's relative success demonstrates that feelings of regional identity, shared by geographically related states, can provide a basis for development of a common political will to manage interdependencies and to broaden the scope for their evolution.

The European Community is a challenge for industrialized democracies elsewhere. The United States and Japan are the most important of these democracies, and both confront very complex choices regarding the Community, their own neighbors, and their mutual relations. The Community tends to assert its interests quite firmly in dealings with the United States and Japan, especially on matters of reciprocity concerning access to its large market. In the North American context there are growing requirements for

1

cooperation between the United States, Canada, and Mexico, especially with regard to energy and trade. In East Asia, rapidly growing economic bonds between Japan and the Association of Southeast Asian Nations (ASEAN) are making policy coordination within that group and between it and Japan highly desirable. At the same time the very active trade and investment links between the United States and Japan are calling for more extensive joint regulation, not only in the interests of these two states but also for the benefit of their neighbors on each side of the Pacific.

Three related areas of foreign economic issues thus demand attention in U.S. and Japanese policy planning and in the research of concerned international scholars working on designs for regional and transregional systems. In the North American, East Asian, and trans-Pacific contexts there is scope to promote integrative activity in line with the neofunctional logic of the founders of the European Community. They envisaged that significant initial ventures in regional economic cooperation would yield benefits sufficient to motivate wider collaboration. These expectations were substantially validated, although an unanticipated upsurge of French nationalism under de Gaulle seriously hindered progress toward economic integration.

The configuration of the North American group of states is much less favorable for integrative activity than that of Western Europe in the early 1950s, when the first stage of the European Community was launched. The East Asian configuration is even less favourable, and transPacific cooperation is hindered by vast distances and major contrasts between the North American and East Asian cultures. There is, however, a complex and extensive congruence of interests between the United States and Japan, and their neighbors on which Pacific collaboration can be planned.

PACIFIC RELATIONS

The Pacific Ocean is a vast expanse separating the North American states from those of East Asia. The bridging of distances across this ocean through communications and trade is not assisted by cultural affinities like those that aid understanding and cooperation across the Atlantic. The Pacific trade and investment flows, however, are large factors in the total pattern of exchanges within the international political economy. In magnitude they rank next after those between the North American states and the European Community. The Pacific interchanges, moreover, are growing relative to those in the Atlantic pattern, because of the great vitality of the Japanese economy and the rapid development of the East Asian states into which the Japanese industrial establishment is expanding. Japan's exports to the United States in 1978 totaled $25,357 million, that is, only about $5,000 million less than the exports of the European Community to the United States, and more than double West Germany's. The European Community's exports to the United States, Canada, and Mexico in 1978 were $35,231 million, while exports to those North American states from Japan, South Korea, Hong Kong, Taiwan, the ASEAN states, Australia, and New Zealand totaled $54,562 million.   Figures for transnational production are not available, but these are known to be very large in the Atlantic pattern, chiefly because of the great volume of goods produced in Western Europe by America-based firms, through subsidiaries or in joint ventures.(1)

As terms common in the language of diplomacy and commerce, North America and East Asia identify groups of states in geographic proximity and carry certain implications regarding the effects of such relatedness. States in these and other geographic clusters tend to have some cultural affinities, they tend to trade more with each other than with distant countries as their economies grow and diversify, and they usually develop a consciousness of regional identity. Such an awareness often becomes a basis for cooperation in dealing with "outside" states and for consulting on matters of common interest within the grouping. This is not to deny that neighboring states in many parts of the world have long histories of mutual antagonism. Economic, political, and social development, however, do increase possibilities for collective rationality, and, while raising levels of interdependence, facilitate advances in communications that shorten distances in the immediate environment.

All terms that designate clusters of geographically related states have great richness and complexity for area specialists.   To such experts, then, each configuration of national attributes, cultural and political affinities, and foreign policy orientations in regions such as Western Europe and Latin America is totally unique. Area specialists thus tend to be very conscious of the factors that hinder the growth of regional cooperation, especially insofar as they sustain each national administration's emphasis on preserving its autonomy and advancing its own interests. In addition, area specialists can fail to appreciate the comparative significance of the characteristics of the regions they study, because of a lack of interest in other groups of states, although comparative studies can direct attention to factors that have positive significance for ventures in regional collaboration.(2)

Instructive contrasts in levels of cooperation are evident within the clusters of geographically related states on the world scene. The European Community is a relatively advanced international system, in which interdependencies are managed collectively, for the common benefit, although somewhat to the advantage of the stronger economies. In Latin America moderate levels of subregional and regional collaboration have been reached for short periods, and, although the resolution of the participating states has fluctuated, fairly extensive awareness of the need for cooperation tends to motivate renewed attempts to develop viable schemes for trade liberalization and complementary industrial development.(3) In East Asia, subregional cooperation has developed on a small scale within the Association of Southeast Asian Nations.

Differences in levels of regional cooperation are related to differences in levels of national political and economic development, but such development in any group of states is not a sufficient condition for the growth of integrative activity. Advanced states, as has been stressed, need partnership in macroeconomic policies with other advanced states for effective management of their political economies. Social progress in these advanced states, moreover, tends to increase public awareness of the need for cooperation and moderates antipathies towards neighboring countries that derive from nationalist, communal, and other affective factors. Yet in several respects the political processes of industrialized democracies can restrict cooperation with advanced neighbors. The industrialized democracies shape their foreign economic policies under the pressures of strong interest group pluralism, and the decision processes are mostly incremental, disjointed, and narrowly focused, especially in the light of each executive's political interests. Policy coordination with other industrialized democracies is sought competitively, rather than with integrative intent, and with sensitivities to disparities in bargaining power and uncertainties about the behavior of the other administrations.(4)

Great differences in bargaining power of course can have quite negative effects. Small neighbors of a large industrialized democracy will tend to limit cooperation with it in order to avoid accepting greater dependencies, and will also tend to be guarded in their collaboration with each other because of a lack of mutual trust. Large states can benefit more from dealing with small states individually than would be possible in a multilateral context, and thus can be disinclined to support ventures in regional cooperation.

In the North American context there is little regional cooperation, and this state of affairs reflects aspects of each national policy process, especially as influenced by disparities in size and economic power. U.S. foreign economic policy is strongly affected by interest group pluralism, which tends to cause incoherence in trade and investment matters. Canada and Mexico deal guardedly with the United States, because of their weak bargaining power, and collaborate with each other only to a minor degree.

In East Asia the members of the Association of Southeast Asian Nations are closely related geographically but restrict their mutual cooperation because of culturally based antipathies and distrust, and are reluctant to enter into arrangements for substantial cooperation with Japan. That country's foreign economic policy is highly coherent and functional, and this, together with its great bargaining power, tends to make the ASEAN governments very cautious in their dealings with Tokyo.

The possibilities for transPacific cooperation are limited because of the absence of substantial collaboration in the North American and East Asian contexts. Of course if such collaboration developed it could take forms that would make transPacific interdependencies more difficult to manage, but if such difficulties could be prevented the prospects for transPacific cooperation would be improved. Cooperation within the North American and East Asian patterns, however, need not assume large proportions before transPacific collaboration becomes more comprehensive. The major disparities in size and bargaining power within both contexts will remain serious hindrances to integrative ventures, but, if the states in both groups begin to form a Pacific community, the inhibiting effects of the differences in bargaining power may be reduced by the multilateralism of the larger setting, especially if solidarity is fostered between the smaller states.

Of the Pacific nations, the United States has the widest scope for transregional initiatives because of its size and its capacities to relate to and influence its immediate neighbors and the East Asian states. Significant levels of understanding, trust, and goodwill are maintained in U.S. dealings with Japan, South Korea, the ASEAN states, and Australia, as well as with Canada and Mexico. The United States, moreover, has a capacity for international leadership, although this is affected by presidential idiosyncrasies and congressional assertiveness. Japan, although a much more unified, coherent, and purposive international actor, has a very distinctive culture that has not yet been sufficiently adapted for communication with other states. Politically, this culture is expressed in highly consensual incremental policy making, but in ways that tend to inhibit leadership.

The United States, of course, is well placed to provide leadership in the Atlantic context as well as in Pacific relations. Much of the literature on the international political economy concerns policy options for the United States vis-a-vis Western Europe. The United States has strong economic incentives to work for close cooperation with the European Community, especially because most of its overseas investments are concentrated in Western Europe. U.S. interaction with most of the Community members, moreover, is facilitated by cultural affinities. Yet the Community is relating to the United States more and more on a competitive basis, and its members are not inclined to support the development of an Atlantic system for the management of common interests. Community politics has an inward-looking quality, because of the diversity of intra-Community issues affecting each member and the necessity for broad consensus for settlement of these issues.(5)

Japan relates to the European Community across very long social distances, and, lacking acceptance within that grouping, can look only to the United States for substantial partnership in macroeconomic policies. This state of affairs, together with Japan's significance as the core member of a group of East Asian states with high growth rates, gives great importance to the U.S. Pacific options. Japan is implementing a vast strategy for the establishment of overseas production bases, especially in the more advanced Southeast Asian states, and the integrated transnational pattern of industrial establishments that is emerging is becoming a major feature of the world economy.(6)

The principal choices open to the United States in the Pacific context concern guiding the evolution of interdependencies regarding trade and investment through joint decisions with neighbors and East

Asian states.   Collective trade liberalization, in addition to simply diverting commerce, can stimulate production for the larger market. Wide-ranging cooperation for the assistance and regulation of direct investment can assist rational specialization in industrial development.

In principle, the United States is committed to the development of a liberal international economic order, in which all tariff and other barriers to trade will be removed.   Mainstream formulations of this concept by members of the business, bureaucratic, and academic elites who shape economic policy envisage little collective management of this future order and imply opposition to the formation of regional trading groups that discriminate against outside states.   The development of such trading groups, however, accords with the perceived interests and preferences of many advanced and developing countries, especially because their administrations are more willing to collaborate with neighbors than with the world at large.   The United States, moreover, has not been in a strong position to obstruct the setting up of new trading groups since its economic performance began to deteriorate after the first oil crisis in the 1970s.   Further, the expansion of the European Community and the gradual increases in its degrees of policy integration are challenging other states to seek association with it or form their own common markets.(7)

The option of participating in the development of new regional trading schemes thus deserves very active consideration by U.S. policy planners, and the most important choice concerns the possibility of developing an economic community with Japan and the East Asian countries into which Japanese production processes are being extended. Japan's interests call for the formation of such a community, especially because it would enhance the stability and growth prospects of affinitive East Asian political economies and would commit the United States to more integrative engagement with transPacific issues. Moreover the developing East Asian countries linked with Japan would benefit from closer association with both the United States and that country, and would not have to contemplate the necessity of accepting greater dependence on Japan alone, because of the dynamism of its economy.

THE GLOBAL CONTEXT

The most important global influences on transPacific relations are in the Trilateral pattern.   These influences are pressures and inducements in the economic diplomacy of West European states, and they have differing effects on the United States and Japan.   They tend to draw the United States into extensive but often inconclusive interactions for the resolution of commercial, investment, and monetary issues, while generally discriminating against Japan.   As U.S. policies are influenced, to Japan's disadvantage, Tokyo is given incentives to increase its bargaining power in relation to the United States, and to compete against the United States in the East-West context by increasing exports of technology to China and the USSR. Japan is the largest exporter to China in the Trilateral group and by strengthening the connection with Peking can to some extent influence Chinese policy and the evolution of Sino-American relations. The United States, meanwhile, lacking full European cooperation on large issues of trade and investment policy, tends to resort to graduated protectionist measures that nevertheless fail to reduce its decline as an actor in the international economic system.(8)

In East-West relations the United States and Japan for the present have secondary roles, except with respect to China. Most of the trade with the Communist regimes is handled by West Germany and France. West Germany is the largest exporter and has strong political and strategic motivations to maintain its lead, especially in order to maximize the effectiveness of its strategy of economic interdependence with the USSR and to promote liberalization in East Germany. Japanese policy is much less friendly to the USSR because of historic antagonisms and Soviet retention of islands seized from Japan in 1945, but is influenced by inducements that the USSR holds out concerning its need for technology to develop its Far Eastern territories. Soviet management of this economic diplomacy has been clumsy and erratic, but the inducements remain significant, especially because of the slow growth in China's economy and the strengthening of the Soviet strategic position in East Asia, at China's expense, since the 1979 Sino-Vietnamese war.(9)

In the north-south pattern the forces that influence transPacific relations are weak, except with respect to the OPEC countries. The ASEAN members and Mexico are associated with Third World demands for Trilateral acceptance of a New International Economic Order, in which the primary export earnings of developing countries will be raised and stabilized, and in which foreign assistance programs will be increased. The primary external concerns of the ASEAN states and Mexico, however, are their own terms of trade with Japan and the United States. The price exactions of the OPEC states have major effects through the transPacific pattern, and impose severe strains on Japanese and U.S. economies. Mexico and Indonesia are secondary oil exporters within the pattern, and their presence would make it possible to evolve a common energy policy for the Pacific, but thus far there have been no initiatives to develop such a policy. U.S. attempts to promote an energy policy for the industrialized democracies have concentrated on Western Europe, with little success.(10)

The main international influences on the transPacific pattern, then, are those of the European Community and the OPEC members, and for the present they tend to cause strains rather than increase cohesion in U.S.-Japanese relations. West European discrimination in commercial policy tends to antagonize both the United States and Japan but, together with the collusive pricing of the OPEC countries, stimulates Japanese competitiveness and drives for greater efficiency, thus indirectly adding to the tensions in U.S.-Japanese relations. In partnership, the United States and Japan could meet the challenges from the European Community and OPEC much more effectively than is possible for either at present. The combination of U.S.-Japanese bargaining power would be very powerful, and, while each state's vulnerability to OPEC pressures would be reduced, the West Europeans could be induced to trade on more favorable terms. This, however, is not to deny that the management of a U.S.-Japanese economic alliance would be difficult for each side. There would continue to be major asymmetries between each nation's involvement in the international political economy, and each administration's external policy would be subjected to very differing internal and external pressures. Problems of advanced political development, moreover, would affect the quality of Japanese and U.S. economic policy. Leadership in the Japanese system tends to be inhibited by the very strong orientation of the political culture toward widely consensual and incremental policy making. In the United States the pronounced individualism of the political culture makes for leadership assertiveness, but also for institutional weaknesses and aggregating failures that contribute to pluralistic stagnation and incoherence.(11)

TWO REGIONAL SYSTEMS

The transPacific pattern of relations is heavily dominated by the interactions between Japan and the United States because the smaller states in East Asia and North America have done little to expand their ties with their immediate neighbors and with their counterparts across the Pacific. Canada and Mexico have been absorbed in the problems of their unequal relationships with the United States and have failed to diversify their foreign economic connections. Mexico sends roughly three-fifths of its exports to the United States, and 75 percent of Canada's sales are to the United States; there is little trade between Canada and Mexico or between these two countries and the states of East Asia, except for Japan. Canada's exports to Japan are larger than those of any West European state and are about half of those from Australia and New Zealand. The ASEAN states, while conducting about 26 percent of their trade with Japan, and about 20 percent with the United States, have little commerce with Japan and Mexico.

In the North American context the most prominent factor is the hegemonic position of the United States. Because of the great size of its economy and its geographic situation, the United States exerts strong influence on Canada and Mexico, while dealing with each bilaterally. As little cooperation has developed between these two smaller states, issues that have arisen in relations with them have had only moderate salience for the United States. With the weakening of the U.S. role in the international economy during the 1970s, however, questions of cooperation with its immediate neighbors have become more significant. Yet thus far no policy design for North American collaboration has emerged. The evolution of such a design, of course, would be hindered by the strong pluralism of the U.S. policy process, and especially by the congressional assertiveness on external issues that developed in the 1970s.(12)

East Asia is a larger and more complex cluster of states, in which Japan's position is central but not hegemonic. The ASEAN states, South Korea, and Taiwan have more diversified external economic ties than Canada and Mexico, although their bonds with Japan are growing faster than their other foreign economic connections. They are less vulnerable to leverage by Japan, despite its great bargaining power, than the small North American states are to U.S. pressures. There is some solidarity in the ASEAN group, although theirs is a loose association, and the United States' rather active economic competition in dealings with these states and with South Korea and Taiwan imposes limitations on Japan's influence. Chinese and Soviet involvement in East Asia, moreover, obliges Japan to be cautious about asserting its interests.

The ASEAN states, because of their rich endowments, their rapidly developing economies, and their substantial trade and investment links with Japan, attract much interest in Tokyo's regional policy. Japan needs strong ties with East Asian states that can offer assured supplies of raw materials and provide suitable locations for overseas production bases. The ASEAN governments seek Japanese investment but tend to be apprehensive and resentful at the growing Japanese economic presence in their societies.

China adds complexity to the East Asian context for Japan and the ASEAN members. Peking has a strong interest in expanding commercial ties with Japan and the ASEAN states but shows ideological hostility to all non-Communist societies and experiences intraelite conflicts that could well result in a shift to leftist policies. Most Japanese leaders see a need to strengthen bonds with China, especially through technology transfers, in order to reduce the danger of a possible Chinese shift to the left, as well as to retain access to the Chinese market. For the ASEAN governments China is not a major trading partner but is a security problem, because Chinese support is given to local revolutionary groups that are endeavoring to build up campaigns of political violence. China is also an unwelcome rival for U.S. attention, yet has moved into a weaker strategic position in relation to the USSR since failing to coerce Vietnam into withdrawal of its forces from Cambodia early in 1979.(13)

The East Asian pattern of relations is linked with that in North America chiefly through U.S.-Japanese interactions, but also through U.S. dealings with China. These influence and are affected by the Sino-Japanese connection and by interchanges between the USSR, China, Japan, and the United States.

The United States interacts with Japan mainly over economic issues of high salience for each side. The levels of understanding and goodwill are moderate, and the exchanges are constant and extensive, ranging over numerous trade and investment issues and involving many bureaucrats and legislators. The issues posed are due to the superior unity, vigor, and competitiveness of the Japanese economy and to the cultural factors that limit its receptivity to foreign products. On the U.S. side there are tendencies to resort to drastic pressures in order to reduce trade imbalances with Japan, and these pressures tend to be more severe than those used by the European Community in order to reduce its normally large imbalance in trade with the United States.

Security issues are involved in the U.S.-Japan relationship, as the United States endeavors to encourage higher defence spending by Japan in order to reduce the need for U.S. deployments in the West Pacific. For the present the Japanese economy benefits from a low level of military spending, which was set as a rather firm precedent during the 1960s when Chinese-influenced leftist groups in Japan were vigorously opposing the revival of the nation's armed forces. The U.S. desire is to have Japan associated with the modified security role that the United States has assumed in Southeast Asia since the end of the Vietnam War. Japan, however, has been sensitive to the uncertainties in U.S. external security policy that were evident under the Carter administration, as well as to the more fundamental problems that affect that policy because of congressional assertiveness.(14)

U.S. dealings with China are less active and evidence much more ambivalent behavior on each side, attributable to low levels of understanding and trust, and mutual perceptions of uncertainties. The interchanges deal more with security and political issues, but rather obliquely, because of problems caused by the Chinese value orientation and communication styles, and by a somewhat manipulative attitude on the U.S. side. The principal Chinese aim is to encourage stronger U.S. opposition to Soviet global ambitions, but the main U.S. purpose is to develop an association with China that will persuade the USSR to accept genuine detente. The intention, it seems, is that such a favorable shift in Soviet international behavor will be rewarded by technology transfers and by reduced U.S. emphasis on the China connection. This approach, however, has stimulated rather than restrained Soviet conflictual behavior. Moreover, the connection has become more difficult for the United States to manage because of the strengthening of the Soviet strategic position in East Asia after the unsuccessful Chinese attack on Vietnam early in 1979. The United States now has to observe caution about the danger of being drawn into association with provocative Chinese moves that threaten Soviet interests.(15)

The United States does not appear to be coordinating its China policy with that of Japan. At its inception, this China policy was implemented by the Nixon-Kissinger administration without honoring well-established commitments to consult with Japan, and little has been done by subsequent U.S. administrations to restore Japanese trust. Japan thus has to reckon with uncertainties in U.S.-China relations, and opts for a mixed response: while the position Japan has gained as China's main supplier of technology is to be consolidated, there is also a precautionary strategy of expanding economic cooperation with the USSR, although with resentment at the close proximity of the large Soviet military presence.

U.S. interaction with the USSR in the Pacific is linked with the management of superpower relations in the Atlantic and global contexts. The values at risk in East Asia are seen to be much less significant than those threatened by the USSR in the European theatre. To preserve detente in Europe, then, the United States is inclined to caution when responding to forms of Soviet coercive diplomacy in East Asia, as in other parts of the Third World. Moreover, congressional restraints on U.S. security policy, which are often not attuned to strategic realities, tend to have more inhibiting effects on U.S. military statecraft in Asia than in Europe. China, of course, is affected, and expresses strong concern that the U.S. quest for coexistence with the Soviet Union tends to become a form of appeasement.(16)

Because the projection of Soviet power in East Asia has become stronger since 1978 due to the acquisition of Vietnam as an ally and the demonstration of China's military weakness, the United States' need for friends in this area has increased. Yet while the relationship with Japan has been strained by pursuing an independent policy toward China, and by the use of pressures related to the U.S. trade deficit, U.S. connections with the ASEAN states have been rather neglected. Japan also needs friends in East Asia, because the increased security problems posed for the United States by the strengthening of the Soviet position have had adverse implications for Japan's own immediate interests.

DEVELOPMENTAL ISSUES

In the North American, East Asian, and transPacific patterns of interaction there is considerable potential for the development of international systems, in which substantial allocations of values will be negotiated, on a continuing basis, with participatory and distribution arrangements conducive to equity and growth. At present there are several bilateral systems in the three contexts, and among these that of the United States and Japan ranks highest in terms of outputs. These networks of interaction, however, and the others that include many of the smaller North American and East Asian states, are evolving with little overall direction. Incremental and disjointed efforts to manage the configurations of interdependencies are producing a frag- mented pattern, in which high-order values tend to be neglected and the interests of the small states inadequately represented.

The deficiencies in foreign policy management result largely from problems of political development, particularly in the advanced states which manage the most important interactive processes. But planning for the development of more comprehensive and responsible policies often cannot engage issues of national political development and must focus on regional and transregional contexts. The activation of holistic motivations in the political psychology of executives and leaders of interest groups is more feasible in regional and transregional contexts than at the global level because of the effects of social distances on values and normative commitments. Among most political elites, feelings of global identity and obligation tend to be weak. Identification with regional and transregional systems of interaction, however, can develop without difficulty if there is substantial cooperation that increases awareness of interdependencies and rouses expectations of equity and reciprocity.

Shared consciousness of common identity in a geographically related cluster of states is necessary for the development of a regional system, especially because it provides a basis for concepts of obligation to neighbors and of collective self-determination with respect to the management of regional interests and dealing with "outside" states. Such awareness is fostered by the communications and activities of states within a region that express trust, respect, understanding, and goodwill toward neighbors. The acceptance and reciprocation of such forms of external behavior is made possible by social progress and cultural enrichment, which diminishes primordial antagonisms toward other communities and which aids understanding of the needs for transnational communication and exchange in modernizing and postindustrial societies. State and nongovernment efforts to promote regional solidarity and cohesion, however, are often hindered by established popular and elite images of neighboring countries and their governments, especially because these images tend to be perpetuated by parochial socialization processes that are little influenced by cultural advancement. In general, such problems are more serious in East Asia than in North America, as the ASEAN group is in various stages of late modernization, and Japan's culture, as has been seen, is highly distinctive and resistant to interchanges with other societies.

Increasingly frequent interactions between states, occasioned by rising interdependencies, tend to make elites and sections of their societies more knowledgeable about each other. Strains in such interactions, however, which can develop easily as substantial issues of equity arise in trade and investment matters of high salience, tend to make executives, bureaucrats, and legislators more reliant on negative images of other states. This happens in part because national leaders who see the interests of their states challenged by neighboring governments will seek to identify with nationalist feelings that are aroused among their secondary elites, and may well do so with a resolve not to be outdone in displays of patriotism by political rivals. Such tendencies affect the development of understanding and goodwill within the Association of Southeast Asian Nations and have been evident in Latin American schemes for regional cooperation.

The evolution of a normative dimension in regional interactions, especially through the development of shared notions of equity applicable to trade liberalization and industrial complementarity, depends on the growth of regional consciousness, and is influenced by levels of modernization in the national cultures as well as by their mixes of instrumental and consummatory values. Some interpenetration of these cultures tends to develop with modernization, and this process can be given impetus by various forms of transnational communication that transmit meaning and commitment across national boundaries. Political communications that articulate regional interests can be especially potent; in Western Europe after the Second World War they encouraged the growth of a collective will to begin economic integration, and they have had considerable effect in Latin American drives for regional cooperation.   In East Asia they have aided the development of subregional consciousness within the Association of Southeast Asian Nations.(17)

The development of a normative dimension capable of supporting the evolution of a regional system is likely to be more difficult in East Asia than in North America because of the diversity of cultures and the differences in levels of modernization and size.   Producing such a dimension for a transregional system across the Pacific would be quite difficult but would be a feasible objective of political designing, particularly if this envisaged a vigorous leadership role for the United States. One of the main concerns of the political design would be to plan ventures in cooperation that could produce benefits sufficient to reinforce the initial motivations to collaborate, while aiding conciliatory treatment of disputes about the distribution of such benefits.

Equity in the terms of participation in regional interaction and in arrangements for trade liberalization and complementary industrial development will tend to promote the development of a normative dimension in an emerging regional political culture, as is evident in the European Community.   At the same time, efforts by national leaderships to build up such a dimension will help to secure general acceptance of schemes that will allow appropriate representation of national interests in regional decision-making institutions.   Perceived failures in equity, of course, will disturb whatever regional value consensus has been produced, as has happened in the operation of the European Community's common agricultural policy, but if the basic imperatives to manage interdependencies collectively remain strong there is likely to be fairly effective invocation of shared norms to promote concord.(18)

Problems of joint and collective decision making and performance have to be anticipated at various stages in the development of a regional or transregional system.   States accustomed to settling many issues of mutual interest bilaterally, such as the United States and Canada, can be reluctant to reduce the scope for such joint decision making when participating in the development of multilateral networks for collective policy making.   When a sufficiently inclusive collective decision-making system is established, moreover, its operation is likely to be affected by unresolved issues concerning unanimity, consultation, and bargaining, and by the growth and decay of coalitions between the participating states.   A unanimity rule in the European Community makes the decision process very slow and cumbersome, but a Franco-German coalition has provided leadership in recent years.(19)

The main substantive issues in a developing regional or transregional system normally concern the growth of economic cooperation. Laissez-faire market integration, however affected by sectoral bargaining, tends to result in greater gains for the larger and more vigorous economies. Questions of redistribution are thus posed, for settlement through the agreed collective decision-making mechanisms or through direct uses of bargaining power to alter the contexts in which such mechanisms can operate. The problems of redistribution are likely to be greater, of course, in a group of advanced and modernizing states, such as East Asia, than in a region of developed states such as the European Community, and the issues of equity and reciprocity are likely to be more difficult in a transregional context than in a regional trading network. Such issues have been much more intractable in the Atlantic pattern than within the European Community, largely because there is considerable solidarity and cohesion within that community, and much rivalry between it and the United States.

Questions about the distribution and redistribution of gains from trade liberalization would tend to strain transPacific relationships and of course would be very difficult if separate processes of market integration were under way in both North America and East Asia. To the extent that problems of transregional and regional leadership are seen, then, the planning of moves toward trade liberalization will require careful calculations of advantage to reinforce the initial tentative motivations to engage in regional and transregional cooperation.

Designs for regional and transregional economic cooperation, however, will also have to be concerned with the collective regulation and direction of transnational production. The volume of such production is large in relation to trade flows and a substantial proportion of it is production for export from the host country, which entails much intrafirm trade. The enterprises involved may be international in the sense of having few national ties, or they may be distinctly national in their affiliations and loyalties and may be closely related to their home administrations, as is the case with the major Japanese international companies.

The magnitude and complexity of the problems that would have to be dealt with in a design for North American, East Asian, and transPacific cooperation can have discouraging effects on policy planners. The trends that can be projected from the current pattern of interplays between narrowly focused and excessively competitive national policies, and largely apolitical activities by transnational enterprises, have many negative features. On present indications the relationship between the United States and Japan is likely to become more destructively competitive, especially because of the pressures of U.S. firms to increase effective rates of protection against Japanese products entering the U.S. market. Meanwhile, both the United States and Japan can expect to face increasingly severe pressures from the European Community because of the weakening of the U.S. role in the international political economy and because of European resentments at past efforts by the United States to extract trade concessions from the Community. The fortunes of Canada, Mexico, and the ASEAN members will of course be affected by the economic strains in the Trilateral context, but these smaller states will have little opportunity to assert their interests.

Substantial progress toward more inclusive and comprehensive interaction is needed in the transPacific pattern of relations, that is, for order, equity, and development. Planning for such progress, of course, must begin with careful examination of the problems of regional development in East Asia and North America. The very asymmetric interdependencies of these areas set exacting requirements for political designing, and for rational choices by governments to harmonize and integrate their foreign economic policies.

NOTES

(1) See Bernard Mennis and Karl P. Sauvant, Emerging Forms of Transnational Community, (Lexington, Mass: D.C. Heath, 1976); John H. Dunning, ed, The Multinational Enterprise (London: George Allen and Unwin, 1971); and Don Wallace, International Regulation of Multinational Corporations (New York: Praeger, 1976).

(2) For discussions of the influence of area studies, see Lucian W. Pye, ed., Political Science and Area Studies (Bloomington: Indiana University Press, 1975).

(3) See Robert D. Bond, "Regionalism in Latin America: Prospects for the Latin American Economic System," International Organization 22, no. 2 (Spring 1978): 401-423.

(4) See Peter J. Katzenstein, ed., Between Power and Plenty (Madison: University of Wisconsin Press, 1978); and Stephen D. Krasner, "The Tokyo Round: Particularistic Interests and the Prospects for Stability in the Global Trading System," International Studies Quarterly 23, no. 4 (December 1979): 491-531.

(5) See Werner J. Feld, "Western Europe" in Comparative Regional Systems, ed. Werner J. Feld and Gavin Boyd, (Elmsford, NY: Pergamon, 1980), pp. 97-148.

(6) See Terutotomo Ozawa, "International Investment and Industrial Structure: New   Theoretical   Implications   from   the   Japanese Experience," Oxford Economic Papers 31, no. 1 (March 1979): 72-92.

(7) See Alfred Tovias, "Differential Country Size as an Incentive to the Proliferation of Trading Blocs," Journal of Common Market Studies 16, no. 3 (March 1978): 246-266.

(8) See Krasner, "The Tokyo Round."

(9) See Hiroshi Kimura, "Japan-Soviet Relations: Framework, Developments, Prospects," Asian Survey 20, no. 7 (July 1980): 707-725.

(10) See Robert F. Ichord, "Pacific Basin Energy Development and US Foreign Policy," Orbis 20, no. 4 (Winter 1977): 1025-1054.

(11) See Masataka Kosaka, "The International Economic Policy of Japan," in The Foreign Policy of Modern Japan, ed. Robert A. Scalapino (Berkeley: University of California Press, 1977), pp. 207-226; and Between Power and Plenty, cited, chapters 3 and 9. See also obsrevations on policy making in Leon N. Lindberg, "Energy Policy and the Politics of Economic Development," Comparative Political Studies 10, no. 3 (October 1977): 355-382.

(12) See Harvey G. Zeidenstein, "The Reassertion of Congressional Power: New Curbs on the President," Political Science Quarterly 93, no. 3 (Fall 1978): 393-410; and Lee H. Hamilton and Michael H. Van Dusen, "Making the Separation of Powers Work," Foreign Affairs 57, no. 1 (Fall 1978): 17-39.

(13) See Richard H. Solomon, ed., Asian Security in the 1980's: Problems and Policies for a Time of Transition (Santa Monica: Rand Corporation, 1979).

(14) See the symposium on Japanese International Perspectives in Asian Survey, vol. 20, no. 7.

(15) Stronger projections of Soviet power are forecast in Solomon, Asian Security in the 1980's; these may cause the Chinese to intensify their efforts to influence U.S. policy.

(16) See James C. Hsiung and Samuel S. Kim, eds., China in the Global Community (New York: Praeger, 1980).

(17) See Ross Garnaut, ed., ASEAN in a Changing Pacific and World Economy (Canberra: Australian National University Press, 1980).

(18) See Ghita Ionexcu, ed., The European Alternatives (Netherlands: Sijthoff and Noordhoff, 1979).

(19) Ibid.; see also Paul Taylor, "Interdependence and Autonomy in the European Communities: the Case of the European Monetary System," Journal of Common Market Studies 18, no. 4 (June 1980); 370-387.

2 Problems of Regional Development: East Asia

Gavin Boyd

East Asia is a more extensive and more diversified group of states than North America and is more penetrated by outside influences. The relatively large number of states and the contrasts between them, especially in size, cultures, levels of modernization, and political characteristics, are major hindrances to regional and subregional cooperation. Nevertheless several East Asian states, including Japan, have rather positive orientations toward such cooperation. In Southeast Asia, Thailand, Malaysia, Singapore, Indonesia, and the Philippines are loosely united in an Association of Southeast Asian Nations (ASEAN), through which they are gradually liberalizing trade between themselves and are endeavoring to coordinate their industrial policies. Relatively frequent consultations between these states and Japan on trade and investment matters are extending their network and are opening up possibilities for quite productive interaction, despite the asymmetries in bargaining power and interests.

In the North American system, the United States has a hegemonic position, but in East Asia there are two core powers, Japan and China, and their potentials for regional dominance are limited and constrained by numerous factors, including military weaknesses, the policy orientations of the smaller neighboring states, and the involvement of the two superpowers in the politics of this area. The Soviet Union is an active intrusive power, in close proximity; and the United States, although operating at a distance, is very deeply involved in East Asian affairs, on the basis of significant levels of rapport with Japan, South Korea, and the ASEAN group.

An interactive network centered on Japan is the dominant feature of the pattern of East Asian economic relations. Large-scale commercial and capital flows link this country with the ASEAN group, South Korea, Taiwan, and China. The very substantial dependencies of these less developed economies on Japan are managed bilaterally at the governmental and transnational levels, and on the Japanese side locally

17

based international firms operate in close partnership with government agencies including especially the powerful Ministry of International Trade and Industry. Significant proportions of the exchanges in the pattern are movements of goods and investment funds within and between subsidiaries of Japanese transnational enterprises.

The Japan-centered network of economic interactions is penetrated by a similar but less coherent pattern centered on the United States and the principal connecting link is a vast flow of commercial exchanges and financial transactions between Japan and the United States. In this second pattern the less developed East Asian economies dependent on Japan are also dependent on the United States, but at the transnational level the international firms with which they deal are more individualistic than those based in Japan and are much less closely linked with Washington's policies, which tend to be put into effect incrementally, with short-term perspectives.

The two large configurations of economic interactions are managed in relative security because the United States has assumed an extensive regional military role on the basis of bilateral defense understandings with Japan and the ASEAN group, as well as with South Korea and Taiwan. This involvement is strongly opposed by the USSR, from a position of growing strategic superiority and with important location advantages, including the use of base facilities in Indochina. The Soviet Union's regional activity stresses the projection of military power for political purposes, and especially to exert pressures against China for accommodation and against the non-Communist East Asian states for the acceptance of a new regional order that will eliminate the U.S. "imperialistic" presence in the area.

The United States, although an outside power, has very wide scope for constructive interaction within East Asia, especially because of cultural factors that facilitate rapport with most of the ruling elites in the area and because of the possession of large resources for economic and military statecraft. Washington's capabilities for interaction, however, are underused, especially in terms of what would seem to be required for adequate management of the interdependencies and dependencies linking the United States with Japan and the ASEAN members.

REGIONAL CONFIGURATION

The East Asian pattern of relations is imbalanced, penetrated, and modestly productive. Within this pattern Japan is the most energetic and coherent actor, but relates to smaller and less developed political economies whose mutual bonds are too weak for collective decision making. The involvement of the United States, while constructive, is on a scale that would influence each East Asian state's perceptions of its choices if regional cooperation became feasible. The governmental and transnational interchanges of the region are expanding and diversifying its interdependencies and dependencies, but engagement with the issues they pose is limited because of the bilateral character of most of the interactions and a common tendency to deal only with small and short-term options.

Japan is a highly industrialized and highly integrated democracy, with cultural and structural features that ensure strong government and advanced capabilities for the management of neomercantilist foreign economic policies. The bargaining strength derived from the great size of the country's financial and industrial resources can thus be used with great effect in trade and investment negotiations with all the other East Asian states, as these rank far below Japan, in terms of gross domestic products and foreign commerce. Any use of leverage by Tokyo is gentle and cautious, but the size and dynamism of the Japanese economy tends to cause fears that it will increasingly dominate the region.

Japan's powerful economic position is sustained principally through trade with and investment in countries outside East Asia, that is, through large-scale involvement in the global economy, which is beyond the capacity of the nation's small neighbors. The resulting imbalance in industrial capacities and in the resources for investment and trade could be reduced through the formation of strong coalitions between the small modernizing East Asian states, but there is little cohesion between these minor actors in the regional pattern. The ruling elites of the ASEAN members show significant awareness of their common interests, but levels of rapport and trust between them are moderate to low, and their outlooks tend to be deeply affected by problems of generating domestic support, in conditions made difficult by institutional weaknesses and factionalism.

The absence of solidarity between the small modernizing East Asian states and their general avoidance of close ties with Japan partly explain the high degree of U.S. involvement in this region. The penetration is cooperative and diffuse but shows disjointedness and low coherence attributable to pluralistic decision making. Altogether the political factors that affect this involvement are quite favorable; the most important is China's interest in the United States as an adversary of the USSR, and this has influenced the attitudes of Japan and the ASEAN group. Nevertheless the United States operates under major constraints: executive directiveness in foreign economic relations is made difficult by legislative assertiveness and interest group pluralism, and congressional restraints on presidential war-making powers limit the scope for military involvement on behalf of East Asian governments that may be threatened by revolutionary violence.(1)

Soviet penetration of East Asia involves much less interaction with governments than that undertaken by the United States, and more emphasis on the display of armed strength. Economic exchanges have only minor significance in the USSR' diplomacy, and the main thrust is toward influencing the policies of Japan and ASEAN members through continuing changes in their immediate environments. China is also an object of USSR military statecraft but does not resort to significantly accommodative moves, whereas Japan and some of the ASEAN group do attempt limited forms of cooperation that in varying degrees benefit Soviet international objectives and limit the effectiveness of the U.S. security involvement.

Productive exchanges occur mainly within the interactions centered on Japan and the United States; they are primarily bilateral and deal principally with economic issues. On the Japanese side these are managed rather holistically and rationally, in line with a national economic strategy, but on the U.S. side the decision making is incremental and lacks continuity. There is considerable issue avoidance in the relationship between these two large political economies, and, because this relationship is strongly competitive, it gives the smaller modernizing East Asian states some opportunities for bargaining with both Japan and the United States. For these states, however, many of the most important questions are posed at the transnational level, in dealings with Japan- and U.S.-based international firms, and the interactions are highly asymmetrical, because of the vastly superior resources of those enterprises and their wide opportunities to exploit competition between developing states that are seeking to attract investments.

The levels of modernization attained by the various East Asian states largely determine their needs for economic exchange with neighbors and polities outside the region, but of course this is not to suggest that the modernizing political economies of the area are significantly integrated. In most of them the subsidiaries of Japanese and Western international firms are active on a large scale, and enjoy much autonomy, because the regulatory capacities of the host governments are weak. These capacities may indeed remain weak while industrialization proceeds, because international firms have incentives to invest in states that will allow extensive scope for independent operation. Ongoing modernization, however, obliges administrations to evolve more and more comprehensive public policies, including especially industrial and foreign trade policies, and these must respond to the problems of external dependence and interdependence.

The relatively more developed modernizing East Asian states are South Korea, Taiwan, and the ASEAN members. Fairly rapid industrialization is under way in these states, with varying mixes of expansion and diversification by national and international firms, under public policies that differ in comprehensiveness and competence. In terms of these criteria Singapore ranks highest and has the most active international economic exchanges. The authoritarian states in the ASEAN group rank low to medium, as their public policies are affected by the neopatrimonial practices of their ruling elites; rapidly growing involvement in the international political economy is obligating more responsible and more competent management of their dependencies, and of all areas of their foreign economic policies, but is not stimulating better performance.

The less developed modernizing East Asian states are the small Communist regimes and Burma. Each one's involvement in the international political economy is quite minor because of strong autarkic tendencies in their policies, their low levels of advancement, and their slow economic growth. In the regional strategic context, however, the small Communist states have special significance: Vietnam, the principal Soviet client state in the region, dominates Indochina and enables the Soviet Union to maintain a strong presence in Southeast Asia, while North Korea looks to the USSR for military support in the struggle to unify Korea under a Communist regime.

China's level of involvement in the international political economy is approaching that of the more active members of the group of rapidly growing East Asian states, notably South Korea, Singapore, and Indonesia. Large technology imports are assisting the growth of a modern Chinese industrial establishment, parts of which are exporting light manufactures to finance further development.   High degrees of control are exerted over the regime's external economic dependencies, but the self-reliant policy that is at the basis of this control precludes engagement   in   schemes   for   regional   economic   cooperation. Strategically, China is important in the regional configuration as an adversary of the USSR engaging in limited military cooperation with the United States, and as a state hostile to Vietnam.

SOCIETIES AND CULTURES

The East Asian states differ in levels and patterns of modernization, and degrees of social integration. The more industrialized and more rapidly growing states, which are developing more substantial and more diversified links with other relatively advanced political economies, are promoting growth on a basis of private enterprise, in the context of dependency relationships that in several respects hinder comprehensive economic development. The less industrialized and slower growing states in the region, on the periphery of its economic interactions, are committed to forms of socialist modernization. In most of the modernizing states of the first group, laissez-faire economic policies under strongly self-interested authoritarian governments contribute to fairly rapid growth, with societal strains due to distribution inequities. In the second group of states, weak command economies are growing slowly, and social strains are resulting from extreme forms of political repression.

Japan, the fastest growing political economy in the world, is the mostly highly modernized nation in East Asia. Its transition from feudalism has been rapid, with selective absorption of values from the West.   Contemporary Japanese society has a more autonomous and more distinctive culture than the other industrialized democracies and experiences less social and political strain.   The vigor of the national culture provides considerable insulation against the penetration of destabilizing influences from the outside world, and great achievements in the promotion of economic growth have been raising living standards toward the highest levels of the older industrialized states.

Japanese culture gives individuals strong orientations toward the service of group, community, and national well-being and toward the acceptance of a very hierarchical authority structure that will realize and allocate social values. In the political process, decision making is consensual, and very active roles are played by middle-level officials, under a primary elite that presides over rather than directs the exercise of collective choice by bureaucrats in consultation with legislators and interest group leaders. There is a highly potent mobilization of social energies by the administration and by enterprises throughout the vast private sector, together with an intense stimulation of creative skills at all levels. Some social tensions are present because welfare concerns have been neglected in public policy management during the postwar economic recovery, but this failing is being overcome by more equitable allocations in response to popular pressures.(2)

All of Japan's neighbors except the USSR are late modernizing societies in which traditional cultures are being penetrated by influences from the highly industrialized nations, depending on their degrees of openness to the outside world. In general the external influences are tending to politicize all social strata, especially in the urban areas, stimulating assertions of interest and demands for accountable administration.   Long-established value orientations, however, mostly associated with traditional beliefs, are responsible for passive acceptance of authoritarian government by the bulk of the population in most of these other East Asian states. Industrial growth is contributing to the politiciziation of the urban areas, especially by increasing the size of the middle and working classes, expanding the gaps between them, and strengthening the presence of foreign-based international firms.   Autocratic administrations tend to resort to more and more repressive measures in order to contain the growing popular pressures for representative government, and for this purpose can take advantage of the passivity of their rural populations.

The Confucian traditions of Taiwan, South Korea, and of the Chinese minorities of Southeast Asia have been conducive to acquiescence in strong government, but, because of an emphasis on the duties of rulers, have been open to the influence of democratic ideas. These traditions, moreover, have been receptive to and adaptable to the requirements for modern technological and administrative development – more so than other long-established belief systems in East Asia. Thailand's Buddhist culture has been considerably less compatible with imperatives to modernize because of its fatalism and stress on renunciation and withdrawal rather than achievement; but it has accepted the penetration of Western values without serious strain because of the absence of anticolonial nationalism, as this country did not experience foreign rule.   In Malaysia the Islamic culture of the dominant ethnic group has been somewhat more open to modernization, partly because of the influence of a relatively enlightened form of colonialism, and, through that experience of foreign rule, has been penetrated – much more than Thai society – by Western concepts of individual rights and responsible government.

Indonesia's traditional culture is divided by a deep cleavage between the abangan societies of Central and East Java, in which Islamic and Hindu elements are mixed, and the orthodox Islamic santri of West Java and the other islands. Within each of these two major groupings are modernizing and more tradition-oriented segments, and their outlooks have been affected by experiences of repression and exploitation under Dutch colonial rule and of blatant corruption and mismanagement by civilian administrations during the first two decades of independence. Arbitrary rule by a neopatrimonial military elite is accepted by the bulk of the population, especially among the abangan, as most of the army leaders are drawn from their cultural grouping and evidence shared antipathies toward the santri.(3) The acceptance of modernization by the abangan, however, tends to be hindered by forms of mysticism that derive from the Hindu elements of their tradition, while among the santri it is affected by feelings of obligation to impose orthodox Islamic beliefs in all areas of national life.

Philippine society has been deeply penetrated by Western values during the long Spanish colonial period, in which the bulk of the population converted to Catholicism, and the short experience of U.S. rule, which was marked by the introduction of universal education and the development of political institutions for highly autonomous government. The political culture has been profoundly influenced by democratic ideas, but it gives all forms of political behavior a strongly personal character which is conducive to the growth of clientelism. The development of large political organizations is thus made difficult, and accordingly the fragmented character of Philippine society prevents the development of strong resistance to authoritarian rule. General orientations toward the imperatives of modernization, however, are more positive than in any of the other Southeast Asian states.

Clientelism is not peculiar to the Philippines – it is quite pervasive in the other authoritarian ASEAN states, as well as in South Korea and Taiwan – but in the Philippines it has had more seriously negative implications for the development of political parties than in Malaysia and Singapore, the only other East Asian polities that have been rather deeply penetrated by Western notions of democracy. Clientelist practices by the ruling elites in the authoritarian East Asian states of course tend to increase social cleavages by alienating the large disadvantaged sections of the population, and, in certain cases, by intensifying ethnic, religious, linguistic, and other differences.

Overall, the degree of social integration is higher in Thailand and the Philippines than in Malaysia and Indonesia. Malaysian society is sharply divided into Malay and Chinese communities, and Indonesian society is fragmented by ethnic and cultural divisions that complicate the primary cleavage between the abangan and the Santri. Thailand has a high degree of ethnic and cultural homogeneity, and this persists despite cleavages that tend to develop because of the alienating effects of military rule. In the Philippines ethnic differences are minor, and the effects of longstanding cultural and linguistic divisions have been greatly moderated by the broad social changes introduced during colonial rule.

Class tensions generated by laissez-faire industrialization, with large-scale participation by international firms, are serious in the Philippines, Indonesia, and Thailand. The authoritarian administrations in these states exert strong pressures on the industrial workers in order to hold down labor costs, so as to attract foreign capital, and their heavy reliance on such capital results in imbalanced growth, with inflationary pressures generated by the channeling of international investment into import-substituting manufacturing. Competent management of the social and economic problems associated with foreign direct investment is evident only in Singapore and Malaysia, and in the latter state administrative bias against the Chinese community is a source of social tension.

The forms of socialist modernization that are being imposed in China, Vietnam, and North Korea are intended to produce drastic changes, of unproven viability. Their consequences are much less visible than those of the modernization processes in the more open East Asian states, but it is clear that the attendant social strains are significant. In each of these states the adaptability of the Confucian culture to imposed socialist values has been affected by severe regimentation and by the mobilization of large numbers of people for vindictive campaigns against alleged class enemies. In China, where the vast scale of the attempted social changes has given them great importance for the entire region, the value orientations of the intelligentsia have been divided and somewhat confused by acutely controversial issues concerning the realization of revolutionary ideals in the modernization process.(4) Thus far Vietnam's socialist modernization has not been affected by such issues, and is being aided by motivations deriving from intense nationalism, but it involves heavy dependence on the Soviet Union, and this is a potentially serious source of social and political tensions. North Korea's gradual transformation into an industrialized revolutionary state is further advanced than Vietnam's, and there have evidently been no serious intraelite tensions that would affect its social consequences; economic aid is being received from both China and the USSR, however, and this may be causing some social disorientation.

Regionally, the patterns of social and cultural affinity are very limited in extent, and there are no major processes of expansion or interpenetration that are altering the overall East Asian configuration. The two core powers, Japan and China, relate to each other partly on the basis of past cultural affinities, but do not share such affinities with any of the Southeast Asian states. An exception is the Chinese relationship with Vietnam, as the Vietnamese absorbed much Confucian culture during long periods of Chinese rule.

The Peking regime's severe repressions of traditional value orientations and its attempts to build up a revolutionary culture have drastically affected its significance in the regional context, especially with respect to Japan, but the post-Mao shift toward somewhat pragmatic modernization has produced a new limited affinity with that country. Similar new affinities with the more advanced Southeast Asian states have also resulted from the contemporary Chinese policy orientation, but their utilities as bases for interaction are marginal. The new Chinese revolutionary culture is intended to be a vigorous and autonomous expression of radical ideals with a universal appeal, but it has become more distinctly national with the rejection of subordination to the USSR, dating from the early 1960s, and this change has in effect been opposed to the relational implications of the current emphasis on meeting the technocratic requirements of industrialization.

Japan, while changing rapidly into a postindustrial society, has retained the cultural vigor of its society while becoming fairly open to the outside world and thus has maintained the considerable social distances separating it from other East Asian states. Meanwhile the distinctive blends of tradition and modern culture in the ASEAN members have been little influenced by each other, or by Japan. In East Asia as a whole the principal form of cultural change has been extraregional penetration – a more pervasive intrusion of Western culture, principally from the United States, that has expanded the educated English-speaking segments of each national elite. This change has been associated with increases in economic ties across the Pacific, yet these have not been as rapid or as substantial as those that have brought the ASEAN members into close association with the Japanese economy.

POLITICAL ECONOMIES

The various national cultures of East Asia, with their modern and traditional elements, sustain political economies at different levels of development. These political economies affect the national cultures, contributing to both growth and decline, and the two-way relationships are in many cases partly conflicted as well as supportive. The possibilities for institutional evolution and growth are determined to a considerable extent, within each national context, by cultural factors, but are also affected by the overall performance of the different polities.

The Japanese political economy operates in a society whose culture is largely congruent with the polity's functional requirements. The strong societal orientations toward consensual decision making within a hierarchical pattern sustain effective bureaucratic leadership of comprehensive aggregating functions that involve interest groups and the middle and upper layers of the ruling Liberal Democratic Party, while the decision processes within the bureaucratic structures are characterized by extensive consultations and by considerable middle-level autonomy. The authority structure is a form of parliamentary democracy, and continuity in the political process is ensured by the dominant position of the Liberal Democratic Party, a relatively conservative organization identified with the business elite. This party has been in power for more than two decades, and the parliamentary opposition comprises mostly incompatible groups – the Japan Socialist Party, on the extreme left, the Democratic Socialist Party, in the center, and the Komeito, a fundamentalist Buddhist association. Also in opposition is the Japan Communist Party, which has been estranged from the two major Communist powers, but which is improving its relations with the Soviet Union.

The Liberal Democratic Party's leadership is normally factionalized. Prominent figures in these factions contend for the position of Prime Minister, on the basis of capacities to mobilize support within the organization and of promises to cope with policy issues. New cabinets comprise members of the Prime Minister's faction and representatives from other factions that have agreed to give their support in exchange for participation in the top decision-making bodies. Public support for the Liberal Democratic Party fluctuates around 48 percent of the total vote, ensuring narrow majorities that have to be maintained by demonstrating achievements in management of the political economy and by continually adapting policies on the basis of consultations with interested groups throughout society. The party's fortunes were aided by a slightly higher popular vote in the 1980 elections and by shifts to the right in the policies of some of the opposition parties, which indicated that some feasible coalition arrangements could be considered if electoral support for the organization declined. The main opposition group, the Japan Socialist Party, is one of the political associations that has shifted its policy to the right but, for the Liberal Democrats, the Komeito and the Democratic Socialists would be more acceptable coalition partners. The Japan Socialist Party's seats in the lower house are usually about 35 percent of the Liberal Democratic Party's total and have been tending to decrease slowly over the long term. An influential segment of the Japan Socialist Party's leadership has long drawn inspiration from Chinese Communism, and the organization's move to the right in its policy orientation appears to have been attributable in part to the post-Mao changes in China, including Peking's support for Japan's military links with the United States, which the Chinese formerly opposed.(5)

Factional rivalries in the higher levels of the Liberal Democratic Party and fluctuations in its popular support do not affect the consistently high level of achievement in public policy management. This is made possible by long-established customs of accommodative behavior by factions represented in the cabinet, and by the strong roles of government departments in shaping and giving expression to cabinet decisions and in guiding the strategies of large enterprises. Levels of institutional development in the bureaucracy are high and help to sustain the confidence and support of politicians and the leaders of peak economic associations.

Japan's foreign economic relations, accordingly, are managed with a high degree of autonomy, and very effectively. There is little penetration of the decision process by outside influences, and the various bureaucratic, legislative, interest group, and other contributors to that process share commitments to exclude external influences and to act in concert for the advancement of national interests. Trade, investment, and monetary matters are directed by the national administration with high degrees of control over the activities of banks, trading companies, manufacturing enterprises, and extractive firms, while these organizations rely heavily on bureaucratic support and guidance in their domestic and foreign operations. The extraordinary degree of effective economic sovereignty has made it possible for Japan to implement an ambitious strategy of export-led economic growth while overcoming the inflationary effects of rising oil prices. This achievement has been especially significant because the country is poorly endowed with natural resources and is entirely dependent on imported oil.

The high-growth modernizing East Asian political economies contrast unfavorably with Japan, for the most part. Singapore is the only polity with a comparable level of achievement in public policy, but its administration is much less accountable, formally and informally, and has authoritarian tendencies. Malaysia ranks next, in terms of public policy achievement, accountability, institutional development and what may be called collaborative participation, conducive to comprehensive demand aggregation.

In the regional pattern Singapore has only minor significance, because of its small size and atypical combination of structural, functional, and normative characteristics. A form of parliamentary government is heavily dominated by a democratic socialist party that is strongly committed to private sector growth. Almost all the population are Chinese, mostly engaged in trade and industry, and there is a substantial Western and Japanese economic presence, attracted by investment opportunitites. The administration demonstrates vigorous application to problems of distribution and infrastructure development, and to the mobilization of general support through community projects. Substantial manufacturing for export is ensuring rapid economic diversification and high growth rates. Bureaucratic competence is an important element in this polity's overall achievements, but the roles of government departments are less powerful than in Japan, and leadership functions at the primary elite level are less diffuse, as there is a considerable concentration of power in the hands of Prime Minister Lee Kuan Yew.

Malaysia has a system of parliamentary government that is controlled by a political party identified with the dominant ethnic group, the Malays. Small parties drawing support mainly from within the Chinese community are induced to collaborate with the leading Malay party. The principal concerns of this organization are to strengthen the political power and what is felt to be the rightful cultural dominance of the Malays, and to improve the education and living conditions of the Malays, so as to reduce disparities between them and the economically dominant Chinese. A related concern is to strengthen the influence of the Islamic religion within the Malay community; this is attemped with considerable zeal by communally minded leaders whose roles in the leadership of the administration have become fairly strong over the past ten years.

The Malay-dominated government allocates relatively large resources to rural development and to redistribution policies, in line with its concerns for its own ethnic group. This group makes up the bulk of the agricultural population, and overall that large part of Malaysian society has higher living standards than their counterparts in the authoritarian ASEAN states. Support for the administration thus tends to be very extensive among the Malay population, but large numbers of Chinese feel resentment at the ethnic bias against them in the government's redistributive measures. The fragmentation of political parties identified with the Chinese community prevents the emergence of strong parliamentary opposition, but frustration with this state of affairs causes some Chinese to opt for a radical solution by joining the underground Community Party. This organization is mainly Chinese and can make strong appeals to their communal feelings, but it has been affected by internal strife associated with upheavals in China, including the Cultural Revolution and the purge of the Maoist elements known as the Gang of Four.

Overall, principally because of the vigor and resourcefulness of the Chinese community, a bureaucracy that has attained a fairly high level of institutional development, and basically rational public policies emphasizing export-led growth, Malaysia is maintaining a high growth rate. The present level of economic discrimination by the Malay leadership is tolerable for the bulk of the Chinese, but there is a grave danger that this discrimination may increase. The economic conditions of the Malays are improving very slowly, especially because they are not responding to educational opportunities provided under the government's redistribution policies, and the influence of communally minded elements in the Malay leadership is evidently tending to increase, partly because of the activities of Islamic revival groups — some financed from Middle East countries.(6)

Thailand, Indonesia, and the Philippines, associated with Singapore and Malaysia as members of the Association of Southeast Asian Nations, are authoritarian states whose levels of performance, institutional development, and integration are medium to low. In each the ruling elite's legitimacy is weak, central control depends heavily on the use of the armed forces, the leadership has little charisma or administrative ability, and there is pervasive high-level corruption. Stability in these states is basically a matter of societal acquiescence rather than equilibrium and is often threatened by intraelite conflicts that reflect failures in consensus building.

Thailand and Indonesia are under military regimes that permit limited political participation through controlled representative assemblies. In each polity the leadership relies heavily on neopatrimonial practices to retain the collaboration of the secondary elite, but these forms of corruption stimulate rather than restrain factional rivalries, erode personal loyalties, prevent the growth of normative commitments, hinder institutional development, and are responsible for mediocre administration. Vicious cycles of authoritarianism, in which new ruling groups display modernizing zeal and then alienate their populations through repression and failures in performance, tend to prevent the emergence of conditions appropriate for competent and accountable government. In each case the degree of societal alienation represents revolutionary potential, and this is especially serious in Thailand because of Vietnam's efforts to supplant China as the main source of external support for the Thai Communist movement.(7)

Thailand and Indonesia are "bourgeois" praetorian systems. The psychology of their military leaders is oriented towards the enjoyment of status and power, personal enrichment, and the promotion of economic growth, with emphasis on the well-being of supportive elements in the middle and upper classes. Few restraints are imposed by commitments to traditional values, or by feelings of obligation to the national welfare. Intense preoccupation with the cultivation of support from colleagues and subordinates of doubtful loyalty affects each leadership's interest in and application to substantive policy issues.

As in most other praetorian systems, the Thai and Indonesian ruling elites' absorption in problems of support mobilization remains intense because of their incapacities to build up institutions for demand articulation, the promotion of consensus, and the provision of more substantial policy outputs. Over time, leadership failures to evolve potent ideological, nationalist, or charismatic appeals are reflected in heavier reliance on neopatrimonial methods of promoting elite solidarity, but these tend to have diminishing results as elite factions emerge and decline and as the potential dangers of the ruling group's lack of societal support are dramatized by the activities of protest groups. Such groups are often provoked by leadership indifference to social justice issues and by severely repressive measures that evidence high-level insecurity and incompetence.

The public policies of the Thai and Indonesian military regimes are negatively affected by neopatrimonialism. Each army leadership adds a large parasitic dimension to its management of trade, investment, and monetary policies and secures favors from international firms that are given generous conditions for manufacturing and trading. As in other Third World dependency relationships, sound administration is made very difficult, despite the efforts of responsible technocrats in each administration and the advice of foreign experts. Economic growth, largely determined by foreign investment patterns that lack coherence, tends to be unbalanced, entails unnecessary social costs, involves losses of economic sovereignty, and is accompanied by alienation of the lower strata of society. Meanwhile considerable emphasis on import-substituting industrialization, providing opportunities for monopolistic and oligopolistic exploitation of local markets by foreign firms, causes inflationary pressures and hinders transition to export-oriented industrialization.

Basically similar failures in public policy are evident in the Philippines, where authoritarian rule is imposed by a single figure who attempts to exercise personalistic and somewhat charismatic leadership in a society that is more intensely politicized than any other in

Southeast Asia. Power is concentrated in the hands of President Marcos, who was originally elected under a system of democratic government, and his administration is backed by the armed forces, whose leadership benefits substantially from the regime's policies. This army leadership will probably be in a position to seize control if there are upheavals that dramatize the President's lack of popular support. Marcos does not project his personality very well, and his appeals for public cooperation are seriously hindered by his government's blatant corruption. As in many other Third World autocracies there is much use of official power to confer favors on large numbers of the secondary elite, while top figures enrich themselves virtually at will. Popular acceptance of the regime is sought through demonstrations of commitment to promote rapid modernization with large infusions of foreign capital, but the benefits of economic growth flow mainly to the middle and upper classes, and severe deprivations are imposed on the workers and peasants. Labor organizations are under heavy pressure from the administration, and strikes are outlawed; the real incomes of urban workers have fallen substantially over the past decade. Inflationary pressures are generated by the monopolistic and oligopolistic practices of firms engaged in import-substituting manufacturing behind high protective barriers, by high prices for imported oil, and by the high administrative costs and low efficiency of the Marcos government.

Foreign investment in the Philippine economy is large and is growing. Inflows come mainly from the United States and Japan and are attracted by generous concessions that contribute to progressive losses of economic sovereignty because of the autonomy enjoyed by the local subsidiaries of international firms and their increasing acquisition of strategic roles in the extractive, manufacturing, and service industries. These foreign interests show little concern at the gross social inequities caused or tolerated by the Marcos government.

Selective repression is used to enforce the administration's authority, and the United States is indirectly associated with this, as it provides arms for the Philippine military establishment. Popular resentments at the repression, together with discontent caused by the regime's economic policies, represent a considerable potential for revolutionary violence. For the present the only active protest movements are groups within the Catholic Church, Moslem insurgents in the South, and a Chinese-inspired Communist organization based in rural areas of Luzon. The Catholic groups exert diffuse pressure for democratic government and represent a major challenge because the bulk of the population is Christian. The Moslem rebels are a localized threat and are concerned mainly with securing autonomy for their community; they have been receiving some external aid, and some of this has come from Eastern Malaysia. The Communist movement is in a position to exploit general hostility to the regime, but its morale and orientation have been negatively affected by China's upheavals and policy changes over the past two decades. Peking's official endorsement of the U.S. military presence in Southeast Asia has tended to hinder the Communist movement's attempts to encourage and utilize anti-U.S. Philippine nationalism.(8)

Outside the ASEAN group, the other high-growth modernizing East Asian states are South Korea and Taiwan. Both have been making rapid economic progress under authoritarian regimes, but South Korea has been experiencing serious political instability, while Taiwan, although placid under the rule of the Chinese Nationalists who lost control of the mainland in 1949, has been seriously disadvantaged by the Carter administration's withdrawal of recognition in 1979 in order to meet the Peking regime's demands for full diplomatic relations.

The South Korean political system is a military dictatorship, with many of the problems of praetorian regimes, including weak legitimacy and low levels of institutional development. The present administration, headed by General Chun Doo Hwan, established in 1979 by a coup following the murder of President Park, is attempting to mobilize popular support by eradicating evils associated with the former Park regime, while contending with strong pressures from student organizations that are agitating for democratic government. The new administration is sponsoring political campaigns to enlist public cooperation but does not have an effective national political organization for this purpose. President Park's Democratic Republican Party had become a very weak organization several years before his death. The main opposition group, the New Democratic Party, which had gained considerable support under the Park regime despite official restrictions, is the principal challenge to the new administration, and for the present is not free to operate.

The new military regime has inherited a bureaucracy that had implemented highly effective economic policies under President Park. Economic growth had been promoted with considerable skill and with fairly active concerns for the welfare of the lower strata of society. During 1980, however, the economy went into a decline because of the political uncertainties that resulted from the murder of President Park and because of the increased burdens imposed by rising oil prices. The prospects for recovery depend heavily on trends in exports to the United States and Japan, which normally constitute nearly 50 percent of South Korea's foreign exchange earnings, and on direct investments from those two countries, which make up the bulk of the nation's capital inflows. Before the decline in 1980 exports constituted about 38 percent of South Korea's GNP.(9)

Taiwan is a one-party state that has begun a transition to representative government. The ruling party is the political organization of the Chinese Nationalist movement dominated by mainland Chinese, but the gradually increasing scope for popular representation will allow more participation in the administration for the local Taiwanese who make up the bulk of the population. The authority of the ruling party is backed by the armed forces, which have been receiving U.S. military equipment for defense over the past 30 years. The outlook and policies of the ruling group are being challenged by the effects of the Carter administration's decision to renege on its obligations to Taiwan and strengthen ties with Peking. The regime's leadership has evidently seen a need to democratize the system in order to draw more sympathy and support from the United States and to cope with ostensibly friendly overtures from Peking. Domestic acceptance of a high degree of continuity in the present administration is being encouraged by a new emphasis on welfare in the regime's policies, which are ensuring, meanwhile, the maintenance of a high growth rate.

An impressive record of industrialization has placed Taiwan high on the list of modernizing Third World states, and rapid growth is being aided by substantial flows of U.S. and Japanese investment. Because of its relative stability and its advanced level of modernization, Taiwan is tending to attract more foreign private capital than most of the other high-growth developing East Asian states. Taiwanese economic progress, however, will be adversely affected if the gradual democratization is followed by vigorous popular agitation for rapid and complete change to a representative system. The danger of such unrest may well be quite serious if the ruling party fails to expand and consolidate its ties with social groups in the Taiwanese community.

The slow-growth Communist political economies of China, North Korea, and Vietnam have political structures based on that of the USSR. In each case a party apparatus exercises virtually absolute power, directly through its own social control organizations, and less directly through a government bureaucracy. Modernization policies are based on socialist beliefs and values and have strong autarkik orientations, but China is attempting to finance industrial development through exports of primary products and light manufactures to non-Communist states and through utilizing credits from international lending agencies, the United States and Japan.

The Chinese regime, because of its great size, overshadows all the small East Asian states, but its significance for them is affected by major uncertainties regarding its stability and policy orientation, because of its recent history of intraelite conflicts and of political campaigns that have affected economic growth. Institutional development and consensus formation of this system have been made very difficult for two and a half decades by acute antagonisms within the upper levels of the Communist party, and the quality of the party and government structures has been seriously affected by the recruitment of large numbers of poorly qualified individuals chosen in the late 1960s and early 1970s on the basis of their support for former party leader Mao Zedong, who stressed revolutionary qualities rather than administrative and technical skills. The post-Mao leadership exercises power with strong military support, and strong army representation in the higher levels of the party complicates a pattern of institutional and personal alignments that may be destabilized by policy issues and succession problems. Policies appear to be decided by a small ruling group that has little interaction with the secondary elite, and many of the members of this group are aged revolutionaries who are evidently reluctant to give up power.(10)

Anti-Soviet nationalism is a powerful social force within the Chinese regime, but there is some ambivalence in its orientation, as the emphasis on revolutionary values during the Maoist period, in opposition to Soviet "revisionism," has been drastically modified by pragmatic recognition of the requirements of technocratic modernization.   In Vietnam, anti-Chinese nationalism is now intense because of resentment at Peking's aggression against the Hanoi regime early in 1980, following the Vietnamese invasion of Cambodia.   The anti-Chinese nationalism reinforces zeal for socialist modernization, and this is unaffected by fears that industrial growth will cause "revisionism," but the Vietnamese regime's strong spirit of independence is in conflict with its heavy reliance on Soviety military and economic support, which has become necessary because of China's hostility.   The dependence may well become controversial, as the collaboration is probably being managed with distrust on both sides, but the Vietnamese polity may be more integrated and more adaptable than the Chinese regime and thus may be able to manage relations with both Communist powers rather effectively, without serious internal strain. North Korea has a political system with a much heavier concentration of power at the top than either Vietnam or China and a higher degree of closure against external influences.   There is intense cultivation of nationalist feelings directed againt South Korea, and, while this is done with political and economic support from both the USSR and China, the leadership evidently has to contend with the effects on its secondary and tertiary elites of the antagonisms between the two Communist powers.   A more immediate source of tension within the regime, however, may be an advance solution that has been devised for a succession problem.   Power is being gradually handed over to the son of President Kim, bypassing older leaders of the regime whose support for this arrangement may not be firm.

DEPENDENCIES AND INTERDEPENDENCIES

The ASEAN members, South Korea, and Taiwan have relatively diversified external dependencies which are being managed with varying degrees of competence.   Most of these states send more than 20 percent of their exports to Japan, and for each this trade is a significant proporation of the GNP.   Considerable quantities of each state's commerce are handled by international firms, and a growing volume of these transactions are intrafirm transfers, often artificially priced to take advantage of tax differences and loopholes.   Between these high-growth modernizing East Asian states there are modest levels of interdependence, evidenced mainly in subregional trade which is well below its potential.   Within the ASEAN group perceptions of common interest relating to this trade and to commerce with Japan are motivating attempts at collective decision making, and these are giving rise to forms of policy interdependence.

Indonesia, the principal oil-exporting country of the region, sends about 50 percent of its exports to Japan, that is, more than twice the proportion reflected in the foreign commerce of the other ASEAN members and South Korea. Djakarta's capacity to bargain with Tokyo on questions of access to the Japanese market is thus fairly weak, and of course the development of an effective political will to engage in such bargaining is hindered by the self-interested pursuits of Indonesian military leaders and the deficiencies of their foreign trade bureaucracy. Indonesia's dependence on Japanese investment is also heavy. The size of the Indonesian market and its relatively strong demand for consumer goods, attributable to the substantial although skewed distribution of high oil revenues, are attracting large Japanese investments into manufacturing ventures. Total Japanese investment is estimated to be more than $4,000 million, that is, about four-fifths of the amount for the ASEAN group as a whole, and two-thirds of Japan's investments in the United States.

The high levels of dependence on Japanese trade and investment call for wide-ranging interaction with Tokyo to ensure diversification and balanced growth in the Indonesian economy. Most of Japan's imports from Indonesia are primary products, and Japanese investment tends to flow mainly into import-substituting manufacturing rather than export-oriented ventures. Djakarta's will and capacity to deal with this problem, however, are weak, and, while the terms of entry and expansion for Japanese international firms remain extremely favorable, the nation's economic growth is assuming more pronounced imbalances and is thus opening the way for wide conflicts of interest between the two governments. These problems, moreover, are tending to become more intractable because of highly potent cultural factors that hinder the assimilation of Indonesians into the management cultures of Japanese international firms. Political risk considerations of course give these firms incentives to maximize their advantages over the short and mid terms, although the social and economic costs for Indonesia are substantial and tend to assume growing political significance.(11)

Outside the Japanese connection, Indonesia's foreign commerce has a low level of diversification. Almost 50 percent of the remaining exports go to the United States, and there is substantial reliance on U.S. capital inflows. The leverage utilized by the United States in bargaining on trade and investment issues, however, is considerably smaller because U.S.-based international firms have more distant relationships with their national administration and cooperate less with each other, and because the general orientation of U.S. foreign economic policy is liberal.

The other ASEAN members and South Korea send 20 to 25 percent of their exports to Japan and roughly comparable proportions to the USA, except in the case of Thailand, which sends to the United States only about 10 percent of its exports. For each of these four high-growth modernizing states, exports to other industrialized countries moderately offset dependence on the Japanese and U.S. markets, but tend to grow slowly, by comparison with sales to Japan, because of stagnation in the West European economies and the growing protectionism of West European administrations. In the cases of Malaysia and Thailand, exports to other Asian countries contribute to further significant diversification (20 to 25 percent of total foreign sales), but for the Philippines and South Korea such exports are relatively low. In the South Korean case total exports constitute about 36 percent of the GNP, and therefore the level of dependence on trade with the United States and Japan is relatively high, but for the Philippines exports amount to only 19 percent of the GNP. Within the ASEAN group the Philippines are relatively isolated, because of apparent neglect of opportunities for trade with neighbors. Thailand's significantly higher level of commerce with other Asian countries has added importance because this state's total exports represent about 22 percent of its GNP. Thailand and the Philippines are thus vulnerable to disturbances in the international market for primary products, as these constitute the bulk of their exports. Within the ASEAN group, however, the highest degree of dependence on export revenue is Malaysia's – 47 percent of GNP. This state's foreign sales show a high degree of commodity concentration, but the level of geographic concentration is moderate, and the Malaysian administration has a superior capacity for managing its foreign commerce.(12)

The ASEAN members, together with South Korea and Taiwan, finance their economic growth largely through export earnings, and, to improve their terms of trade and enlarge their overall external revenues, seek to increase their international sales of manufactured goods, especially to advanced countries. Efforts are made to promote the development of export-oriented national firms, but because of inadequate domestic capital and management resources there is heavy reliance on foreign direct investment, mainly from Japan and the United States. This dependence necessitates caution, and only gradual modification of the very prominent roles that foreign firms have acquired in the export and import trade of most of these countries (especially the ASEAN members), as well as in manufacturing for domestic and external markets. Increases in host-country controls and guidance tend to discourage further foreign investment, and such investment tends to flow to countries offering the most favorable location advantages, including tax concessions and market privileges. The high-growth East Asian modernizing states are thus interdependent as host countries with common as well as competing interests in their dealings with international firms. As there is little cooperation between them for the management of dependencies on transnational enterprises, the location decisions made by such firms depend mainly on comparative market opportunities, the scope for resource extraction, and the quality of each nation's administrative services and economic infrastructure.

The high-growth East Asian modernizing states are also interdependent because of their shared interests in gaining wider access to the Japanese and U.S. markets, and of course in overcoming protectionist tendencies that restrict access to those markets. In the absence of collaboration to bargain with Japan and the United States the problems of access are serious and are tending to increase. They are especially significant for the Philippines, Thailand, and Indonesia, the three authoritarian states that are experiencing difficulties in their efforts to move from import-substituting industrialization to large-scale manufacturing for export.

A further form of interdependence between the high-growth East Asian modernizing states relates to their trade with each other, which is relatively small and is growing only at a slow pace. There is little complementarity between these states as exporters of primary products, and the scope for trade in these is relatively small because their established patterns of commerce, which have been shaped largely by international firms, make them rather heavily dependent on extraregional sources of food and other commodities. Trade in manufactured goods is at moderate levels, as these states are mainly competitors in such commerce, and its prospects are limited by relatively high tariff and nontariff barriers, especially in the Philippines, Thailand, and Indonesia. Within the ASEAN group, some efforts have been made to liberalize trade in manufactures, but with little result.(13)

Outside the group of high-growth modernizing economies China is the most important developing country in the region and influences the pattern of East Asian commerce mainly by importing technology from Japan. Chinese industrialization is financed by exports of primary products and manufactured goods, and within the region these are sent in significant quantities mainly to Hong Kong and Malaysia. The degree of dependence on Japanese support for the expansion of productive capacity is high and reflects both Japan's location advantages and the dynamism of the Japanese economy, but Peking exerts strong bargaining power in the relationship because of the attraction of its large potential market.

Of China's total exports, which are slightly less than those of South Korea, about 25 percent go to Japan and roughly the same proportion are sent to Hong Kong. Sales to the United States and Western Europe constitute approximately another 25 percent, but penetration of these markets is difficult. After Japan, the United States and West Germany are Peking's main sources of technology, and there are large unfavorable balances in trade with each of these nations. The imports are assisted by credits, and those extended by Japan are the most substantial. Peking's foreign exchange earnings are being augmented by international firms which are being encouraged to produce in China for export, but the volume of outside investment that is being attracted is quite small.

The Soviet Union has a minor role in East Asian commerce. The only substantial trade is with Japan, and the flow each way is slightly more than 50 percent of China's exports to and imports from that country. The USSR, however, is endeavoring to utilize Japanese technology for the development of its Far Eastern territories and for this purpose is holding out major inducements.(14) On the Japanese side, interest is conditioned by threatening displays of Soviet military power, the USSR's intransigence on the question of returning the Kurile Islands, and Japan's strongly felt imperatives to maintain friendship with China.

Japan's large and very complex interdependencies with the United States are the most important links between East Asia and the global economy, and the evolution of these interdependencies is affected mainly by the vigor of the Japanese economy and the growth of Japan's bonds with other major trading partners. The interdependencies are largely commercial, in contrast with the mainly production interdependencies between the United States and Western Europe, as the Japanese economy has been relatively closed to U.S. investment, while Japanese international firms have been cautious about entering the U.S. economy.

The high level of trade interdependence has developed principally because of the dynamism of Japanese export promotion and the politically motivated willingness of U.S. administrations to accept deep Japanese penetration of the domestic economy during the fifties, sixties, and seventies. Japan's rapid export-led growth opened the way for large increases in U.S. exports to that country, and it became well established as the largest national market for U.S. products, with imports roughly double those of West Germany from the United States. U.S. imports from Japan were considerably higher, however, because of strong internal demand and a liberal orientation in foreign economic policy, and by the mid 1970s these imports were roughly double the value of U.S. exports to Japan. Earlier substantial deficits in this trade were tolerated by the United States because of security concerns relating to Japan's importance in the East Asian strategic balance, but the magnitude of the unfavorable balances and their significance in the overall U.S. trade deficit caused Washington to exert strong leverage against the Japanese government for export limitations and for the reduction of Tokyo's tariff and nontariff barriers.

The Japan-U.S. trade interdependencies give rise to serious strains because Japanese exports cause severe restructuring problems for U.S. industries, while contributing to U.S. unemployment, and also because U.S. pressures on Japan to accept larger U.S. exports cause misunderstandings and resentment. The United States appears to be more willing to use leverage against Japan than against the West Europeans, partly because of the size of the trade gap, and partly because of the greater importance that is being given to security issues affecting the European Community. Because of the volume of trade each way, of course, each of these two major industrialized economies is affected by the other's performance, and there is constant U.S. pressure on the Japanese government to induce measures that will stimulate domestic consumer demand. The degree of policy interdependence is high, but collaborative management of this interdependence is difficult, and it must be stressed that Japan, because of its weaker bargaining power, has incentives to maximize its advantages without increasing its overall level of cooperation as long as the U.S. policy process remains highly pluralistic and thus hinders the evolution of a coherent commercial statecraft.(15)

The strains in the Japan-U.S. trading relationship add to the significance of Tokyo's effort to spread its industrial establishment into suitable host countries, especially in East Asia, through the establishment of overseas production bases. The vast scale of this endeavor, while increasing the dependencies of the high-growth modernizing East Asian states on Japan, has important consequences for the mutual relations of those developing political economies. Each one's industrial policy is affected, and in each case a growing share of foreign trade is taking the form of transfers within and between networks of Japan-based transnational enterprises.

REGIONAL FOREIGN POLICY BEHAVIOR

The mixed attributes of the East Asian states are reflected in their international behavior and in the relatively autonomous activities of transnational enterprises to which they relate as homes or hosts. The resulting configurations of external engagement exhibit different levels, ranges, and forms with constructive, competitive, and conflictual elements.

National administrations in the region interact with each other on economic, security, and political issues, with varying degrees of understanding, trust, and goodwill. At the same time, each gove n e 's management of its political economy affects the political economies of its trading partners, and its dealings with locally based and foreign transnational enterprises affect the expansion and interpenetration of national and international production processes. Further, these transnational enterprises relate to each other, competitively and cooperatively, with much autonomy but also with the support of various direct and indirect governmental ties.

The largest, most extensive, and most diversified pattern of external activity is Japan's. The highly integrated Japanese political economy relates to the rapidly advancing modernizing states of the region and to China and the slower-growing nations, as well as to the USSR. The interaction deals mainly with trade, investment, monetary, and development issues but is spreading into security and political matters. Through dependencies associated with the economic issues the states that have substantial trading relations with Japan are affected by changes in the pace and direction of its growth and by the activities of Japan-based international firms, which function in close collaboration with Tokyo's policy.

Japan's regional policy is a complex form of integrative and expansionist neomercantilism, combined with a type of alliance management that is sensitive to the proximity of the USSR and China. The economic component is shaped by a powerful bureaucracy, interacting with highly cohesive business leaders and top figures in the ruling Liberal Democrat party, on the basis of a pervasive consensus to continue the strategy of export-led growth, while spreading production bases into nearby developing states with significant location advantages. The strategic element of foreign policy is determined almost entirely by officials in the defense and external affairs ministries, interacting principally with cabinet leaders, and the most fundamental operating principle is the retention of U.S. military protection against a highly visible Soviet threat. A secondary principle is the maintenance of ties with China, in cooperation with the United States, to encourage Peking's policy of independent development and opposition to the USSR.

The regional economic policy is integrative in the sense that it aims at broad collaboration with the high-growth East Asian developing states in the management of trade, investment, developmental, and monetary issues. The implementation of this policy is incremental and cautious, recognizing that the prospective regional economic partners have historically based fears of Japanese strength and wish to avoid excessive dependence on the Japanese economy. The development of a more favorable Southeast Asian atmosphere is awaited in the hope that this will facilitate initiatives for substantial policy coordination. For the present, however, relations with each of the high-growth modernizing states are managed almost entirely on a bilateral basis, while these states compete to attract investment from the Japanese international firms that are spreading their production processes into Southeast Asia and South Korea.(16)

The regional security policy is implemented with low allocations for defense. The conventional forces that are maintained are small, and accordingly any Soviet aggressive moves against Japan would have to be countered immediately by massive U.S. responses. For the United States the imperative to respond would be less compelling if the Japanese forces had a greater defense potential, but Tokyo's policy expresses a consensus against major increases in defense spending. These are opposed because they would slow economic growth and would evoke protests from Japanese groups fearing a return to militarism. The weak strategic position which thus has to be accepted obligates heavy reliance on U.S. capacity to deter the USSR and gives much importance to the Japanese connection with China, as Peking could be expected to react in a spirited fashion if its major source of technology were seriously endangered, and thus could help to trigger a determined U.S. response. Yet close association with the U.S. security role in Southeast Asia is to be avoided, in this form of alliance diplomacy, because memories of Japanese militarism in this area are still strong, there are concerns about currents of economic nationalism generated by the Japanese economic presence, and there is some lack of confidence in Washington's capacity to manage security ties with weakly legitimized authoritarian regimes in East Asia.

The rapidly growing East Asian states that are linked with the Japanese economy undertake little regional interaction. These polities have few resources for diplomacy, the orientations of their governments are affected by dependencies and by domestic preoccupations resulting from weak legitimacy, and a general lack of understanding and trust between these administrations prevents collective endeavors on behalf of their common interests.

South Korea, although having some modest capabilities for economic diplomacy, has little scope to use these in East Asia because of relative political isolation. Japan is this state's only non-Communist neighbor, but the relationship is strained because of historic antagonisms and because the oppressive character of the South Korean regime gives it low status in the eyes of the Japanese political elite. Heavy military dependence on the United States, moreover, and the high level of U.S. concern with South Korean security, tend to limit interest in the possible advantages that might be gained through diplomatic activity outside the U.S. connection.

Within the ASEAN group, Indonesia's size represents a potential for subregional leadership, but there appears to be only moderate interest in developing such a role. The military leaders of the Indonesian regime tend to be absorbed in problems of solidarity building, show reluctance to promote cooperation with ASEAN members, and attempt little significant diplomatic activity outside that association. On questions of trade liberalization within the ASEAN group the Indonesian attitude is mainly negative, because of reluctance to lower the high protective tariffs that are intended to foster local industries. Political coopera-tion in the ASEAN group on issues relating to Vietnamese control of Cambodia, the Soviet presence in Vietnam, and Chinese hostility to Hanoi is sought with emphasis on consultations with Malaysia. The Indonesian orientation, apparently shared with Kuala Lumpur, is based on fears that China is seeking to dominate Southeast Asia and on assumptions that Peking's ambitions will be checked by the Soviet presence in Vietnam. Hence there is opposition to Thailand's support of Chinese-inspired guerillas in Cambodia and an active concern to improve relations with Hanoi, but there is support for Thailand as an ASEAN member threatened by Vietnamese military power.

Thailand has weaker resources for the support of international activity and does not have close ties with any neighboring state, but for geographic reasons is more exposed to Chinese and Soviet pressures than any other ASEAN member and has been obliged to respond to the challenges presented by Vietnam's domination of Cambodia and Laos. Influenced by fears of China, especially because of Peking's support for Communist guerillas in the Northeast provinces, and by heavy dependence on U.S. economic and military assistance, as well as by the U.S.-China connection, the Thai regime tends to favor China against Vietnam, although not wishing to see the emergence of a new Peking supported government in Cambodia. On economic issues within the ASEAN group, and in their relations with other states, Thailand is moderately active, showing cautious support for incremental moves towards trade liberalization in the association and a readiness to consult with other ASEAN members regarding trade with and the acceptance of investment from Japan and the United States. The Thai administration's main extraregional concern is to maintain military cooperation with the United States, especially to deter any aggression by Vietnam, and to ensure preferential consideration in allocations of U.S. economic aid. Overall support for U.S. policies in East Asia is thus forthcoming, and there is no attempt to secure increased bargaining power in relations with the United States by developing links with other East Asian states. Interaction with the United States is managed almost entirely on a bilateral basis.

Malaysia, ranking next after Singapore as the most advanced member of the ASEAN group, has relatively large resources for external statecraft but is less challenged on regional security issues than Thailand and has a more diversified pattern of extraregional economic relations. For the Malaysian administration there are no major incentives to engage in regional diplomacy, but a significant level of involvement in Southeast Asian affairs is facilitated by ties with Indonesia. Regional and extraregional policy is managed with some concern to prevent any increase in Peking's status and influence that would encourage the Malaysian Chinese to be more assertive in defense of their interests. Within the ASEAN group the Malaysian attitude to questions of trade liberalization is more positive than Indonesia's, but Malaysia has less need than Thailand to work for market integration within the association, because of successes in global trade promotion and more competent management of commercial policy.

The Philippines, relatively isolated within the ASEAN group because of cultural differences and a strongly extraregional foreign trade orientation, as well as because of a low level of diplomatic activity, has very close economic and military ties with the United States. The management of these ties is the principal concern of Philippine foreign policy, and there is little interest in developing bonds with other Asian states for more effective interaction with the United States, or for collective dealings by ASEAN with Japan and the United States on trade and investment issues. The Marcos regime endeavored to develop a cordial relationship with China in the 1970s, but Peking's responses were only moderately enthusiastic, possibly because of consideration for U.S. special interests in the Philippines. Subsequently the Vietnamese seizure of Cambodia and China's aggression against Vietnam apparently evoked little concern and were evidently viewed as matters to be dealt with by the United States.

All the ASEAN members, together with South Korea and Taiwan, are affected by trends in the Japanese economy, and, to a lesser extent, by changes in the U.S. economy, as well as by the movements of Japanese and U.S. investments in East Asia. The effects of expansion and contraction in Japan are the most pronounced because of the extraordinary dynamism of this nation's economy. These effects, and those resulting from growth or decline in the United States, could be moderated and adjusted in the general interest, but there are no institutionalized arrangements to facilitate policy harmonization between the high-growth East Asian economies and the United States.(17) Japan, because of the large-scale expansion of its industrial establishment into the ASEAN members, has increasing incentives to encourage harmonization of their economic policies with its own, and with each other, but has to reckon with their fears of external economic domination.

The U.S. international activities in East Asia have wide-ranging effects, penetrating and providing security for the interactions between the high-growth political economies of the region. This extensive involvement in East Asian affairs has developed with much emphasis on strategic considerations, relating to the USSR and China, that have strongly influenced U.S. regional economic policies. Accordingly, while Japan's engagement in regional affairs has not involved a strong projection of national purpose, being restricted mainly to trade and investment, U.S. regional engagement has had an important normative dimension, resulting from moral justifications advanced to legitimize military cooperation with Japan, South Korea, the Philippines, and Thailand, as well as Taiwan. The principal justification has been to prevent Soviet political or strategic gains through the promotion of revolutionary change in East Asia, but the concerns with human rights that are associated with that justification have assumed some ambiguity because of pragmatic alliances with oppressive and corrupt East Asian states. These forms of collaboration can be counterproductive because of the social tensions generated by the dependent authoritarian regimes.

U.S. security involvement in East Asia may be seriously affected by violent political change in some of the repressive modernizing states. This danger is becoming more serious because demands for popular participation are tending to grow in the authoritarian regimes and the USSR is assuming a stronger role in the East Asian strategic balance, with Vietnamese collaboration. The Soviet Union's projections of power in the region are increasing, relative to those of the United States, and U.S. behavior is conditioned by major societal and legislative restraints on the use of force and of military aid in Third World conflicts. The U.S. administration thus has to rely more than in the past on economic and political methods of advancing security objectives, but its regional economic policy has become much less subordinated to strategic goals in recent years because of difficult trade issues with Japan and on account of strong internal pressures to manage foreign commercial policy more effectively, in order to cope with the inflationary consequences of high oil prices. The domestic pressures that have been operating, moreover, have made the decision process of foreign economic policy more pluralistic, thus limiting the degree of coherence in U.S. regional investment and commercial policy.

U.S. regional security involvement is directed primarily against the USSR, and it is managed by maintaining a military presence in Japan and the Philippines, and in South Korea, as well as by providing various forms of military support to Thailand, Taiwan, and Indonesia. Overall the power projected is inferior to that of the USSR, but for the present it is sufficient to limit fairly effectively the political effects of displays of Soviet armed might. The Japanese administration, although apprehensive at the growth of the Soviet military presence in the Southern Kuriles, is not discouraged from continuing its security collaboration with the United States, its moderate rearmament program, and its policy of friendship with China. The Philippine regime, while aware of the Soviet involvement in Vietnam and willing to use connections with the USSR for leverage against the United States, is of course anxious to preserve its security links with the United States as these help to attract substantial economic as well as military aid, part of which is used to strengthen the coercive state apparatus. The authoritarian Thai and Indonesian regimes have similar reasons for preserving links with the United States, due to their greater sensitivities to the growing Soviet presence in Southeast Asia and to the dangers of Soviet aid to their local revolutionary groups. Low-level security cooperation with China is a secondary feature of the U.S. regional involvement, but its utility is uncertain and its current benefits are not motivating increased collaboration by either side. The Peking regime's military modernization program is very slow and is being managed with much emphasis on self-reliance, which adds to the uncertainties affecting U.S. decision making. The United States administration cannot be sure that China would accept substantial military assistance if this were offered and has to reckon with the possibility that such aid would have a provocative effect on the USSR. There is a strong commitment to preserve the connection with China, but an incidental cost is that this virtually prevents independent approaches to Vietnam that might help to draw that state away from the USSR.(18)

The regional economic policy of the United States is dominated by the management of interdependencies with Japan. Issues in this relationship arise mainly because of energetic Japanese penetration of the U.S. market. The U.S. administration seeks voluntary Japanese restraints on such penetration and increased access to the Japanese market for U.S. goods, while urging Tokyo to adopt expansionary policies that will increase consumer demand. For Japan, however, continued export expansion is imperative to cope with the high prices of imported oil, which are less burdensome for the United States.

The interaction on economic issues between Japan and the United States is almost exclusively bilateral and on the U.S. side tends to be increasingly influenced by demands from industries affected by Japanese imports. Resolution of the basic problems of mutual economic penetration and cooperation is made difficult by the disjointedly incremental decision processes on the U.S. side, which produce uncertainties that sustain and may even increase the forces of economic nationalism in Japanese trade policy.

At the transnational level there are asymmetries because U.S.-based international firms do not operate in close collaboration with Washington and encounter major barriers to entry into the Japanese economy. The centrally guided expansion of the Japanese industrial establishment strengthens Tokyo's capabilities for economic diplomacy, while of course increasing the commercial competitiveness that is a source of trade issues for the U.S. administration. These transnational contrasts have effects in Southeast Asia, where the United States relates to the ASEAN members as a less coherent international actor, and where the movements of U.S. investments are largely uncoordinated. The ASEAN members deal with the United States as dependent states, but the most substantial economic issues with which they have to engage arise in negotiations with U.S.-based international firms. For these firms the Philippine and Indonesian regimes appear to offer the most advantageous terms of entry and operation, because of their corruption, although this does mean that international companies, like national firms, are vulnerable to the parasitic behavior of high-level Philippine and Indonesian officials.

The interaction of Japan, the ASEAN members, and the United States is penetrated to some degrees by China, constructively, but with conflictual transnational involvement through Peking-oriented Communist movements. The most significant engagements are with Japan and the United States, and for the present they tend to draw Tokyo and Washington toward deeper involvement with China, while in effect imposing restraint on Chinese dealings with the ASEAN group.

The Chinese regime overshadows the region, and, as a revolutionary state, stands apart from its non-Communist neighbors. For most of these neighbors China's great size is the most prominent feature of the immediate environment, and Chinese strength is associated with radical commitments to modernize and to restructure the international community while absorbing technology from its industrialized nations. Peking's behavior sets difficult conditions for coexistence but in a less demanding fashion now than in the recent past, because high priority is given to the development of friendly relations with East Asian states, in competition against the USSR, and to displays of respect for U.S. interests in the region. China's resources for constructive diplomacy are modest because of economic underdevelopment and the restrictive effects of ideology on communications, but the strengthening of Chinese ties with Japan and the United States tends to facilitate the expansion of Peking's contacts with the ASEAN members.

Within East Asia the most active forms of cooperative Chinese behavior are directed at the Japanese administration, in order to strengthen its emphasis on supporting China's industrialization with generous credits, and to discourage it from accommodating with Soviet pressures. This diplomacy involves tacit respect for the domestic political interests of the ruling Liberal Democratic Party and relative neglect of the strongly independent Japan Communist Party, alienated by Peking during the Maoist era. Since Japan has become the main supplier of technology to China, there is evidently no wish to see the Liberal Democratic government replaced by a coalition that could be less effective in managing the Japanese economy, or to contribute to social tensions that might disrupt that economy. On the Japanese side, most factions in the Liberal Democratic leadership appear to believe that their nation's strategic and economic interests require a close relationship with China, through which the evolution of Peking's policies can be influenced, especially to prevent any shifts toward cooperation with the USSR, and of course to minimize the danger that a new leadership in China may revert to Maoist policies. Such policies would slow the Peking regime's modernization and introduce much conflictual behavior into China's relations with Japan and the United States, and thus would give advantages to the USSR.

Chinese behavior toward the United States seeks to utilize the U.S. need for a major Asian ally against the USSR and encourages Washington to increase its opposition to Soviet expansionism. The tendency of U.S. decision makers to view the China connection as a means of leverage against the USSR, however, exposes U.S. policy to Soviet influence, in that relatively more cooperative Soviet behavior toward the United States will tend to be rewarded by reduced U.S. collaboration with China. The U.S. concern to ensure flexibility in the China connection, moreover, is linked with an unwillingness to provoke the USSR by establishing a very close relationship with Peking. From the Chinese point of view, then, the connection is of limited utility and certainly does not promise an improvement in security that would sufficiently offset the risks incurred by antagonizing the USSR through collaboration with its adversary. The limitations of the connection were dramatized after the Chinese attack on Vietnam in 1979, when it was clear that China could not expect any U.S. support in coping with Soviet air and naval deployments that were intended to force a Chinese withdrawal from Vietnam. Nevertheless the United States, like Japan, is an increasingly important source of technology for China, and offers large-scale credits to finance Chinese imports, in competition against Japan and the major West European states.(19)

Soviet activities in East Asia are highly conflictual and are directed mainly against the United States, China, and Japan. By demonstrating that it is acquiring a position of great strength in the region, the USSR seeks to influence Japanese policy, as well as the policies of the smaller East Asian states, so as to restrict U.S. scope for involvement, isolate China, and encourage the emergence of affinitive leftist or revolutionary regimes. This strategy is implemented from a position of relative political isolation, despite regional strategic superiority over the United States, and with only small resources for the support of economic diplomacy. Threatening projections of Soviet power are directed at Japan and China, but in the Japanese case major inducements are held out relating to participation in the development of Siberian resources and significant levels of trade each way are maintained. The USSR secures modest benefits from imports of Japanese technology, but the Liberal Democratic government's alignment with the United States remains unchanged, like its policy toward China, and Soviet behavior does little to foster the emergence of a more friendly Japanese administration. From the Japanese point of view, the USSR is a secondary trading partner with a minor economic role in East Asia, and much of its current behavior reinforces widely felt Japanese antipathies toward the Soviet Union. Japanese attitudes of course are influenced by the USSR's very conflictual behavior towards China, which stimulates Peking's hostility and causes the Chinese to maintain their bonds with the United States as well as Japan.

The Southeast Asian states are moderately exposed to Soviet pressures but show little susceptibility to the USSR's small-scale economic diplomacy. Thailand, because of proximity to Cambodia and Laos, is very sensitive to the Soviet presence in Vietnam, but is also apprehensive about China's longstanding ties with the Communist movement in its Northeast provinces and thus seems anxious to establish a basis for coexistence with Peking, while utilizing U.S. military aid for the suppression of local revolutionary elements. Malaysia, Indonesia, and the Philippines, while relating to Vietnam as a more distant neighbor, are directly affected by the USSR's efforts to project its power in the South China Sea and to remove U.S. influence from Southeast Asia. The principal implication of Soviet communications aimed at these states is that they must accommodate by terminating forms of military cooperation with the United States and initiate "progressive" changes in their domestic affairs.

ISSUES IN REGIONAL INTERACTION

The issues posed in East Asia's intersecting patterns of foreign policy behavior differ in substantive importance and susceptibility to resolution, over the short or long terms. The weakly legitimized Southeast Asian states confront security issues in which their own social and political tensions can be utilized by revolutionary groups, with support from the USSR as a power forcefully asserting its commitment to the promotion of radical change. The levels of internal strain in the Southeast Asian states are affected by each national administration's management of its political economy, and that is conditioned by the evolution of external dependence issues, principally in relations with Japan and the United States. The terms on which these matters are handled by those two nations are influenced by the interdependencies between them, which are managed competitively rather than integratively.

The most significant security issues, for the present, are those confronting Thailand. Vietnam's efforts to control and build up the Communist movement in the Northeast provinces represent a serious threat, especially because of the USSR's military collaboration with Hanoi. The Vietnamese-Soviet interest in promoting political change in Thailand is not negotiable, while on the Thai side the question of continuing to aid guerillas in Cambodia is a matter affecting ties with China, and it seems that the Chinese are resolved that this cooperation must continue. The United States is an interested party but is evidently unwilling to risk antagonizing China by opposing further Thai cooperation with Peking in support of the anti-Vietnamese guerillas operating against the new Cambodian regime. Thailand is not able to press resolution of the problem through discussions between China and the United States, and accordingly the complex pattern of hostile indirect interaction is undergoing little change.

The internal security problems of the Philippine regime rank next after those of Thailand and have smaller external dimensions. The local Communist elements have links with China and possibly also with the USSR, but operate, of necessity, with greater self-reliance, and with no immediate prospect of receiving substantial aid from Vietnam. No negotiations with either of the two leading Communist powers on the domestic security issue are feasible for the Philippine ruling elite, and those two powers may well consider that the Marcos administration is basically more vulnerable to political violence than the military regime in Thailand.

For Malaysia and Indonesia, externally related internal security problems are less serious than those of the Philippines, and the perceived issues relate to China rather than the USSR. There are incentives to seek understandings with Peking regarding the local Communist movements that will provide a basis for coexistence, but thus far only Malaysia has shown an active interest in the pursuit of such understandings, and the Chinese attitude indicates that renunciation of ties with those revolutionary movements is not contemplated. Concerns about China's aims and future role cause the Malaysian administration and the Indonesian regime to oppose the Thai policy of cooperating with China in the support of guerillas in Cambodia, but there is evidently no meaningful interaction with Vietnam or the USSR regarding its manifest determination to gain influence and spread revolutionary change in Southeast Asia.

The political economy issues for the ASEAN states that arise out of their external dependencies are matters of infrequent bilateral interaction and continual transnational interchanges. Asymmetries in bargaining power and capabilities at each level largely determine the outcomes, mostly at some costs to the ASEAN members, but fail to inspire collective ASEAN efforts to negotiate with Japan and the United States on the basis of common interests. The most salient issues are problems of access to Japanese, U.S., and West European markets. Tariff and nontariff barriers constitute major obstacles to entry for ASEAN primary products, goods at various stages of processing, and manufactured articles. Sales of larger quantities of manufactures and goods at intermediate and higher stages of processing are necessary to finance comprehensive industrial development but are made difficult for the ASEAN members by the tendencies of the major industrialized democracies to increase their protectionism if there is greater penetration of their markets by ASEAN and other Third World products. For the present the ASEAN members have the same terms of access as other Third World states and are associated with the global efforts of those states to negotiate a New International Economic Order, with improved access, but it would be feasible for them to seek preferential trading arrangements with Japan because of the great importance of their primary products for Japanese industries. The negotiation of such arrangements, however, would require a high degree of cohesion within ASEAN, and on the Japanese side would necessitate difficult calculations about the effects on other Third World markets, where access could diminish unless generalized concessions by Tokyo were in prospect.

To increase their export earnings and improve their terms of trade, the ASEAN administrations, with varying degrees of competence, seek to draw more foreign investment into manufacturing for the markets of the industrialized democracies. Competition between these ASEAN governments to offer the most favorable terms of entry prevents the evolution of a common policy for the guidance of international firms, and the results of the interactions with those firms are generally in their favor, especially on questions of location in the Philippines, Indonesia, and Thailand. Malaysia and Singapore have important bargaining advantages because of their superior administrative services and infrastructures and show more responsible concerns with economic sovereignty than do the authoritarian ASEAN governments. Indonesia's vast natural resources and large internal market have great drawing power, especially for Japanese capital, and this asset is being utilized in order to build up an industrial establishment that will be sufficiently large and diversified to compete with those of the more advanced ASEAN economies.

The trade and investment concerns of the ASEAN states are affected, in ways outside their control, by issues in the complex interdependencies between Japan and the United States. These are basically trade issues, complicated by U.S. efforts to link them with demands for stimulation of the Japanese economy, and by Tokyo's commitment to maintain the nation's high rate of export-led growth. The interaction is asymmetrical not only with respect to contrasts in economic vitality but also with regard to the coherence of the actors. Japan's main interest is to utilize the still substantial U.S. commitment to an open international trading system, while retaining advantages on the nonnegotiable matters of growth strategy and administrative directiveness in private sector guidance, and while recognizing the degrees to which pluralistic incrementalism on the U.S. side limits the possiblities for comprehensive issue engagement.

Japan's nontariff barriers and the relative openness of the U.S. economy are the main sources of issues. The Japanese nontariff barriers of course have cultural as well as administrative dimensions, and some of the most important of the latter derive from the intimate links between the powerful Japanese bureaucracy and national firms of all categories which can only be strengthened rather than weakened by U.S. pressures. The relative openness of the U.S. economy, which provides major opportunities for Japanese exporters, is being reduced because of strong demands from industries affected by imports from Japan, and this is being done principally through the use of nontariff barriers, often with the collaboration of U.S. firms that resort to discriminatory trade practices. The U.S. administration tends to respond to domestic pressures for a balance of trade with Japan, to be achieved through reduced Japanese market penetration, although in the overall U.S. balance of payments the deficit with Japan is partially offset by a favorable balance with Western Europe.

The Japan-U.S. interaction on trade and related issues is strained, mainly because of the strong demands by disadvantaged groups in the United States that affect Washington's management of the relationship. On each side, levels of trust and goodwill tend to be moderate to low, and the results of the interchanges are mostly Japanese accommodations with U.S. demands for export restraints and import liberalization. There are few jointly realized benefits that would build up commitments to further cooperation, and such commitments are not likely to develop unless the interaction becomes oriented toward the attainment of common values through policy coordination rather than forceful readjustment of the terms of trade. For the present, modest concessions are feasible for Japan because of the great importance of access to the U.S. market, but there is no compelling incentive to accept demands for balanced trade which the United States cannot put forward for general acceptance in the international economy.

The issues in Japan's economic relations with China and the USSR are of minor importance in the regional pattern, and for the present Japan is well placed to manage those in the China connection by utilizing its bargaining assets as Peking's main source of technology. This indeed is being done without jeopardizing trade with the USSR, and the economic ties with both the Soviet Union and China are of some help to Japan in negotiating on trade issues with the United States. The basic issue of Japanese trade policy toward the two Communist regimes is the extension of further substantial credits to finance technology exports. There are incentives to be more generous than West Germany and the United States, the main suppliers of technology to the USSR, but also to limit economic cooperation with the USSR because of its threatening behavior, and to avoid major political and economic risks in dealing with the Chinese, especially because of their record of instability and fluctuating administrative performance. The immediate issue for China is that of increasing or reducing dependence on Japanese credits for technology imports, and this is linked with the more fundamental question of accepting Japanese inputs into the regime's planning and administrative functions and the separate but related issue of utilizing Japanese direct investment for joint ventures to expand Chinese exports. The discussion of these questions is evidently difficult and protracted, because of basic features of the Chinese policy process, and the uncertainties posed by the current practices of the Peking regime evidently tend to restrain Japanese initiatives for a closer relationship.

DEVELOPMENTAL ISSUES

The emergence of a sense of regional identity in East Asia is being aided by moderately productive interactions on common problems between the ASEAN members, by Japanese efforts to develop cooperation with them as a group, by the expansion of economic bonds and political ties between Japan and China, and by communication flows between Japan and the ASEAN members which increase awareness of certain shared interests in dealing with the United States, although ASEAN consciousness of conflicts of interest with Japan is also tending to grow.   Various domestic and external constraints, together with deficiencies in resources for statecraft, affect the scope for Japanese and ASEAN efforts to broaden the current pattern of constructive interactions.

The interchanges within the ASEAN group of course tend primarily to increase each member's sense of identity with that association, although it remains a loose community.   Consciousness of regional identity, that is, of sharing basic interests with Japan and possibly China, and of having to contend with the USSR and Vietnam, results from interactions concerning ASEAN's external relations.   The awareness of regional identity, however, remains weak, especially because of insufficient capacities to influence events in the environment outside ASEAN and because of each national elite's consciousness of dependence on military and economic support from outside East Asia, as well as of the bilateral character of the interchanges through which such forms of support are managed.

Japanese efforts to develop cooperation with ASEAN naturally increase awareness of the Southern environment within the Japanese elite, while making ASEAN elites more conscious of Japan as a state with whom dependencies have to be managed.   The possibilities for rational joint and collective choice, however, are negatively affected by Japanese perceptions of the political and economic weaknesses of the ASEAN members and their slow and cautious attempts to collaborate.   Japanese forecasters have grounds for anticipating that significant integrative activity within the ASEAN group may not develop unless Indonesia, after advancing to the levels of industrialization reached by Singapore and Malaysia, emerges as a leader of the association.   On the ASEAN side, awareness of insufficient progress toward the formation of a community tends to discourage efforts for solidarity building that would be aimed at collaborative dealings with the Japanese.

The Japan-ASEAN pattern of relations, however, will remain the potentially most significant feature of the core network of East Asian interactions.   If some working out of neofunctional logic results in substantial policy integration between Japan and the ASEAN members, this will be an important advance toward the evolution of a new subregional international system, and it will have a capacity to spread, because it will tend to draw in outside states that wish to share in its trade and investment opportunities. This long-term possibility may well have a growing influence on Japanese forward thinking, especially if such thinking is stimulated by further U.S. pressures on trade issues. Japan, it must be stressed, has the very potent option of initiating, with the ASEAN members, a Lome type agreement that would help to stabilize their primary export earnings, allow them better access to the Japanese market, set levels for Japanese investment in and aid in their economies, and open the way for broad coordination of their basic economic policies with Japan's.

NOTES

(1) For a discussion of the substantive security problems, see Richard H. Solomon, ed., Asian Security in the 1980's: Problems and Policies for a Time of Transition (Santa Monica: Rand Corporation, 1979).

(2) See discussion of cultural factors in Bradley M. Richardson, The Political Culture of Japan (Berkeley: University of California Press, 1974).

(3) See Harold Crouch, "Patrimonialism and Military Rule in Indonesia," World Politics 31, no. 4 (July 1979): 571-587.

(4) See Problems of Communism, vol. 30, no. 1 (January-February 1981), symposium issue.

(5) For a brief review of recent trends in Japanese politics, see Lee W. Farnsworth, "Japan in 1980: The Conservative Resurgence," Asian Survey 21, no. 1 (January 1981): 70-83.

(6) See Fred R. von der Mehden, "Malaysia in 1980: Signals to Watch," Asian Survey 21, no. 2 (February 1981): 245-252.

(7) See Martin Stuart-Fox, "Tensions within the Thai Insurgency," Australian Outlook 33, no. 2 (August 1979): 182-197.

(8) See trends discussed in Clark D. Neher, "The Philippines in 1980: the Gathering Storm," Asian Survey 21, no. 2 (February 1981): 261-273.

(9) For brief recent assessments of the South Korean regime, see Chong-Sik Lee, "South Korea in 1980: The Emergence of a New Authoritarian Order," Asian Survey 21, no. 1 (January 1981): 125-143.

(10) For a discussion of issues affecting Chinese development, see Lowell Dittmer, "China in 1980: Modernization and its Discontents," Asian Survey 21, no. 1 (January 1981): 31-50.

(11) See Franklin B. Weinstein, "Multinational Corporations and the Third World: The Case of Japan and Southeast Asia," International Organization 30, no. 3 (Summer 1976): 373-404.

(12) See tables on ASEAN trade in John Wong, ASEAN Economies in Perspective (Philadelphia: Institute for the Study of Human Issues, 1979).

(13) Ibid., See also R. J. G. Wells, "ASEAN Intraregional Trading in Food and Agricultural Crops – The Way Ahead," Asian Survey 20, no. 6 (June 1980): 661-672; and ASEAN: Challenges of an Integrating Market (Hong Kong: Business International Asia Pacific Ltd.).

(14) See Herbert S. Levine, "The Soviet Union's Economic Relations in Asia" (Paper presented at Conference on Soviet Policy in Asia, Seoul, Korea, April 1980, sponsored by Asiatic Research Center, Korea University, the Federation of Korean Industries and the Council on Foreign Relations).

(15) See Leon Hollerman, ed., Japan and the United States: Economic and Political Adversaries (Boulder, Col.: Westview Press, 1980).

(16) See Terutotmo Ozawa, "International Investment and Industrial Structure: New   Theoretical   Implications   from   the   Japanese Experience," Oxford Economic Papers 31, no. 1 (March 1979): 72-92.

(17) See Lawrence B. Krause and Sueo Sekiguchi, eds., Economic Interaction in the Pacific Basin (Washington: Brookings Institution, 1980).

(18) See Solomon, Asian Security in the 1980's.

(19) U.S. options toward China are discussed in ibid., and in James C. Hsiung and Samuel S. Kim, eds., China in the Global Community (New York: Praeger, 1980).

3 Japan's Regional Policies

Sueo Sekiguchi

Since the mid-1970s Japanese political scientists and economists have shown increasing interest in the possibilities for cooperation between Pacific states, especially on trade, investment, industrial, and monetary policies. These possibilities have attracted attention because of high growth rates in Japan, South Korea, and the ASEAN members; the persistence of tensions in Japan's commerce with the United States; the emergence of protectionist trends in both Western Europe and the United States; the inflationary pressures of high oil prices; and the rapid expansion of Japanese investment into manufacturing and extractive ventures in Southeast Asia. Other factors drawing attention to the opportunities for Pacific regional cooperation have been the development of the ASEAN group as a subregional association, the growth of exchanges between Japan and the ASEAN members on questions of economic collaboration, and the holding of regional conferences by private and semiofficial groups, including the sponsors of a September 1980 meeting at the Australian National University. This meeting had been preceded by the publication of a report on Pacific Basin Cooperation by a private advisory group commissioned by the late Japanese Prime Minister M. Ohira.

Japan has strong incentives to seek wide-ranging economic cooperation with nearby high-growth modernizing states, including, especially, the ASEAN members. Large quantities of primary products imported from these states are essential for the resource-deficient Japanese economy, and substantial Japanese investments are establishing overseas production bases on their territories for the export of manufactured goods to Japan and to states outside East Asia. Some exports of manufactures from these states, by national firms and non-Japanese transnational enterprises, are challenging the strong positions of Japanese companies in West European and North American markets. More fundamentally, the evolution of industrial policies in the high-growth modernizing East Asian states affects the roles of

Japanese enterprises within their economies, and, thus, in the pattern of regional transnations.

Japanese foreign economic policy is more consensual, and in many respects more functional, than that of any other industrialized democracy, for cultural and institutional reasons. If current public and official discussions of the nation's Pacific relations produce broad support for the promotion of regional cooperation, a vigorous and highly integrated strategy for that purpose will probably be implemented. Restraints, however, will be imposed by ASEAN fears that Japan's economic strength will enable it to dominate any emerging Pacific association for market integration and policy harmonization. Japan relates to the ASEAN members across considerable social distances, and the interaction is affected by great differences in size and levels of overall development, as well as by sharp contrasts in cultures and in types of political systems.

Regional security considerations influence Japanese views of the possibilities for Pacific cooperation. There is concern at the weakening of the U.S. security role in the area, the unfriendly behavior of the USSR, and the Soviet collaboration with Vietnam. The development of ties with China is welcomed, especially inasmuch as this helps to counter Soviet influence in the environment, but there appears to be growing sentiment in favor of developing an independent and rather active Japanese regional statecraft. This, it is expected, would ensure some influence on events in East Asia, and especially on the management of U.S. policy, which from the Japanese point of view has been insufficiently collegial.

THE POLITY

Japan is an advanced industrial society with a distinctive culture that is still fairly traditional and that is evolving in considerable isolation from neighboring countries, which are much less developed, and from other postindustrial societies, which are geographically remote. Japanese attitudes to the outside world are shaped very much by the national culture and by general awareness of the national economy's needs to draw large quantities of primary products from resource-rich nations and to export great volumes of manufactured goods, especially in high technology categories. Domestically, the national culture fosters strong orientations toward group solidarity and group decision making, and toward acceptance of authoritative policy making by the national administration as the institutional expression of the state and of a common political will.(1)   The Japanese bureaucracy gives strong administrative guidance to private enterprise, and the two work in partnership, with much consultative interaction between the middle echelons on each side, whose contributions to the shaping of policy are considerably more autonomous than those of their counterparts in other industrialized democracies. Consensual decision making in Japanese institutions is oriented toward what may be called consensual directiveness and compliance, in which the principal managerial function is to elicit sound policy from the working levels. The decision processes can be slow, but they maintain high degrees of integration in the authority structures.(2)

The economy is heavily industrial, with an emphasis on high and rapidly advancing technology, and there is a very large services sector in which financial institutions fulfill major entrepreneurial functions. There is a strong orientation toward export-oriented growth, and for this vital roles are played by large diversified trading companies that handle roughly 50 percent of the nation's commerce. Large yearly increases in total output are made possible by high rates of domestic investment, substantial allocations for research and development, an intense and very pervasive work ethic linked with a spirit of partnership, and the close cooperation between government and the private sector. With levels of domestic saving well above those in the United States, capital input in Japan has rapidly overtaken that in the United States since the early 1950s, a technological lead has been gained over the United States, and a U.S. lead in capital intensity of production is being swiftly reduced.(3) Vigorous private and official export promotion is ensuring large yearly increases in foreign trade that secure the additional resources needed for the maintenance of a high overall growth rate. At the same time the dynamism of the economy is facilitating heavy investment in both Third World and advanced countries by Japanese international firms manufacturing for local and world markets.

Japan's growth is export-led because the economy must function with acute resource deficiencies. Imports of manufactured goods tend to be restrained by various social barriers, as well as by some remaining official barriers, which can be resented by aggressive salesmen from other countries. Export promotion is basically a matter of concentrating energies and all relevant resources to take advantage of the relative openness of foreign markets. Competitive advantages are gained by liberal export credits, superior information and distribution networks, and a foreign policy that avoids potentially costly positions on international security or political issues, while nevertheless deriving security from U.S. military protection. Other advantages are derived from the expansionist economic policies of major trading partners among the industrialized democracies, which are responsible for levels of consumer demand higher than those in Japan, where there are fairly strict limitations on budgetary and monetary measures that might stimulate domestic sales.(4)

Until recently growth requirements have been given a higher priority over welfare considerations than has been common in other postindustrial societies, but this allocative failing has been remedied by the pressures of opposition parties against the ruling conservative Liberal Democratic party, which had been losing votes steadily before it sharply increased its popularity in the 1980 elections. This party, which has been in power since the 1950s, enjoys majority support primarily because of the general prosperity that has resulted from its successful growth policy, and because none of the opposition parties can hold out credible promises of superior performance in public policy. These other parties are small, several of them are mutually incompatible, and the most important – the Japan Socialist Party, which has derived some ideological inspiration from China – is being obliged to adjust to the pragmatic shift in Chinese policies and to the effects of Chinese cooperation with the Liberal Democratic administration on public attitudes.(5)

REGIONAL TIES

Japan's traditional culture has been deeply influenced by Confucian beliefs and values derived from China. Strongly felt affinities with China pervade Japanese society, although there is general awareness of that nation's backwardness and of the authoritarian features of its Communist system. The felt affinities tend to be strengthened by friendly official interaction with the Chinese regime and are influenced by awareness of some shared attitudes towards the USSR. The USSR's unfriendly and often hostile behavior is viewed with some apprehension, especially because of the large deployments of Soviet military power in the Kuriles and in nearby parts of the Soviet Far East.

The traditional Japanese culture is penetrated by Western instrumental values, absorbed through vast communication flows from the United States relating to educational, scientific, technological, economic, and other forms of cooperation. The foreign values tend to introduce varieties of individualism that threaten established orientations toward group responsibility and group behavior, yet in some respects they assist the development of understanding if not trust between Japanese elites and those in the United States, as well as between Japanese politicians, entrepreneurs, and bureaucrats and their somewhat Westernized counterparts in the more advanced Southeast Asian states. The traditional cultures of these states, however, are quite different from Japan's, and the attitudes of their peoples toward Japan are still influenced in part by memories of the Second World War.(6)

Traditional Japanese culture is strongly nationalist, and nationalist orientations tend to evolve in the very competitive contexts of encounters with the United States and other industrialized democracies on trade, investment, and monetary issues. What is commonly experienced is an insensitivity to Japanese needs for large export revenues to cover necessary imports of primary products and fuels. Nationalism, however, is also stimulated by awareness of superior achievements in management of the national political economy and by consciousness of the need to preserve the close partnerships between business enterprises, the bureaucracy, and the ruling party in order to maintain the high overall growth rate.(7)

To the extent that Japanese nationalism is evidenced in dealings with other Asian states, the social distances from those states remain fairly large. These distances can of course be reduced by cultural diplomacy and by shifts towards integrative and less competitive economic statecraft, as well as by attempts to develop political bonds. The present level of cultural diplomacy is relatively modest, and the integrative elements in Japan's regional foreign policy behavior are quite small, being directed towards the ASEAN group, which, because of weak internal cohesion, does not make encouraging responses. Politically Japan has some affinities with the representative political systems in Singapore and Malaysia, but major cultural differences affect interaction between the Liberal Democratic Party and the communally based modernizing party which dominates the Malaysian system, while the democratic socialist outlook of Singapore's Peoples Action Party is ideologically somewhat more distant from the Liberal Democratic Party and yet closer to it in terms of pragmatic commitment to private sector growth.(8)

Japan relates to the authoritarian states in the Association of Southeast Asian Nations and to South Korea on the basis of their policies rather than their political characteristics and principally with reference to the management of their relatively open economies. Ties resulting from volumes of trade and investment are developing mainly with South Korea and Indonesia, and on a smaller scale with Thailand and the Philippines. All these bonds, as well as Japan's economic links with Malaysia and Singapore, are growing rapidly and contribute substantially to the high rates of increase in trade and gross national product that are maintained by the ASEAN members and South Korea.(9)

Outside East Asia, Japan has strong economic, political, and security ties with the United States. These are based on extensive complex interdependencies that have evolved with a longstanding U.S. commitment to the preservation of Japan's security and with the rapid emergence of this country as a global economic power. Serious strains have developed in the relationship because of U.S. concern at heavy trade imbalances and at problems of industrial restructuring posed by large imports of Japanese-manufactured products. Other sources of strain have been U.S. demands for expansionist policies that would stimulate consumer demand in Japan, and for higher Japanese defense spending. Expenditures on the armed forces are kept to a low level by the Liberal Democratic administration, in line with a policy that became established in the 1950s because of desires to avoid arousing Chinese, Soviet, and Southeast Asian fears of Japanese rearmament.(10)

SOURCES OF REGIONAL POLICY

The primary source of Japan's East Asian policy is a broad elite consensus on security and economic matters in the immediate environment. This consensus is well established and is stable because of a congruence of external and domestic factors that have tended to confirm the logic of earlier policy choices from which the consensus derived. Japan's military ties with the United States are endorsed by

China, the Chinese need for technology is being met principally by Japan, and the new pragmatic Chinese policy orientation evidences respect for the methods by which the Japanese political economy is managed.   Indirectly, then, electoral support for the Liberal Democratic Party is encouraged, while this party continues to benefit from general satisfaction with the prosperity that has been maintained under its rule.

The consensus on external security problems is based on noncontroversial assessments of Soviet behavior over three decades, from a position of serious vulnerability, and, of course, proximity. The USSR has long been showing deep ideological hostility to the Japanese political system, and it has built up large concentrations of military power in the area around Vladivostok, while retaining control of the Kurile Islands which it seized from Japan at the end of the Second World War. Threatening displays of Soviet armed strength, including provocative approaches and overflights, and seizures of Japanese fishing vessels, have evoked grave evaluations from the Japanese defense authorities.   These have underlined the importance of continuing the military relationship with the United States, although concern has been shown at the relative weakening of the U.S. position in the regional strategic balance, and at Washington's present confrontation policy against the USSR. It is expected that Peking's attitude to the USSR will not undergo any major changes.(11)

A new element that has emerged in the security consensus is a fairly explicit recognition that an active and independent role will have to be assumed in the East Asian strategic context, although without major increases in defense spending or serious modification of the practice of avoiding stands on political issues that could affect the growth of economic ties with most East Asian states.(12)   The present Chinese attitude suggests that the new role could be assumed without straining the relationship with Peking and that a considerable identity of interest would be seen by the Chinese, especially with respect to the security of Japanese shipping movements through the South China Sea and the Indian Ocean.   Large quantities of Middle East oil come to Japan through those shipping routes.

The consensus on economic policy concerns China and the high-growth modernizing East Asian states. China is seen as a vast potential market and as an industrializing nation in need of technology and of allies against the USSR.   Support for China's economic growth, on generous terms, is expected to open up large commerical opportunities for Japan to cope somewhat more effectively with protectionist pressures from the industrialized democracies, especially the United States.(13)   Meanwhile, expanding trade with and investment in the ASEAN members and South Korea, it is clearly understood, will strengthen economic bonds with those high-growth developing nations, secure access to their raw materials, and facilitate their industrial development on a basis of intimate production links with Japanese enterprises.   Because of resource deficiencies and space limitations, more and more Japanese manufacturing processes are to be moved to overseas bases, and the ASEAN members, together with South Korea, are high priority locations bescause of their proximity and their importance as suppliers of primary products.(14)

The elite consensus on policy pervades the leadership of the Liberal Democratic Party, the managements of large manufacturing and trading firms, and the bureaucracy. The higher levels of the ruling party are factionalized, however, and leaders of factions who gain control of the administration can give distinctive orientations to the management of East Asian affairs within the general consensus.(15) In recent years, Prime Ministers Fukuda, Ohira, and Suzuki have all taken personal initiatives to raise levels of understanding, trust, goodwill, and cooperation in relationships with the ASEAN members, and with China. The large national enterprises, while accepting strong adminstrative guidance from the bureaucracy, especially the Ministries of International Trade and Industry and Finance, express their interests through powerful associations of industry and commerce which have close links with the upper levels of the Liberal Democratic Party. Liberal Democratic Party leaders in office rely heavily on the expertise of the high bureaucrats in the major economic ministries and in general seek to work with rather than direct these officials, while respecting the power they enjoy as a matter of well-established precedent. Industrial policy is decided mainly by the Ministry of International Trade and Industry, and this bureaucratic structure influences the expansion of the national industrial establishment into the ASEAN group and South Korea.(16)

Societal views and preferences on questions of regional policy are articulated weakly and their influence is modest and indirect.   There are no pressure groups waging strong campaigns for change in the established lines of East Asian policy, as the extreme left parties have been somewhat disoriented by the Sino-American detente, and there are no powerful currents of nationalism with which the small right wing opposition parties can identify.   Fluctuations in voter support partially express popular attitudes to the administration's management of external relations, but the basic expectations manifested in this way are that the administration will continue to ensure that the nation has a peaceful international environment, except insofar as this is made difficult by the USSR, and that fundamental forms of cooperation with the United States will be maintained while U.S. demands for slower Japanese export expansion are resisted.(17)

The state of the regional environment and the behavior of other East Asian states influence the perceptions, expectations, and preferences of Japanese cabinet members, Liberal Democratic Party leaders, bureaucrats, and business managements. The main effects are that general agreement on economic and security policy is sustained, while attention is fixed on issues of cooperation with the high-growth modernizing states, and with China and the United States.

The resource-rich ASEAN members, especially Indonesia, invite foreign investment in manufacturing and the extractive industries, with generous concessions regarding terms of entry, tariff and nontariff measures, taxes, profit remittances, and local participation in ownership and management. All the conditions are negotiable, because of the significance of the large outflows of Japanese capital for each ASEAN member's industrialization, and because the bargaining strength of the Japanese international firms is very great, especially on account of their intimate links with their national administration.(18)   The ASEAN group also attracts U.S. investment, in smaller flows, and while this limits the expansion of Japanese influence in the ASEAN economies it reduces fears of that influence and contributes to overall growth in ways that indirectly benefit Japan investment and trading interests. To increase their exports, the ASEAN members seek improved access to the Japanese market, but do not press their demands, although, with the exception of Indonesia, their trade with Japan is usually in deficit.(19)

The volume of Japanese trade with and investment in the ASEAN members (see tables 3.1 and 3.2) raises issues for planning over the mid and long terms. For the present, each ASEAN member relates to Japan more as a competitor than a partner of its associates in that organization, and the resultant asymmetries work to Japan's advantage on immediate issues. If the ASEAN members began to coordinate their industrial policies, however, there would be scope for wide-ranging cooperation between them and Japan, although their increased cohesion would enable them to bargain more effectively for the advancement of their own interests.

South Korea, Taiwan, and Hong Kong trade with Japan on a larger scale than the ASEAN members but attract much less Japanese investment. On this account, and being relatively isolated from each other, these states have less significance than the ASEAN group for Japan's regional economic policy, but of course would assume more importance if they were associated with ASEAN members in a large regional grouping. In such a grouping, shared interests with the ASEAN group as trading partners of Japan's would be a basis for cooperation, although the ASEAN governments might well be seriously divided over issues of collaboration with Japan in that larger context. For Japan's security policy South Korea assumes significance, but the Japanese public believes that South Korean defense policy leads to an arms race on the peninsula and that there is a real prospect for peaceful coexistence. There is little interaction on this issue, however, and South Korea relies heavily on US military support.(20)

China, because of its size, overshadows the regional environment; there is intense awareness of its presence and much sensitivity to Peking's international activities.   The apparently firm Chinese commitment to a pragmatic industrialization policy is seen to have great implications for Japan's future technology exports, while Chinese fears of the USSR are regarded as a firm basis for the current Chinese policy of friendship with Japan and the United States. The principal message in Chinese communications is that the Soviet threat must be confronted by a broad alliance of industrialized and developing states. This is accepted to the extent of showing friendly attitudes to China and concern at threatening Soviet behavior, but with caution about

Table 3.1. Japan's Trade with Selected Countries in the Pacific Basin (in millions of U.S. $ and %)

	Japan's Exports						Japan's Imports					
	1960		1970		1979		1960		1970		1979	
	$	%	$	%	$	%	$	%	$	%	$	%
Canada	119	2.9	563	2.9	1738	1.7	204	4.5	929	4.9	4105	3.7
U.S.	1083	26.7	5940	30.7	26403	25.6	1545	34.4	5560	29.4	20431	18.5
Australia	144	3.6	589	3.0	2607	2.5	344	7.7	1508	8.0	6298	5.7
New Zealand	24	0.6	114	0.6	584	0.6	32	0.7	158	0.8	805	0.7
Mexico	18	0.4	94	0.5	841	0.8	103	2.3	151	0.8	483	0.4
(East Asian market economies)	(358)	(8.8)	(2218)	(11.5)	(14263)	(13.8)	(106)	(2.4)	(572)	(3.0)	(6498)	(5.9)
Republic of Korea	100	2.5	818	4.2	6247	6.1	19	0.4	229	1.2	3359	3.0
Taiwan	102	2.5	700	3.6	4337	4.2	64	1.4	251	1.3	2476	2.2
Hong Kong	156	3.8	700	3.6	3679	3.6	23	0.5	92	0.5	663	0.6
(ASEAN)	(501)	(12.4)	(1808)	(9.4)	(9646)	(9.4)	(509)	(11.3)	(1866)	(9.9)	(16276)	(14.7)
Thailand	118	2.9	449	2.3	1714	1.7	72	1.6	190	1.0	1169	1.1
Singapore	87	2.1	423	2.2	2679	2.6	14	0.3	87	0.5	1473	1.3
Malaysia*	32	0.8	166	0.9	1507	1.5	194	4.3	419	2.2	3257	2.9
Philippines	154	3.8	454	2.4	1622	1.6	159	3.5	533	2.8	1583	1.4
Indonesia	110	2.7	316	1.6	2124	2.1	70	1.6	637	3.4	8794	7.9
(Centrally planning economies)	(124)	(3.1)	(1084)	(5.6)	(6562)	(6.4)	(113)	(2.5)	(780)	(4.1)	(5066)	(4.6)
China	3	0.1	569	2.9	3699	3.6	21	0.5	254	1.3	2955	2.7
USSR	60	1.5	341	1.8	2461	2.4	87	1.9	481	2.5	1911	1.7
Democratic People's Republic of Korea	NA	NA	23	0.1	284	0.3	NA	NA	34	0.2	152	0.1
Vietnam**	61	1.5	151	0.8	118	0.1	5	0.1	11	0.1	48	0.0
Subtotal	2371	58.5	12410	64.2	62689	60.8	2956	65.8	11524	61.0	59962	54.2
World Total	4055	100.0	19318	100.0	103032	100.0	4491	100.0	18881	100.0	110672	100.0

Note: Custom clearance statistics in calendar year.
*Total of North and South Vietnam.
**Figures for Malaysia 1960 are for Malaya.

Source: Japan Tariff Association, Summary Report: Trade of Japan, December, 1979.

Table 3.2. Japan's Direct Foreign Investment in Selected Pacific Basin Countries:
Cumulated Approval Amount (in millions of U.S. dollars and %)

End of Fiscal Year	1970		1978	
	$	%	$	%
Canada	211	5.9	715	2.7
U.S.	701	19.6	6049	22.6
Australia	210	5.9	1168	4.4
New Zealand	33	0.9	117	0.4
Mexico	40	1.1	217	0.8
(East Asian market economies)	(147)	(4.1)	(2006)	(7.5)
Republic of Korea	33	0.9	1007	3.8
Taiwan	85	2.4	284	1.1
Hong Kong	29	0.8	715	2.7
(ASEAN)	(490)	(13.7)	(5499)	(20.5)
Thailand	91	2.5	309	1.2
Singapore	33	0.9	544	2.0
Malaysia	50	1.4	473	1.8
Philippines	74	2.1	434	1.6
Indonesia	242	6.8	3739	13.9
(Centrally planning economies)	(0)	(0)	NA	NA
China	–	–	NA	NA
USSR	0	0	NA	NA
Democratic People's Republic of Korea	–	–	–	–
Vietnam*	–	–	–	–
Subtotal	1832	51.2	21270	79.3
World Total	3577	100.0	26809	100.0

*Total of North and South Vietnam.
Source: Toyo Keizai Shinposha, Japanese Multinationals: Facts & Figures 1980.

associating Japan with U.S. global defense policy. Chinese management of the commercial relationship with Japan encourages optimism regarding the development of this trade, but in a long-term perspective because current prospects have been affected by drastic revisions of Chinese procurement plans.(21)

The slow pace of China's modernization affects perceptions of the Soviet presence, but no encouraging trends are seen in Soviet behavior, and the growing projections of Soviet military power tend to increase awareness of the USSR as a power striving forcefully to effect changes in the international community. There is awareness of an enormous potential for cooperation in the development of Siberia's resources, as this potential is stressed in Soviet economic diplomacy, but its significance is somewhat negated by the military dimension of Soviet behavior and its ideological hostility.

The East Asian activities of the United States assume great prominence in Japanese views of the regional environment, because of the magnitude of the values that are realized in the complex interdependencies with that nation, and because of the difficulties of managing those interdependencies. As Japan's largest trading partner, the United States has a potent influence on the operation of Tokyo's growth strategy and must be engaged with as a nation that is making significant protectionist revisions in its liberal trade policy and that is demanding larger entry to the Japanese market. Because of its great size, the United States is first of all a challenge to Japan's capacity for coalition building, since the acquisition of allies would remove the asymmetries in bargaining power that for the present oblige Japan to accommodate U.S. demands. Stronger ties with the ASEAN members, for example, and possibly also with China, could strengthen the Japanese bargaining position. For the present, however, the U.S. attempts to change the trading relationship are obliging Japan to intensify its export promotion in other markets and attain a strong lead in international sales of high technology manufactures, and with this stimulus to a global endeavor the commercial and investment opportunities in East Asia become elements in a very wide context that extends to Latin America and the Middle East.(22)

In the military relationship with the United States its demands on Japan to increase defense spending and assume a regional security role are viewed as dangers to the Liberal Democratic Party's electoral support, since there would be agitation by the Japan Socialist Party, the leading opposition force in Japan's parliamentary system. Higher defense spending, moreover, would reduce allocations for the support of the nation's technological advancement and economic growth, while of course drawing more hostility from the USSR.

DECISION MAKING

Japan's regional policy is managed on the basis of elaborate informal consultation, in which autonomous inputs of bureaucratic expertise interact with the preferences of key cabinet figures who are identified with leading factions in the ruling party and operate with the support of that party's representatives in the Diet. The strong articulation of business interests, through the ruling party and through the bureaucracy, is responsible for a heavy concentration on economic issues. The orientation is toward comprehensive guidance of the spread of national production processes and resource extraction ventures into the ASEAN group, and of related trade matters. Resource ventures on a large scale, involving the construction of industrial complexes that benefit host countries while ensuring vital raw material supplies for Japan, are undertaken with the support of vast government funds, and constitute a form of public and private economic aid.

The close cooperation between business interests and the government generally produces coherent and functional policy. The degree of collaboration, however, can alienate sections of the public if it appears that the common welfare is being neglected, as has happened within the past decade because of major environmental problems. The representation of community interests through the Liberal Democratic party and the opposition groups can be inadequate.(23) In another important respect, moreover, the business-government partnership can be affected by sectionalism in the ministries; they tend to pursue organizational interests and adhere to their distinctive policy orientations. The scope for bureaucratic pluralism has increased with a relative decline in the influence of the Ministry of International Trade and Industry, although it remains a powerful structure in the bureaucracy.(24)

The Ministry of Finance and the Ministry of Foreign Affairs are the main structures associated with the Ministry of International Trade and Industry in the direction of regional economic policy. The influence of these ministries in decision making of course varies with the substantive issues, but it also varies with the status of the Ministers in the hierarchy of the ruling party and with the pressures exerted by business organizations. The Ministry of Finance is deeply involved in guiding the outflow of investment, and the Ministry of Foreign Affairs has an important coordinating role on Pacific cooperation matters, which may be the concern of the Energy Agency, the Ministry of Agriculture, Forestry and Fishery, or the Ministries of Transportation and Communications.

Business interests are expressed mainly through Keidanren (Federation of Economic Organizations – FEO), Nikkeiren (Japan Federation of Employers' Associations – JFEA), Nihon Shoko Kaigisho (Japan Chamber of Commerce and Industry – JCCI), and Keizai Doyukai (Japan Committee for Economic Development – JCED). While proposals from these organizations are very influential in the decision processes, they are often very forward-looking, in the sense of engaging with new policy issues before these are taken up by the economic ministries. This can happen partly because individuals and groups in these economic organizations have exchanges with economic associations in the ASEAN members, the United States, Canada, and Australia, especially through the Pacific Basin Economic Council. Some of the exchanges are assisted by private economic research institutions, in Japan and other Pacific countries.(25)

Labor interests are weakly articulated because of the fragmented structure of the Japanese trade unions. Pressures for protectionist measures by workers in labor-intensive industries are of minor significance, although employment opportunities in these industries have been declining because of losses of comparative advantage. Significant protectionist pressures, however, are exerted by farmers and small-scale manufacturers, affecting trade in beef, fruits, silk, textiles, and sundry goods.

The highly consensual character of the decision processes, while functionally biased in favor of the economic elite, is a source of dynamism in the business-bureaucratic-Liberal Democratic partnership, and this enlists vigorous cooperation from the middle and lower levels of the economic and government structures because of the culturally based emphasis on autonomous contributions from those levels. There are operational problems, however, and the most serious is that the extensive and protracted consulting makes the decision process very slow. There is a general unwillingness to overrule dissenters, and intransigent opponents of an emerging consensus can delay a final decision.(26) A further difficulty is that issues can be avoided because of the wide spread of responsibility and the limited possiblities for leadership. For these reasons, moreover, planning tends to be difficult: consensus cannot be generated about emerging and future issues.(27)

Decision making on immediate questions of regional economic policy is facilitated to a considerable extent by general awareness of achievements — the expansion of production and trade links with the ASEAN members, on a scale larger than the U.S. economic involvement in Southeast Asia, and the consolidation of Japan's role as the leading exporter of technology to China. Adaptions of policy to continue these achievements are not difficult. The emerging and future issues that seem to call for attention, however, are affected by major uncertainties and evidently discourage engagement. The issue that appears to deserve the highest priority is that of managing the forms of policy coordination that are becoming necessary with the ASEAN members and the partnerships that are developing with their local economic elites. With the expansion and diversification of Japanese production and extractive processes in the ASEAN group, the need for policy harmonization is becoming greater for each side, and the likely political costs of failures to collaborate are growing, expecially for the ASEAN administrations. Questions of effective economic sovereignty are increasing in salience for those governments, and an important common dimension of those questions is the extent to which ASEAN entrepreneurs, technocrats, and specialized staffs are drawn into the unique Japanese management subcultures. It can be argued very strongly that these matters call for farsighted political designing rather than pragmatic incremental consultative decision making that is highly susceptible to variations in its domestic inputs but rather unresponsive to the interests of other states.(28)

REGIONAL STATECRAFT

Japan's regional economic diplomacy seeks firstly to maintain high levels of understanding, trust, and goodwill in relations with East Asian states that experience balance of payments problems in part because of deficits in their commerce with Japan. These are mostly modernizing states that are attempting transitions from import-substituting to export-oriented manufacturing. To increase their foreign exchange earnings they wish to have better access to the Japanese market for their primary products and manufactured goods as developing countries they lack bargaining power on major trade issues. The overall exporting capabilities of these countries, however, are being strengthened by the large flows of Japanese investment into their industrial establishments, and accordingly the guidance of those flows is the second major feature of Japan's East Asian economic diplomacy.

Large favorable balances are customary in Japan's trade with Thailand and the Philippines, and, although there is a substantial deficit in trade with Indonesia, this is due to the high price of oil imports from that country, and a better trading relationship, from the Indonesian point of view, will necessitate the development of exports of manufactures to Japan on a relatively extensive scale. Thailand and the Philippines experience unfavorable balances in their overall foreign commerce, principally because of high production costs associated with heavily protected manufacturing, and the absence of export incentives for international firms engaged in such manufacturing. There are major flows of Japanese investment into these two states, and these evidently help to preserve friendly relations. Larger flows of Japanese capital, however, are attracted by Malaysia, whose trade with Japan is in surplus, and a great volume of that capital is drawn into Indonesia.(29)

On trade issues, then, the interests of the ASEAN members are not sufficiently identical to motivate vigorous collective bargaining, and Japan has no major incentives to grant trade concessions to Thailand and the Philippines, especially as these would have to be given to the ASEAN states as a group. Indonesia's large benefits from Japanese trade and investment evidently tend to prevent the development of empathy with Thailand and the Philippines as states lacking access to the Japanese market. The possibilities for cooperation between Thailand and the Philippines are quite limited, moreover, especially because the Philippine position within the ASEAN group is relatively isolated. Further, Japanese policy on the question of trade preferences for ASEAN members has to be decided with reference to the interests of numerous modernizing states elsewhere in the Third World that are important in Japan's foreign commerce.(30) These interests do not rule out trade preferences for the ASEAN group but they affect Japanese calculations about the demands of the two ASEAN members – Thailand and the Philippines – for whom trade concessions by Tokyo would have vital significance. For the present Japan does not have to reckon with strong pressures from these states, and the overall pattern of commercial and investment benefits in the connections with the ASEAN group can be maintained without significant costs. The relatively large flows of Japanese investment to Singapore and Malaysia respond to the attractions of well-developed economic infrastructures, and the very large flow of Japanese capital into Indonesia is encouraged by great resource endowments and market opportunities. There may be increases if there are significant improvements in the quality of its infrastructure and if it attains a higher level of stability and internal security. A larger volume of foreign direct investment could be of crucial importance for the development of this country's export manufacturing, and, thus, its capacity to enter new markets. Thailand's industrialization has been seriously affected by high oil prices.(31)

The major regional trading partners outside the ASEAN group have to cope with heavy imbalances in their commerce with Japan, but there is little political collaboration between them and each one's overall economic strength enables it to perform much better than Thailand and the Philippines in East Asian and world trade. South Korea, Taiwan, and Hong Kong are dealt with bilaterally and cannot exert much pressure to secure better access to the Japanese market. South Korea is the most important trading partner and attracts more Japanese investment than the other two, but politically it is rather isolated in the region and, like Taiwan and Hong Kong, it cannot compete against Indonesia's potent attraction for Japanese investment.(32)

Altogether, Japan relates to the ASEAN members and to South Korea, Taiwan, and Hong Kong from a position of economic and political strength, handling large shares of their foreign trade and providing much of their foreign investment. Most of the interaction is bilateral, with great asymmetries that protect Japan from pressures to grant these neighbors concessions on trade or investment issues. The volumes of Japanese trade and investment, however, as shown in tables 3.1 and 3.2, together with the differences in bargaining power, tend to cause fears of Japanese economic dominance.(33) Hence bilateral trade consultations are held frequently with these partners, and a positive attitude is shown to initiatives for regional cooperation which otherwise might develop mainly on a basis of opposition to the spread of the Japanese economic presence.

Support for regional cooperation can be ranked as the third major feature of Japan's East Asian economic diplomacy. The first major step was an initiative to establish the Asian Development Bank (ADB), for financial cooperation, in 1966. The bank was established with an initial capital of U.S. $1.1 billion, and Takeshi Watanabe became the first president of the institution. Japan has since played an important role in financing regional development projects and has offered large-scale assistance to ASEAN members as a group for five major industrial enterprises that had been planned for the promotion of complementarity in that association. Although disagreements within the ASEAN group have affected the development of these projects, Japanese support can be anticipated by the ASEAN members if they reach agreement on major schemes for regional industrial collaboration.

Japan, moreover, is in a position to link its large-scale technology exporting projects for resource development in any ASEAN country, especially Indonesia, with those under way or contemplated in other members of that grouping.(34)

As an extension of the principle of support for regional cooperation, Japan seeks to promote approval of the concept of Pacific collaboration between North American and East Asian states. This is done with sensitivity to ASEAN fears of possible Japanese and U.S. domination of a future Pacific economic community and with hopes of encouraging participation by Mexico and several Latin American states, as well as the United States, Canada, Australia, New Zealand, and South Korea. In September 1980, Japan cosponsored with Australia a conference on Pacific cooperation which was attended by government, business, and academic representatives from the ASEAN members, the United States, Canada, Japan, and Australia.(35) Official and private Japanese advocates of Pacific cooperation see possibilities for harmonizing the industrial, trade, ocean, investment, and energy policies of East Asian, North American, and Latin American states. There is a reluctance to propose security cooperation on such a broad basis, but there is an interest in regional collaboration between the security and economic issue areas, especially for the protection of Pacific sea and air routes, as most of Japan's commerce passes through the Malacca Strait and the Panama Canal. There is also an interest in developing a common policy on the use and disposal of nuclear fuel, in line with the purposes of the nuclear nonproliferation treaty, which Japan has ratified. Cooperation in foreign aid programs is also envisaged, and it is anticipated that goodwill generated in this way will be increased with wider cultural exchanges.

Japanese official development assistance is extended mainly to Pacific countries, on a scale somewhat below the U.S. level. The volume, shown in table 3.3, represented a .23 percent of GNP in 1978, i.e., $2.2 billion, of which 75.2 percent was in the form of grants. As a proportion of GNP, this aid is lower than the average of the Development Assistance Committee of OECD. In the Japanese view, however, a substantial volume of the nation's government-aided private investment in Third World countries is a form of economic assistance and makes vital contributions to growth, especially through joint ventures with local firms, that might not be matched if equivalent funds were provided as official development aid. In response to proposals from OECD countries Japan's official development assistance is tending to increase, as a proportion of GNP, although this is difficult to achieve because of heavy budget deficits attributable to revenue losses associated with high prices for imported oil.(36)

The management of official development assistance and the guidance of private investment into developing Pacific countries, although vital areas of regional policy, have much less prominence than the interaction with the United States on trade, monetary, and investment issues. This is a matter of global as well as Pacific policy, and the interchanges with the United States take the form of Japanese

Table 3.3. Japan's economic cooperation toward selected Pacific Basin countries (net disbursement in 1978)

	Official Development Assistance (ODA)					Direct invest-ment	Portfolio invest-ment	Other Official Funds & Private Funds			Grand total
	Grants funds technology		Subtotal	Gov't loans etc.	Sub-total			Export credits OOF	PF	Sub-total	
(East Asian market economies)	(3,4)	(8.9)	(12.3)	(43.1)	(55.4)	(309.6)	(88.7)	(161.1)	(22.2)	(581.5)	(636.9)
Republic of Korea	3.4	8.1	11.5	54.6	66.1	171.8	71.1	293.4	31.9	568.1	634.2
Taiwan	-	-	-	-11.4	-11.4	24.6	-2.2	56.2	-112.5	-33.9	-45.3
Hong Kong	-	0.8	0.8	-0.1	0.7	113.2	19.8	-188.5	102.8	47.3	48.0
(ASEAN)	(33.1)	(72.4)	(105.4)	(344.0)	(449.5)	(614.5)	(561.6)	(81.7)	(102.5)	(1196.4)	(1645.7)
Thailand	6.1	20.0	26.1	77.6	103.8	20.4	105.7	-6.5	5.3	125.0	228.7
Singapore	-	4.2	4.2	-0.6	3.6	94.6	-0.1	-45.1	45.2	94.6	98.2
Malaysia	2.9	7.8	10.6	37.4	48.0	73.6	109.2	-25.3	6.8	163.6	211.6
Philippines	9.8	15.4	25.2	41.3	66.5	46.9	249.9	11.9	85.8	394.5	460.9
Indonesia	14.3	25.0	39.3	188.3	227.6	379.0	96.9	-16.7	-40.6	418.7	646.3
Oceania	(2.5)	(3.8)	(6,4)	(-1.7)	(4.6)	(16.5)	(-0.3)	(-3.9)	(-0.8)	(13.2)	(17.8)
Mexico	0.6	4.3	4.9	-0.2	4.7	32.4	209.7	43.9	30.4	316.4	321.0
Panama	-	0.3	0.3	-	0.3	89.2	348.5	-3.0	-31.2	403.5	403.8
Colombia	1.4	0.8	2.2	-	2.2	0.5	-1.7	-2.8	-0.1	-4.1	-1.9
Ecuador	1.9	1.2	3.1	4.1	7.1	-0.1	-	-3.0	-1.7	-4.7	2.4
Peru	-	4.9	4.9	6.6	11.5	19.7	-0.3	-3.5	0.3	16.1	27.6
Chile	-	2.3	2.3	-1.3	1.1	-10.8	23.8	-7.6	-0.3	5.1	6.2
Vietnam	19.5	1.2	20.7	7.8	28.5	-	59.4	-	-	59.4	87.9
Subtotal	62.4	100.1	162.5	402.4	564.9	1071.5	1289.4	99.5	122.9	2582.8	3147.4
World Total	162.2	221.2	383.4	1147.6	1531.0	2025.8	3692.4	1286.5	412.1	7416.8	8947.8

Notes: - signe indicates net repayment   Fiscal year

Source: MITI, White Paper on Economic Cooperation 1979.

responses to U.S. official demands stimulated by U.S. interest group reactions to Japanese export promotion. Japan, valuing highly the access that has been gained to the U.S. market, tends to accommodate gradually to U.S. pressures and threats of pressure, although these often violate rules of the General Agreement on Tariffs and Trade, and does not accept U.S. charges that the large trade imbalance is a cause of overall U.S. balance of payments difficulties, since these can be attributed to very heavy payments for oil imports and to the failures of U.S. manufacturers to meet the expectations of foreign consumers. U.S. demands for expansionist Japanese policies that might increase imports are resisted, but U.S. efforts to attract large Japanese investments evoke positive responses.(37) On each side the interaction is managed without reference to questions of regional cooperation, and for the present neither Japan nor the United States attempts to draw other Pacific states into the interchanges. If Japan could enlist the support of such states its capacity to bargain with the United States would be strengthened, of course, but the United States would retain considerable leverage because of its options for introducing strong protectionist modifications into its basically liberal foreign trade policy.

The principle of regional cooperation partially covers relations with China, although this state is not considered a potential participant in the initial stages of a scheme for Pacific collaboration. Japan is consolidating itself as the leading exporter of technology to China, making available credits in coordination with the U.S. and West European suppliers, and showing a firm commitment to the support of China's industrialization that evokes Soviet hostility, although the military benefits for China are presently small and indirect. The exports to China are about 20 percent less than those to Taiwan and about 30 percent more than those to the USSR (see table 3.1). There is a substantial balance in Japan's favor, and this is likely to persist because of the Chinese need for technology and relatively weak Japanese demand for Chinese light manufactures. The commercial exchanges have a relatively long recent history, beginning with small-scale unofficial trade in the early 1950s, before the confrontation between China and the USSR. A Chinese objective was to utilize trade diplomacy in order to secure Japanese derecognition of the Chinese Nationalist government on Taiwan and the establishment of full diplomatic relations between Tokyo and Peking. Japanese business interest in China's industrial growth is active partly because of problems of access to North American and West European markets, and the possibilities for future coordination of areas of economic policy with China have some significance for Japan's regional diplomacy.(38)

On the periphery of the large zone of constructively interacting nations is the Soviet Union. Japanese regional policy responds to that power's formidable volume of conflictual behavior and to its moderate initiatives for economic cooperation. Relations with the USSR were normalized in 1956, and trade with that power expanded with the detente between it and the United States. Japan began to assist in the development of Siberia's resources during the late 1960s, and more actively in the early 1970s, but the relationship deteriorated in the later 1970s as Soviet policy became intransigent on the question of returning the Kurile Islands seized from Japan in 1945. The islands have been used increasingly for military purposes, and the USSR has assumed a more aggressive image since its invasion of Afghanistan. The USSR had reacted in a hostile fashion to a Sino-Japanese Peace and Friendship Treaty in 1978 which had included an "anti-hegemony" clause. In Chinese rhetoric this was directed against the USSR, but for Japan it was acceptable as a general principle.(39)

Relationships with the Indochinese states are distant, because of Vietnam's alignment with the USSR and hostility to China and because of Japan's sympathy for ASEAN condemnations of Vietnamese military activities against Thailand.   Japan has no incentive to strain its friendship with China by developing ties with Vietnam but has an interest in persuading Vietnam to reduce its dependence on the USSR and to build up friendly relations with the ASEAN members.   Japan began providing economic assistance to Vietnam after the Communist victories in Indochina during the mid 1970s, but discontinued this aid when the Vietnamese invaded Cambodia. A resumption of economic assistance will be possible if Hanoi shows a willingness to observe the principles of coexistence in its regional policy.

Of more immediate concern is the possibility that North Korea's policy will undergo a significant change. The relationship with Pyongyang is even more distant than that with Vietnam, but the adverse security implications of this are more apparent because of North Korea's proximity to Japan and to the Soviet Far East. The shifts in China's policy over the past decade are expected to have some influence on North Korea, and for the present Japan is expanding trade with North Korea and increasing economic contacts with the North Korean government.

The overall emphasis on developing commercial relations with the East Asian Communist states, to consolidate and extend ties based on peaceful coexistence, is partially responsible for an avoidance of security questions in Japan's regional diplomacy, except with respect to the immediate dangers posed by threatening Soviet nearby deployments. There can be no major projections of Japanese power for purposes of deterrence without large increases in defense spending, which politically are not feasible, and the scope for Japanese military cooperation with Southeast Asian states is still limited because of their memories of World War II sufferings. The evolution of a Japanese security role in East Asia, moreover, would require a high degree of policy coordination with the United States, and this could be difficult to achieve because of the strains that have been present in the relationship with Washington since the Nixon administration's disruption in 1971 of what had been a collegial partnership.   At that time the United States had failed to honor obligations to consult with Japan before making any changes in its policy towards China, and the political costs for the then Prime Minister Sato had been serious.

PROSPECTS

Japan's characteristics as the central economic power of East Asia are not likely to change in the foreseeable future. The distinctive qualities of the political culture will remain largely unaffected by external influences, general public satisfaction with the Liberal Democratic Party's management of the political economy is likely to remain fairly high, the major business enterprises will continue to respond to administrative guidance from the economic ministries, the Japan Socialist Party's challenge to the Liberal Democrats will be of moderate proportions because of problems of policy adjustment, and the dynamic growth associated with export promotion is not likely to slacken. With the spread of extractive, processing, and manufacturing operations in the ASEAN group, South Korea, and Taiwan, and to some extent in China, levels of dependence and interdependence affecting Japanese interests in the immediate environment will rise. Japan's capabilities to manage its regional economic connections will increase, absolutely and in relative terms, while the high-growth East Asian states will remain rather isolated from each other and thus unable to engage in collective decision making for improvement of the terms on which they interact with Japan.

All the elements of societal, normative, structural, and functional continuity in the Japanese postindustrial system will be attributable mainly to the potency of the collective thrust in the general culture and to its expression in vigorous forms of autonomous task orientation in the middle and lower levels of the economic and political institutions. Any introductions of Western individualism would tend to fragment the patterns of collaboration, but it must be stressed that their vitality seems to be assured. The export of this culture on a scale that will match the spread of Japanese production processes into the modernizing East Asian states, however, will be difficult because of basic dissimilarities that seem to discourage intensive diplomacy for this purpose.

For resolution of the large and complex issues of cooperation with other East Asian states and with the United States, extensive and sustained consultations will be necessary, especially because the dimensions of these issues are growing, and also because the cultural problems of interaction will remain substantial. The industrial, trade, investment, and monetary policies of the high-growth East Asian modernizing states will require more and more substantial Japanese cooperation as their economies are more deeply penetrated and invigorated by transnational production processes under Tokyo's administrative guidance. At the same time the planned expansion of the Japanese industrial establishment will necessitate, from the Japanese point of view, more and more comprehensive collaboration from the host governments. For Tokyo, the best results, at least for the time being, will be realized within the present pattern of bilateral relations, which facilitates separate handling of the issues in each dyadic context. It will be important for Japan, however, to maintain a positive attitude to proposals for regional cooperation. An elementary consideration here is that other states advocating such cooperation should not be given an opportunity to coalesce on the basis of antipathies to and fears of Japan. A more important concern is that Japan can expect to evolve a natural leadership role, because of the size of its national economy, if its regional diplomacy inspires sufficient trust and goodwill.

Long-term planning is needed for the development of a regional leadership role that will be directed toward broadly consultative exchanges with the high-growth modernizing East Asian states and that will draw them into collective decision making for policy harmonization. Through participation in multilateral endeavors those states, hopefully, will acquire a sense of community that will reduce their fears of Japanese economic domination while enabling them to expand their production and trade links with Japan and with each other. In such a context Japan's bargaining capabilities will be less than they are in the current pattern of bilateral relations, but the altered terms of interaction will facilitate cooperation on a larger scale, and with less risk. Of course the consultative processes may be obstructed by the intransigent behavior of some participating states, but the risks of this will be reduced if Japanese business associations support their government's leadership activities by developing extensive ties with economic groups in those other East Asian states.

The diversification and expansion of Japan's East Asian economic role, in conditions of increasing political harmony and cooperation, will support and in turn be strengthened by the continuing growth of Japanese involvement in the global economy. Large proportions of the necessary supplies of primary products for the nation's industrial establishment will be acquired from the East Asian trading partners, under firm arrangements through which those states will receive technology and accept extensions of Japanese international manufacturing enterprises. Meanwhile Japan's global trading and investment activities will be sustained by the outputs of industries utilizing raw materials from the East Asian trading partners and will assist those purchases as well as the exports of technology and manufactures to those partners. But all this will be predicated on diplomacy aimed at promoting confidence, understanding, and constructive interaction, and at the development of a wide consensus on the realization of a comprehensive design for regional policy collaboration.

A security dimension can be expected to evolve in Japan's East Asian diplomacy, differentiated from that of the United States and mostly keyed to the major forms of economic cooperation. A politically important element of this dimension may well be the Japanese contribution to the development of a common commitment to the building of an international community in the region. If such a community begins to emerge the authoritarian administrations in some of the member states will be drawn into the acceptance of forms of international accountability that hopefully will make them more responsible domestically, and thus less vulnerable to externally supported political violence. In addition, solidarity within the community will make the member governments less inclined to accommodate the political demands of the USSR that are tending to become more insistent with the projection of its military power. Japan is seeking to draw the USSR into the acceptance of widening interdependencies that will favorably influence its external policy but must also take politically feasible steps to promote an effective balance of social and other forces in the East Asian strategic context.

The development of more active Japanese statecraft in the immediate environment will hopefully involve stronger partnership with the United States. There is a danger that economic nationalism will increase on each side, especially because of the persistence of tensions and conflicts arising out of issues that are avoided by the disjointed incrementalism of the United States and the more coherent incrementalism of the Japanese. The United States will remain Japan's most important source of imports, although its share of these will tend to decrease as Japan's global trade expands, especially in response to opportunities presented by the more advanced Third World states, and imbalances are likely to persist in U.S. trade with Japan, because of the greater vigor of the Japanese economy and the inflationary factors that maintain a high level of consumer demand in the United States. For Japan it will be increasingly necessary to seek deeper understanding with U.S. policy makers on questions of basic economic policy, and it would seem that the necessary initiatives will have to come from the business groups that make potent inputs into the management of Japan's foreign economic relations. While contributing to the shaping of economic diplomacy, moreover, such groups will have to engage more actively, on long-term issues, with their counterparts in the United States, who represent the more permanent and more influential sources of U.S. foreign economic policy. For dialogue oriented towards joint decision making, of course, each side's difficulties with respect to planning will have to be overcome, and, in the bargaining dimension of such dialogue, Japan's position will be stronger if broad cooperation is developing with national manufacturing and trading enterprises in the high-growth modernizing East Asian states.

NOTES

(1) See Bradley M. Richardson, The Political Culture of Japan (Berkeley: University of California Press, 1974).

(2) See T.J. Pempel, "Japanese Foreign Economic Policy: The Domestic Bases for International Behavior," in Between Power and Plenty, ed. Peter J. Katzenstein (Madison: University of Wisconsin Press, 1978), pp. 139-190.

(3) See Kazuo Sato, ed., Industry and Business in Japan (White Plains, N.Y.: M.E. Sharpe); and Leon Hollerman, ed., Japan and the United States: Economic and Political Adversaries (Boulder, Colo.: Westview Press, 1980).

(4) See Pempel, "Japanese Foreign Economic Policy."

(5) See Lee W. Farnsworth, "Japan in 1980: The Conservative Resurgence," Asian Survey 21, No. 1 (January 1981): 70-83.

(6) See Gavin Boyd, "East Asia," in Comparative Regional Systems, ed. Werner J. Feld and Gavin Boyd (Elmsford, N.Y.: Pergamon Press, 1980), pp. 195-236.

(7) See Masataka Kosaka, "The International Economic Policy of Japan," in The Foreign Policy of Modern Japan, ed. Robert A. Scalapino (Berkeley: University of California Press, 1977), pp. 207-226.

(8) See references to Malaysia and Singapore in Boyd, "East Asia."

(9) See Lawrence B. Krause and Sueo Sekiguchi, eds., Economic Interaction in the Pacific Basin (Wasington: Brookings Institution, 1980); and Ross Garnaut, ed., ASEAN in a Changing Pacific and World Economy (Canberra: Australian National University Press, 1980).

(10) See Scalapino, The Foreign Policy of Modern Japan, part IV.

(11) Ibid.

(12) Isaac Shapiro, "The Risen Sun: Japanese Gaullism?" Foreign Policy 41 (Winter 1980-81): 62-81.

(13) See Hollerman, Japan and the United States.

(14) Terutomo Ozawa, "Japan's New Resource Diplomacy: Government Backed Group Investment," Journal of World Trade Law 14, no. 1 (January/February 1980): 3-13; and "International Investment and Industrial Structure: New Theoretical Implications from the Japanese Experience," Oxford Economic Papers 31, no. 1 (March 1979): 72-92.

(15) See Kosaka, "The International Economic Policy of Japan."

(16) Ozawa, "Japan's New Resource Diplomacy"; and Chalmers Johnson, "MITI and Japanese International Economic Policy," in Scalapino, The Foreign Policy of Modern Japan, pp. 227-280.

(17) See Takashi Inoguchi, "Economic Conditions and Mass Support in Japan, 1960-1976," in Models of Political Economy, ed. Paul Whiteley (Beverly Hills: SAGE Publications, 1980), pp. 121-154; and Scalapino, The Foreign Policy of Modern Japan, part II.

(18) Ozawa, "Japan's New Resource Diplomacy" and "International Investment and Industrial Structure."

(19) See tables in John Wong, ASEAN Economies in Perspective (Philadelphia: Institute for the Study of Human Issues, 1979).

(20) See Hahn Bae-ho, "Korea-Japan Relations in the 1970s," Asian Survey 20, no. 11 (November 1980): 1087-1097.

(21) See Shinkichi Eto, "Recent Developments in Sino-Japanese Relations," Asian Survey 20, no. 7 (July 1980): 726-743.

(22) See Hollerman, Japan and the United States.

(23) Hugh Patrick, Japanese Industrialization and its Social Consequences (Berkeley: University of California Press, 1976).

(24) See T.J. Pempel, ed., Policymaking in Contemporary Japan (Ithaca, N.Y.: Cornell University Press, 1977).

(25) See Sir John Crawford, ed., Pacific Economic Co-operation (Singapore: Heinemann).

(26) Kosaka, "The International Economic Policy of Japan."

(27) Ibid.

(28) See observations on necessity for policy coordination by major Pacific actors in Krause and Sekiguchi, Economic Interaction in the Pacific Basin.

(29) See Garnaut, ASEAN in a Changing Pacific and World Economy, part III.

(30) Ibid.

(31) See references to Thai production and trade in Krause and Sekiguchi, Economic Interaction in the Pacific Basin.

(32) See Hahn Bae-ho, "Korea-Japan Relations in the 1970s"; and Krause and Sekiguchi, Economic Interaction in the Pacific Basin.

(33) See comments in Crawford, Pacific Economic Cooperation.

(34) See Ozawa, "Japan's New Resource Diplomacy."

(35) See Crawford, Pacific Economic Cooperation.

(36) White Paper on Economic Cooperation (Tokyo: Ministry of International Trade and Industry, 1980).

(37) See Hollerman, Japan and the United States.

(38) See Eto, "Recent Developments in Sino-Japanese Relations."

(39) Ibid.

4 Asean Regional Policies

Gavin Boyd

The regional policies of the high-growth Southeast Asian states that have strong economic ties with Japan significantly affect the prospects for Pacific cooperation. For Japan the participation of these states would be essential in the planning of large scale policy collaboration between East Asian and North American nations. Individually, then, and as members of the Association of Southeast Asian Nations, the faster-growing Southeast Asian states influence Japanese attitudes toward proposals for a Pacific Economic Community. North American views of such proposals are similarly influenced because of the importance of economic exchanges with Southeast Asia for the United States and Canada.

The growth rates of the members of the Association of Southeast Asian Nations have been attained through the maintenance of substantially open market economies, the attraction of large flows of foreign direct investment, and the expansion of primary and manufactured exports, especially to Japan and the United States. Each national growth strategy has been highly self-interested, often to the exclusion of concerns with the interests of neighbors, and has been implemented with intense domestic preoccupations, some related to distributive bias favoring the upper and middle classes, but there has been increasing consciousness of common subregional interests among the political and economic elites of the ASEAN members. Awareness of shared security interests grew significantly after the Communist victories in Indochina and was increased by Vietnam's invasion of Cambodia and the Chinese attack on Vietnam early in 1979. Appreciation of the advantages of consultations and cooperation on economic matters increased during the mid- and later 1970s because of the inflationary effects of high oil prices and the shifts towards protectionism in the policies of the major industrialized democracies. Trade between the ASEAN members grew slowly, however, despite modest advances towards trade liberalization, and little progress was made towards the development of common institutions to support initiatives for policy coordination within the grouping.

There is some political cooperation between the ASEAN members on major external issues, principally relating to Vietnam and the Sino-Soviet confrontation, but large areas of each member's foreign relations are managed with little use of opportunities for consultation in the context of ASEAN interests. There appear to be no substantial efforts to coordinate foreign investment policies or to evolve common positions on questions of trade with the United States, Japan, and the West European countries. The collective bargaining potential of the Association is thus not utilised. The development of a common political will to engage in integrative activity on a significant scale is made difficult by relatively low levels of understanding, trust, and goodwill. This situation reflects the self-interested concerns of the mostly authoritarian leaderships in the ASEAN group.

Proposals for Pacific economic cooperation tend to arouse fears among ASEAN elites that Japan and the United States would dominate an emerging economic community of East Asian and North American nations. Indications of possibly growing Japanese and U.S. interest in Pacific cooperation, however, are not stimulating increased collaboration between the ASEAN members, although the development of more cohesion within their association would enable them to work more effectively for the protection of their interests in the context of any schemes for regional trade liberalization and complementary industrial development.

ATTRIBUTES

The ASEAN members are developing states with largely traditional cultures that facilitate the imposition of forms of authoritarian rule and that in some respects hinder modernization. These nations began to modernize during the colonial period, and, because of the influences of that period and of subsequent dependencies on unequal economic interchanges with major industrialized democracies, have been experiencing imbalanced growth, with little of the complementarity that could facilitate trade expansion within the association. Levels of interdependence between the ASEAN members are low, and their ruling elites thus do not see compelling incentives to manage those interdependencies collectively. In their behavior toward each other, moreover, these national leaderships are conscious that their levels of mutual understanding and of cooperative intent tend to be moderate to low because of their own characteristics as mostly authoritarian elites, as well as because of fairly restricted communication flows within the association and inadequate experiences of the benefits of policy coordination. Further, the attitudes of these elites are influenced by awareness that they compete against each other in their attempts to hold out incentives to foreign investors and that the acquisition of foreign capital and the penetration of markets in the industrialized countries is of greater immediate importance for economic growth than the promotion of commercial exchanges within the association. There is a large potential for such exchanges, subject to the reduction of high protective barriers by most of the members, and to the development of a viable consensus for planning industrial complementarity, but, if there were substanital trade liberalization within the grouping, the more industrialized states – Singapore and Malaysia – would benefit disproportionately, and there would probably be no common resolve to redistribute the benefits to freer commerce, and to collaborate for the guidance and control of the transnational enterprises that would be most active in such trade.

The three authoritarian states within the ASEAN group – Indonesia, Thailand, and the Philippines – are highly protectionist, but commerce within the grouping is considerably higher than within the Andean Pact, whose members have to contend with very difficult dependency problems. Nevertheless the ASEAN members lack the political will that the Andean governments showed, until recently, to engage with problems of distributing the benefits of freer trade and with the requirements for common foreign investment policies.

The orientations of the ruling elites among the authoritarian ASEAN members largely determine this group's prospects for community formation; Malaysia and Singapore are the smaller members, and, although there are few affinities between Indonesia, Thailand, and the Philippines, they have compatible if not shared interests in maintaining their high protectionist barriers, which have been set up to facilitate import-substituting industrialization.(1) The political psychology of the ruling elites in these authoritarian regimes is influenced by parasitic connections with international firms operating in their national markets and is strongly affected by preoccupations with the generation of political power through intensely personal clientelist connections, in parochial contexts, involving the manipulation of communal attachments and sentiments. Interest in and capacities to engage with questions of regional policy are negatively affected, and the inevitable failures to build up effective political institutions also tend to prevent leaderships from applying their energies to issues of regional cooperation and from becoming sufficiently open to constructive policy inputs from their bureaucrats, who generally observe caution because of the arbitrary tendencies and the ignorance of their political masters.

Of the authoritarian members, Indonesia and Thailand are military regimes. They can be described as middle class praetorian systems, as their army leaderships largely identify with and show bias toward the interests of their urban middle classes and the better-off elements of their rural populations, and as only their middle classes – not their workers and peasants – have undergone significant degrees of politicization. Both military elites endeavor to modernize their countries, utilizing the skills of relatively able civilian technocrats, and their growth strategies emphasize private sector development, with generous concessions to international firms and moderate concerns for the encouragement of national enterprises. The demonstration of zeal for economic development is a major element in each leadership's attempts to mobilize popular support, but there is little concern with equity in the distribution of benefits from industrialization, and, especially in Indonesia, maldistribution causes severe deprivations for large sections of the rural populations and for the urban workers, who cannot articulate their interests effectively because of the heavy repression they have to endure.

The Indonesian military regime imposes its controls on a culturally divided society, identifying with the abangan communities of Central and East Java, and in a somewhat restrained fashion with their deep antipathies toward the orthodox Moslem communities of West Java and the other islands, who are disliked because of their aspirations to establish a political system based on Islamic beliefs. Abangan fears and resentments towards the orthodox Moslems were directed into the support of extreme leftist policies by former President Sukarno and by the once powerful Indonesian Communist Party which flourished during his rule; but currents of abangan sentiment were turned against Communists and extreme socialists when the present military leaders began to establish their regime after the failure of an attempted Communist coup in 1965. Orthodox Moslem feelings were also turned against the leftist political groups, but after the military authorities consolidated their power, opportunities for the representation of orthodox Moslem interests were severely restricted, and the armed services were almost entirely dominated by abangan elements. An officially sponsored political party, organized with an emphasis on functional representation, receives large majorities in a weak legislative body through regular elections held under the auspices of the military authorities, but this party is not significantly open to interest articulation from local groups, and is not utilized as a means of transmitting leadership views and values to Indonesian society on a constant basis. Opportunities for other political groups to compete against the vote gathering functions of the official party are greatly limited by open and covert administrative measures. Opposition from the media is discouraged by threats of drastic reprisals, and demands by university students for more representative government are countered by forceful assertions of control, in circumstances that leave the students without allies among the repressed urban workers. For the present the regime is stable, although its methods of operating produce little equilibrium and tend to generate much discontent. As in other military regimes, there are intraelite rivalries that may lead rapidly to severe conflict, and the danger of destabilization through these will increase if the status of the dominant figures is adversely affected by their responses to any upsurge of popular unrest.(2)

The Thai praetorian system operates within a culturally homogeneous society and, despite considerable corruption at the higher levels, identifies fairly effectively with the predominantly Buddhist values of that society, while deriving a measure of legitimacy from respect for the King as the head of the nation. The military leaders in this system are less repressive than their Indonesian counterparts, because of memories of a popular revolt that removed an army-dominated regime in 1973, and because of a need to demonstrate a capacity for responsible government that will make some impression on U.S. legislators and officials. Thailand is heavily dependent on U.S. military support, for protection against any large-scale attacks by the Vietnamese forces occupying Cambodia, and for the suppression of Communist guerillas operating in the Northeast provinces.   These guerillas have been supported by China, but Vietnam is seeking to gain control of their movement and is well placed to give them military assistance through Cambodia and Laos.

A degree of accountability is maintained in the Thai system because of the presence of a consultative assembly, set up through elections much freer than those in Indonesia, and the toleration of considerable activity by political parties, several of which compete effectively against government-sponsored organizations.   Rivalries within the military elite, however, threaten the stability of the system.   In the rural areas, moreover, and especially in the Northeast, there is much poverty and exploitation that is ignored by the regime, and this provides opportunities for the growth of protest movements.   In the urban areas there has been some politicization of the students and workers, especially because of the experiences of the 1973 upheaval and the limited freedoms allowed for parties contesting national elections, but the emergence of a strong political organization capable of mobilizing general support for democratic government is made difficult by the tendencies of Thai politicians to unite in factions and cliques rather than combine in large numbers for the building of nationwide parties.(3)

Thailand's prospects for political development, like Indonesia's, have been affected by experiences of military rule because these have restricted opportunities for the acquisition of organizational and mobilization skills by the civilian elite and have affected public attitudes by limiting opportunities for political participation.   In each of these military regimes, however, the leadership is to some degree collective, and this has positive implications for stability and for the possibilities of evolution toward more responsible government, although both military elites exhibit disdain for civilian politicians and show confidence that army leaders can provide more enlightened and more effective administration.

The Philippine regime is a contrasting form of authoritarianism, as its main feature is a heavy concentration of power in a civilian politician, President Marcos, who enjoys military backing. He has done little to institutionalize his power, and, because he is reluctant to delegate it, except to close friends and relatives, the functioning of the regime is heavily dependent on his personal capacities to dominate, administer, persuade, and bargain. His style of rule is patrimonial, and its alienating effects are not mitigated by any projection of charisma, although this is attempted. There is blatant administrative corruption, and, as in Indonesia, as well as in Thailand to a lesser extent, the political economy is managed with a strong bias toward upper and middle class interests and with a callous indifference to the welfare of the lower strata, especially the urban workers, whose real incomes have fallen very much since Marcos established himself as a dictator. Yet there is little organized opposition to the regime; army loyalties have been maintained by generous budget allocations, supplemented by U.S. military aid, and the two main political parties that functioned in the former democratic regime have been too factionalized and too deeply affected by clientelism to exert pressures for a return to representative government. A Chinese-inspired Communist movement contests the regime's control of some rural areas in Luzon but evidently receives little aid from Peking.(4)

Malaysia and Singapore are the democratic polities in the ASEAN group, and their administrations enjoy relatively high levels of legitimacy because of substantial voter support and significant achievements in the promotion of economic growth and social welfare. Each state is dominated by one party, and in Malaysia it is a communal organization, the United Malays National Organization, which identifies with Malay interests rather than those of the Chinese community. This community has very strong control of the national economy, and the ruling United Malays National Organization promotes economic development with emphasis on improving the lot of the Malays, through measures that discriminate against the Chinese, especially in educational opportunities and government employment. The political parties that draw support from the Chinese community are weak, and some of them function as coalition partners of the United Malays National Organization, which exploits their rivalries and their interests in acquiring some participation in the work of government. Communal antagonisms between the Malays and the Chinese tend to grow because of the discriminatory aspects of the effort to give the Malays a stronger economic role and because the ruling party is under pressure to make more use of its administrative power in order to uplift the Malays. The pressure comes from extreme Malay communal groups, and from militant Islamic revival associations; it has some effect because the economic advancement of the Malays is very slow, despite the degrees to which they are favored by the government's education and employment policies, and by the use of public funds to facilitate Malay ownership of manufacturing and trading enterprises.

Levels of competence and integrity in the Malaysian administration are medium to high, and it manages a fairly open economy that attracts foreign investment mainly because of the quality of its infrastructure. Similar observations can be made about Singapore, where the ruling party is a multiracial social democratic organization that is strongly committed to private sector development and to substantial allocations for welfare. The population of this small state is mostly Chinese, and it enjoys a high degree of stability because of its administration's successes in promoting racial harmony and in maintaining fairly rapid economic growth. Much of this growth results from well-administered foreign direct investment that is guided into manufacturing for export.(5)

REGIONAL AFFINITIES AND TIES

Within the ASEAN group the Philippines are relatively isolated, culturally, politically, and economically, while Indonesia and Malaysia have significant cultural bonds and political links. The principal trade flows of the Association are between Indonesia, Singapore, Malaysia, and Thailand.

The Philippines were deeply penetrated by Western culture during periods of U.S. and Spanish rule. The experience of Spanish colonialism resulted in an almost total acceptance of Christianity, and under American control during the first half of this century the country enjoyed a high degree of internal autonomy, which ensured much openness to U.S. culture. After independence the political elite exhibited little anticolonial nationalism and could not identify with the strongly anti-Western orientation that Indonesia assumed under President Sukarno between the mid-1950s and the mid-1960s. As moderate nationalists the Philippine leaders could relate to Thailand's elites, since these had escaped colonial domination and had not become strong opponents of Western imperialism, but few economic exchanges with Thailand had developed under U.S. rule, and the nation's trade remained centered on the United States.

Because the Philippines is on the periphery of the main economic exchanges within the ASEAN group and has closer economic and military ties with the United States than any of the other members, its political links with those members have been relatively weak. Constructive interchanges with Indonesia have been possible only since the ending of the Sukarno regime in that country, and the basis for rapport with that state's military leaders has been narrow. The possibilities for interaction with Malaysia were limited until the abandonment, in the 1970s, of a Philippine claim to the East Malaysian state of Sabah, and the imposition of Malaysian restraint on the movement of military supplies from East Malaysia to Moslem insurgents in the Southern Philippines. Communication with Malaysia, and also with Singapore, is facilitated by the widespread use of English in both states, but for geographic reasons the Philippine authorities are more aware of their need to relate to Indonesia, their nearest neighbor in the ASEAN group. Indonesia is the only ASEAN member with which Philippine trade is above the $100 million level each way, and Philippine trade with Malaysia is roughly half that level.

The Philippines has the most extensive and most developed education system in the ASEAN group, and thus has a potential to serve as a major center for scientific and technological advancement and for cultural exchange. Schools and universities were established in large numbers during the period of U.S. rule, and since independence their growth has been assisted under U.S. aid programs. Philippine administrations, however, have done little to develop cultural and educational ties with the other ASEAN members, and as a group these members have not built up a common resolve to promote close cultural bonds between their societies.

Between Indonesia and Malaysia there are significant linguistic and religious affinities. Indonesian, the common language of Java, the most populous island in Indonesia, is almost identical with Malay, the language of the dominant ethnic group in Malaysia. This group's Moslem faith, moreover, which has been somewhat penetrated by Western influences, has affinities with the Islamic elements of abangan culture in Central and East Java, and these facilitate some rapport between Indonesian military leaders and Malaysian government figures. Shared antipathies to the local Chinese communities and to the Peking regime contribute to the maintenance of a significant level of understanding, and, thus, to common opposition to Thailand's policy of collaborating with China in the support of anti-Vietnamese guerillas in Cambodia. The development of bonds through economic cooperation, however, is hindered by the sharp contrasts between Malaysia's relatively open and more industrialized economy and Indonesia's high tariff barriers and relatively less-developed industries. Indonesia's growth, moreover, is becoming heavily dependent on Japanese investment, while Malaysia's external dependencies are remaining quite diversified, especially because of the attraction of West European as well as U.S. and Japanese capital.(6)

Thailand, despite geographic proximity, stands apart from Malaysia and Indonesia because of linguistic and cultural differences. The Thai language has no affinities with Malay, and Thai Buddhism has little in common with the Islamic culture of the Malays. The development of Thailand's external contacts has been strongly influenced by military and economic dependence on the United States, which has been accepted because of acute concerns with dangers to security posed by China and Vietnam as well as because of the needs of Thai military elites for external resources to strengthen their domestic controls. Malaysia's external contacts have been much less influenced by proximate threats to security, and more active economic ties with West European states have been responsible for a quite different orientation in commercial and foreign investment policy. Thailand, like Indonesia, is strongly protectionist and would have to expect that Malaysia's relatively more open and more industrialized economy would benefit greatly from trade liberalization within the ASEAN group.(7)

Outside the subregional context, the ASEAN members have ties with the former colonial powers and Japan but no significant bonds with other developing states or with the major Communist regimes. The traditional Islamic cultures of Malaysia and Indonesia are moderately open to revivalist Moslem influences from Southwest Asia and the Middle East, but Thailand's Buddhist culture is evolving in considerable isolation. Philippine culture is being deeply affected by trends in U.S. culture, especially through the entertainment media, and this is a source of concern for Philippine intellectuals who wish to see a more vigorous and autonomous development of creative energies within their society. American cultural influences penetrate the other ASEAN societies to lesser degrees but more than West European literature and art. U.S. contributions to educational development in general and to the growth of technocratic elite cultures are substantial and tend to build up a pervasive consensus, within each national administration, in favor of continuing pragmatic economic growth strategies based on moderately guided private sector development. Japan's very active economic involvement and smaller cultural programs contribute to the expansion of each national policy consensus on modernization policy, although the activities of Japanese international firms tend to stimulate economic nationalism.(8)

In the authoritarian ASEAN states general endorsement of the growth strategies that are being implemented is affected by bitter reactions to administrative corruption, repression, and violations of social justice. Social democratic groups in these regimes, however, are small, exist precariously, and have no significant ties with similar political organizations in the West. On the extreme left the local Communist movements are fragmented and have experienced some disorientation because they had strong ideological ties with China in the 1960s and in recent years have had to adapt to Peking's new pragmatic domestic and external policies.

As a grouping the ASEAN members are being challenged to manage their growing dependencies on Japan more actively and more comprehensively. This requirement has to be met collectively, because each member lacks bargaining strength in bilateral dealings with Tokyo, and Japan's economic involvement in Southeast Asia is a highly integrated process that is increasing functional links between the ASEAN economies, especially because of the diversification of Japanese manufacturing enterprises within each member and their growing emphasis on regional and global exporting.

Outside the connections with Japan, the principal economic ties of the ASEAN members are with the United States. These rank next in importance because, although very large, they are growing less rapidly and are not expressions of a centrally directed U.S. economic strategy with which engagement is necessary for the implementation of each ASEAN member's public policies. Links with the United States and with U.S.-based international firms are useful sources of leverage for the ASEAN members in bargaining with Tokyo and with Japanese transnational enterprises. Ties with Japan, similarly, are advantageous in dealings with the United States, but the United States is seen as a very pluralistic actor that is less committed to the advancement of its economic interests in Southeast Asia.

SOURCES OF REGIONAL POLICIES

The policies of the ASEAN members toward each other and toward the rest of East Asia are shaped with strong executive direction, at various levels of generality, and this largely determines the character and strength of what may be called the inputs into the decision processes. In the authoritarian regimes executive directiveness in foreign policy is very strong, while bureaucratic and societal influences are weak, and of course the patterns of reciprocal causation are restricted, especially because the ruling elites are not open to new knowledge from their staffs and supporters and are not challenged to become self-critically rational in their choices. The two democratic ASEAN members exhibit less directiveness, and the decision structures are relatively developed institutions; there is more extensive and more active reciprocal causation, and this involves more diffuse socializing processes, some associated with significant degrees of formal and informal accountability.

Each ASEAN executive utilizes the expertise of a foreign affairs bureaucracy that functions in strict subordination, under senior officials chosen mostly on the basis of personal ties and experience rather than skills. These officials have strong incentives to identify with the outlooks and preferences of foreign affairs decision makers in the primary elite, and to avoid challenging these with new assessments of external situations and new policy proposals. Leadership quests for such assessments and for innovative policy proposals are generally not stimulated by contributions to public debate from prominent nongovernment opinion leaders, as such figures have little scope to express their views, even in the democratic states – Malaysia and Singapore. Communications on external affairs from major foreign governments can activate executive reviews of policy options, but the officials obliged to contribute have to operate with caution, not only in order to anticipate new executive preferences, but also to be able to cope with abrupt idiosyncratic executive determination of surprise policy choices.

On matters that are recognized as ASEAN concerns, of course, consultations between the members entail exchanges that challenge the outlooks of government leaders and officials, but it seems that the most common result is a hardening of established views by each administration. To the extent that this happens, it affects the operation of the foreign affairs structures, which become more firmly committed to the reaffirmed policies. On the major divisive issue of Thai government support for Chinese inspired insurgents in Cambodia, it appears that Malaysian and Indonesian opposition has not significantly influenced the views of Thai government leaders and has not stimulated more open-minded policy assessments in the Thai bureaucracy.

Malaysia and Singapore are the only ASEAN members in which significantly active legislatures can contribute to foreign policy making, but the possibilities for this are limited by fairly strong executive control of each ruling party's parliamentary members and by traditions of cabinet secrecy derived from Britain, as well as by the rather parochial context of most legislative business. The spoken and tacit views of the legislative majorities on basic foreign policy orientations, however, have to be taken into account by each administration. In the Malaysian case this means that the relationship with China has to be managed in ways that will not stimulate stronger assertions of the local Chinese community's interests and that interaction with the Soviet Union should be fairly cordial, to discomfort radical elements among that community, as well as to expand sales of rubber and other primary products to the USSR.(9)

Societal expectations and hopes on foreign policy issues are articulated on a modest scale in Malaysia and Singapore. A prominent question for Malaysia has been the influx of refugees fleeing by boat from Vietnam. Many of these refugees have been Chinese, and Malay attitudes to them have been hostile. Malaysian policy towards these unfortunate people has been ruthless, and its more severe expressions have been restrained only by public criticisms from the United States and Britain.

Major currents of popular sentiment on external affairs influence the Thai, Indonesian, and Philippine regimes. The Marcos administration responds in some degree to any manifestations of public ill feeling toward the United States over questions relating to local U.S. military bases, levels of U.S. military and economic aid, and the effects of U.S. investment in the Philippine economy. Indonesian policy toward China is affected by popular hostility to the Peking-oriented Indonesian Communist Party, which was almost exterminated by a violent mass campaign against its members after the failure of its attempted coup in 1965. Thai regional policy reflects societal antipathies towards the Vietnamese and weaker antipathies towards the Chinese.

While influenced by popular feelings on salient foreign policy matters and by needs to identify with such feelings, leaders of the ASEAN administrations give expression to personal understandings, sentiments, and calculations in the direction of their external relations and have considerable freedom to do this on issues that attract little public attention. Most questions of foreign economic policy are in this category, and in this area the financial and political interests of government leaders as well as their perspectives on substantive issues can strongly affect their decision making. In the authoritarian ASEAN governments, key figures are linked, often extensively, with international firms producing for highly protected local markets and accordingly are reluctant to implement trade liberalization proposals that they may publicly endorse at ASEAN meetings. Issues of foreign investment policy, however, can stir popular feelings if there is highly visible exploitation of markets and labor by foreign firms with apparent government connivance. This was made evident by the anti-Japanese riots during Prime Minister Tanaka's 1974 visit to Indonesia. Nevertheless, Indonesian policy on Japanese investment did not change, yet potentially explosive issues of public regulation and guidance continue to affect general receptivity to the overall benefits derived from this foreign capital.(10)

Questions of economic cooperation within the ASEAN group have political dimensions, affecting the status, autonomy, performance, and domestic support of the participating governments. Such concerns restrain ASEAN administrations from committing themselves to wide-ranging schemes for policy collaboration that would entail some losses of independence and that would make economic growth and export promotion partly contingent on cooperation by governments with manifest weaknesses.   Other considerations that influence ASEAN government leaders are that any large ventures in cooperation will raise difficult questions about the distribution of benefits and that the outcomes of subsequent negotiations would probably not accord with the expectations of vital domestic support groups.   The avoidance of uncertainties and risks, then, is an important source of constraints on any integrative impulses that ASEAN ruling elites may show in formulating their foreign economic policies.

Each ASEAN leaderships's interest in, knowledge of, and disposition to engage with foreign policy issues is limited by pressing domestic concerns, as well as by the cautious information processing and counseling of the officials in the foreign affairs bureaucracies, and by awareness of deficiencies in resources for diplomacy that are common in developing states.   Cognitively the Indonesian ruling elite appears to be relatively isolated; it relates to an intelligentsia that is smaller, more repressed, and less exposed to international influences than that in Singapore, or Thailand, and is less informally accountable than the Thai military regime.   Because of the absence of significant immediate external dangers, moreover, the Indonesian army leadership is less challenged than the Thai ruling elite to seek friends and allies in the international community.   Similarly, the Philippine administration, enjoying the benefits of U.S. military protection, and somewhat removed from mainland Southeast Asia, does not confront external problems that would obligate close attention to the international evironment.

The Thai ruling elite has to cope with serious external security problems that necessitate interaction with Vietnam, China, the United States, and the USSR, as well as other ASEAN members.   Awareness of the complexities of the environment thus tends to be high, despite the urgency of attending to problems of domestic support mobilization within a factionalized military establishment.   The Malaysian administration's external security difficulties are less serious but demand much attention because of proximity to Thailand and Vietnam; this government, moreover, is served by a relatively more developed bureaucracy and appears to be more open to the views of its indigenous intelligentsia and the foreign diplomatic and business communities.

As a group, the ASEAN members do not have a regional leader.   This state of affairs reflects the fairly modest diplomatic skills of the ASEAN government leaders and the social and cultural differences that limit their capacities to relate to elites in each others societies.   The socialization processes that have shaped the political psychology of ASEAN government figures have been distincly national, and indeed rather parochial.   Their high-level interchanges within the ASEAN group, moreover, have been infrequent, and their status concerns have evidently tended to impose caution on each one's tendencies to assert regional interests, while making it probable that any attempts to provide active leadership would be resented.   Indonesian government figures have evidenced aspirations for a strong regional role and of course are suitably placed because of the size of their country and their links with Malaysia, but it does not seem easy for them to develop rapport with either the Thai or the Philippine leaderships.

Because of the low level of cohesion within their association and their lack of resources for international activity, ASEAN leaders are dependent on economic and military cooperation with major industrialized democracies and tend to be open to policy inputs from those democracies. The United States is the principal source of information and advice, but its communications evidently relate mainly to its incremental management of security, trade, and investment issues and thus seem to contribute only in small degrees, positively or negatively, to the shaping of basic ASEAN economic policies.

On external security matters, the ASEAN ruling elites incline toward cautious collaboration with the United States, seeking to maximize its military support, in whatever forms this is available, while avoiding close identification with its regional security policies because of insufficient confidence in its capacities to manage those policies effectively and an unwillingness to face domestic criticism that might result from shifts or failures in U.S. regional security engagement. In these respects the attitudes of ASEAN leaderships are similar to those of other Third World states that are dependent on U.S. military support but uncertain about the resolve behind the U.S. security involvement in their areas and the wisdom with which this involvement is managed. Secondary tacit elements in the external security orientations of some ASEAN members thus include contingency plans to open channels for possible accommodation with the USSR, Vietnam, or any anticipated adversary. Confidence in the effectiveness of the U.S. security policies of course has risen above the low levels of the period immediately after the Communist victories in Indochina, but the improvement was quite slow during President Carter's term of office, when it appeared that U.S. policy was neglecting Southeast Asia.(11)

The external security concerns of the ASEAN ruling elites relate primarily to the USSR and Vietnam, but the main domestic threats to their security are posed by Chinese-inspired Communist movements, and, in view of the Sino-U.S. connection, quite diverse contingencies have to be considered by each ASEAN leadership. U.S. ties with China may be strengthened, with gradual U.S. acceptance of efforts by Peking to assert a stronger role in Southeast Asia, especially to offset the Soviet presence in Vietnam. Alternatively, Sino-U.S. relations may deteriorate and Sino-Soviet relations may improve, after which the Chinese may make vigorous efforts to build up Communist movements in the ASEAN group, and, despite that trend, the United States may reduce its engagement in Southeast Asia. Moreover, while Sino-American ties are strengthened or weakened, there may well be a stronger projection of Soviet power in Southeast Asia, with demands by the USSR for the neutralization of the area on terms that may be gradually accepted by a future U.S. administration.

On questions of foreign economic policy, the orientations of the ASEAN leaderships are influenced by the behavior and the apparent options of Japan as well as the United States. The contexts are more competitive than cooperative, and, in each, personal interests can strongly affect the decisions of ASEAN government figures, especially in the Philippines, Indonesia, and Thailand. The ASEAN ruling elites of course differ in levels of expertise on foreign economic issues and degrees of concern with national as distinct from personal interests, but all seek to attract large flows of direct foreign investment. This is being sought increasingly for export oriented manufacturing, but apparently with little overall planning by the host governments. In the heavily protectionist ASEAN members moreover the development of suitable domestic environments for such manufacturing is difficult because the high tariffs which shelter import substituting firms and which thus contribute to high costs for exporting firms cannot be dismantled without serious tensions and conflicts that could involve the personal interests of key government figures. U.S. policy in general does not attempt to influence Thai, Philippine, or Indonesian choices regarding shifts towards manufacturing for export, but protectionist trends in that policy, it must be stressed, tend to make such shifts more imperative. Japanese policy, because of its emphasis on building up overseas production bases, contributes to increases in manufacturing for export. Such increases are especially necessary for the Philippines and Thailand, as they are not oil producers, and are experiencing serious balance of payments problems which are tending to increase their heavy indebtedness to Western banks. Pending their development of manufacturing for export, the Thai, Philippine and Indonesian regimes are being challenged to seek new markets for their present exports because of Japanese and U.S. protectionism, but are doing little to realize the potential for intra-ASEAN trade.

DECISION MAKING

ASEAN government leaders manage their foreign economic and security policies with some consultative exchanges in the context of their association, but their commitments to cooperate are relatively weak, and they are unwilling to allow the development of an ASEAN bureaucracy that would serve as a permanent negotiating structure. Consultative exchanges are facilitating the development of some rapport between the foreign affairs establishments of each member state, but the development of these exchanges is affected by each administration's apparent reservations about accepting substantial policy interdependence, that is, by becoming locked into a potentially wide-ranging program of collaboration. Trade liberalization within the Association is the most prominent issue that has been raised in ASEAN discussions of economic cooperation, and the subjective preferences of leaders of most of the ASEAN governments are opposed to the initiation of a series of major negotiated cuts in tarrif and nontarrif trade barriers. The promotion of industrial complementarity within the Association appears to rank next in salience, but it has been clear that the difficulties of agreement on the five industrial projects proposed several years ago, and encouraged by Japanese aid offers, have reflected the reluctance of most if not all of the member governments to move into a context of substantial collaboration on industrial policies.   There is a general lack of confidence that initial commitments would be honored by all members and that each member's interests would be handled fairly in future negotiations to coordinate industrial policies.

The most authoritative forms of collective decision making within the Association have been summit meetings of heads of the member governments. The first of these was in 1976, some nine years after the foundation of the ASEAN group, and it appears to have been more concerned with problems of political and security cooperation raised by the Communist victories in Indochina than with the promotion of subregional economic collaboration, although commitments were made to liberalize trade.   Exchanges between ASEAN members on issues relating to Indochina were stimulated by the outflow of refugees from Vietnam, the Vietnamese seizure of Cambodia, and the Chinese attack on Vietnam early in 1979, but the summit meetings were discontinued after 1977.   Yearly meetings of foreign and economic ministers now give overall direction to the evolution of the Association, but the integrative momentum provided by these is limited.   There is no supporting committee of permanent representatives, as in the European Community; the ministers are aided by a Standing Committee without permanent staff or location.   Each year this Committee is headed by the foreign minister of the country in which the ministerial meeting is to be held, and the members comprise the ambassadors to that country from the other ASEAN members, the Secretary General of the ASEAN Secretariat, and the directors of national ASEAN secretariats.   The ASEAN Secretariat, which was set up by the 1976 summit and which is located in Jakarta, has little power to promote policy collaboration, and its scope for operation is restricted by its subordination to the Standing Committee, which, of course is generally located in one of the other member states.   The Secretariat has an international staff, but the restrictive attitudes of most of the ASEAN administrations have discouraged any attempts to expand the role of the organization.   The secretary general holds office only for two years, and this post rotates between member countries.   The national ASEAN secretariats in the members other than Indonesia are not extensions of the Association's Secretariat in Jakarta, and each operates under its own national government.(12)

The weaknesses of the ASEAN institutions reflect the difficulties of community formation in this subregional grouping, and the absence of collaborative achievements that could reinforce national motivations to expand the areas of policy cooperation.   The member governments shape and implement their external policies in very independent ways, and, although confronting many common economic and security issues, are not being drawn toward more active consultations within their grouping.

While ASEAN institutional weaknesses limit collective engagement with issues that are significant for the Association's development, there can be considerable issue avoidance by member governments, to the detriment of their own and subregional interests. The feasibility of issue avoidance is quite substantial for the authoritarian governments in the ASEAN group, especially Indonesia and the Philippines, whose levels of formal and informal accountability are low. Issue avoidance is in general less feasible for the Malaysian and Singapore administrations, as these must relate to critical legislators and to interest groups and media representatives as well as to foreign business and diplomatic communities which are less inhibited than those in the authoritarian ASEAN states. A general indicator of issue avoidance is a low level of international activity in foreign economic or security policy, within and outside the ASEAN context. As a group the ASEAN members appear to have devoted little effort to the problem of stabilizing the prices of their primary exports to Japan, while individually and collectively they seem to have given only moderate attention to the acquisition of better access to the markets of the industrialized countries.

To the extent that issues of economic policy are taken up, the main trend is toward the building up of independent diversified economies whose development is not significantly predicated on the evolution of complementary forms of industrialization in other members of the association. This orientation expresses significant degrees of economic nationalism and relatively weak confidence in the possibilities for collective decision making on industrial policy and for significant trade liberalization within the ASEAN group. For the authoritarian ASEAN members, it must be stressed, the desired economic diversification is difficult to achieve because it necessitates manufacturing for export on a rapidly expanding scale. This requires not only reductions of the high protectionist tariffs that shelter import-substituting industries exploiting the domestic markets, but also major improvements in economic administration, especially through the elimination of arbitrary and often parasitic interventions that confuse and discourage national and foreign entrepreneurs. The problems of improving economic management are extremely serious in Indonesia, the most heavily protectionist and strongly interventionist state, where the policy of economic diversification is being implemented in a rather disorderly fashion, posing difficulties with which only strong international firms can expect to cope.(13)

The management of foreign economic policies, in line with the emphasis on building independent national economies, is understandably dominated by relations with major trading partners and sources of investment outside Southeast Asia. Decision making in these contexts assumes qualities that are determined largely by the characteristics of each national administration. Coherent and functional management of relations with Japan and the United States is a routine achievement for Singapore but not for Indonesia or for the other authoritarian regimes in Thailand and the Philippines. An important consequence is that the growth of national firms in these autocratically directed political economies is hindered. The uncertainties associated with opportunities for commerce with Japan and the United States are discouraging and can be overcome only by large transnational enterprises, which can be expected to handle most of this trade.   National manufacturing enterprises, moreover, while lacking the resources and bargaining power that can enable international firms to operate within the administrative disorders of the Indonesian, Thai, and Philippine systems, are unable to compete against the advantages acquired by such transnational companies in negotiating and exploiting their terms of entry. As agreed on and utilized, these terms of entry compensate for disadvantages experienced because of poor administrative handling of foreign investment policies.

Decision making on questions of trade and complementary growth within ASEAN evidences weak commitment, attributable to the low salience of the incentives and to manifest uncertainties about the degrees of cooperation to be anticipated.   The lowest degree of commitment is exhibited by the Indonesian administration, whose poorly administered policies for import-substituting industrialization are in effect making participation in trade liberalization less and less feasible. Thai and Philippine commitments to trade liberalization within ASEAN, while at low levels also because of administrative political interests in high protectionism and because of bureaucratic failings that hinder manufacturing for export, especially by national firms, are nevertheless slightly more positive than Indonesia's.   The Thai and Philippine manufacturing industries are relatively larger and more developed, and, because of the smaller size of the local markets, international firms producing for those markets have incentives to take advantage of any progress towards subregional trade liberalization. Singapore is the only ASEAN member with a strongly positive attitude to trade liberalization within the Association, but this is affected by pessimism about the prospects for such liberalization and by awareness that movement toward market integration, with a common external tariff, could be very disadvantageous because that tariff would in effect impose a high degree of protectionism on Singapore.   This state's rapid economic growth and attractiveness for foreign investors has been due in a large measure to very open trading, with little use of protectionist measures.

Decisions on external security policy tend to be made quite independently by each ASEAN administration, although with some consultations with other members, and are affected by each leadership's personal views on domestic and outside threats.   The Thai administration, confronting the most serious internal and external dangers, and recognizing that other members of the Association lack the will and resources to provide significant military support, makes its security choices primarily in response to its own perceptions of the situation.   Since these are influenced by strong antipathies to the Vietnamese and by hopes of using the Chinese against them, there is a congruence with the main line of U.S. security policy, and this reduces the significance of opposition encountered from Indonesia and Malaysia.(14)   The security policy of the Malaysian administration focuses on the immediate problem of securing full Thai cooperation for the suppression of Malayan Communist insurgents that use havens in

Southern Thailand. Malaysian decision making has been influenced by a lack of cooperation on the Thai side, and this may well have been partly responsible for the emphasis which Malaysian external security policy is placing on collaboration with Indonesia.

REGIONAL STATECRAFT

The foreign policy behavior of the ASEAN members is almost entirely regional, and of course this reflects the limited range of their external interests and the modest dimensions of their diplomatic resources. The level of activity within the Association is medium to low, but it appears to sustain commitments to consultative decision making on major external security problems and, to a smaller degree, on questions of trade liberalization and industrial policy, which are difficult to negotiate. Individually and as a group, the ASEAN members relate mainly to Japan and the Unites States as major trading partners and sources of investment.

In their mutual and group interactions the ASEAN members do not project any potent political symbols for solidarity building, although this would help to raise the low level of community consciousness within their association. Each member's diplomatic style is pragmatic, incremental, cautious, and expresses only modest expectations of collaborative responses. Shared concerns with modernization and the management of dependency relationships constitute a basis for the invocation of values that could inspire the formation of a common political will to engage in substantial integrative activity, but none of the ASEAN leaderships evidence the will and capabilities that would be needed for community formation at that level of commitment. To build up a strong spirit of dedication to a common program of industrialization and trade promotion of course would require a readiness to undertake major steps towards economic integration, and none of the members, it must be stressed, is willing to accept the likely consequences of such interdependence.

There are moderate flows of consultative communications within the Association, and these are intended to support each member's independent pursuit of external objectives rather than the gradual evolution of collective decision making. The contributions to the consultative processes that can be made by the ASEAN Secretariat are relatively small, it must be stressed, because of the restrictive attitudes of the member governments to this common institution. Bilateral consultations are quite active between Malaysia and Indonesia, mainly on security issues related to Vietnam, but there appear to be few bilateral exchanges on policy issues between Indonesia and Thailand, or between the Philippines and Thailand.

Bargaining on security and economic questions develops in response to what are perceived as limited incentives to cooperate within the Association. Exchanges on security questions have been stimulated mainly by Thailand's predicament as a member threatened immediately from Vietnam, through Cambodia, and, indirectly, by China, through Peking-inspired insurgents.   Thailand has not been able to hold out significant benefits to the other members of the Association in return for their political support in condemning Vietnamese border attacks, but has been able to receive such support, although with public manifestations of Indonesian and Malaysian disapproval of Bangkok's partial identification with Chinese policy towards Vietnam.   Little leverage has been applied by Indonesia and Malaysia, and it has been clear that any attempts to use serious pressures would be unsuccessful unless there were major changes in the policy of the United States, Thailand's source of external military support.   There is no collective endeavor to interact with the United States on regional security questions, and this can evidently be explained by a tendency to avoid such issues, which dates from the ASEAN group's early years, and by the established U.S. practice of dealing bilaterally with the ASEAN members on matters affecting each one's defense.

Exchanges within ASEAN on economic cooperation result in low level interaction that is marginally productive.   There is a general willingness to consult on trade liberalization, but most of the member states do not seek to bargain for substantial progress toward market integration and devote only modest efforts to collaborative quests for wider access to the markets of the industrialized states.   The interaction helps to maintain some sense of community within the association, but it also tends to perpetuate awareness of the difficulties of achieving significant results through collective decision making and thus causes each administration to concentrate its energies on its own management of relations with the major outside trading nations – the United States and Japan.

The strongly protectionist practices of the Indonesian, Thai, and Philippine regimes are not negotiable, for the present, and this is so for reasons that tend to preclude agreements for industrial complementarity.   While the personal interests of the elites in these states are linked with the fortunes of international firms producing for the local markets, the tariff structures and the assortments of industrial establishments they protect would make any balanced reductions of trade barriers extremely difficult to negotiate even if there were a common resolve to move toward market integration.   If achieved, moreover, any substantial trade liberalization would almost certainly pose major problems of industrial restructuring, for which indigenous resources would be lacking.   The effective levels of Indonesian and Thai protection for manufactured products are believed to be about 100 percent, and the effective level of protection in the Philippines is estimated to be 60 percent.   The effective level of protection enjoyed by manufacturing enterprises in Malaysia is much lower, and that in Singapore is very low.(15)

As a group the ASEAN members give high priority to the development of their trade with Japan.   Despite their low degree of cohesion they have some significant bargaining power in this relationship because of their importance as suppliers of primary products to the Japanese economy, and Japanese governments have shown very active interests in developing comprehensive cooperation with the Association.   ASEAN products enter Japan under that country's Generalized System of Preferences, and Japan has responded sympathetically to an ASEAN request for a STABEX agreement that would stabilize the earnings of members from exports of primary products to Japan.   This request was based on the provisions of the Lome Agreements governing economic cooperation between the European Community and its associated African, Caribbean, and Pacific trading partners.

Issues relating to the flow of Japanese investment into the ASEAN area are managed by the members individually, in bilateral dealings with Tokyo, and competition between these members to attract Japanese capital is a source of major advantages for Japanese firms and for the Japanese administration.   Indonesia receives a very large share of the investment flow, and its policy appears to be dominated by a concern to maximize this share, in order to build up a larger and more diversified industrial establishment and thus reach a stage of development approximating those of the Philippines and Thailand.   The Indonesian capacity to provide effective administrative guidance, however, is weak, and the pattern of Japanese involvement in the local industrial establishment is largely determined by the individual decisions of Japanese firms.

ASEAN interaction with the United States on trade matters is relatively less successful than it is with Japan, because U.S. interest in the area is weaker, and the pluralistic quality of U.S. foreign economic policy causes it to be somewhat indecisive and lacking in coherence. U.S. responses to proposals for a STABEX scheme have been less sympathetic than Japan's, the ASEAN states have been given no concessions on access to the U.S. market, and the United States has not shown any willingness to support regional projects like those for which Japanese aid has been offered.   On the U.S. side there is no strong group of economic and political associations capable of promoting an emphasis on the ASEAN group in foreign economic policy, and the organization's bargaining strength is relatively more fragmented than it is in dealing with Japan. The Philippines are more susceptible than the other members to assertions of U.S.   interest, and as a group the ASEAN members tend to be more apprehensive of Japan's economic penetration than of the U.S. involvement in their area.   The flow of U.S. investment into the ASEAN group is smaller than the volume of Japanese capital moving into extractive and manufacturing ventures in those nations, and it is difficult for their administrations to hold out incentives that could attract a larger flow of U.S. funds.

The dealings of individual ASEAN states with the United States on security matters are uncoordinated, and on the U.S. side no encouragement seems to be given to regional interaction on these issues.   Thailand's security interchanges with the United States are the most active, and they are managed from a relatively weak bargaining position that is affected by U.S. legislative as well as bureaucratic views of this state's capabilities for overcoming insurgencies and meeting direct aggression.   Thai diplomacy endeavors to secure an increasing flow of U.S. military and economic assistance, while avoiding an appearance of excessive dependence on the United States that would alienate domestic support, and while maintaining some interchanges with China, the USSR, and Vietnam that may facilitate new initiatives for coexistence if these are necessitated by an expansion of the insurgency in the Northeast provinces.   Philippine interchanges with the United States rank next, with respect to the level of activity and the importance than those confronting Thailand; yet they involve the United States more directly in the support of a regime that, because of its repression, invites agitation by protest groups.   Philippine diplomacy seeks mainly to exploit the U.S. administration's need to project power into Southeast Asia from bases in this country, especially for the protection of Japan, and to discourage Soviet aggression against China. Because of this need, the bargaining power of the Marcos regime is considerable and can be utilized to counter U.S. demands for a transition to responsible and representative government in the Philippines, especially because of U.S. fears that attempts to exert strong leverage against Marcos could produce instability that would be exploited by ambitious Philippine military leaders and by extreme left movements.

On security matters Malaysia and Indonesia deal with the United States somewhat remotely, with less urgency, and more independently, but with less leverage. For these nations the United States is the main source of military support, but this is not needed in large quantities to cope with the presently manageable domestic threats of Communist insurgency and the dangers of hostile behavior by Vietnam and the USSR.   Indonesia, because of its large oil revenues, is able to maintain considerable defense spending, and Malaysia, utilizing a security apparatus that was built up during the final years of British colonialism, relies on police rather than military methods of coping with the local Communist guerillas.

PROSPECTS

The regional policies implemented by the ASEAN members, individually, consultatively, and, in a small measure, collectively, produce common benefits of low salience that are sufficient to sustain commitments to periodic exchanges for limited policy coordination on external security and political issues and for incremental progress toward market integration and industrial complementarity.   The levels of diplomatic activity within and outside the Association are not likely to rise appreciably over the next half decade, and the low-to-moderate levels of cohesion within the grouping will probably not increase even if there is more noticeable advocacy of Pacific cooperation by private and governmental groups in Japan and the United States. If serious discussions of policy coordination begin between those two powers and other Pacific states, most of the ASEAN administrations may well tend to limit their participation, in order to encourage substantial offers of economic cooperation by the United States and Japan, as conditions for ASEAN involvement in any schemes for broad regional collaboration. Awareness of Japanese and U.S. perceptions of the need for ASEAN membership of a Pacific economic community would probably give rise to expectations that vigorous bargaining could secure favorable terms for participation in such a community, including liberalized access to the Japanese and U.S. markets for ASEAN manufactured goods and primary products.

As quests for external values, seen nationally and in some respects collectively, the regional activities of the ASEAN members will continue to express characteristics of their elites, structures, and societies. Cognitively, the perspectives of the ruling elites in the authoritarian states, and to some extent in Malaysia, will remain rather inward-looking, absorbed in clientelist support mobilization, with little grasp of the potential for building institutionalized regional cooperation, and distrustful of other Pacific states. Perceptions of national and regional interests and obligations by these elites are likely to remain dominated by personal ambitions and attachments, with negative implications for social justice, political integration, institutional development, overall performance in public policy, and neighborly cooperation. Affectively, primordial and often more distinctly communal sentiments will perpetuate the inward-looking orientations of most of the ASEAN leaderships, preserving their consciousness of long social distances between themselves and the neighboring states, and of their remoteness from North America and Japan. Normatively, the habits associated with repressive and corrupt rule will tend to sustain each leadership's awareness of the weaknesses of the other governments in the Association, thus holding down levels of trust and goodwill within the ASEAN group. Operationally, the growth policies of most of the ASEAN executives will no doubt remain dominated by ambitions for independent and diversified development that will allow little scope for regional cooperation.

Altogether, the problems of political as well as economic advancement in most of the ASEAN members will affect prospects for the development of their grouping as a system. If the ASEAN group is to begin providing substantial collective benefits for its members, their administrations will have to become more accountable, and not only in their domestic contexts. Certain external forms of acountability, it can be argued very strongly, will have to be imposed for the evolution of appropriate domestic accountability. Through having to answer to concerned political and economic groups in countries that are major trading partners, and to administrations in those countries, the authoritarian ASEAN governments could be persuaded to accept political reforms that cannot be pressed for by their weak internal oppositions. Increased domestic accountability of course would not have positive implications for regional development immediately, but it would facilitate the growth of an informed consensus for such development in each state, and the external pressures for reform could be accompanied by solidarity-inducing contributions, from outside states and groups, to the institutional evolution of the ASEAN group as a mechanism for collective decision making, and to the growth of its resources for allocation.

Over the next decade the most prominent issues of foreign economic policy for the ASEAN administrations will probably be questions of integrating the subregional Japanese economic presence, as it enlarges, into national growth strategies, on terms that will contribute to diversification, equity, and expansions rather than contractions of economic sovereignty. For adequate leverage the bargaining will have to be collective, but on present indications this will be difficult to achieve, and if the efforts of individual ASEAN governments fail to resolve major questions relating to the activities of Japanese enterprises there may be serious tensions, affecting not only those firms but also the domestic support of the concerned ASEAN administrations. The more diffuse and less integrated U.S. economic presence will be a less potent source of issues, but these will also have large dimensions and will make it all the more important for the members of the Association to coordinate the management of their external economic relations, to the extent that this becomes possible. Changes in perceptions, attitudes, values, and behavior will be needed, and it seems clear that these will have to be stimulated and encouraged by inputs from regionally oriented associations and government agencies in the United States and Japan. The ASEAN members will have to continue their growth within the context of dependency relationships, but those relationships hopefully can be transformed, through initiatives for a new regional economic order that will be taken by transnational consultative and promotional groups dedicated to permanent private and public interaction for Pacific community formation.

NOTES

(1) See extensive examinations of the ASEAN economies in Ross Garnaut, ed., ASEAN in a Changing Pacific and World Economy (Canberra: Australian National University Press, 1980); John Wong, ASEAN Economies in Perspective (Philadelphia: Institute for the Study of Human Issues, 1979); Lawrence B. Krause and Sueo Sekiguchi, eds., Economic Interaction in the Pacific Basin (Washington: Brookings Institution, 1980); idem, ASEAN, Challenges of an Integrating Market (Hong Kong: Business International Asia Pacific Ltd., 1979); and Bela Balassa et al., The Structure of Protection in Developing Countries (Baltimore: Johns Hopkins University Press, 1971).

(2) See Guy J. Pauker, "Indonesia in 1980:   Regime Fatigue?" Asian Survey 21, no. 2 (February 1981):   232-244; Harold Crouch, "Patrimonialism and Military Rule in Indonesia," World Politics 31, no. 4 (July 1979):   571-587; and Geoffrey B. Hainsworth, "Indonesia: Bonanza Development Amid Shared Poverty, Current History 77, no. 452 (December 1979):   199-230.

(3) See Larry A. Niksch "Thailand in 1980:   Confrontation with Vietnam and the Fall of Kriangsak," Asian Survey 21, no. 2 (February 1981): 223-231; and Ansil Ramsay, "Thailand 1979: a Government in Trouble," Asian Survey 20, no. 2 (February 1980): 112-122.

(4) See Clark D. Neher, "The Philippines in 1980: the Gathering Storm," Asian Survey 21, no. 2 (February 1981):   261-273; and Geoffrey B. Hainsworth,   "Economic   Growth   and   Poverty   in   Southeast   Asia: Malaysia, Indonesia and the Philippines," Pacific Affairs 52, no. 1 (Spring 1979): 5-41.

(5) See Geoffrey B. Hainsworth, "Economic Growth and Poverty in Southeast Asia: Malaysia, Indonesia and the Philippines"; Hans Indorf, "Malaysia in Search of Affluence and Tolerance," and K. Mulliner, "Singapore: Prosperity in a Global City," Current History 77, no. 452 (December 1979): 203-230, 207-209; Fred R. von der Mehden, "Malaysia in 1980:   Signals to Watch," and Chee-meow Seah, "Singapore in 1980: Institutionalizing   System   Maintenance,"   Asian   Survey   21,   no.   2 (February 1981): 245-252, 253-260.

(6) See comments on Indonesian-Malaysian relations in Guy J. Pauker, Frank H. Golay, and Cynthia H. Enloe, Diversity and Development in Southeast Asia (New York: McGraw-Hill, 1977); and in Charles E. Morrison and Astri Suhrke, Strategies of Survival: The Foreign Policy Dilemmas of Smaller Asian States (New York: St. Martin's Press, 1979).

(7)   See Balassa et al., The Structure of Protection in Developing Countries, pp. 203-222; and Krause and Sekiguchi, ASEAN: Challenges of an Integrating Market.

(8) See Franklin B. Weinstein, "Multinational Corporations in the Third World: The   Case   of   Japan   and   Southeast   Asia,"   International Organization 30, no. 3 (Summer 1976): 373-404.

(9) See Bernard K. Gordon, "Southeast Asia," in The Soviet Union in World Politics, ed. Kurt London, (Boulder, Col.:   Westview Press, 1980), pp. 173-194.

(10) See Weinstein, "Multinational Corporations in the Third World"; and J.   Panglaykim,   "Economic   Cooperation: Indonesian-Japanese   Joint Ventures," Asian Survey 18, no. 3 (March 1978): 247-260.

(11) See Bernard Gordon, "Japan, the United States, and Southeast Asia," Foreign Affairs 56, no. 3 (April 1978): 579-600.

(12) See ASEAN: Challenges of an Integrating Market; Morrison and Suhrke, Strategies of Survival; and idem, "ASEAN in Regional Defense and Development," in Changing Patterns of Security and Stability in Asia, ed. Sudershan Chawla and D. R. Sardesai, (New York: Praeger, 1980), pp. 192-214. See also H. Monte Hill, "Community Formation within ASEAN," International Organization 32, no. 2 (Spring 1978): 569-575.

(13) See ASEAN: Challenges of an Integrating Market; Gustav F. Papanek, ed., The Indonesian Economy (New York: Praeger, 1980); and H.W. Arndt and Ross Garnaut, "ASEAN and the Industrialisation of East Asia," Journal of Common Market Studies 17, no. 3 (March 1979): 191-212.

(14) For notes on the history of Thai relations with China, see Shee Poon Kim, "The Politics of Thailand's Trade relations with the Peoples Republic of China," Asian Survey 21, no. 3 (March 1981): 310-324.

(15) See Balassa et al., The Structure of Protection in Developing Countries; Arndt and Garnaut, "ASEAN and the Industrialisation of East Asia"; and John C.S. Tang, Pakorn Adulbhan, and R.P. Nepal, "Intra-Extra ASEAN Trade — The First Decade," The Southeast Asian Economic Review 1, no. 2 (August 1980): 165-178.

5 TransPacific Interdependencies

Martin H. Sours

The use of the term interdependency as a concept in the study of world affairs grew throughout the late 1970s. While many causes may be cited for this trend, several general global developments are particularly persuasive. The increase in world interaction patterns of all kinds has accompanied technical improvements in transportation and communication. General technological breakthroughs, the growth of the worldwide scientific community, and the accompanying knowledge explosion have all contributed to a breakdown of isolation, particularly at the nation-state level. Additionally, economic independence as an achievable goal for nation-states has been acknowledged to be unrealistic. The People's Republic of China, by rejecting the concept of Maoist self-sufficiency after the death of Mao Tse-tung, most graphically demonstrated to the world an imperative need for all nation-states to interact. Further, small, economically underdeveloped states of the world community have called for a "New International Economic Order," which clearly connotes a recognition that their fate is affected by world interaction patterns.

The most obvious case in point revolves around world energy sourcing. Despite political rhetoric directed toward the notion of energy independence, the notion that even a continental state, such as the United States, can achieve true self-suffiency has proved to be a false one. Further, the impact of the worldwide need for energy has affected the economic development of all states, and the non-oil-producing developing nations have been particularly affected, in that foreign exchange that could be used for capital and infrastructure development has been diverted to secure and pay for a supply of imported energy. Thus, while energy is the most visible of the commodities underpinning the concept of interdependence, it is not the only economic element, but rather the one that has created a large ripple effect in world financial circles. Debt servicing and the viability of capital markets also tie the world together and thus reinforce general notions of interdependence.

103

Concurrently, there has been a shift of global military power, in both the symbolic and real senses. Symbolically, the failure of the United States government to project power successfully in South Vietnam has led to an image of a world power structure without a leader. Symptomatic of this drift within the United States were reduced force levels and attrition of naval craft after the Vietnam war, and the 1976 Brookings Institution study calling for the end of the Marine Corps' traditional mission (and by implication, the end of the Marine Corps).(1) With the election of Ronald Reagan as President in 1980, however, such proposals stopped, went out of political favor, and numerous features in the press extolling the Marine Corps' new mission in the Middle East began to appear.

In terms of real force levels and military capacity, a semiparity of forces between the Soviet bloc and the NATO allies has been basic to the theoretical constructs of the work of Robert O. Keohane and Joseph S. Nye in Power and Interdependence.(2) They argue that there are two basic approaches to international affairs. The first is the traditional or realist approach which examines power and power positions. The second, which they present, focuses on interdependencies, and they stress the complexities of these between industrialized democracies.(3) Such complex interdependence, they emphasize, involves multiple connecting channels, ambiguities about the ranking of issues, a minor role for military force in conflict resolution, and a general lack of concern about the relative status of the closely linked nations.(4)

Multiple connecting channels may be seen in earlier analyses of world politics that focused on networks as a measure of interaction patterns. As one analysis posited, "Networks . . . produce public goods even though their 'product' is much harder to identify . . . elite networks are informal patterns of influence, but usually also have significant capacity for order."(5) Thus, earlier work on networks appears to lead directly to Keohane and Nye's definition of international regimes, which they characterize as "relationships of interdependence which often occur within, and may be affected by networks of rules, norms, and procedures that regularize behavior and control its effects. We refer to the sets of governing arrangements that affect relationships of interdependence as international regimes."(6)

The notion of networks and regimes is important for analytic purposes herein because such relationships constitute observable interaction patterns. Given the diversity of the states within the Pacific area in particular, the notion of regimes and networks, being noncultural, is more central to this analysis than would be the case in regions sharing a common cultural heritage, wherein shared cultural perceptions would facilitate communication and bridge specific issue gaps and policy differences.

Nevertheless, commentary of the contemporary interdependency literature has raised questions concerning the apparent lack of emphasis on power as an analytic concept. Stanley J. Michalak, for example, has noted that Keohane and Nye have "misrepresented political realism"(7) by failing to give it the proper and ongoing weight that it continues to deserve in the study of international affairs. This overemphasis on the new intellectual constructs of interdependency needs to be recognized with particular reference to the Pacific area, for while interdependency now appears to be the central concern in the Pacific area, questions of political and military power continue to have importance. This point is true for two general reasons, the interdependent nature of military force levels with regard to Japan and the United States in the post-Vietnam era (about which more will be said below) and the historical nature of previous sytems of regional dependency that have characterized relations between major actors in intraregional affairs.

Prior to the current interest in interdependency within the Pacific area, that region had been characterized by four historical systems of political and economic dependency. The first was the traditional tribute system of imperial China, in which China served as the Middle Kingdom, and other societies related to each other in terms of their tributary relationship to China. As John K. Fairbank noted:

> The relations of the Chinese with surrounding areas, and with non-Chinese peoples generally, were colored by this concept of Sinocentrism and an assumption of Chinese superiority. The Chinese tended to think of their foreign relations as giving expression externally to the same principles of social and political order that were manifested internally within the Chinese state and society. China's foreign relations were accordingly hierarchic and nonegalitarian, like Chinese society itself.(8)

The surrounding societies related to each other in line with a ranking system that reflected not only the geographic proximity of the various states to China but also their relative degree of societal compatibility with Chinese Confucian values. Thus tributary societies that were highly influenced by China were accorded a high status in the view of the Chinese court, and this was, in turn, reflected in the relationships between the various tributary units themselves. The resultant total intersocietal hierarchy was supposed to insure order throughout the region, with China as the undisputed leader of the region not only in terms of political power but social status and economic capacity as well.

The tribute missions to China during this traditional period dramatized these concepts. The act of tribute itself symbolized the subordination of the surrounding societies to China, but in keeping with the concept of mutual obligation codified in Confucianism, the Chinese court had to reciprocate with even more elaborate gifts to demonstrate and perpetuate its superior status. As a consequence, a form of economic interdependency between the ruling houses of the societies of the region emerged within a framework of an overt political order based on dependency. It should also be noted in passing that this form of intersocietal relations was not, strictly speaking, an "international" order because the actors were not nation-states. Rather, they were traditional societies that were neither independent nor sovereign in the Western European sense. Thus, while it may be easier to describe such relationships in modern terms and call them international, in fact, modern nation-states, as such, were not involved. Rather, societies with traditional ruling elites were bound together by a dependency system, and in turn, each of these elite groups bound the people of their respective and individual societies together in ·dependent and hierarchial fashions.

The Chinese traditional order for East Asia was replaced by the globalization of the European international order in the nineteenth century.(9) The spread of European influence into Asia had begun much earlier but had had little effect on basic economic and political structures due to the relative strengths of the Indian and Chinese empires.   After Great Britain achieved world power with the final defeat of Napoleonic France, the nature and scope of the European penetration into Asia, led by the United Kingdom, greatly expanded. The resultant Opium Wars brought a complete collapse of the Chinese-ordered world in the short span of a few decades and replaced it in Asia with colonies and spheres of influence.

Thus a new kind of dependency emerged in Asia, one in which parts of the region were parceled out to various imperial powers. By the end of the nineteenth century, even the United States had a colonial possession in the Philippines, and Japan, partly in reaction to perceived threats to its national security, was preparing to establish a continental base in Korea after the successful acquisition of Taiwan from China. Initially, then, a traditional, centralized dependency system in Asia focusing on China was replaced by a decentralized dependency, with each colony dependent upon its metropolitical colonial master.

Ironically, intra-European conflicts in the form of World Wars I and II led to a fusion of the two earlier forms of regional dependency in the short-lived, Japanese-sponsored, East Asian Co-Prosperity Sphere. While not recognized as such by the European states, the Japanese sought to replace China as the traditional center of Asian power relationships but to do so within a modern framework of a regional empire featuring direct control. This had some intuitive appeal in Asia, for it displaced foreign (i.e., European) imperialism and provided a framework for the rise of indigenous Asian elites under Japanese sponsorship. The excesses of Japanese imperial rule, and its ultimate military collapse, ended this form of regional organization but significantly posited, however briefly, the concept of an exclusively Asian regional organization with modern economic functions, such as a currency block built around the Japanese yen. Therefore, the Japanese imperial period needs to be remembered not because it failed, which is obvious, but rather because within the contemporary context it still serves as one type of model for regional organization with destructive and exclusive characteristics. In particular, the Co-Prosperity Sphere's emphasis on regional self-sufficiency, while inoperative in today's globally interdependent world, serves as a kind of unspoken stimulus to current discussions of Pacific interdependency. The transPacific, or regional and geographic element, was first attempted by Japan in the early 1940s. The economic dimension was regional self-sufficiency, through the harnessing of the region's resources via the principle of comparative advantage. Therefore, for however brief a period of time, a form of regional, Pacific interdependency was achieved under the umbrella of Japanese military force. This very success, however limited in time, has instilled a lingering fear of transPacific inter-dependence among some leadership circles of Asian states because of a fear of a resurgent Japanese domination of the region. As a consequence, the Japanese government's advocacy of a Pacific community has explicity been an inclusive one with regard to the United States, Australia, New Zealand and Canada, precisely because of these residual concerns within the region related to Japanese dominance.

Finally, the defeat of Japan in 1945 ushered in a period of virtual American dominion in the Pacific area. While of course decolonization and national independence appeared to be the obvious characteristics of the post-World War II period, the real nature of the post-war Pacific order was one of new or weak states, including a defeated and occupied Japan, looking out on a Pacific dominated by the U.S. Navy. American military might was employed in the Korean War to preserve this status quo, and therefore the U.S. military became the dominant force for the preservation of a regional order fostered in large measure by the U.S. government. Behind this military shield, and supported by the strong U.S. dollar, American business interests were free to operate in the Pacific rim states, and the People's Republic of China, by carrying out a revolution that was incompatable with this regional regime, was isolated.

The Vietnam War may be seen within this context and viewed as the last great act of the American-dominated period in Asia. The failure of the United States to sustain a client state forced a reformulation of American foreign policy in Asia, first enunciated in the Nixon or Guam doctrine, initially expressed by President Nixon in an interview on Guam in July 1969 and later formalized in the President's State of the World message of February 1971.(10) After the Vietnam Peace Accords of January 1973, a truly regional regime of independent and sovereign states in Asia was assured, and concurrently, the supranational authority of a single dominant regional power was no longer a systemic given in the region. Thus, ironically, the end of the American-dominant period in Asia brought into being for the first time a regional international order within which truly independent nation-states, as actors, existed with some semblance of real sovereignty. While this did not end intraregional conflict – and in fact some of the world's worst conflicts have occurred within this regional framework (Cambodia/Kampuchea and Timor) – the international conditions for an international order based on interdependency could, for the first time, be openly discussed precisely because previous systems of dependency, which had historically characterized the Pacific region, were gone.

SOURCES OF TRANSPACIFIC DOCTRINES

Three main sources have provided specific formulations of transPacific or Pacific Basin regional configurations within the world's international system. These may be categorized broadly as academic analyses, policy papers and studies sponsored by the major governments of the region, and what may be characterized as "the international business community." The first two sources can be recognized by the traditional forms they take, represented by identifiable studies and reports communicating with opinion leaders. The third formulation is imprecisely defined, in that the output of international business commentaries is filtered through a variety of media sources. Nevertheless, business periodicals and journals have exhibited the most flexibility in establishing a title or common conceptual reference point. Hence, multiple references exist in the business literature that make reference to the Pacific Basin, the Pacific Rim, the Pacific Area, and the Asia/Pacific Region.

While exact references as to the composition of the Pacific Basin are difficult to identify, the unofficial consensus that emerges from the literature in general divides the Pacific Basin into the following subcomponents: Northeast Asia; various international entities related to China; the ASEAN countries of Southeast Asia; Australia and New Zealand; and, in the Americas, the United States, Canada, and Mexico. Each of these elements may be further delineated, and some common threads interlock them. Some special considerations also exist with regard to the inclusion of the Soviet Union in the Pacific area.

First, Northeast Asia refers in this Pacific context to Japan and South Korea (the Republic of Korea, or ROK). This is logical in that it builds on classical academic terminology for the region, and also identifies the industrial core of East Asia. It is also nonmilitary in the sense that the U.S. defense relations with both states are an assumed given, and by contrast the isolationist regime in North Korea (i.e., the Democratic People's Republic of Korea, or DPRK) is excluded because it does not interact, to any measurable degree, with other states in the region. Thus Northeast Asia, exclusive of the DPRK, represents an area of the Pacific region characterized by high and advanced levels of international economic activity.

Second, three diverse, yet interconnected entities, constitute the "Chinas" of the Pacific Basin. The Republic of China on Taiwan (ROC) has survived "derecognition" by all the states in Asia except South Korea and has made a smooth transition to become an economic actor without any extensive or meaningful formal diplomatic status. As such, it still continues to attract the interest of the international business community, and, due to internal, domestic American political considerations, expects to receive more political support from the United States government under the Reagan administration which took office in January 1981. Additionally, Hong Kong, while continuing to remain a British colony, is considered a separate economic entity, operating with the dual function as a gateway to the People's Republic of China (PRC) and as a financial, trading, and manufacturing center in its own right. Finally, the PRC itself joined the Pacific Basin by establishing formal diplomatic relations with other states throughout the region, most important by the mutual exchange of formal diplomatic recognition with the United States in January 1979.

Third, the Association of Southeast Asian Nations (ASEAN), composed of Thailand, Malaysia, Singapore, Indonesia and the Philippines, has come to be viewed as a regional market, even though the level of its Southeast Asian regional integration remains low. In the wake of the failed U.S. policy in South Vietnam, the United States focused its attention on the ASEAN group as the centerpiece of its foreign policy for the Southeast Asian region as a whole.(11) Further, the aggressiveness of the united Vietnamese state, with regard to its Laotian and Cambodian neighbors, created a Southeast Asian regional dynamic of closer cooperation among the ASEAN members of the region.

Connected with the emergence of the ASEAN group into the Pacific Basin is the dramatic change in status and policy within Sri Lanka. Prior to 1977, that country had been closely identified with socialist policies and had been clearly outside the mainstream of international business activity. On July 21, 1977, a national election swept the socialist coalition of former Prime Minister Bandaranaike out of power and brought into office Junius Jayawardene and the United National Party.(12) A new constitution featuring a presidential system was inaugurated in February 1978, which was followed by a significant feature article in the Far Eastern Economic Review in May of that year.(13) The story outlined a type of economic alliance between Singapore and Sri Lanka that brought the latter country into the favor of the international business community as a site for low cost, labor-intensive production. During the following years, Sri Lanka followed a policy of openly encouraging international business investment in that country, which finally brought the country to the attention of the American international business community in the form of a front-page story in the Asian Wall Street Journal Weekly in 1980.(14)

Finally, Australia and New Zealand constitute the last area on the Western side of the Pacific within the composition of a Pacific Basin rim. As developed nations in terms of GNP per capita, and with Australia's mineral wealth, they have long been considered an integral resource base for overall regional development. Further, the solidification of the European Community (EC) left these British commonwealth states outside their traditional trading partner's preferential trading area, as Britain joined the Common Market and thus had to accept continental Europe's agricultural products.

On the North American side, Canada and Mexico have long been seen as potential participants within the Pacific Basin area, but the codification of their participation has been more difficult. Nevertheless, the specific frameworks discussed below either implicitly or explicitly include these states, along with the United States, within a broader community concept. The reasons for their inclusion are basically two-fold and were suggested above. Much of the impetus for the Pacific Basin concept has Japanese origins, and Japan, in particular, does not want to revive historical images of a Japanese-dominated region. Also, given the cultural diversity within Asia, the inclusion of non-Asian actors transforms the region into one characterized primarily by economic interaction.

Among the academic writers, the earliest noteworthy attempt at a Pacific regional formulation appeared in the June 1966 issue of Hitotsubashi University's Journal of Economics, authored by Kiyoshi Kojima and Hiroshi Kurimoto, entitled "A Pacific Economic Community and Asian Developing Countries." It was followed in 1971 by Kojima's book Japan and a Pacific Free Trade Area.(15) Within the general global context of North-South issues, that author raised the possibility of expanded trade between the component parts of the Pacific region as outlined above and posited the feasibility of a Pacific Currency area. At the time of that publication, Kojima suggested that

> to date, the United States has been more interested in Atlantic arrangements. However, European integration, through a fusion of E.E.C. and EFTA, could well produce an "inward-looking" Europe, whereupon the United States might find closer integration in the Pacific region desirable. And while, for the time being, the political and economic integration a free-trade area entails is not feasible in the Pacific area, economic cooperation among the advanced countries of the region (i.e. the U.S., Japan, Canada, Australia and New Zealand) could be profitably fostered. Collective measures by the group are especially desirable for assisting economic development and trade growth in South-east Asian countries.(16)

Kojima followed this book in 1977 by a second, broader formulation entitled Japan and a New World Economic Order.(17) In it (Chapter 8, "Economic Integration in the Asian-Pacific Region"), the author candidly assessed the difficulties encountered with his initial proposal and recognized that

> the key problem in fostering Western Pacific economic integration is how to harmonize interest between large and small economies. . . . The principles for integration among economies which are unequal in size and stage of development may be different from those dealt with in the traditional theory of integration dealing with economies which are on a more or less equal footing. . . . Foreign direct investment may have an important role to play in the development of horizontal specialization.(18)

A second generation of writing appeared in the United States in the mid-1970s. It may be characterized by the edited volume by Bernard K. Gordon and Kenneth J. Rothwell entitled The New Political Economy of the Pacific.(19) Rather pessimistically, Rothwell concluded that future economic performance will be governed more by the economic programs of one or two chief actors than by common policies involving a majority of the economies of the region. . . . In the absence of formal or official regional organizations or political relationships, the trend toward a Pacific unification will be fostered instead, but to a lesser degree and on a more narrow basis, by the roles of the multinational corporations.(20)

A more positive tone was set by Endel-Jakob Kolde in his 1976 work, The Pacific Quest: The Concept and Scope of an Oceanic Community.(21) While largely an effort at structuring data, Kolde was highly optimistic concerning the linking of his data to the broader themes raised in his book:

Interdependence is the emerging reality of the Pacific nations. What was a scatter of separate economies of different size on varying developmental stages is slowly becoming intertwined by interlocking goals and transboundary linkages. Although far from forming a cohesive whole as yet – the historic cleavages take time to bridge and the forces of fragmentation impede consolidation – the Pacific Basin is nevertheless moving towards economic integration. The concept of a Pacific economy is, therefore, starting to gain rationale.(22)

Such optimism, however, was not operationalized along policy lines, and the scope of Kolde's concept was too broad, taking into account all the Pacific states of Latin America as well as the Soviet Union. Additionally, the interjection of such issue areas as the seabeds confused and diluted his original conceptual focus.

At the other extreme, works that essentially focus on the nation-states themselves within the Pacific Basin have provided a great deal of descriptive economic data. This was done on an informal level by Lloyd R. Vasey and George J. Viksnins in their edited volume, The Economic and Political Growth Pattern of Asia-Pacific, which contained the proceedings of a Pacific Forum Conference.(23) A more complete formulation has been offered by Lawrence B. Krause and Sueo Sekiguchi in their edited work, Economic Interaction in the Pacific Basin.(24) By focusing on the economic performance of selected Asian states, they concluded that

the Pacific Basin is the most dynamic region of the world. Economic growth and international trade in the region are advancing at rates not experienced elsewhere. Much of the success comes from positive stimuli spilling over from country to country. Thus benefits to economic interdependence are being captured.(25)

To harness this activity, they propose that regular and continual consultative procedures among the governments of the states of the region are now necessary. Their argument is persuasive, and accordingly it is now necessary to examine governmental studies and policy positions regarding Pacific interdependencies.

GOVERNMENTAL POSITIONS AND PROPOSALS

Regional governmental support for an interdependent Pacific community has come primarily from the United States and Japan, with Australian academic and governmental leadership showing active interest in a subordinate way. The major American effort may be seen in the U.S. House of Representatives hearings on the idea of a Pacific Community during the summer and fall of 1979.(26) The hearings largely established a consensus as to the importance of the region both on its own terms, that is, intraregionally, and in transPacific terms. This was presented statistically by demonstrating that over 50 percent of the total national trade for the key states in Asia is now intraregional trade, and also, since 1978, over 50 percent of U.S. trade has been with Pacific Basin states. Thus, the reality of increasing trans-Pacific economic interdependence was emphasized as justification for increased U.S. governmental interest in the region.

The year 1980 also saw a more public formulation of the Japanese government's longstanding support for the idea of a Pacific community. Japanese Prime Minister Masayoshi Ohira established the Pacific Basin Cooperation Study Group on March 6, 1979, as an advisory group to study, among other things, ways to construct a regional community within the Pacific Basin area. An interim report was released on November 14, 1979, and the final report, entitled <u>Report on the Pacific Basin Cooperation Concept</u>, was completed on May 19, 1980. The tasks suggested in that report to facilitate Pacific Basin Cooperation were:

1. Promoting international exchange and mutual understanding
2. Promoting area studies
3. Cooperating in human resource and technology development
4. Promoting trade expansion and adjustment of industrial structure
5. Cooperating in resource exploitation
6. Enhancing the smooth flow of funds
7. Expanding and consolidating transport and communications systems.(27)

Three main areas thus emerged from this Japanese report: an academic or intellectual focus suggested by items 1, 2, and 3; a resource development program represented in items 5 and 7; and, perhaps most significant, the strengthening of international business linkages by freer trade (a trade/import-export dimension) and a better investment climate to be achieved by upgrading the activities of the international financial community within the region, since increased investment in the Pacific Basin would require more open and sophisticated capital markets.

Finally, interest has been expressed in Australia toward formalizing the Pacific Basin concept. A few Australian academics, notably Peter Drysdale and Sir John Crawford of the Australian National University (ANU), have long been interested. Australian Prime Minister Malcolm Fraser became a supporter after consultations with Japanese Prime Minister Masayoshi Ohira, and that resulted in ANU hosting the first of what was to be a series of seminars on the topic in September 1980. Australia, for its part, "has taken the . . . initiative because it makes eminent economic sense for it to do so, and because it is becoming increasingly aware that it is a part of the Asia-Pacific region, not of Europe."(28) The sum of these efforts has been to create a climate of official approval for the concept from the governments of three major market economies of the region.

The real mainspring and emphasis for an interdependent region has not surprisingly come from the international business community. Interest in the business aspects of the Pacific region may have begun as long ago as 1971, when the Chief Director of the Tokyo Securities Exchange, Teiichiro Morinaga, led a business delegation to visit 14 nations of the region and produced a lengthy report on their findings.(29) This was followed in 1974 by the first publication of the Security Pacific Bank's Economic and Financial Series, entitled Financial Markets of the Pacific Rim. The introductory overview of the bank's publication set the tone for the flood of business commentary that followed by saying:

> During the last few decades . . . intraregional trade among the nations of the Pacific has been making inroads into the former, almost monolithic importance to the Asian nations of inter-regional trade with Europe. . . . The Nations of the "Pacific Rim" have, therefore, become increasingly interdependent as some Asian countries developed into manufacturing powers, drawing resources from Asian nations and exporting their output to other Pacific countries. . . . Accompanying the increased intraregional trade has been the development of many of the cities of the area into regional financial centers.(30)

The tempo of both business analysis and advocacy increased in 1977 with a major article in Fortune magazine which not only characterized the business environment in Asia as good, but provided a crude ranking index of the investment climate of the individual states of East Asia. Using ten categories and a scale from 5 (the highest, or most favorable) to 1 (a "very bad" investment environment), table 5.1 shows the order of country preferences from a business perspective.

Inspection immediately indicates a rough division into two categories of states: the Group I division of developed economies that could sustain industrial expansion, and Group II, which are sources of raw materials from a trade perspective, and the sites for low wage or low labor cost manufacturing in the investment area (sometimes characterized as areas for "labor-intensive manufacturing"). The article concluded that "after half a century of wars, Asia is undergoing an unprecedented period of peace. . . . If the present conditions endure, the political climate would truly be right for a Pacific Century."(31)

Table 5.1.

Rank	Country	Composite Score
1	Hong Kong	42
2	South Korea	41
3	Japan	40
4	Singapore	39
5	Taiwan (ROC)	38
6	Malaysia	34
6	Philippines	33
7	Thailand	33
8	Indonesia	28
9	China (PRC)	27

Last four states ranked: Vietnam, Burma, Laos and Cambodia, with scores from 23 to 17.

Source: "A Peaceful Asia Beckons Investors," Fortune, October 1977, p. 194.

This kind of optimistic language was followed by a series of major stories in influential business publications. The Banker devoted 31 pages of its December 1978 issue to a survey of the Pacific Basin from a financial and capital markets point of view,(32) followed one year later by a feature cover story in the Far Eastern Economic Review which comprehensively summarized the academic, business, and governmental inputs to the movement to formalize the concept of an interdependent Pacific area.(33)

By 1980 more specialized analyses and particular events reinforced the Pacific Basin approach in business and governmental circles. Analysis focusing specifically on trade, such as the March-April 1980 article in Europe(34) appeared simultaneously with more detailed explanations of investment options in the various countries of the Asian area as represented by a special report in Business Week.(35) Asian governments themselves began to promote this economic framework with conferences at the same time. On May 26, 1980, the Export-Import Bank of Japan sponsored a "Symposium on Business Cooperation between Asia-Pacific and Japan in the 80s," which featured a keynote address by Nobuhiko Ushba, the Special Trade Representative of Japan for trade talks with the United States, and concurrently an advisor to the Japanese Ministry of Foreign Affairs.(36) In November 1980, the Korean World Trade Center Building in Seoul was the site of a special seminar on the Pacific Community, featuring former American Ambassador to Korea Richard L. Sneider. The event was sponsored by the Korea-U.S. Economic Council, which tied the specific program directly to the semiofficial Korean Traders Association, a Korean government-related association of Korean firms engaged in import-export operations.(37) Thus the tempo, extent, and multifaceted nature of the acceptance of Pacific interdependence spread and became cumulative, creating a self-fulfilling force of its own, and thus the overall Pacific Basin concept came to be accepted within the business community as a fact. Once accepted, actions within that framework were assumed by the business community to follow naturally.

TRADE DIMENSION

Because a major input into the formulation of the Pacific Basin concept has been the notion of expanded trade, an overview of trade mechanisms and an examination of the bilateral trade relationships between the two major economies of the Pacific region are necessary. In the area of export-import operations, the framework for analysis is that of a private firm selling internationally, and for that firm, irregardless of its national identity, the products are sold or marketed; hence the firm views its interactions outside of its own national borders as international selling. There are two general approaches to international selling: direct and indirect. In direct sales, the firm deals with the foreign customer directly, while, in indirect sales, another firm acts as an intermediary. For Japan, the intermediaries have been the general trading companies, or sogo shosha, while U.S. firms have used export management companies (EMCs). In working with a trading company, any seller treats the transaction as though it were a domestic sale. The firm fills an order from the trading company, which in turn takes title to the goods and arranges for shipment to the customers, or end-users. The major disadvantage of selling to a trading company is the loss of marketing control over the product. There is no way to promote the product, evaluate sales, or survey customer satisfaction.

Export management companies have served as the export department for several manufacturers of similar but noncompeting products. Formerly known as combination export manager firms (CEMs), these companies promote, distribute, and finance overseas sales. They may provide financing by buying the goods directly from the manufacturer, thereby relieving the seller of any credit risk, or they may act as a commission agent. Additionally, EMCs handle shipping, documentation, and other mechanics of export selling.

In the area of direct selling, two viable options exist. One is the use of an agent. He is an independent businessman who identifies customers and makes sales or brings buyers and sellers together for a commission that is a percentage of sales. Alternatively, direct sales may be made using a distributor. In this case, a local dealer may receive shipments for resale to customers. He may be a "stocking-distributor," in which case he maintains inventory on hand, or he may receive shipments as needed. The distributor buys directly from the manufacturing firm, adds a markup to cover his costs and profit, and sells at a retail price. This approach would apply if there is a significant volume of sales to warrant an ongoing, as opposed to a case-by-case, sales program. The critical distinction is that an agent is a sales tool facilitating the meeting of the seller/manufacturer and the customer, while the distributor is an additional link in the marketing/distribution chain.

With this framework as to the mechanics of trade, it can be seen that trade is an ongoing and standard form of both business and general economic interaction. Once this point is accepted, specific measures of trade interaction may be utilized to measure broader concerns of interdependence without concern over intervening variables such as unusually high transaction costs. Because Japan and the United States are the dominant economic actors within the Pacific Basin, the bilateral relationship between these two states will carry a disproportionate impact upon the region as a whole, and the degree and nature of their mutual interdependence will influence the region's entire interdependent structure.

THE EVOLUTION OF THE ISSUE OF JAPANESE-AMERICAN TRADE

The American public's attention first focused on Japanese-American economic relations at the beginning of the decade of the 1970s, with the publication of Herman Kahn's The Emerging Japanese Superstate.(38) Kahn's work was widely criticized at the time as being both too optimistic with regard to Japanese economic performance and unrealistic in terms of his comparative analysis of the relative performance of the economies of the United States and Japan. By the closing years of the decade, however, the issue of Japanese-American trade was receiving widespread attention. While Kahn's work was forgotten by that time, concerns surrounding the trade issue were leading into broader inquiries about the nature and survivability of the entire American business system. An example of this concern was reflected in the special June 30, 1980, issue of Business Week, "The Reindustrialization of America."(39)

Serious scholarship concerning Japanese economics and trade began to appear in the mid-1970s. Two major conclusions emerged. Japan was, in fact, a trading nation, and therefore, exports were central to the Japanese economic system. At the same time, exports alone did not account for what was informally called "the Japanese Miracle." Rather, as two authorities put it, "In purely descriptive terms, Japanese growth has been export led in that exports grew faster than the gross national product (GNP), particularly in recent years."(40) Yet later in the same book, they modify their earlier statement by saying, "Even though Japanese growth in the main has not been export led in the analytical sense, it does not mean that exports were unimportant to growth. Export expansion has been of strategic importance principally because it has financed the growing imports of raw materials and capital goods that embody new technology."(41) Japanese exports appear to be part of an overall economic growth pattern, which involves the total economic development of the Japanese economy.

This comprehensive view is important in relation to what follows. The material that has emerged in the literature of the American business community and the general public has presented a picture of Japan as a society obsessed with trade expansion for its own sake. For example, a Newsweek article of December 19, 1977, contained a cartoon of a Japanese fighter plane bombing a Zenith factory with Japanese television sets while the pilot yelled Tora-tora-tora, the famous battle cry of the pilots who attacked Pearl Harbor at the beginning of World War II.(42) The same article contained scattered inflamatory statements such as, "Japan's huge surplus in its trade with the U.S." and "Japan's surpluses have grown so large in the past two years that nickel-and-dime concessions will no longer do."(43) During the same time period, U.S. Ambassador to Japan, Mike Mansfield was quoted by the Associated Press as saying Japanese-American relations were at a crisis.(44)

A review of several journal articles revealed the complex and interdependent reasons for this culmination of events. In the first place, Japanese products attained a non-price sensitive quality; they became inherently attractive because they emerged as high quality goods that responded to market demand in the United States. Put another way, the total marketing ability of Japanese firms became evident after the mid-1970s, when all the elements of successful marketing, including packaging and delivery, became effective.

Also, excesss capacity played a part in the export of Japanese goods. Japan is inherently a more limited market than the United States, so any product line tends to reach saturation in the Japanese market and then seeks markets abroad. This process has been facilitated by the Japanese business institution of the general trading company, or sogo shosha.

The decline in the international value of the floating U.S. dollar also helped to create a balance of trade surplus for Japan. That statement appears to be contrary to logic; yet it is true. Most goods in the world are valued in U.S. dollars. Therefore, because Japan imports most of its raw materials from both the United States and the rest of the world, a declining dollar in relation to the yen not only affects Japanese-American bilateral trade but Japanese worldwide trade as well. With the appreciation of the yen in relation to the dollar, Japanese industry could buy imports more cheaply, because fewer yen are needed to buy dollar denominated imports. This, in turn, reduced the cost of inputs into Japanese industry, allowing Japanese firms to arrive at end product unit prices that were still competitive, in spite of the appreciating of the Japanese yen in relation to the dollar.

Concurrently, the appreciated yen valued the goods sold from Japan more highly than before. Consequently, even the same volume of goods exported from Japan reflected statistically an increase in Japanese exports to the United States. Trade statistics are kept on an f.a.s. basis (free alongside the ship), or transaction price exclusive of shipping costs. This transaction price naturally reflected the changes in the exchange rates between the yen and the dollar. Thus, exchange rates alone impact on trade balances by impacting on their calculation.

Finally, the Japanese economy has been directly and greatly affected by the increases in the world price of oil as a result of the OPEC price increases of the 1970s. Deflationary pressures have emerged in Japan as a result of the sudden price increases, because Japan imports over 90 percent of its petroleum needs. This deflation has led to a record number of Japanese business bankruptcies, the most notable being the Eidai Company, Japan's largest plywood maker.(45) In such a deflationary environment, Japanese firms could not raise capital for expansion and thus could not import from abroad in order to expand. Further, the demand for raw material imports is generally fixed, or inelastic, in economic terms. Inherent limits existed within the Japanese economy as to the amounts of raw materials that could be consumed at one time. By emphasizing reinvestment and increased productivity, more goods could be produced without as great a con-current increase in raw materials consumed.

One specific reaction by the American government to the overall deterioration of the U.S. trade position was the establishment of the International Trade Commission. Its function has been to investigate charges brought by U.S. manufacturers that goods from abroad are illegally "dumped" on the U.S. market. Dumping is defined as selling a product in the U.S. market for a price less than the price utilized when the product is sold in the home market. Assumptions inherent in antidumping actions include notions that such actions are solely to block unfair competition designed to achieve market entry and to drive local producers out of the market preparatory to predatory pricing.

International Trade Commission action, in effect, sets minimum import prices.(46) It is government intervention in free trade. Further, it does not take into account Japan's complicated, many-layered domestic distribution system which has created added costs that are passed along to end-users and retail customers and result in higher domestic retail prices than export prices. Nevertheless, tension continued into 1978 when "the U.S. International Trade Commission issued a 'cease and desist' order directing eleven Japanese companies to stop selling stainless steel pipe and tube in the U.S. market at prices below Japan's production costs."(47)

During this time, both the Japanese and American governments were engaged in restructuring their policies with regard to trade. The Japanese government had enacted an Eight-Point Program on June 4, 1971, which contained the following provisions:

1. Acceleration of import liberalization
2. Implementation of preferential tariffs in favor of developing countries
3. Promotion of tariff reduction
4. Promotion of capital liberalization (i.e., easing of restrictions on direct investment in Japan by foreign firms)
5. Removal of nontariff barriers
6. Promotion of economic cooperation (foreign aid)
7. Orderly marketing and acceleration of imports
8. Elastic operation of fiscal and monetary policy(48)

The impetus for this program was to forestall protectionist policies by the major trading partners of Japan, yet, as indicated above, general structural conditions, both within and outside of Japan, continued to make trade an intensely debated issue throughout the 1970s.

On the American side, the Congress enacted the Trade Act of 1974, which provided for a strengthened position of the Office of the Special Trade Representative. This was the first of a series of steps taken to strengthen the American governmental mechanism in the trade area.(49) Another intent of the bill was to build up the governmental mechanism for the promotion of free trade. "But as of mid-1977, the Act's effect was more to buttress a holding action against protectionism than to bring about major additional trade liberalization."(50)

In the late 1970s, scholars at Harvard University and elsewhere produced works of an explanatory nature in an apparent effort to foster an educated understanding of the Japanese situation in the United States. Edwin Reischauer, perhaps the best known American expert on Japan, a Harvard professor and former American Ambassador to Japan, wrote in his popularized book, The Japanese:

> The nature of the Japanese business system has contributed to the rapid growth of industry since the war, but certain external factors have probably been even more important. There was an open world trading system which Japan could join and a world-wide abundance of raw materials. New technologies had been developed in the West during Japan's period of relative isolation in the war and prewar years and were now made available to the Japanese at modest costs, largely by American companies.(51)

The implications were clear. Systemic factors had contributed to the present business and trade situation, in Reischauer's view, and conflictual efforts to resolve differences would be counterproductive, according to his analysis. This view was even more forcefully argued by Reischauer's colleague at Harvard, Ezra F. Vogel. Vogel argued that Japanese success had less to do with traditional character traits than with specific organizational structures, policy programs, and conscious planning.(52) He posits three basic reasons why American reactions to successful Japanese trading practices in the United States have failed to retard vigorous Japanese penetration of the American market. First, as mentioned above in this study, Japanese costs are determined by raw materials costs. These have remained stable or declined in relative terms for Japanese manufacturers as the yen has appreciated in world markets against the U.S. dollar. Second, Japanese firms traditionally invest funds in research and development which results in reduced manufacturing costs and increased productivity, thus keeping Japanese products price competitive. Finally, "Japanese goods with a superior reputation for quality continue to sell even if prices are raised. If the Japanese . . . face quotas . . . they move into the higher quality market, thus increasing the dollar value of exports to America while continuing to observe the quotas."(53)

As mentioned above, the major organization within the Japanese business system for the promotion of exports is the sogo shosha, or general trading company. These firms were formed during the rapid industrialization period of Japan in the later 1800s and have functioned as a collective of worldwide networks for the gathering of marketing information and the selling of goods. A study of their organization and character described them as follows:

> From their inception in the 1870s to the late 1960s, the trading companies had a clear notion of their chief objectives and main business. Service to Japan's national interest was a chief objective. Operating as Japan's major supply and distribution channels, primarily as importers of industrial raw materials and as exporters of manufactured goods, was their main business. Now the sogo shosha have taken on new roles. . . . But in fact, whatever the future may hold, trading remains the sogo shosha's main business. The hundreds of subsidiaries and related firms in manufacturing, processing, financing, leasing, subcontracting, and sales all have one primary purpose: to support the main business of selling and buying and to generate new business.

A distinction exists between these general trading companies and the notion of the zaibatsu. The latter were family-owned holding companies that controlled a majority of pre-World War II Japan's industrial capacity and were broken up during the U.S. occupation of Japan (1945-1952). Nevertheless, references continue to appear from time to time conveying to the notion that Japan today is similar to prewar Japan. Such references may inflame passions on both sides of the Pacific and distract from efforts at regional community formation.

A more accurate description of the present system revolves around the notion of high debt ratios in Japanese firms today, or stated another way, the concept of debt financing rather than equity financing. This results in highly leveraged Japanese firms, which rely on the sogo shosha to sell goods to generate cash flow for debt servicing. Also, since return on equity is a minor Japanese business concern, Japanese managers are free to use excess profits after debt service for reinvestment in research and development and new product generation. Thus a zaikai, or financial circle system has emerged in Japan today, wherein the major Japanese banks are, in fact, the major "owners" of Japanese corporations through their loan positions, and these banks have a major influence in corporate decision making.

Two authorities from the Boston Consulting Group suggest that, despite the expense, investing in Japan could be an effective way of increasing American sales to Japan. Put another way, "Investment is relevant to the issue of trade because investment in Japan is a powerful stimulant to export sales to Japan. Foreign companies, on average, import more than seven times as much as the average Japanese company imports, while exporting much less from Japan than the average company."(55)

Japanese imports remained a topic for commentary in the American business press throughout the 1970s. One article predicted that Japanese imports would increase, notwithstanding slow-downs in the Japanese economy, causing continual and ongoing concern in both the United States and Europe.(56) For its part, the American government mounted a variety of major campaigns in the 1970s to encourage increased sales activity by U.S. firms in Japan. Major elements in this program included a cruise ship that visited Japanese ports to display U.S.-made goods in 1979, and the publication of two Department of Commerce books on the subject: Japan: A Growth Market for U.S. Consumer Products and U.S. Export Opportunities to Japan. Both publications were produced by the Department's Industry and Trade Administration in February and August of 1978 respectively.

ANALYSIS OF JAPANESE-AMERICAN TRADE DATA

Japanese-American trade data presented herein indicates the nature of the interdependent economic relationships between these two major Pacific Basin actors. The statistics are limited to the last five years of the 1970s, 1975 through 1979. As demonstrated above, this time-frame encompasses the period within which the issue of Japanese-American economic relations had been hotly debated, and thus is relevant to an assessment of the bilateral relations of the two countries within the Pacific Basin.

Three sources of data were utilized: the United States government, the United Nations, and the Japanese government. An examination of Japanese governmental sources revealed that contemporary trade statistics are limited. The White Paper on International Trade: Japan 1976, published by the Japan External Trade Organization, has a section on U.S.-Japanese trade, but contains out-of-date data. By contrast, the White Paper on International Trade 1979, published by the Japanese government Ministry of International Trade and Industry in June 1979, has no reference, nor data of any kind, on Japanese-American trade. The same is true in the case of an editor's background paper entitled "Japan and the World Economy," distributed by the Consulate General of Japan at Los Angeles in June 1979. Consequently, analysis of Japanese-sourced data is not attempted below.

In order to assess the extensive data from the U.S. government, a comparison of selected years' trade statistics with those furnished by the United Nations was conducted.   As Table 5.2 indicates, there is virtually no difference between the U.N. data and that of the U.S. government.   Thus, this study is based on U.S. governmental sources that provide the necessary depth and breakdowns required for comparative analytic purposes.

Table 5.2.
Data Comparison: United States Government
and the United Nations

	Japanese Exports to the United States		American Exports to Japan	
	U.S. Govt. Data	U.N. Data	U.S. Govt. Data	U.N. Data
1975	11,424.8	11,260.0	9,562.7	9,420.0
1976	15,683.0	15,900.0	10,144.7	10,030.0
1977	18,901.9	19,930.0	10,522.1	10,410.0

Sources: United Nations, 1978 Statistical Yearbook, 1979; and United States Department of Commerce, Highlights of U.S. Export and Import Trade, FT 990, Years 1975-1979. Figures in millions of U.S. dollars, f.o.b. (free on board or transaction price).

In selecting data sets, we rejected tables containing Department of Defense figures for military assistance because this analysis is focusing on business-related trade interaction, while military concerns related to interdependency are discussed below at the conclusion of this chapter.

The definition of exports used by the American government is employed herein: Military transfers obscure overall business/trade analysis.

Exports of domestic merchandise include commodities which are grown, produced, or manufactured in the U.S., and commodities of foreign origin which have been changed in the U.S. from the form in which they were imported, or which have been enhanced in value by further manufacture in the U.S. Exports of foreign merchandise consist of commodities of foreign origin which have entered the U.S. as imports and which, at the time of exportation, are in substantially the same condition as when imported.(57)

Finally, all data sets are quoted in millions of U.S. dollars and transactions were on a f.o.b. (free on board) or f.a.s. (free alongside ship) basis, which is a transaction price basis. These figures quote prices utilized in the actual transaction or sale of goods. They do not reflect shipping and insurance costs. Using f.a.s. prices for imports provides a more realistic measure of the magnitude of foreign sales to the United States. Since the purpose of the chapter is to assess the business climate rather than to evaluate total transaction costs, f.a.s. prices are more appropriate.

A breakout of the data indicates that substantial two-way trade has taken place during the time period under evaluation. U.S. exports to Japan have increased 83 percent over the five-year period, with an average increase of 17 percent per year. This fact was not mentioned in any of the literature reviewed. Rather, attention has been focused on the 131 percent increase in Japanese exports coming to the United States over the same period. Table 5.3 summaries these trends.

Table 5.3.
Percentage Change in Bilateral Exports:
Japan and the United States

	U.S. Exports to Japan	Japanese Exports to the United States
1975/1976	+6%	+37%
1976/1977	+5%	+20%
1977/1978	+22.5%	+31%
1978/1979	+36.5%	+5.8%
5-year average	+17%	+23.5%
5-year shift 1975/1979	+83%	+131%

Source: Author's computations based on U.S. Department of Commerce data contained in Highlights of U.S. Export and Import Trade, FT990, Years 1975-1979.

The basic tension in Japanese-American bilateral relations was created in the 1978 time period, when Japanese imports into the United States greatly exceeded the increasing U.S. exports to Japan. This created a trade "gap," a word that connotes a sudden change in bilateral economic relations. Politically, this image was connoted in the Task Force Report on United States-Japan Trade which opened by saying "because of growing trade problems with Japan. . . .(58) The problem is presented in that report as a bilateral one in which the focus of attention is exclusively on Japanese-American trade. Within that framework, the problem for the United States, and thus for American businessmen, is clear as Table 5.4 indicates. The shortfall of U.S. exports implies a lack of American business success in selling to Japan.

Table 5.4.
U.S. Trade Balance with Japan
(in millions of U.S. dollars)

	U.S. Exports to Japan	U.S. Imports from Japan	Balance
1975	9,562.7	11,424.8	- 1,862.1
1976	10,144.7	15,683.0	- 5,538.3
1977	10,522.1	18,901.9	- 8,379.8
1978	12,885.1	24,933.0	-12,047.9
1979	17,579.3	26,397.5	- 8,818.2

Source: Author's computations based on U.S. Department of Commerce data contained in Highlights of U.S. Export and Import Trade, FT 990, Years 1975-1979.

However, a comprehensive analysis of the data indicates that, when taken into the totality of U.S. trade, the relative performance of

Table 5.5
U.S. Imports from and Exports to
Japan as a Percentage ofTotal U.S. Imports and Exports

	Imports from Japan as % of Total Imports	Exports to Japan as % of Total Exports
1975	12%	9%
1976	13%	9%
1977	13%	9%
1978	14%	9%
1979	13%	10%

Source: Author's calculations

Japanese-American trade is not that unique.   Rather, as Table 5.5 demonstrates, both U.S. export performance and Japanese imports into the American market have not fluctuated in terms of total U.S. trade patterns.   This overall trade performance of the American economy shows that the rapid rise of U.S. imports has been followed generally by increased U.S. exports as well.   The Japanese aspect, far from being the main element in the overall trade picture, is but an active component part.

The data suggest that the root cause of much of the concern is the selective impact of Japanese imports on certain segments of the U.S. economy.   Table 5.6 displays three of the most active categories of commodities that compose the goods traded.   It is clear that American businessmen have made substantial progress over the five-year period under study, yet the magnitude of the Japanese imports in the category of machinery and transport equipment (which includes automobiles) has selectively and radically altered the domestic U.S. markets of those industries.

Table 5.6.
Japanese-American Trade by Selected Sectors

	Japanese Exports to the United States		American Exports to Japan	
	U.S. millions of dollars	% change	U.S. millions of dollars	% change
Nonagricultural commodities	1975: 11,204.1 1979: 26,153.8	+133.5%	6,339.1 12,112.9	+ 91%
Chemicals	1975: 387.4 1979: 616.1	+59%	589.0 1,651.6	+180%
Machinery & Transport Equipment	1975: 5,596.2 1979: 17,497.5	+212.7%	1,698.3 3,218.1	+ 89.5%

Source: Author's computations based on U.S. Department of Commerce data contained in Highlights of U.S. Export and Import Trade, FT 990, Years 1975-1979.

This analysis of statistical trade data indicates that during the years in question Japanese imports into the United States have, in fact, increased when viewed in an overall sense.   The year 1978 was particularly dramatic in that regard with a 31 percent increase in Japanese imports over the previous year, and a $12 billion deficit in Japanese-American two-way trade.

However, American exports to Japan have also been steadily rising during the period under study, and in 1979 the United States exports to

Japan increased by 36 percent over the previous year, while Japanese exports to the United States increased only 5.8 percent. Therefore, the relative measure of export performance has limitations as an analytical tool, because clarity is needed in order to infer meaning from data.

One aspect of this process involves putting Japanese-American trade into the perspective of overall trade patterns. A trend emerges from an examination of Japanese-American trade as a percentage of both nations' total trade in which the United States has maintained a steady economic relationship with Japan, in effect "depending" upon Japan for about 13 percent of annual United States imports. Similarly, Japan's economy has consistently imported about 9 percent of its inputs from the United States, indicating mutual interdependence. Further, the United States, rather than reducing general export performance over the period under study, has maintained an expanding export performance posture, even though overall imports have exceeded overall exports since 1975.

If one shifts from a macro to micro focus, the real significance of Japanese-American trade emerges from an examination of the various sectors of commodities involved. The most visible element is the 212 percent increase in Japanese exports of machinery and transport equipment, a category that includes automobiles. From that extreme, an actual decrease of 35 percent has been recorded in the Japanese category exports of oils and fats to the United States. This is an insignificant category, but the very fact of its insignificance demonstrates that data manipulation can produce a variety of results.

Throughout the period under review, certain sectors of American exports show steady increase in shipments to Japan over the years examined. These include agricultural commodities (70 percent), food and live animals (82 percent), and miscellaneous manufactured articles (175 percent), in addition to the shifts reflected in Table 5.6. Thus generalizations about all export or all import performance in all cases cannot be properly made from these data. Each case needs to be analyzed on its own merits.

Additionally, a preliminary analysis of data on the export and import performance of the Pacific Basin countries in general indicates some general increase in imports from the Pacific Basin. Yet in terms of overall United States imports, the great bulk of such imports comes from outside the region during the years in question. This pattern accords with the Japanese-American trade pattern, and indeed the two trade relationships, Japanese-American and Pacific Basin-United States, are compatible and mutually reinforcing. A primary finding that demonstrates the complexity and potential subjectivity of this matter is the one-year 476 percent increase experienced in 1979 in American exports to the People's Republic of China (PRC), now considered a member of the Pacific Basin, especially after the mutual recognition of the governments of the United States and the PRC on January 1, 1979. However, the 1979 figure that contributes to this impressive-appearing increase amounts to only .01 percent of U.S. worldwide exports in 1979. In both relative and absolute terms, the rate of change in the U.S.-PRC relationship, while great, is insignificant in relation to worldwide American export performance.

INVESTMENT ENVIRONMENT

To complement the trade dimension, a descriptive measure of the investment climate in the Pacific Basin may be derived from an examination of the action of regional capital markets, in that private business investments rely on capital for the financing of their operations. Principle sources of public sector investment capital for Asia have come from the Asian Development Bank; private investment banks such as the Private Investment Company of Asia, S.A. (PICA), an investment bank that takes minority positions in the financing of public sector projects; and new capital instruments such as the Asian Pacific Capital Corporation or Apco, a unit of Citibank.(59) The regional investment climate however is being changed by the liberalization of capital and stock markets in major centers, the most noteworthy of which is Japan.(60)   That country's new and more liberalized Foreign Exchange and Foreign Trade Control Law went into effect on December 1, 1980.   It constituted a change in philosophy from one in which investments were restricted in principle to one of freedom in principle.

One area greatly impacted by the new law was the securities market, especially in equities. Foreign investors now had easier access and, in principle, faced no restrictions on the purchase of stock in the Tokyo Stock Exchange. This reflected increasing global interest in the Japanese stock market: a growing influx of capital into Japan on a global sourcing basis.(61) Restrictions used to state that a single foreign investor (individual or company) could not purchase more than ten percent of a Japanese company's stock and no more than 25 percent in total could be foreign-owned.   Under the new law, the 25 percent ceiling has been lifted, but the ten percent restriction still applies insofar as the foreign investor must give 30 days advance notification and await approval from the Japanese Ministry of Finance (MOF).   In the wake of this change, the South Korean government announced in January 1981 a program of liberalization that will lead to freer access to the Korean stock exchange by foreign investors.(62)

Another indicator of investor interest is the growth of bond markets. In 1978, yen-denominated bonds, the so-called "samurai" bonds, were offered to non-Japanese, allowing buyers to gain on exchange rate fluctuations and also participate in this form of capital investment, especially since there were no restrictions on foreign ownership in secondary (resale) markets.   By 1980 banking and investment houses were setting up special investment funds, such as the Merrill Lynch Pacific Fund. The Association of International Bond Dealers created a Far East region in early 1981 reflecting the growing role of bonds in Asia.(63) All of the region's members have offices in either Hong Kong or Singapore, reflecting the fact that Singapore had become the center for the issuing of bonds, a logical extension of the established Asian Dollar Market, while Hong Kong had emerged as the center for bond trading.

In order to try and promote Manila and compete with Hong Kong and Singapore as a regional international financial center, the Philippine government abolished in 1981 a 5 percent income tax formerly levied on offshore banking units in an effort to help the Philippines attract international banking activity.   Offshore banking consists of international loans made outside of the country, so that such activity would not compete with domestic Philippine banks. A major result has been the creation of Asian Drawing Rights or ADRS, which are U.S. dollar denominated negotiable certificates that represent underlying foreign securities.   The four major U.S. banks most active in this market are Morgan Guaranty Trust Company, Irving Trust Company, Chemical Bank, and Citibank.(64)

Another dimension of the investment interactions within the Pacific Basin consists of the particular relationship between Japan and the market economies of Southeast Asia which make up the Association of Southeast Asian Nations (ASEAN).   The patterns of interaction have grown along both trade and investment lines, so that during the 1970s Japan became both the major trading partner and major source of direct investment in the region.   By the time Japanese Prime Minister Zenko Suzuki made his January 1981 trip to the region, Japan had invested over $4 billion in the ASEAN group, accounting for 44 percent of the region's total foreign direct investment, as against 25 percent by the United States.   Additionally, Japan had become ASEAN's largest trading partner, buying 30 percent of the group's exports by value.(65) While Japan had been running small trade surpluses with the Philippines, Singapore, and Thailand, its massive deficits with Indonesia (due to oil imports) and Malaysia have created systemic regional deficits, so that as an example, during the month of November 1980 alone, Japan had a $400 million deficit with ASEAN.(96) This has become a regional trend, with increased imports into Japan from the high-growth economies of Asia in general.   Research by Gene Gregory has demonstrated that lower costs and vigorous export promotion programs by other states are cross-pressuring Japanese industry in general, so that whole industries heretofore thought to be Japanese strengths are themselves under import pressures from neighboring countries.(67) The net effect has been to push Japanese firms to seek either protection from imports or to abandon industries that cannot compete and move to higher value added manufacturing and more sophisticated product lines, which compete directly with European and American manufacturers in the same markets.

There have been a number of reactions to this development.   One continues to be a fear that the ASEAN states will become dependent upon Japan.   Another may be measured in such approaches as the "Fukuda Doctrine," named after the former Japanese Prime Minister who articulated it after the August 1977 ASEAN summit meeting in Kuala Lumpur, Malaysia.(68) Greater developmental aid and questions of Japan's defense role for the region will continue to be raised in regard to this relationship. Even Japanese aid is controversial in this regard, for much of Japanese aid to the region has been in the form of tied loans, which are designed to subsidize indirectly Japanese exports that will feed into Southeast Asian regional developmental projects.(69)

It can be seen, therefore, that on both a transPacific and intra-regional basis, Japan is central to the entire web of interdependencies that have emerged in the Pacific Basin. Its strong economic links with both the United States and Southeast Asia show that the high productivity of the Japanese economy serves as a sort of gateway into which linkages flow. Yet this is not dominance, for Japan is a major importer from Southeast Asia and North America as well as an exporter, so that the ongoing search for formalized channels for conflict resolution between these major entities of the region (Japan, the United States, and the ASEAN group) is central to the region as a whole.

OTHER PACIFIC ACTORS: MEXICO, CANADA, AND THE USSR

When Herman Kahn's Hudson Institute, among others, discussed the Pacific Basin, the formulation was inclusive and contained more than just the high-growth states discussed above. Mexico and Canada in North America, rich in resources and developing along their individual national policy lines, have intersecting links with the Pacific area. Additionally, both economic and military/political factors make a discussion of the USSR's regional role important as well. The issues involved revolve around Soviet influence in the interdependency process. The potential for an impact now appears much greater than had previously been the case.

The basic policy of the Mexican government has been, and continues to be, the promotion of economic growth and development without totally abandoning its sovereignty to the United States. Yet the discovery of large oil deposits in Mexico has created a natural economic compatability between the Mexican production of oil and its consumption in the United States. This, in turn, creates a naturally expanding market for U.S. exports. Yet protectionism has always been a feature of Mexican import policy; restrictions are effectuated through two types of controls – tariffs and quantitative restrictions. Article 131 of the Mexican constitution gives the federal government exclusive power to regulate imports, and the Mexican Congress has historically delegated this power to the national executive. Thus the President of Mexico can fix tariffs and quotas and needs only to inform the Mexican Congress.

The Mexican governmental policy has been restrictive in order to protect domestic manufacturing and to combat unfavorable balances of trade. Its tariff system is based on "ad valorem" duty rates, which are assessed on either the invoice value or the "official valuation," whichever is higher. The policy is designed to restrict the importation of products   that   compete   directly   or   indirectly   with   Mexican manufacturers. These restrictions are implemented by the setting of a license requirement on all imports. However, licenses are routinely granted under a wide variety of conditions, among which are the inability of Mexican manufacturers to supply products needed in sufficient quantities or in time to meet a reasonable deadline, and/or the inability of a domestic product to fill reasonable technical specifications for a particular application.

A central problem in the managing of trade, as it affects the Pacific Basin, revolves around the development of infrastructure. In seeking a participative position within the Pacific Basin, the Mexican government is encouraging joint venture investment in Mexico toward the end of manufacturing and processing within its borders for ultimate shipment to the U.S. market. Two major obstacles affect this effort: rail service and port facilities. The Mexican rail system is basically single track, which has been expanded by only 600 miles since the turn of the century.(70) Shortages of capacity have inhibited the flow of goods and resulted in delays in which capacity is underutilized. Such conditions tend to reduce the effectiveness of Mexican firms in their dealings with both Asian and U.S. enterprises.

Compounding the problem, port facilities on the Pacific coast are substandard for transPacific trade. The Mexican development plans call for the establishment of major port facilties at Salina Cruz, which is supposed to be a terminal for a "land bridge" across Mexico for container shipping through the Gulf of Mexico to Atlantic ocean ports, and Lazaro Cardenas. These port facilities are essential for Mexico to capitalize on potential business investment by manufacturers from Korea, Taiwan, and the Philippines, who have expressed interest, along with the Japanese, in participating in the U.S. border area's low wage rate manufacturing under the Mexican government's Border Industrialization Program. Part of the motivation of Asian manufacturers is to use Mexican plants as sites for the production of goods for sale to the rest of Latin America. Thus issues of infrastructure directly affect not only internal Mexican development but also its participation in the region as a whole.

On the investment side, Japanese firms have been heavily committed to the Mexican plan to create a major steel complex at Las Truchas, adjacent to Lazaro Cardenas. Technical know-how for the project is being supplied by Kobe Steel Company, the Sumitomo Metals Industry, and the Nippon Steel Corporation, which collectively have contributed about one-third of the total financing costs, or about $124 million.(71) Yet efforts at creating a "Pacific Pittsburgh," as the project is unofficially known, still exhibit operating, financial, and production problems, due to the underutilization of capacity and poor infrastructure, raising questions concerning the viability of such projects in the Mexican environment. What cannot be questioned is the commitment to the project, and thus to the concept of Mexican development with a Pacific Basin context.

The interaction patterns do not always originate externally. In late December 1980, the Mexican government entered into negotiations with the Philippine Board of Investments concerning Mexican supplies of raw materials for a future petrochemical plant funded by the Philippine National Oil Company. The Mexican state-owned oil company, Petroleos Mexicanos, S.A., also expressed interest in taking delivery of some of the plant's output.(72)

The Canadian perspective is somewhat different. Canadian governmental pronouncements concerning Canada's interest in Asia build upon a foundation of British Commonwealth associations with many of the states in the Asian region but go beyond that to stress new commercial ties and business interests. This stems from the natural markets in Asia for the raw materials produced in Canada and the desire for Canada to have more active commercial relations of its own in the region. The large-scale nature of the contracts that have been discussed is illustrated by the 1981 multi-billion-dollar coal supply contract reviewed in the business press that was under negotiation between two Canadian mining companies and a group of Japanese steelmakers. Such agreements automatically would bring large-scale infrastructure development to Western Canada, particularly the expansion of the Canadian National Railways.(73) Yet at the same time nationalistic feelings continue to mitigate against an entirely open relationship between Canada and the outside economic world. The Candian Banking Act of 1980, while directed against American branch banking operations in Canada, had the effect of limiting banking activity of all foreign banks, including Asian banks, by limiting such enterprises to an 8 percent share of total domestic Canadian assets.(74) This could restrict foreign participation in the very developmental projects that underpin the Canadian compatability with the other states of the Pacific.

The Canadian experience is similar to that of Australia's, but the Australian government had to come to grips with the shift from a Commonwealth focus to a Pacific Basin focus earlier, for obvious geographic reasons. Yet both have vast land areas, small populations, strong Commonwealth ties, and thus a British cultural orientation, and economies in the process of transition. In the Australian case, the interdependency with Japan reached the point that, by the end of 1980, the Fraser administration had dispatched a full-time labor attache to the Australian embassy in Tokyo to explain Australian labor relations to Japanese business and governmental leaders. The Japanese, observing what appeared to be a violent labor environment, had been reluctant to increase direct investments in Australia. The Australian position and response has been historically to pledge long-term supplies of energy and other commodities to Japan in return for better access to Japanese markets for Australian goods and investment capital for the development of Australian mineral resources.(75)

The situation with regard to the Soviet Union (USSR) is complicated due to its particular role in both economic and military affairs in Asia. Economically, the USSR impact is felt primarily through competition in Far Eastern shipping. The Trans-Siberian Railway (TSR) has established a land bridge across the whole of the Soviet Union and has provided reduced-rate shipping of goods to and from Europe and Asia. This has had a particular impact on the Far East Freight Conference (FEFC), a consortium of 29 large shipping companies that had traditionally dominated the ocean transport industry by shipping via the Suez Canal at established rates.   According to the Overseas Containers Ltd. Company, the TSR's Asian operations have grown at a compound annual rate of 20 percent during the late 1970s, giving it an overall market share of about 10 percent by 1979.(76)   This simply reinforced the already existing competition from Soviet shipping which had long provided a challenge to the shipping conference with its low sea rates. According to a detailed analysis by Wayne Decker, staff researcher for the Woods Hole Oceanographic Institution, this combined merchant fleet/land bridge approach has provided leverage for Asian shippers in bargaining with the traditional conference member shipping lines. These lines are faced with increased fuel costs and do not receive the subsidies   allocated   by   the   Soviet   maritime   administration, MOREFLOT.(77)   It is not possible to determine whether the destabilization of the shippers conference, represented by the pull-out of the U.S. corporation, Sea-Land, in March 1980, is reflective of this general competitive situation, since other shipping lines based in Singapore and Taiwan are not members of the conference either. In any event, Decker's analysis convinced him that the Soviet Union could not be kept out of the Asia/Pacific transportation theater, even with a concerted intergovernmental exclusivity approach. Thus, in the area of ocean transporation, increased activity has produced the effect of fragmenting existing corporate and governmental relationships and creating new alignments, the results of which are not clear. While it appears that Sea-Land Corporation might rejoin the shipping conference, its corporate goals of controlling costs and gaining market share have more influence in corporate rate setting matters. The Japanese shipping lines, supported in their policy position by the South Korean shipping lines, have opposed the concept of individual rates for selected lines, and collectively they dominate the FEFC.(78)

Parenthetically, the same set of issues impact the other major mode of transpacific travel, airlines. A series of interlocking problems arose in the late 1970s over landing rights; treaty provisions; and the routes of airlines that were not members of IATA, the International Air Transport Association. U.S. carriers, in particular, were in conflict with Asian airlines over landing rights, through service, especially to the PRC, and the relationship of a deregulated U.S. airline industry to those state-supported flag carriers from Asian countries.(79)

MILITARY-POLITICAL DYNAMICS

In the area of security affairs, the role of the Soviet military, and particularly the Soviet Navy, has had a direct effect on the entire international political dynamics of the region. While not recognized at the time, the U.S. defeat in Vietnam created a perception of great change in the military balance of the region, and thereafter increasing attention to the Soviet military position in Asia began to appear in a number of authoritative works. Two major dimensions of military analysis initially appeared: the relative decline of U.S. military power vis a vis the USSR and the accompanying concern of Asian allies as to their national security and the tenor of the international political environment in which they existed. A third dimension, which emerged later, was the impact of these two leading concerns on the nature of the Pacific Basin, with particular implications for interdependence.

An initial statement of the naval issues in particular appeared in a lengthy feature article on the front page of the Los Angeles Times in April 1978,(80) which was followed by a Rand Corporation study the following year.(81)   These studies established the premise that an expanded Soviet military capability existed, based at the established port of Vladivostok, with a new base complex at Petropavlovsk on the Kamchatka Peninsula.   Furthermore, the overall increase in Soviet naval strength was graphically represented in the increase of surface combatants.   The most noteworthy addition to these forces, beyond boats consigned to submarine service, was the arrival in 1980 in Pacific waters of the aircraft carrier Minsk, the second of the Soviet's Kiev-class carriers. A carrier task force under Soviet command projected a psychological image of power projection which up to that time had been exclusively American.

These developments were met with debate regarding two major policy issues for the U.S. and Japanese governments.   The U.S. government's position, on the one hand, was to encourage Japan to increase its defense budget as the United States redeployed (in fact) part of its Western pacific military assets to the Indian Ocean.   The Japanese government, for its part, undertook a national defense debate in its own right, prompted by a perception of weakened U.S. security guarantees. By 1980, the joint military maneuvers in exercise "RimPac 80" were clearly seen by outside observers and the press as an effort to increase U.S. military credibility in Asia in return for continued movement by the Japanese government toward increased defense spending.

The Japanese government, for its part, apparently needed a specific issue around which to rally public support for greater military preparedness. The 1977 fishing rights disputes with the USSR, triggered by the extension of Soviet territorial waters north of Japan, served as a prelude. By 1980, the issue of the Soviet militarization of the occupied islands in the Kurile Islands group provided the specific focus for an ongoing policy debate inside the Japanese government. It now appears that a consensus was achieved by 1980, in which the Soviet threat was perceived as real, that increased military spending was required, and that a shift, however incremental, in Japanese policy away from an evenhanded and low-key relationship with both the PRC and the USSR, archrivals on the Asian mainland, was required. This may be the real meaning of the first Japanese government sponsored "northern territories days" in February 1981, during which demonstrations against the Soviet occupation of the southern Kuriles took place throughout Japan. The significance of these developments go beyond purely military matters. They signal a relative decline in influence and policy advocacy importance of those Japanese international business leaders who wished to participate in the development of Soviet Siberia.   Those business interests obviously wanted to modify somehow the attitude and posture of confrontation so that joint development contracts, which had been sought off and on for years, could be brought to fruition.

Yet, while Japan appeared to put aside purely economic concerns in the Siberian case and opted for an emphasis on military security matters, the U.S. position appeared mixed. The report of the U.S. House of Representatives 1980 Special Study Mission to Asia formally recognized the military dimension mentioned above:

> The growing Soviet naval presence is a matter of particular concern to the United States and its Asian allies. During the past decade, the Soviet Pacific Fleet was upgraded with the newest classes of submarines and missile cruisers and the much-publicized Kiev class aircraft carrier – the Minsk. All indicators point to a continuing expansion and modernization in the decade ahead. Given the fact that the prosperity of the Asian-Pacific region overwhelmingly rests on seaborne commerce, the political and strategic implications of the Soviet naval buildup cannot be overlooked.(82)

Concerning this threat, however, Keith Dunn, writing in the Naval War College Review, has pointed out that the Soviet navy is still constrained by geography, in that its Pacific naval forces do not have open access to the sea but must pass through the Tsushima or LaPerouse Straits. Thus only the new base at Petropavlovsk has a direct access to the sea, but it is totally depended on resupply by sea from Vladivostok.(83) These limitations were more fully discussed by Stuart Johnson and Joseph Yager in The Military Equation in Northeast Asia, published by the Brookings Institution in 1979.

A most comprehensive public discussion of these issues is contained in the 1981 Far Eastern Economic Review Yearbook. Remarkably, the first two sections of the volume, entitled "The Region" and "The Power Game," are devoted exclusively to an in-depth discussion of the Soviet military/political position in the Pacific, with particular reference to Soviet influence in Vietnam. Not only is the extent of analysis remarkable, but its appearance in an international business publication that has emphasized the interdependencies of the states of the region demonstrated the reemergence of military and political affairs as a critical dimension of the international business environment. While arguing that the Pacific idea is an idea whose time has come, these writings evidenced considerable concern that Soviet military might, linked to bases in Vietnam, could disrupt the interdependencies of the entire region. The implied, but unstated, thrust of the analysis was that the Soviet Union is a negative factor in the Pacific area and that its growing military power should be seen as a force pushing the other states of the region into closer cooperation. The editors conclude that,

> if the Soviet Union succeeds in securing naval and air bases in Vietnam and in having Soviet forces permanently stationed there, the problem that the Soviet Pacific Fleet now has of having to pass through narrow straits in order to gain access to

the Pacific will be partly solved. The resulting change in the U.S.-Soviet naval balance in the South China Sea and the Indian Ocean could seriously affect vital Western sea lanes in those waters.(84)

It appears, however, that, ironically, the Soviet military presence has created a political climate more conductive to transPacific co-operation. A little-recognized result of the international movement to boycott the 1980 Summer Olympics in Moscow after the 1979 Soviet invasion of Afghanistan has been the extent of boycott support by the governments of the Pacific Basin states. While the Western media, in general, emphasized the extent of European nonparticipation in the games, the list of nonparticipants from Asia is more impressive, particularly when viewed in terms of an implied commonality of political purpose. As figure 5.1 indicates, only Australia and New Zealand, where sports have a strong domestic constituency, and Sri Lanka, which continues to maintain a public posture of nonalignment in spite of its market economy orientation and close ties with Singapore after 1977, sent teams. The other Asian states participating were either neutralist states, states with pro-Soviet policies, or Communist states.

Fig. 5.1. Pacific Basin Nations

States Boycotting the Olympics	States Attending
Japan	Australia
People's Republic of China	New Zealand
Hong Kong	Sri Lanka
The ASEAN States:	Burma
Philippines	Nepal
Thailand	Pro-Soviet:
Malaysia	India
Singapore	Laos
Indonesia	Mongolia
Pakistan	North Korea
South Korea	Vietnam

Note: Taiwan does not participate in the Olympics.

No other region, including Europe or Latin America, displayed such an overwhelming coherence and congruence on the issue.

CONCLUSIONS

It appears from the analysis above that some modifications may be in order in the utilization of the dimensions described at the onset of this chapter. While multiple channels connecting the states of the Pacific do exist, the common thread that unites them is a general commitment to economic progress, primarily through market forces. In a sense then, there exists a hierarchy of issues, but the hierarchy is nonconflictual in that the overall goals of the states in the region all revolve around the attainment of individual progress for their respective individual national economies, and thus, through the progress of each state, the progress of the entire region as a whole.

This has led, in turn, to a primacy of international business concerns in building interdependencies, and, as a result, the international business community has been in the forefront in promoting international interaction. The specific issues involved vary on a case-by-case basis and reflect the widely differing economic capabilities of the Pacific states, to say nothing of their differing cultural and historical traditions. This makes the establishment of a single agenda of issues and policies difficult. Efforts to overcome these shortfalls have led to the positing, as a given, the geographic dimension of the states in the sense that they all border the Pacific Ocean and thus have a common geographic variable around which to rally.

Mere economic goals alone are insufficient, however, to forge an interdependent community and may even be conflictual, as in the case of Japanese-American trade. Some sort of larger regional political framework is needed as a conflict resolution mechanism. On this issue, the passing of former hierarchial orders, experienced in Asia in the past, has given way to a sense that the nation-state system, foreign to Asia, is now a fact of life for the region and must be the milieu for any future regional order. The United States, once seen as the dominant power in the region in modern times, is no longer seen as playing an overarching, dominant role, and there is no enthusiasm for a replacement of U.S. power in the form of either Japanese economic domination or Soviet military hegemony. Thus the convergence of policy for all the Pacific states revolves around international economic interaction, precisely because economic and business affairs are, in the sense of pure market theory, politically neutral. In designing a regional system then, the overall objective is to put into place mechanisms that are culturally neutral and capable of resolving intraregional economic conflicts arising over conflicting strategies or divergent domestic goals.

To allege that the interdependencies of the Pacific do not exist because they are not formalized, or because they are supported only by international business interests seeking stable business environments, is to beg the point. Rather, the need for a more formalized system to manage the multiple and ongoing interdependencies of the area is now recognized on a variety of levels: academic, governmental, and economic. In the last analysis, the Pacific area has never been without some sort of encompassing regional order; now the goal of all these groups is to create a new and forward-looking order that will encompass the independent states of the Asia-Pacific region and facilitate the promotion of the developmental strategies implemented by the high-growth societies of the region.

NOTES

(1) See Martin Binkin and Jeffrey Record, Where Does the Marine Corps Go from Here? (Washington, D.C.: Brookings Institution, 1976).

(2) Robert O. Keohane and Joseph S. Nye, Power and Interdependence: World Politics in Transition (Boston: Little, Brown, 1977).

(3) Ibid., p. 8.

(4) Ibid., pp. 24-27.

(5) George Modelski, Principles of World Politics (New York: Free Press, 1972), pp. 13-14.

(6) Keohane and Nye, Power and Interdependence, p. 19.

(7) Stanley J. Michalak, Jr., "Theoretical Perspective for Understanding International Interdependence," World Politics 32, no. 1 (October 1979): 145.

(8) John K. Fairbank, ed. The Chinese World Order (Cambridge, Mass.: Harvard University Press, 1970), p. 2.

(9) For details, see Modelski, Principles of World Politics, pp. 44-46.

(10) Richard M. Nixon, U.S. Foreign Policy for the 1970s: Building for Peace (Washington, D.C.: GPO, February 25, 1971).

(11) See U.S. Department of State, "The Dominoes That Did Not Fall," Current Policy, no. 36, Bureau of Public Affairs, Office of Public Communications, October 1978.

(12) For details, see W.A. Wiswa Warnapala, "Sri Lanka 1978: Reversal of Policies and Strategies," Asian Survey 19, no. 2 (February 1979): 178-190; and James Manor, "A New Political Order for Sri Lanka," The World Today 9, (September 1979): 377-386.

(13) "Singapore Looks Further Afield," Far Eastern Economic Review, May 12, 1978, pp. 40-46.

(14) "Sri Lanka Is Offering American Investors A Place in the Sun," Asian Wall Street Journal Weekly, September 22, 1980, pp. 1, 20.

(15) Kiyoshi Kojima, Japan and a Pacific Free Trade Area (Berkeley: University of California Press, 1971).

(16) Ibid., p. 49.

(17) Kiyoshi Kojima, Japan and a New World Economic Order (London: Croom Helm, 1977).

(18) Ibid., pp. 184-185.

(19) Bernard K. Gorden and Kenneth J. Rothwell, The New Political Economy of the Pacific (Cambridge, Mass.: Ballinger, 1975).

(20) Ibid., p. 90.

(21) Endel-Jakob Kolde, The Pacific Quest: The Concept and Scope of an Oceanic Community (Lexington, Mass.: Lexington Books, D.C. Heath, 1976).

(22) Ibid., p. 107.

(23) Lloyd R. Vasey and George J. Viksnins, The Economic and Political Growth Pattern of Asia-Pacific (Honolulu: The Pacific Forum, distributed by the University of Hawaii Press, 1976).

(24) Lawrence B. Krause and Suceo Sekiguchi, eds., Economic Interaction in the Pacific Basin (Washington, D.C.: The Brookings Institution, 1980).

(25) Ibid., p. 243.

(26) U.S. Government, House of Representatives, Committee on Foreign Affairs, Subcommittee on Asian and Pacific Affairs, Hearings: The Pacific Community Idea, Ninety-sixth Congress, first session, July 18, October 23 and 31, 1979.

(27) The Pacific Basin Cooperation Study Group, Report on the Pacific Basin Cooperation Concept (in English translation), Govt. of Japan, May 19, 1980.

(28) "Clearing Hurdles in the Pacific," Far Eastern Economic Review, February 1, 1980, p. 44.

(29) John Scott, The Pacific Community. A Report to the Publishers of Time, the weekly newsmagazine, n.p., n.d.

(30) Financial Markets of the Pacific Rim, Economic and Financial Series, vol. 1, Security Pacific Bank, Los Angeles, 1974.

(31) Roy Rowan, "A Peaceful Asia Beckons Investors," Fortune, October 1977, p. 196.

(32) "The Pacific Basin: A Survey," The Banker 129, no. 634 (December 1978): 43-82.

(33) "Exploiting the Pacific Tide," Far Eastern Economic Review, December 21, 1979, pp. 47-59.

(34) Howard Banks, "Pacific Basin Trade," Europe, March-April 1980, pp. 21-24.

(35) "Asia's New Bidders for Western Plants," special report, Business Week, March 17, 1980, pp. 48-D to 48-P. This special report may have appeared only in the magazine's West Coast edition.

(36) For his remarks see, "Economic Cooperation in the Asia-Pacific Area: Prospects for the 21st Century," Speaking of Japan (Japan Institute for Social and Economic Affairs, (Keizai Koho Center) 1, no. 1 (January 1981): 1-4.

(37) "Stress on Pacific Basin," Korea Newsreview, November 29, 1980, p. 16.

(38) Herman Kahn, The Emerging Japanese Superstate (Englewood Cliffs, N.J.: Prentice-Hall, 1970).

(39) "The Reindustrialization of America," Business Week, June 30, 1980, pp. 55-142.

(40) Lawrence B. Krause and Sueo Sekiguchi, "Japan and the World Economy," in Asia's New Giant, ed. Hugh Patrick and Henry Rosovsky (Washington, D.C.: The Brookings Institution, 1976), p. 398.

(41) Ibid., p. 401.

(42) "Half a Loaf," Newsweek, December 19, 1977, p. 41.

(43) Ibid.

(44) "Japan Trade Proposals Insufficient U.S. Envoy Says," The Arizona Republic, December 13, 1977, p. A-8.

(45) "Eidai, Four Affiliates Ask Court Protection; Failure May Be Postwar Japan's Biggest," The Wall Street Journal, February 21, 1978, p. 14.

(46) "Dumping of Steel by Japan Ruled Far Less Severe," The Wall Street Journal, January 10, 1978, p. 28.

(47) "Cease, Desist Order is Issued to Japan Firms," The Wall Street Journal, February 24, 1978, p. 10.

(48) Leon Hollerman, "Foreign Trade in Japan's Economic Transition," in The Japanese Economy in International Perspective, ed. Isaiah Frank (Baltimore: Johns Hopkins University Press, 1975), p. 192.

(49) For a detailed analysis of this law, see I.M. Destler, "United States Trade Policymaking During the Tokyo Round," in The Politics of Trade: U.S. and Japanese Policymaking for the GATT Negotiations, ed. Michael Blaker (New York: Occasional Papers of the East Asian Institute, Columbia University, 1978), pp. 25-52.

(50) Ibid., p. 55.

(51) Edwin O. Reischauer, The Japanese (Cambridge, Mass.: Harvard University Press, 1978), pp. 188-189.

(52) Edgar F. Vogel, Japan as Number One: Lessons for America (Cambridge, Mass.: Harvard University Press, 1979), page ix.

(53) Ibid., p. 227.

(54) Alexander K. Young, The Sogo Shosha: Japan's Multinational Trading Companies (Boulder, Colo.: Westview Press, 1979), p. 214.

(55) James C. Abegglien and Thomas M. Hout, "Facing Up to the Trade Gap with Japan," World Politics 52 (June 1978): 163.

(56) "Japan: A Slowing Economy Triggers Export Fever," Business Week, February 25, 1980, p. 64; and "Europe: Japanese Exports Have Carmakers Quaking," Business Week, April 7, 1980, p. 44.

(57) U.S. Department of Commerce, Highlights of U.S. Export and Import Trade, FT 990, December 1978, p. 4.

(58) Subcommittees on Trade, Committee on Ways and Means, U.S. House of Representatives, Task Force Report on United States-Japan Trade, January 2, 1979, p. 1.

(59) "Citibank Sparking Competition in Asia," Wall Street Journal, Thursday, January 15, 1981, p. 28.

(60) "Japan Eases Foreign-exchange Rules," Christian Science Monitor, Tuesday, December 2, 1980, p. 11.

(61) "Tokyo Exchange Handling Foreign Investment Surge," Christian Science Monitor, Monday, June 9, 1980, p. 11.

(62) "Securities Trading to be Okayed for Aliens," Korea Newsreview, January 24, 1981, p. 16.

(63) "International Bond Dealers See Growing Role for Asia," Asian Wall Street Journal Weekly, January 26, 1981, p. 23.

(64) "U.S. Banks Boost Offerings of Asia, Australian ADRs," Asian Wall Street Journal Weekly, January 19, 1981, p. 23.

(65) "Japan Goes Courting in Southeast Asia," New York Times, Sunday, January 11, 1981, p. E5.

(66) "ASEAN-Japan Trade," Asian Wall Street Journal Weekly, January 12, 1981.

(67) Gene Gregory, "Japan's Asian Challenge," Columbia Journal of World Business, Summer 1979, pp. 65-73.

(68) For details, see "ASEAN and Japan '78," Far Eastern Economic Review, March 10, 1978, pp. 32-64.

(69) Donald C. Hellmann, "Japan and Southeast Asia: Continuity Amidst Change," Asian Survey 19, no. 12 (December 1979): 1192.

(70) "Boxcars Snarl Mexican Trade," Business Week, February 9, 1981, p. 46.

(71) Lloyd's Mexican Economic Report, April, 1980, p. 1.

(72) "Mexico May Provide Help for Philippine Petrochemical Plant," Asian Wall Street Journal Weekly, December 29, 1980, p. 19.

(73) "Canada Nearing Completion of Contract to Sell Japan $400 Million of Coal a Year," Wall Street Journal, Friday, January 23, 1981, p. 32.

(74) "Canada: A Strict New Law Limits Foreign Bankers," Business Week, February 2, 1981, p. 30.

(75) "Australian Labor Envoy Is Aimed for Tokyo," Asian Wall Street Journal Weekly, February 2, 1981, p. 13.

(76) "Railroads: Yet Another Soviet Threat," World Business Weekly, March 31, 1980, p. 9.

(77) This section is based on Wayne R. Decker (Woods Hole Oceanographic Institution) "The Global Shipping Regime: An Asian Focus" (Paper presented at the twenty-first annual conference of the International Studies Association, Los Angeles, March 1980), and the author's conversations with Dr. Decker.

(78) "Tempest Brewing Over Pacific Shipping Rates," Asian Wall Street Journal Weekly, March 17, 1980, p. 19.

(79) For details, see "Transportation: Is the U.S. Sabotaging Its International Airlines?" Business Week, January 26, 1981, pp. 74-80. Also

with regard to China, see "Pan Am Begins Flights to China that Include Stopovers in Tokyo," Wall Street Journal, Thursday, January 29, 1981, p. 28.

(80) San Jamesen, "Growing Soviet Fleet Raises Pacific Alarms," Los Angeles Times, Sunday, April 9, 1978, p. 1.

(81) Richard H. Solomon, ed., Asian Security in the 1980s: Problems and Policies for a Time of Transition (Santa Monica, Calif.: The Rand Corporation, November 1979).

(82) U.S. House of Representatives, Committee on Foreign Affairs, Asian Security Environment: 1980, Report by a Special Study Mission to Asia, January 5-23, 1980 (Washington, D.C.: GPO, May 1980), pp. 3-4.

(83) Keith A. Dunn, "Power Projections or Influence: Soviet Capabilities for the 1980s," Naval War College Review, September-October 1980, pp. 40-41.

(84) "The Power Game," Asia 1981 Yearbook, Far Eastern Economic Review, Hong Kong, 1981, p. 23. See p. 23 also for a complete breakdown of the strengths of the Soviet Pacific Fleet as of June 1980.

6 Problems of Regional Development: North America

Gavin Boyd

As a geographic expression, North America is the area comprising the United States, Canada, and Mexico. In the literature on international relations the term has a richer meaning, for it refers to the attributes of those three political economies and their interactions, and it has relational and comparative significance in the much larger pattern of world politics. The United States is a large, well-integrated, strongly polyarchic postindustrial democracy; a global power; and a very active intrusive state in the politics of Western Europe, East Asia, Latin America, Africa, South Asia, and the Middle East. In North America the United States is the core power, and its transnational enterprises deeply penetrate both Canada and Mexico. Canada is a culturally affinitive, less integrated, smaller, and less polyarchic postindustrial democracy, relatively isolated in world politics and marginally involved in the politics of Latin America. Mexico is culturally part of Latin America, integrated socially but with notable class division; it is a modernizing democracy, heavily dependent on trade with the United States, and, like Canada, lacks external ties that could enable it to interact with the United States on a more equal basis. Geographically Mexico is better situated to develop such ties, but it is somewhat estranged from its Latin American neighbors.

There is little interaction between Canada and Mexico, because of cultural differences, geographic separation, political contrasts, low interdependencies, and a weak congruence of perceived interests. Hence in North America values are negotiated at the government level and allocated transnationally through two bilateral patterns – the U.S.-Canada system, with high and complex interdependencies, and the U.S.-Mexico system, based on a complex dependency relationship. Interaction between the United States and Canada is managed pragmatically, with a considerable separation between the governmental and transnational levels, and the major asymmetries are effective principally at the latter, where their operation is mostly

143

autonomous.   In the U.S.-Mexican relationship, however, emotional factors with a long history influence each side, Mexican behavior is spirited and expresses strong economic nationalism, and there are close bonds between the Mexican administration and national firms whose interests are involved in the transnational interactions with the United States.

CONFIGURATION

The territorial size, endowments, and locations of the North American states are primary determinants of the pattern formed by their characteristics and relationships.   Each has a large territory, with resources sufficient to support a diversified modern economy, and in these respects differs from Japan and some of the ASEAN members. Exchanges between the two smaller North American nations and the United States are facilitated by extensive land communications, as they share long common borders.   Outside the continent, communications must bridge the long distances across the Atlantic or the Pacific for interaction with major powers.   Geographically, and because of the size of its human resources, the United States is the most advantaged nation: it relates to Canada and Mexico as neighbors and has the capabilities needed for extensive interchanges with Latin American states, and also with West European and East Asian powers.   Relative geographic isolation, however, has been responsible for a distinctive tradition in U.S. foreign policy that emphasizes the preservation of security and independence through the avoidance of entanglements with other powers and the use of a preventive diplomacy to exclude major outside states from the politics of Latin America.   Canada, dis-advantaged by location and a small population, has close cultural bonds with the United States, but major asymmetries affect the quality of cooperation in this relationship.(1)   Mexico, with a national territory that was substantially reduced in size by U.S. encroachments during the colonial period, relates to the United States under the influence of strong historical resentments and from a position of considerable economic weakness.

The transnational expansion of the U.S. economy has occurred largely because of the autonomous activities of U.S.-based international firms.   These have been capable of allocating large resources for foreign investment because of powerful oligopolistic and monopolistic positions in their home market and have had strong incentives to invest abroad, including tax concessions, opportunities to dominate markets, and relative freedom from government regulation, especially with respect to intrafirm trade and transfer pricing.   By cross-subsidizing their subsidiaries in order to undercut national firms in the host countries, U.S. transnational enterprises have been able to consolidate strong positions in the Canadian and Mexican economies and ac-cordingly have been able to draw local and especially Canadian invest-ment that might otherwise have gone into national firms.

The pattern of governmental interactions in North America is not fully triangular because of the low level of interchange between Canada and Mexico.(2) The ties between these two states are weak, and there is a danger that the existing asymmetries in U.S.-Canada and U.S.-Mexico relations will increase, with serious political costs on each side, or that the U.S.-Canada link may be strengthened while the bonds between the United States and Mexico are subjected to further strains. For the development of a regional system, the North American pattern of relations would have to become fully triangular, so as to facilitate Canadian-Mexican interaction on common interests and to prepare the way for decision making on regional issues – not through three separate bilateral systems but collectively. That is hindered, for the present, by geography, disparities in size, differences in economic advancement, and cultural contrasts. These factors tend to obstruct the development of a general sense of area identity, and thus, of feelings of obligation to work for the common good of the region. Consciousness of area identity can be fostered by cooperation on equitable terms, if this can be promoted through a shared political will that is committed to overcoming distances, bargaining inequalities, and cultural differences; but if the general resolve to collaborate falls short of such a will the smaller states will need coalition partners. The region, then, will have to be enlarged, that is, Canada and Mexico will have to secure or receive the cooperation of other states, and this can be envisaged within the larger context of an international community comprising North America and East Asia.

The possibilities for understanding, goodwill, and policy coordination in North America are determined principally by the basic characteristics of the U.S., Canadian, and Mexican political systems. Structurally, functionally, and in terms of their political cultures, these polities differ substantially, with consequences that affect their policy orientations and capabilities for constructive regional diplomacy and for the guidance of transnational interactions that affect their economies.

The United States, the largest polity, is highly pluralistic because of a fragmentation of power between its executive and legislative structures, the politicization and impermanence of the upper levels of its bureaucracy, the extensive scope for interest group activity that is permitted by the institutional weaknesses of its major political parties, and an intense individualism that pervades its political culture, giving rise to conceptions of government as the outcome of competitive manipulation by self-interested groups. All the negative effects on executive decisional efficacy cause a lack of coherence in foreign economic policy. The numerous agencies involved are inadequately coordinated, and the policy is managed in a disjointed and incremental fashion, with shifting sectoral bias. The substance of foreign economic policy expresses the concerns of powerful domestic economic groups, but it also evidences a general orientation toward the development of a liberal international economic order in which competitive pressures will stimulate free exchanges that will help to maximize welfare for most of the participants.(3)

Canada has a parliamentary system that is structurally more suited for coherent management of foreign economic policy. The collective executive exerts strong downward pressures for the aggregation of interest group demands, through the organization of the ruling party and the legislature, and operates through a permanent bureaucracy. The degree of political and social integration, however, is lower than in the United States and it is threatened by a strong movement for independence in Quebec, the predominantly French province. Coping with this problem necessitates bias in federal allocative policies and concessions on questions of provincial autonomy that tend to strain Ottawa's relations with other provinces. Overall growth policies are thus affected, but external economic relations are dominated by trade and investment problems between Canada and the United States which are difficult to manage because of weak bargaining resources and which call for strong federal direction of the Canadian economy.(4)

Mexico's polity is a presidential system dominated by a rather deradicalized revolutionary party. There is a heavy concentration of power in the chief executive, who emerges as the common choice of the party elite, serves a six-year term, and presides over the choice of his successor. The ruling party is a corporatist structure, held together by a large network of patron-client relationships that are affected by numerous executive appointments at the beginning of each president's rule. Many of these appointments concern the management of a very extensive public sector in the economy. The efficiency of enterprises in this sector is impaired by pervasive forms of patronage, and their administrations are influenced by a general bias against private enterprise that derives from the ruling party's philosophy. Economic growth is negatively affected, but government resources for the support of the public sector and for infrastructure development are relatively large because of revenue from oil exports. Development in the private sector is of critical importance for the diversification and expansion of exports, especially to reduce dependence on the U.S. market, in line with the objectives of the current Mexican administration. Foreign economic policy stresses the need for such diversification and expansion, but, while this policy can be shaped with strong executive directiveness, its implementation is difficult because of the poor relationship with the private sector and the shortcomings of the regime's bureaucracy. Foreign investment is sought to assist overall growth, and the main sources of capital are the United States, Western Europe, and Japan.(5)

Altogether, the configuration formed by the North American political economies allows scope for continuing expansion by U.S.-based transnational enterprises, in reponse to opportunities for entry set by Candian and Mexican requirements, within distinctive limitations imposed by forms of economic nationalism, and, in the Mexican case, by administrative deficiencies. For the United States these opportunities have special significance because of losses of competitiveness in world trade and strains in economic relations with Western Europe and Japan. The global reach of U.S. foreign economic policy, however, is still growing relative to the external commercial, investment, and monetary affairs of Canada and Mexico, which to a considerable extent are confined to the North American context.   Associated with these contrasts, of course, are major differences in perspective that result from quite separate interests and from diverging value orientations.

SOCIETIES AND CULTURES

In the United States and Canada the expectations and demands of social groups are fairly potent determinants of foreign economic policy, operating through representative structures, but in Mexico such inputs have only weak influence on executive decision making.   Vast communication flows between the United States and Canada tend to preserve what is virtually a common culture and ensure general awareness, in Canada, of the main directions of U.S. economic diplomacy. Some of these communication flows result in penetration of the Canadian political processes, but a more important consequence of the shared values and language is a large pattern of intergovernmental exchanges that facilitate diverse forms of functional cooperation.(6) Between the United States and Mexico cultural and political differences limit societal interchanges, and Mexican culture develops with a high degree of autonomy.

As postindustrial societies the United States and Canada have characteristics similar to those of the advanced West European nations. High social mobility, mass communications, and the competitive pressures of rivalries between national parties are breaking down barriers between ethnic and regional groups, but the integrative results are negatively affected by forms of alienation.   These are consequences of employment practices that lack the paternalism of Japanese enterprises, and of the displacement of consummatory values by instrumental values, leading to the pursuit of self-interest by expedient means.   Other contributing factors are the growth of monopolistic and oligopolistic concentrations of wealth and the emergence of problems of governability, due to the difficulties of aggregating forcefully articulated interests.(7) In the U.S.-Canadian mix of value orientations there is stronger individualism and less commitment to the general welfare than in West Germany and Japan, and this affects the character of elite-mass relations.

Social alienation in the United States and Canada, especially as aggravated by problems of governability that reduce trust in the national administrations while stimulating aggressive interest articulation, limits possibilities for the development of bonds with other societies. This happens despite rising levels of interdependence with other industrialized democracies and advances in communications technology that reduce distances from such democracies. If the U.S. and Canadian problems of governability were less serious, less parochial politics would be associated with the higher levels of performance and the improved degrees of social integration. Being under less stress, then, social groups in these countries could relate more actively to their counterparts in other nations. This could be envisaged if the United States and Canada were members of a large regional grouping such as a Pacific Community, but of course it must be added that the existing competitive pressures in these two states that give their politics an inward-looking character could be increased by problems concerning the distribution of gains from trade liberalization in a Pacific grouping.

Culturally the United States and Canada have affinities with Western Europe, but these are diminished by social distances that have prevented the growth of bonds across the Atlantic between political groups and economic associations but that have facilitated the development of a sense of area identity within the European Community, together with feelings of antipathy towards the United States. U.S. and Canadian interaction with Japan and the high-growth East Asian states is aided by cultural affinities with their relatively Westernized elites, but general social interchanges are severely limited by linguistic and value-based differences, as well as by distances. These hindrances to societal interaction would represent major barriers to community formation in a Pacific economic grouping, but they could be partly overcome through vigorous programs of cultural exchange and diplomacy.

Mexico, culturally, is further removed from East Asia and has strong affinities with Spain. These affinities would facilitate cultural interaction with the Philippines, but Mexico's foreign policy has given little attention to that country or to others in East Asia, because of preoccupations with the immediate environment, and especially with the United States. Mexican society is evolving with little external cultural penetration but is experiencing stresses associated with modernization, rather authoritarian rule, and the divisive effects of clientelism. As in other newly industrializing countries there is a deep class division between a small wealthy elite and the large mass of poor peasants and workers. This is a source of social tensions that are utilized by small extreme left parties and that of course challenge the ruling party's leadership to bring about a more equal distribution of wealth and to encourage more vigor in the private sector. The autocratic quality of the regime and the size of its public sector tend to restrict the scope for entrepreneurial initiative while limiting confidence in the regime's capabilities and in its sensitivities to public concerns. The clientelism that links large numbers of individuals to the patronage of the revolutionsary party tends to perpetuate its hold on Mexican society but diminishes respect for its administrative performance.

The pervasive clientelism is a major hindrance to institutional development, in the ruling party and in the administrative structures. As in other modernizing societies it is due in a large measure to the intensely personal quality of social and political behavior, and the forms of support it generates for the chief executive allow him considerable scope for the expression of his personal views and motivations in determining policy and indeed foster expectations that this will be done.   Popular value orientations have been profoundly influenced by Catholicism, the main religion, but to a considerable extent through the medium of Spanish culture, which has been responsible for an emphasis on authority and hierarchy rather than accountable government and social equality.   The ruling revolutionary party has an anticlerical tradition, but its authoritarianism and clientelism tend to fit the cultural context that has been derived from Spain.(8)

POLITICAL ECONOMIES

North American is dominated by the vast political economy of the United States.   The evolution of this major polity will to a large extent determine the future of the region, especially by affecting the growth and autonomy of the Canadian and Mexican political economies. Because of the strong pluralism of the U.S. system, however, and the institutional weaknesses of its main political parties, its processes of change may lack coherent direction, and its interactions with Canada and Mexico may on the whole fail to draw them into fully collaborative relationships on equal terms.

The U.S. political economy is distinguished by a dispersal of powers among government structures that was designed to foster responsible collaboration between elected officials and that reflected distrust of political institutions and of politicians.   The spread of powers becomes functional only through extensive bargaining between legislators and the executive, with much bureaucratic involvement.   The policy process is disjointedly incremental, with bias occasioned by needs for support from groups in Congress that are associated mainly with powerful business interests.   The strong individualism of the political culture, by preventing institutional development in the major political parties, tends to perpetuate a situation that allows much greater freedom for the expression of interest groups demands than is possible in most other industrialized democracies.   Excessive aggregating responsibilities are thus imposed on the executive, but these have to be managed in line with requirements for legislative support, while coping with the problems of directing the bureaucracy through a layer of mostly inexperienced political appointees who have separate career interests. The chief executive, moreover, emerges from socialization and recruitment patterns that often involve little experience in national government and that are distinguished by pressures to excel in the projection of a popular image rather than to provide leadership for and work with a representative political elite.

The U.S. authority structure was framed for limited government that would allow wide freedom for the individual, especially in economic matters.   The political thinking behind this has remained strong and has been responsible for a liberal ethos in Congress and the bureaucracy.   The state has moderately regulated production, trade, and finance to prevent heavy concentrations of economic power and serve the general interest, to the extent that has been made possible by an unequal distribution of resources for the articulation of demands. In this system the potential for converting economic power into political leverage is high, but such leverage tends to be more useful for blocking rather than facilitating government action.   There is no coherent expression of strong economic interests in policy, because rivalries and conflicts   divide   the   major   industrial,   trading,   and   financial organizations, and because there are no adequate institutions for comprehensive aggregation of the demands of these bodies.(9) The type of pluralism that results thus makes disjointed incrementalism the normal mode of decision making.   This, in turn, reinforces pragmatic habits that severely limit the possibilities for planning.

• The orientation of foreign economic policy is basically liberal, with qualifications deriving from the state of the domestic economy.   The objective is an international trading system in which tariff and nontariff barriers will have been reduced to low levels through harmonious negotiations. In such as system competitive challenges will stimulate U.S. firms to utilize their managerial, financial, and technological advantages for the overall benefit of the national economy. In general there is to be no state support for those firms, as they are expected to operate independently, and there is opposition to the diverse forms of official assistance given to enterprises in other industrialized democracies.   Discriminatory measures can be taken against the products of such enterprises when these enter the U.S. market.   Canadian and Mexican exporters can be affected in this way, at considerable political cost, because assistance to those exporters from their governments can be justified with reference to the oligopolistic positions of many of their U.S. competitors.

•   The fundamentally liberal orientation of U.S. foreign economic policy entails advocacy of scope for virtually unrestricted private investment in other states and of equitable arrangements for compensation if international firms are nationalized. There has been a great outflow of private direct investment from the United States since the end of World War II, mainly to take advantage of manufacturing opportunities in the European Community, but also to secure resources and serve markets in the relatively more advanced Third World nations. Overseas operations have been attractive because of lower labor costs, tax concessions by foreign governments, opportunities for tax evasion through transfer pricing, the vulnerabilities of local firms, and the forms of economic support offered by host administrations.   U.S. labor unions have demanded restrictions on the outflow of investment, citing losses of employment, and the question of guiding if not regulating this outflow is a major unresolved issue of economic policy.(10)

A larger and more difficult issue is a strong tendency towards imbalance in U.S. foreign trade. This is attributable to strong consumer demand, associated with inflationary pressures in the United States; the competitiveness of other trading nations; and relatively high rates of effective protection in those nations. The U.S. administration tends to respond with protective measures or threats, directed principally against Japan.   The U.S. has had to cope with large unfavorable balances in trade with that country, and, although these have been offset to considerable extent by favorable balances in trade with Western Europe, Japan has been vulnerable to pressure and the dislocations experienced by U.S.industries have been serious.

Because of the demands of disadvantaged internal economic groups, U.S. commercial policy has tended to become more protectionist, but the pluralistic character of the U.S. political economy and the continuing commitment to a future liberal economic order have prevented imitation of the active neomercantilism practiced by the Japanese and the West Germans. Meanwhile U.S. hegemony in the international economy has weakened, especially because of upsurges in Japanese and West German exports and increasing competition from Japanese and West German firms in manufacturing for foreign markets through local subsidiaries.   With the weakening of hegemony it has become less easy for the United States to bargain with the European Community for tariff and nontariff reductions that would favor U.S. exporters. Accordingly the nearby markets of smaller states, including Canada and Mexico, have become more significant for the U.S. political economy.   Yet these states, affected by slower growth in the major industrialized democracies and by West European protectionism, have strong compulsions to seek wider access to the U.S. market, especially for their manufactured products.

The Canadian political economy is to a considerable extent a dependency of the United States because of the deep transnational penetration that it has experienced and because it is administered with only moderate economic nationalism that allows much of that penetration to continue.(11)   The Canadian governmental system provides a usable concentration of power that facilitates decisional efficacy, but the exercise of this power has to contend with the transnational ties and attractions of what can be considered national firms. The implementation of economic policy is also affected by the parliamentary position of the ruling party or coalition and by the difficult requirement to attract support from Quebec without alienating other provinces. Strong administrative guidance of the private sector could promote growth and reduce the element of dependence to manageable proportions.   The highly functional Japanese-style administrative guidance, however, is not feasible in the Canadian culture, and if it were attempted it could be made dysfunctional by bureaucratic inertia. For the present the Canadian political economy is affected by stagflation, attributable to many of the factors that have caused Britain's very serious combination of inflation and slow growth, but rapid recovery would be possible if there were an energetic policy to develop extractive industries and energy resources for export.

Canadian foreign economic policy focuses on issues in the unequal • relationship with the United States and gives some attention to problems of diversifying external trade. Inadequate bargaining power makes this policy difficult to manage, but the relationship with the United States is not exclusively competitive; on each side negotiating is guided by shared norms that tend to result in greater equity than would be expected in other bilateral contexts. There have been phases of assertive nationalism in Canadian economic diplomacy, but in recent years this has been relatively accommodative toward the United States, partly in appreciation of considerate U.S. attitudes to the issue of Quebec's independence.

About 25 percent of U.S. imports come from Canada, and Canada receives roughly 25 percent of U.S. exports, but for Canada this commerce represents about 70 percent of total trade and about 11 percent of the Canadian GNP. Much of this trade is duty-free, and after current liberalization measures are completed in 1987 it will be 80 percent free. Canada's main concern is to increase the proportion of manufactured goods in sales to the United States, as this tends to be held down by the competitiveness of U.S. products and by the local market orientations of U.S. firms manufacturing in Canada. The ongoing trade liberalization will tend to work more to the advantage of U.S. manufacturers, most of whom can use their large resources to subsidize their sales to Canada and their enterprises in Canada. Canadian firms exporting to the United States will benefit from the progressive tariff reductions but in general will remain disadvantaged by their smaller resources and distribution networks. In trade negotiations with the United States, Canada can seek marginally preferential treatment for sectors of industry that will still be affected by tariffs after 1987, and these may be justified by invoking principles of complementarity, but the scope for bargaining is limited, even if leverage can be used on the supply of basic resources, including minerals, to the United States. Canadian resource conservation policies can be an indirect means of leverage.

The Mexican political economy is relatively more autonomous. The degree of trade dependence on the United States is high, and there is substantial transnational involvement by U.S. firms, but the ruling revolutionary party has a strong nationalist ethos, and this, together with cultural differences, greatly limit the possibilities for cooperation between Mexican and U.S. interests on matters affecting Mexican policy. The heavy concentration of power in the presidency also contributes to the greater autonomy of the Mexican political economy; if power were more dispersed, coalitions between Mexican and U.S. interests would undoubtedly have considerable scope for operation. The Mexican political will to diversify foreign economic relations is stronger than the resolve behind Canada's similar policy, but the effectiveness of this commitment is reduced by administrative failings, an emphasis on regulation rather than guidance of the private sector, and continued reliance on state enterprises as instruments of policy.(12)

Growth in the Mexican political economy is hindered by the size and inertia of its patronage-ridden public sector, its ideological bias against encouraging entrepreneurial initiatives in the private sector, and its tolerance of acute inequalities in the distribution of wealth and income that prevent the emergence of strong consumer demand. The deradicalized revolutionary leadership, however, does not appear to be open to critical assessments of its performance, and its attention tends to be diverted from substantive policy matters by the engrossing demands of patronage. Competition from political parties on the right is made difficult by the use of administrative power and by the revolutionary party's historical identification with the main currents of Mexican nationalism. Popular attitudes to the country's high unemployment and economic inequalities are influenced to a considerable extent by ideological and nationalist bias in the media, which tends to encourage beliefs that solutions to the nation's basic problems will be found only if there are major policy shifts to the left.

The Mexican political economy thus has more in common with India's than with the more open and more dynamic systems of some of the smaller modernizing East Asian states. A foreign economic policy that stresses diversification, however, is leading to increased cooperation with Japan, as well as with Western Europe, and this may result in the absorption of new perspectives on the role of the private sector and, thus, in more effective utilization of U.S. and other foreign direct investment. Foreign firms manufacturing in Mexico, as in other developing states with relatively weak administrations, tend to produce luxury items for upper income groups, because of the lack of broad consumer demand, while exploiting oligopolistic market positions that are protected by tariff and nontariff barriers. The high prices charged for products keep them beyond the reach of lower income groups, result in a drain on the economy as profits are remitted, facilitate the use of resources to obstruct national firms producing for low income groups, and contribute to high costs in export-oriented manufacturing enterprises. Meanwhile the denial of opportunities to national firms perpetuates problems of technology transfer, while limiting the mobilization of resources for research and development.

REGIONAL INTERACTION

The patterns of interchange between the United States and its North American neighbors are shaped by incentives seen to be significant for the functioning of each political economy, at the governmental and transnational levels. The contexts are distinguished by varying degrees of understanding, trust, and goodwill, and there are differences in bargaining styles, methods, and resources. The interactions between the United States and Canada are more intimate and productive, but great values are at stake in the U.S. dealings with Mexico because of the potential for change in this state and its involvement in the politics of Latin America. The Soviet Union is not a significant intrusive power in the U.S.-Canadian context, but it is in the U.S.-Mexican context, because of its economic and cultural ties with Mexico, and because the Mexican regime maintains some links with Cuba.

The interaction between the United States and Canada is mainly economic but also concerns North American and West European defense. For the United States this security dimension has high importance, especially because Canada is the only other NATO member associated with the protection of North America as well as the maintenance of the central strategic balance. The interchanges are marked by high levels of rapport and confidence, attributable in part to professional military relationships based on common task orientations, and initiatives come mainly from the United States because of perceived needs to encourage a larger Canadian defense effort. Canadian allocations for the armed services have been held low to maximize spending on welfare and to stimulate growth, and in the recent past have also been restricted because of compulsions to express nationalist sentiments directed against the United States. Canada's forces in West Germany were halved in the early 1970s, and overall force levels were reduced to 79,000, that is, approximately 19,000 below the 1969 level. In the later 1970s, however, Canada reversed a policy of not replacing outdated tanks used by its forces on the Central Front in Europe and purchased 142 aircraft for North American and West European defense.(13)

The changes that expressed stronger commitment to West European defense occurred in part because of a new awareness of West German security concerns, and this developed in the course of Canadian efforts to broaden economic links with the European Community. Canada seeks to reduce dependence on the United States, while controlling the entry of U.S. investment and seeking to improve terms of access to the U.S. market for Canadian goods. On the U.S. side there is a quest for partnership in a liberal international economic order, but the management of specific issues is a highly pluralistic process in which bureaucratic structures operate with considerable autonomy in constant dialogues with their Canadian counterparts.

The most prominent economic issues concern energy, and the United States is the principal initiator of consultations and bargaining. The Canadian scope for leverage is considerable, because of major resource advantages, but questions of cooperation involve the interests of Canadian provinces that resist direction from Ottawa, and thus can be settled only through protracted negotiations. Canada's treatment of energy issues has to be sensitive to extensive interdependencies that set requirements for comprehensive collaboration with the United States, and there are similar needs for restraint and for a broad perspective on the U.S. side.

Canada is a large net exporter of natural gas, crude oil, and electricity to the United States, and its gas and oil conservation policies are moderated to help reduce U.S. energy imports from other sources, as well as to assume a stronger position in North American trade.   There is a high degree of coordination between U.S. and Canadian energy agencies, although there is a lack of agreement regarding the role of private interests in energy development, and Canada's views are affected by the very strong position of U.S. investment in that nation's oil and gas industries. That investment was attracted before the 1973 oil crisis in order to expand domestic production and widen access to the U.S. energy market. In the late

1960s the U.S. administration had imposed restrictions on oil imports from Canada, but after the 1973 Middle East war the U.S. administration sought to increase such imports, while Canada endeavored to reduce them in order to become self-sufficient. Serious strains ensued in the relationship, but each side's understanding of the other's concerns increased, and the overall level of cooperation rose, partly as a result of shipments each way across the border to meet local needs under a swapping arrangement that began in 1976.

In 1977 the level of cooperation increased greatly with the conclusion of an agreement for joint construction of a northern pipeline system to transport Alaskan natural gas to the United States. This is to be the largest collaborative project undertaken by the two countries, and, while the benefits for the Western states in the United States will be very great, Canada's exports of gas will be aided because its gas fields in the Mackenzie Delta will be connected with the pipeline. Implementation of the agreement, however, has been delayed by financial, environmental, and native rights issues in Canada, and by financial and regulatory problems in the United States.(14)

The interaction on trade in primary and manufactured products has been more unequal than the interchanges on energy and has been managed within the framework of GATT arrangements affecting commerce between industrialized nations. Trade liberalization agreements resulting from the Tokyo Round have tended to go against Canadian interests by cutting tariffs on manufactured items more than on raw materials and processed goods, but, as outcomes of multilateral negotiations, have not been serious irritants in the Canada-U.S. relationship. The application of GATT trade liberalization agreements regarding nontariff barriers, however, involves difficult issues because of the diversity of industrial assistance measures on each side and the subjectivity of judgments about damage suffered by producers in the state importing what are viewed as subsidized products. Canadian attitudes are influenced by memories of the countervailing duty imposed by the U.S. administration in 1973, under pressure from domestic interests, against tires exported from the Michelin Tire Company plants in Nova Scotia, on the ground that this company had been assisted by grants from Ottawa. Various industrial and agricultural subsidies are utilized by both the U.S. and Canadian administrations, and by U.S. state and Canadian provincial governments. Both national administrations have overall incentives to reduce what are commonly regarded as nontariff barriers, but for domestic political reasons tend to increase their use of subsidies, grants, and other forms of aid to both advantaged and disadvantaged producers and are not inclined to regard these as negotiable issues in U.S.-Canada relations.

The trading relationship is closely linked with the large U.S. transnational presence in Canada, which appears to be growing relative to the nationally owned segments of the economy, because of continuing inflows of U.S. capital and comparable outflows of Canadian investment into the United States. The attitudes of the two administrations are basically permissive, and there is no interaction to harmonize industrial policies, but on the Canadian side there is a regulatory effort to ensure that takeovers of national firms by U.S. enterprises will be in the general interest. This is a responsibility of the Foreign Investment Review Agency, and its activities have not occasioned significant interchanges at the governmental level, in part because a high proportion of its decisions have been affirmative. There has been considerable popular opposition in Canada to the penetration of U.S. investment, but this opposition has decreased since the late 1970s because of a decline in Canadian economic nationalism and slow growth in Canada's trade and GNP.(15)

Because of a need to acquire greater bargaining power in all areas of its relations with the United States Canada has sought increased contacts with Latin America, but with only modest results. In 1976 Prime Minister Trudeau visited Mexico, Cuba, and Venezuela to increase exchanges with those states his administration had begun to promote in the late 1960s. Mexico ranked well below Venezuela as a trading partner, but Canada had received a Mexican trade mission in 1972, and the President of Mexico in the following year. Trade with Mexico increased in the late 1970s, but has remained a small element in each side's total commerce because of their protective barriers. Mexico's balance in this trade has been persistently unfavorable, and this has been a source of dissatisfaction. Political ties between Canada and Mexico have been weakened by disappointments over the slow growth of their mutual trade, and Mexican administrations appear to have had little confidence that bonds with Canada would ensure added bargaining power in dealing with the United States. President Lopez Portillo rejected suggestions that there should be a North American Community when he visited Canada in May 1980, and, although his remarks evidenced fears of U.S. economic strength, they implied that the cooperation that might be forthcoming from Canada in such a community would not be sufficient for the protection of Mexican interests.(16)

U.S.-MEXICAN RELATIONS

Interaction between the United States and Mexico involves more strain and uncertainties than the U.S.-Canadian interchanges, but in this relationship the United States has strong incentives to raise the level of cooperation because of the results that could be expected in its dealings with other Latin American states. For Mexico the principal imperative is to change the terms of the interaction while reducing its dimensions relative to the total pattern of external relations, that is, by developing ties with other industrialized democracies. The sources of strain in the interaction are Mexican nationalist and ideological antipathies towards the United States, and U.S. failures to overcome those antipathies by working consistently to establish a basis for comprehensive cooperation. U.S. management of the relationship over the past few decades has been disjointedly incremental, with idiosyncratic improvisations under some administrations that have not been given continuity by others.

The United States and Mexico relate to each other mainly over commercial issues.   Mexico has become very heavily dependent on exports to the United States and has failed to build up trade with Latin American neighbors.   The commerce with the United States has grown because of geographic proximity and U.S. demand for primary products and light manufactures.   In recent years the exploitation of Mexico's large oil and gas reserves has made the United States very much aware of the importance of these nearby energy supplies, but there has been considerable opposition in U.S. government circles to the granting of a special trading relationship to Mexico.   After Canada and Japan, Mexico is the United States' largest trading partner, and has been urged by the United States to join GATT, which would entail reduction of the protective barriers that are intended to foster the development of Mexican industries.   Mexico is seeking reductions of trade barriers that affect the entry of its manufactures into the large U.S. market, and lack of satisfaction on this matter is partly responsible for restrictions on the volume of oil available for purchase by the United States. Roughly 50 percent of Mexico's oil exports are sent to the United States, and if this continues the United States will be much less dependent on Middle East oil within half a decade.   Mexico's oil production, approximately two million barrels a day in 1979, has been growing at a rate that suggests a level of seven million barrels a day in 1988.   Mexican gas is also being exported to the United States, under a 1979 agreement that followed intervention by Washington to obstruct an earlier arrangement between the Mexican government and private U.S. companies for the sale of this gas.(17)

On the Mexican side the limitation of oil exports to the United States, for leverage on questions of access to the U.S. market for primary products and manufactured goods, is feasible because the concentration of power in the president makes possible strong central direction of the nation's economic diplomacy.   On the U.S. side, however, responsibility for energy policy and for commercial policy is spread through numerous government structures that are often poorly coordinated and that are affected by the discontinuities between U.S. administrations.   Uncertainties about future U.S. energy policy clearly dictate diversification of Mexico's oil exports, but for the United States greater reliance on these is certainly desirable, for strategic as well as economic reasons.

A problem overshadowed by the energy issues and not altogether open to negotiation is the presence of large numbers of undocumented Mexicans in U.S. border states.   Most of them are workers, and they remit an estimated $2,000 million a year to relatives at home.   The Mexican administration, seeking to cope with high unemployment, does not wish to see tight immigration controls imposed by the United States, and within the United States such controls are opposed by business interests that employ low-wage Mexican labor, as well as by civil rights groups.   Opposition from such sources defeated moves by the Carter administration to establish more effective border controls. U.S. policy toward the immigrants is influenced by the presence of some 17 million Hispanic citizens who constitute a potentially important minority, and who would sympathize with the undocumented Mexicans if it appeared that they were being treated unfairly. Tight restrictions on the inflow of Mexicans, however, are being demanded by the American Federation of Labor/Congress of Industrial Organizations, which is a major source of pressure for higher tariff protection against imports of Mexican manufactures.(18)

Investment issues in Mexican-U.S. relations have large dimensions but are more manageable than the commercial, energy, and immigrant questions. Mexico seeks to attract U.S. direct investment and offers relatively favorable terms of entry. U.S. banks provide large-scale financing for the Mexican government and hold more than half of its foreign debt; their loans provide crucial support for the current six-year development program of the state oil company, PEMEX. The overall growth strategy now being implemented with support from oil revenues is directed toward capital-intensive industrialization, to build up export capabilities, and this strategy emphasizes reliance on U.S. direct investment, especially because capital is not available in sufficient quantities from alternative sources. The Mexican private sector is assisting this policy and is maintaining friendly relations with U.S. business interests, mainly through a Mexican-U.S. Chamber of Commerce. U.S. firms operating in Mexico can be subject to strong direction by the host government, but none is likely to be threatened with nationalization unless that administration's policies make a drastic shift to the left. In that event compensation issues could surface in U.S.-Mexican relations, but for the present most U.S. enterprises in Mexico have relatively secure roles within the framework of the regime's industrial policies. For the U.S. administration the volume of investment flowing to Mexico and the conditions that affect it are matters of significance for overall domestic growth policy, on which there is little interaction with that country. The immediate questions concern possible checks on the outflow of funds, which could antagonize Mexico and reduce the availability of its oil, and the terms on which goods manufactured by U.S. firms in Mexico can enter the U.S. market. These questions, especially the latter, could assume prominence on the negotiating agenda, and there is a danger that that may happen because of small measures by the U.S. administration that will be judged inconsiderate and that will cause Mexican protests.

A submerged issue in the relationship is the question of Latin American security, of special concern to the United States because of the USSR's involvement in the region and its ties with Cuba. Mexican leaders feel affinities with Cuba, for cultural, ideological, and nationalist reasons, and maintain cordial relations with the USSR. There is sympathy for revolutionary movements opposing conservative regimes on the continent and a readiness to protest against any U.S. interventionist measures on behalf of such regimes. Yet this does not prevent Mexico from developing substantial economic cooperation with strongly anti-Communist Latin American administrations, including that in Brazil. The United States can anticipate that Mexican ties with such governments will grow, on a basis of economic rationality, but cannot expect that Mexico will be induced to moderate its policy of maintaining bonds with Cuba and the USSR. This is clearly not negotiable, especially because of Mexican pride and nationalism, and the difficulties of achieving rapport through encounters between U.S. pragmatism and Mexican ideology.

PROSPECTS

Most academic discussions of the future of North America deal with U.S.-Canada relations because of the scale of economic cooperation between these states and the existence of conditions favorable for comprehensive rational joint decision making, that is, for extensive policy integration. Canadian scholars, however, tend to see the relationship as a heavy dependency that requires a strong resolve by their government to assert greater control over their economy, while U.S. scholars are conscious mainly of the interdependencies between the two nations and are inclined towards optimism about the possibilities for managing these more cooperatively. Relatively little attention is given by U.S. scholars to the Mexican connection, and relations with that country arouse only minor interest in the Canadian academic community. In Mexico, academic thinking is dominated by problems of managing the dependency on the United States, and the little attention given to Canada does not result in any appreciable awareness of that country as a prospective coalition partner in relations with the United States.

The United States is the only North American state confronted by problems of world as well as regional order. Comprehensive engagement with these problems is difficult because of the strong pluralism of the U.S. decision process, its pragmatic bias against planning, and the absence of a basic policy consensus that might accompany the liberal policy orientation. This orientation, it must be stressed, is exposed to serious challenge by the pervasive selective protectionism of major trading partners committed to neomercantilism. What the United States needs, clearly, is a network of strong associations with industrialized and developing nations who will collaborate in shaping a regional, and later, a world order, and whose capacities for planning will hopefully draw U.S. decision makers toward a comprehensive policy consensus. The network will have to be large enough to give the partners independence and security and to have a potent influence on the international political economy, but not so large that a sense of community will fail to develop.

North America, it can be argued very strongly, is simply too limited in coalition possibilities and too divided by inequalities to serve as an appropriate network. Canada and Mexico, however, could be members of such a network in association with other states, and, of these, the most necessary prospective member would be Japan. For the United States, Japanese partnership will be essential in the evolution of a statecraft for comprehensive engagement with issues of regional order and growth. For Canada and Mexico, meanwhile, ties with Japan can promise measures of security and flexibility that will be needed for more equal dealings with the United States. It must be stressed, however, that the leading role in a regional scheme that will be larger than North America will have to be assumed by the United States, with some internal political designing for greater policy coherence and, hopefully, with a profound and comprehensive commitment to human rights that will develop with an internal struggle against moral decline.

NOTES

(1) See David Leyton-Brown, "North America," in <u>Comparative Regional Systems</u>, ed. Werner J. Feld and Gavin Boyd, (Elmsford, NY: Pergamon Press, 1980), pp. 173-194.

(2) See J.C.M. Ogelsby, "A Trudeau Decade: Canadian-Latin American Relations 1968-1978," <u>Journal of Interamerican Studies and World Affairs</u> 21, no. 2 (May 1979): 187-208.

(3) See Stephen D. Krasner, "United States Commercial and Monetary Policy: Unravelling the Paradox of External Strength and Internal Weakness," in <u>Between Power and Plenty</u>, ed. Peter J. Katzenstein, (Madison: University of Wisconsin Press, 1978): 51-88.

(4) See Harald von Riekhoff, John H. Sigler, and Brian W. Tomlin, <u>Canadian-US Relations: Policy Environments, Issues and Prospects</u> (Montreal: C.D. Howe Research Institute, 1979); and Robert O. Keohane and Joseph S. Nye, <u>Power and Interdependence</u> (Boston: Little, Brown, 1977); part 3.

(5) See Susan Kaufman Purcell, "Business Government Relations in Mexico: The Case of the Sugar Industry," <u>Comparative Politics</u> 13, no. 2 (January 1981): 211-234; George W. Grayson, "Oil and US-Mexican Relations," <u>Journal of Interamerican Studies and World Affairs</u> 21, no. 4 (November 1979): 427-456; George Philip, "Mexican Oil and Gas: The Politics of a New Resource," <u>International Affairs</u>, Summer 1980, pp. 474-483; and Laurence Whitehead, "Mexico from Bust to Boom: A Political Evaluation of the 1976-1979 Stabilization Programme," <u>World Development</u> 8, no. 11 (November 1980): 843-864.

(6) See Roger Swanson, <u>Intergovernmental Perspectives on the Canada-US Relationship</u> (New York: New York University Press, 1978).

(7) See Leon N. Lindberg, ed., <u>Politics and the Future of Industrial Society</u> (New York: David McKay, 1976).

(8) For reviews of the Mexican polity, see Susan Kaufman Purcell and John F. H. Purcell, "State and Society in Mexico: Must a Stable Polity be Institutionalized?" World Politics 32, no. 2 (January 1980): 194-227; and Douglas Bennett and Kenneth Sharpe, "The State as Banker and Entrepreneur: The Last Resort Character of the Mexican State's Economic Intervention, 1917-1976," Comparative Politics 12, no. 2 (January 1980): 165-190.

(9) See Krasner, "United States Commercial and Monetary Policy."

(10) See Anant R. Negandhi, ed., Functioning of the Multinational Corporation: A Global Comparative Study (Elmsford, N.Y.: Pergamon Press, 1980).

(11) See von Riekhoff, Sigler, and Tomlin, Canadian-US Relations.

(12) See Bennet and Sharpe, "The State as Banker and Entrepreneur."

(13) See Leyton-Brown, "North America"; and von Riekhoff, Sigler, and Tomlin, Canadian-US Relations.

(14) Ibid.

(15) Ibid.

(16) See Ogelsby, "A Trudeau Decade."

(17) See Grayson, "Oil and US-Mexican Relations."

(18) See Viron P. Vaky, "Hemispheric Relations: Everything is Part of Everything Else," and Alfred Stepan, "The US and Latin America: Vital Interests and Instruments of Power," Foreign Affairs 59, no. 3 (Winter 1980/81): 617-647, and 58, no. 3 (Winter 1979/80): 659-692.

7 U.S. and Canadian Pacific Perpsectives

Charles Doran

In many ways the countries on the perimeter of the Pacific constitute a region that is the wonder child of the post-1945 economic system. Included here are countries, such as Japan, that have enjoyed some of the highest sustained growth rates in the system. More interesting is the statistic that Taiwan, South Korea, and a number of the developing countries in the ASEAN group have enjoyed higher economic growth rates and larger percentage increases in per capita wealth (albeit shared perhaps less equally) than many of the world's advanced industrial countries. The region includes a number of the most richly endowed mineral producers. It also includes countries with some of the most modern mineral-processing facilities and some of the most sophisticated markets for raw materials and processed goods.(1) Trade among these widely dispersed countries has increased at a remarkable rate in terms of both the volume and value of exchanged services and materials. Given all of this rather phenomenal economic and commercial achievement, Canada and the United States must each independently ask themselves two questions. First, is the pattern of rapidly growing trade and commerce among Pacific countries likely to continue at least through this decade?(2) Second, can some form of agreement or limited trading association among the Pacific partners sustain or possibly accelerate these very promising trends?(3)

The former question is important because it will determine whether or not greater trading emphasis on the Pacific is justified in political as well as economic terms. Since political attention and leadership are as scarce as physical resources, allocation of these commodities toward one region of the world has opportunity costs elsewhere.(4) A government must have some confidence that such an allocation, or reallocation, is likely to produce significant benefits that override the opportunity costs. But what makes the question more difficult to answer is that the decision to so allocate scarce resources and political effort by two such major participants as Canada and the United States

162

is to some extent self-fulfilling: more active involvement will affect the activity of other Rim countries to a considerable, if unknown, degree; lack of such enhanced involvement is likely to reduce the growth of trade among Pacific countries with corresponding significance for the growth of GNP and wealth especially for the smaller and more regionally oriented economies, but again the degree of such reduction is largely unknown.(5) Certainly there are few anticipated obstacles to a continuation of past patterns of high trade and commercial interaction, but how important the impact of any single actor is, even one so large as the United States, is open to much speculation in situations where so many other actors are available either as substitutes or counterweights.

Concerning the second question – the impact that formal agreement can have as opposed to a continuation of status quo informal relationships – the responses are perhaps even more open-ended. The question is manageable only in the context of clearly specified proposals for regional agreement. Proposals, however, range from some form of common market with congruent public policies, through a customs union with only a common external tariff, to association that merely exchanges information and attempts to coordinate research on mutually interesting trade questions.(6) Each type of association deserves comment varying in length perhaps with the size of expected benefits and the political feasibility of the project. But since economic benefits and political feasibility are sometimes inversely correlated for curious, sometimes spurious, reasons, even this guide to analysis is less than totally reliable.(7)

POLICY ISSUE

As far as Canada and the United States are concerned, the policy issue at stake is very genuine. Will involvement in some type of formal association assist the Pacific countries in coping with problems that they mutually experience or help them to obtain economic and commercial benefits that would otherwise be unobtainable? From the governmental point of view there is little enthusiasm for the creation of yet another international organization unless that organization can perform in such a way as to provide net benefits to the participants. Moreover, there is much interest in how the possible benefits would be distributed.

Without asserting that we are entering a period of greater economic nationalism, one must still note the deep interest expressed by governmental bureaucracies regarding who the gainers and losers might be from closer association, even assuming that this notion only has meaning when considered in relative terms. Gone in this period of intellectual history is the amicable assumption of the 1960s that bigness is automatically better. Awareness of the unequal benefits that some actors received through participation in, for example, the Central American Common Market (notably El Salvador, as opposed to

Honduras), raises doubts in some minds about the mutually advantageous impact of trade discrimination on industrialization.(8) While one can quickly point out that with foresight such locational effects can be avoided by the proper use of subsidies or other incentives to establish industries in poorer areas in the way that the European Common Market has attempted, the anxiety in governmental circles tends to remain.

At the analytic root, perhaps, of some of the skepticism regarding the Common market idea is a problem that has plagued the evaluation of market performance everywhere. This is the problem of the counterfactual.(9) In order to demonstrate the value of market association, one must be able to say that in the absence of association, benefits would be less. But an absence of association is a counter-factual, and counterfactuals cannot be tested empirically; they can only be simulated. If one can observe a decisive break in a time series that corresponds to the initiation of the market, causation can perhaps be inferred. But in the absence of such a decisive change in trend line, the causal impact of association remains quite ambiguous.

To those possible critics of this discussion who point out quite correctly that this is an analytic problem that transcends the study of market behavior, we must return to the specific question at issue as far as Canada and the United States are concerned. The issue of causal validity is particularly troubling in the Pacific because past growth in GNP and trade has been so striking for countries along the Rim. The burden of proof is even tougher here than elsewhere in demonstrating that any form of association could improve the current high levels of economic performance. Of course, if evidence existed that in the absence of some kind of association, performance of individual countries or the group as a whole was likely to fall off, the value of association could be defended on the basis of the capacity to sustain the previous high level of performance. But even here one must be able to show in theoretical or policy terms specific obstacles that tighter affiliation can overcome. One must also demonstrate that any limitations imposed either on government or the private sector by some form of closer trade relationship will not serve to undermine the positive contributions that association can make to the economic performance of Pacific nations. This is a much more generalized statement of the old customs union dichotomy between trade creation and trade diversion.(10) In this more general case, any of the achievements of closer association among Pacific countries must be net achievements, certainly in the economic sense but perhaps in the political sense as well.

Having argued the standard against which the proposals for associa-tion must be measured, and in fact are being measured today by Canada, the United States, and other governments, we must also consider the very important reasons why these governments should take the Pacific idea seriously. First, given the confluence of very high rates of inflation and unemployment, the global economy needs a shot in the arm. This stimulus is even more necessary since higher cost energy is a negative factor in the development of all the Pacific economies with the possible exception of Indonesia and Canada. World trade has adapted to an adjustable exchange rate regime without the negative consequences on trade expansion that many opponents of adjustable exchange rates once feared.(11) But the combination of all of these economic and financial occurrences means that world trade may not grow as rapidly in the last decades of the twentieth century as it did in the middle decades. Yet growth in world trade is needed more than ever in order to pump up the global increase in GNP in the face of sluggish productivity and continuing high rates of global population growth.(12) Second, governments should take the Pacific idea seriously because the momentum in trade liberalization, from the Kennedy Round to the Tokyo Round, is being seriously threatened by protectionist sentiment especially in the form of nontariff barriers such as buy-nation policies and subsidies. An effort in the direction of a new Pacific trade association might continue the dynamic of trade liberalization, to the benefit of the leading trading countries as well as the smaller trading partners, provided that such matters as protectionism were faced realistically. Of course some proponents might object that the Pacific is not the correct forum for such discussions and that these might better be left to a more mature organization (GATT and OECD being the more obvious choices). My own feeling is that regional associations may be increasingly appropriate for discussions of trade liberalization.

Third, the potential is large for the Pacific to occupy a more significant share of the total trade of each trading partner, especially since the first positive effects of European postwar trade expansion followed by consolidation through the European community have begun to wear off.(13) The European Community is not so much a threat, or trade rival, to Canada or the United States as it is a partner unable to match the potential for trade growth exhibited by the Pacific countries that as a group have a much different mix of resource capabilities and market requirements.

Finally, in an era when tensions between the North and South are so visible, an association that includes countries from both categories in a market setting that has worked for all is a welcome relief. Whether or not this stems from the recognition that the Pacific Community is more regional than other associations is debatable. But what is not open to debate is that this group of countries seems more interested in the substance of trade and trade negotiations than in rhetoric, more interested in the price of manufactured goods than in jockeying for political power. Thus an association that could enhance the prevailing commercial and trade patterns, while eliminating discontinuities and trouble spots along the way, would demonstrate to the global system that advanced industrial and developing countries can mutually benefit from trade and commercial interaction, a lesson not to be lost perhaps by other actors, some of whom are not as richly endowed with resources or as highly motivated as the actors around the Pacific seem to be, but who nevertheless would gain confidence from the demonstrated success of this venture.

For all of these reasons the Pacific idea deserves more than passing interest by Canada and the United States, two actors with a large international political as well as economic stake in a stable world system. But the two prior questions will not disappear, namely, (1) Will the phenomenal increase in GNP, per capita wealth, and trade continue for the Pacific countries? and (2) Will some type of formal association among those countries sustain or accelerate these patterns of growth? Paradoxically, a strongly positive answer to the first question may make an affirmative answer to the second more difficult. If these countries have been able to sustain their growth for an extended period without a formal association, how will new, more formal ties strengthen the relationship?   Or will such ties merely get in the way of the virtually unimpeded development that some of the actors foresee? A slightly less optimistic answer to the first question might create a larger role for a formal association as the growth of trade begins to plateau and new arrangements are therefore sought to consolidate the gains.   It is this latter reality that perhaps must become evident if the Pacific idea is to gain greater bureaucratic approval from within many of the principal governments now considered for participation.

But as far as Canada and the United States are concerned, perspectives are even more multifaceted, requiring analysis in the detail that we shall subsequently attempt to provide. Before we turn to this analysis, however, we must give some attention to the composition and characterization of the Pacific area as community, region, or other country grouping.

COMMUNITY, GEOGRAPHIC REGION, OR WHAT

Often the terms Pacific Community, Pacific Region, and Pacific Rim are used interchangeably to characterize the countries bordering the Pacific Ocean. Sometimes the terms are used to describe relationships as they now stand; at other times they are employed as though they have normative content regarding what these countries collectively might become.

We find little basis in other than the loosest sense for describing the countries bordering the Pacific as a community. More conventionally, a community implies "a sense of belonging."   Culture, tradition, and historical affinity contribute to that feeling of belonging.   Identical political ideologies and regime structures are not essential to community, but they help. Likewise, geographic proximity of the members is helpful but not mandatory. Community also implies that affinity is close enough to overcome strains and stresses regarding distributional questions where short-term sacrifices are demanded from the individual members for the long-term benefit of the collective.   A strong foundation in community can absorb the stresses of policy dissonance, whereas a weak community cannot; a nonexistent community is not even likely to try to contend with such dissonance.

Looking at the countries on the edge of the Pacific, one sees that the qualifications regarding culture, historical affinity, and tradition can be dismissed quickly. Japan and Australia share as little in common as Canada and the Philippines or Mexico and South Korea. Provided that one excludes the People's Republic of China, most of the possible members of a Pacific Community are democratic with some substantial differences in attitude toward the degree of pluralism encompassed by that term. But the concept of community that transcends distributional difference has never been tested in the Pacific area because self-awareness of community has been so weak. Community cannot be used to describe the area in contemporary terms and only with great optimism in the normative context.

Perhaps the term "region" is more appropriate.(14) Region in the geographic sense is both an inclusive and an exclusive term. In general, all the countries considered for inclusion in any form of Pacific association are located within this very broad geographic area, an area that spans the largest ocean in the world and that includes travel distances as great as any found world-wide. Yet, while all potential candidates for association are located within this very broad region, the region itself does not serve to exclude countries that are not considered as serious participants. For example, both China and the Soviet Union have Pacific shorelines, yet for a variety of reasons their participation is not envisaged; on quite different ground, the countries of Central America and South America are less active candidates although geographical location is not the criterion. Hence in only a very partial sense are the Pacific countries the members of a well defined geographic region.

Instead, what seems to bring these countries together is a common interest in the rapid increase in trade and commerical ties with each other. The Pacific is really a functional grouping of countries, able because of modern transportation and communication to overcome some of the disadvantages of vast distance. In this functional, commercial, and trade sense, the Pacific exists as contemporary reality, and, in various alternative forms, as a normative ideal. It is never likely to be a political or economic community; geography is more an obstacle than a criterion of association; but as a functional grouping of countries with a rather focused set of policy objectives, the Pacific has perhaps the necessary and sufficient grounds for being and for becoming. What it may become as far as the United States and Canada each is concerned is the topic toward which we next turn.

CANADA AND THE UNITED STATES: COMMON PACIFIC INTERESTS

From Hegemony to Interdependence

One of the ironies of the literature on political economy is that, when American economic dominance was a reality, virtually no one spoke of "DEPENDENCIA" or economic dependence; now that American economic hegemony is a thing of the past and interdependence is the reality, the literature suddenly has discovered the imperialist argument. In any case the structure of the world economy has changed since 1945. Canada and the United States have a common interest in acknowledging these changes.

Prior to the 1971-1973 interval, the U.S. economy could act as a focal point for initiatives in trade and monetary policy.   Other economies could extrapolate trends from U.S. performance and adjust their own strategies accordingly. The United States could afford to be lenient in its attitude toward reciprocity, demanding less than equivalence in tariff reduction, for example, as long as other countries financed the U.S. trade deficit and supported the Western alliance system.   The United States assumed the bulk of Western security expenditures, creating an umbrella under which the allies – Germany and Japan in particular – had a financial edge reinvesting funds more productively (in economic terms) than in tanks and missiles.   This contributed to a better growth performance than in the United States.

But this propitious arrangement began to falter. U.S. productivity in relative terms began to slip; the U.S. share of world trade declined; governments began to balk at continued financing of the U.S. deficit; the Bretton Woods monetary system of fixed rates collapsed; and the era of cheap energy disappeared. All of these blows to the old economic system meant that henceforth governments would have to look to a new set of relationships of greater relative equality and interdependence. While some analysts would hail this new era as one of greater fairness, there is little evidence that it is either likely to be one of greater ease in management terms or one in which global output will increase at the rate it did over the prior three decades.

But given the new era of economic and commercial relationships, the Pacific concept might begin to furnish some much-needed opportunities.(15) Canada and the United States both recognize that interdependence really means intervulnerability. Managing the triangular balance of payments situation among Japan, Canada, and the United States is one such problem of intervulnerability. Similarly the use of fiscal and monetary policy to cure domestic political ills requires communication in a fashion that goes beyond discussions in the OECD or the IMF. Perhaps more regionally oriented associations could facilitate such communication in a way that the larger associations have not. Finally both Canada and the United States would benefit from a dispersal of information regarding the commercial objectives of Pacific countries. Interdependence suggests encouraging investment to move in those directions where it is most needed and wanted while conversely taking the pressure off those areas where political resistance to higher levels of investment has mounted. A Pacific Association could not and should not attempt to channel private foreign investment. But it could perhaps raise awareness regarding opportunities, and signal shifts of policy, so as to avoid situations of forcible divestiture. Both Canada and the United States share interests in making the new era of increasing interdependence work more efficiently.

Economic Growth with Political Stability

Both Canada and the United States have a general interest in the prosperity and political stability of the Pacific.(16) Since both countries are democracies and have open economies, the fate of Thailand, Indonesia, the Philippines, and South Korea as well as of the larger trading partners is of much concern. Vietnam was a bitter experience for the United States. It was also very stressful for Canadian-U.S. relations. Neither North American country wishes to see this experience repeated. Stable growth among democratic or quasidemocratic polities in Southeast Asia is a kind of guarantee there against the recurrence of Vietnam-like situations. Hence both Canada and the United States can see benefits in an association among Pacific countries that would reinforce the mutual economic and political achievements of the members.

Distrust of Tightly Integrative Structures

While both Canada and the United States participate in various international organizations, neither government favors tightly integrative structures. Canada is especially cautious about any form of association that would integrate its economy, culture, or political apparatus any more closely with that of the United States.(17) Indeed, insofar as one can summarize the ethos of a people, especially a people as diverse and richly varied in outlook as the Canadians, that ethos is found in the stubborn effort by Canadians to maintain their autonomy in all spheres. An argument can be made that economic integration does not proscribe any other form of autonomy and may indeed create the material foundation to better defend other types of autonomy. But insofar as this is a valid view, and we have not the time here to probe all the interesting aspects of the argument, the view is definitely a minority one in Canada especially at the seat of federal power. With virtually no qualifications, Canadian prime ministers, from MacKenzie King to Pierre Trudeau, have been unwilling to accept closer economic association with the United States.(18) Sections of Canada, notably Alberta and Quebec, for quite dissimilar reasons, are much more enthusiastic about closer participation with the United States than Ottawa has been. Over time, the political attitudes of these sections of Canada may play a larger role in the composite attitude of the federal government itself. But such a shift is not predictable today.

In short, both Canada and the United States share a distrust regarding closely integrative international structures. Neither is willing to sacrifice autonomy for posited economic gains. Canada would probably have difficulty gaining acquiescence from certain of the provinces, especially those traditionally accustomed to wield economic and political power. The United States would have considerable difficulty getting a treaty through the Senate advocating significantly closer economic ties and somewhat less political autonomy, notwithstanding the possible advocacy of such policies by the President himself.

What this means for the Pacific idea is that any very integrative form of association is likely to be politically less acceptable than a less integrative but nonetheless functionally still quite useful form of association. These common held suspicions of tight international organization mean that the lower profile versions of the Pacific idea are more likely to be attractive to the majority of Canadians and Americans, albeit in each case for quite different reasons.

CANADA AND THE UNITED STATES: CONTRASTING INTERESTS

In contrasting the interests of the United States and Canada regarding participation in a Pacific association, we must begin by examining two sets of "grand perspectives." The first contrasts the overall foreign policy priorities of the two countries. The second contrasts the internal developments in each polity that establish underlying foreign policy motivations and set limits on foreign policy conduct. By starting at this level of analysis we will be better able to articulate differences of viewpoint with respect to the nature of participation in a Pacific association. Our approach will be to discuss each set of perspectives separately showing the implications for the specific policy orientation of each state toward the Pacific idea in turn. Only through this larger discussion is it possible to appreciate how Canada and the United States, so similar in many economic respects, can choose to emphasize different aspects of participation.

Concerning the first set of perspectives, the United States tends to emphasize strategic/military considerations while de-emphasizing economic factors. Economic factors have traditionally been regarded in Washington circles as matters of "low politics." This means, according to this view, that such matters are treated incrementally. "High politics," on the other hand, involves national security and global political involvements and is "crisis-prone."

In contrast, Canada tends to relegate military/strategic questions to a rather low priority and to emphasize the primacy of economic and commercial policy.(19) Economic and commercial policies are most important because they affect the average Canadian very directly. They are also important because Ottawa traditionally has been very activist regarding such policies and has confidence in its capacity to shape them and to negotiate abroad to the advantage of the country as a whole. Strategic/military questions, for the most part, are left for other governments to resolve. They are questions that emerge episodically and often to the detriment of Canada. They have normally involved high cost both humanly and financially, and they are regarded by many, but not all Canadians, as outside the range of significant Canadian influence.

In short, because of their different sizes and foreign policy roles, Canada and the United States hold diverging perspectives on what ought to receive priority in foreign policy making.

The second set of contrasting "grand perspectives" involves a substantial and perhaps growing ideological and political contrast.(20) Although scarcely as far in that direction as critics have feared, a movement to the right has occurred in American politics following the landslide victory of President Reagan. Similarly, a shift has taken place in Canadian politics toward the left, although it is not as pronounced. This shift is not measured in terms of greater levels of welfare spending; rather it is discernible in the greater commitment to government intervention in the private sector, especially regarding the energy industry, through government subsidies and incentives in other areas of the economy, and in general through very confident government-led entrepreneurship. The upshot is a divergence of political perspective. This is certainly not disturbing. Government interaction continues at all levels, and the private sector on both sides of the border continues to carry weight in all decision making. But the difference in governmental philosophy and viewpoint is bound to have some impact on the external policies of the respective countries, including participation in any type of potential Pacific association.

Some analysts see these ideological shifts as very transitory and thus without much political consequence. But this may be a misreading of the history of each polity and a misunderstanding of how the stage of development of each polity has mandated certain new orientations. In other words, these shifts of political ideology and behavior may be more real than apparent, and more lasting.

The explanation for these ideological shifts lies not in an artifact of electoral politics or a temporary rejection of long familiar approaches to politics. As far as the United States is concerned, the country is reacting to an altered global power position where the financial burdens of strategic parity are becoming more arduous, where the productivity of the economy has slipped, where belt-tightening will become evident in a number of domestic programs, and where the high costs of increasing amounts of imported energy are beginning to bleed the nation. An index of these problems is the fall in the value of the dollar; floating exchange rates are an adjustment mechanism that is only partially self-correcting, leading to an improved trade position (thus putting pressure on neighbors to import more American goods.) These are problems that have invited a tough conservative response in the political sense, although free trade-oriented externally. Neither the problems nor the conservative tone of leadership will soon disappear even if a change of government should occur in four years.

As far as Canada is concerned, the country is in a much different stage of development. Canada is enjoying a steady increase in its relative power position globally. The federal government now feels it has the financial capacity to Canadianize certain sectors of its industry in part because the energy industry, for example, seems to be self-financing. This invites greater government interventionism in the economy. So does the need to promote greater federal/provincial coordination of the economy. The balkanization of commercial and investment policies on a provincial level, for instance, requires a stronger federal stand in many areas despite disagreements over cultural autonomy and the distribution of regional power. While Prime Minister Trudeau may epitomize the strong, confrontationist Federal leader, the problems his government must face – personal leadership style apart – certainly encourage an activist stand. Thus the apparent movement toward the left in terms of Canadian industrial policy, abetted by the need for New Democratic Parliamentary support in the West in a critical constitutional period, is not likely to disappear quickly.

We now turn to the effect that these two sets of contrasting perspectives may have on the willingness and capacity of each government to participate actively in discussions regarding some new form of Pacific association.

Implications of the "Grand Perspectives" for Pacific Policy

U.S. objectives regarding a Pacific policy stem rather directly from the first set of perspectives noted regarding the strategic/military versus the economic policy emphasis. The United States sees some prospect that a Pacific association could help fortify the area by making the members more self-consciously interdependent. This is regarded as especially important in a period of Soviet assertiveness in Afghanistan, Ethiopia, and Eastern Europe as well as of Soviet-backed Vietnamese assertiveness. It also sees this venture as helping to devolve some leadership responsibilities on other governments, notably Japan, Canada, and Australia. In particular, the United States hopes that the Pacific concept would make Japanese political and security initiatives more acceptable in East Asia.

Regarding the economic dimension, the United States tends to emphasize the difficulties inherent in "managing interdependencies," notably the problems of serious bilateral imbalances on current account, and "beggar-thy-neighbor" trade policies.(21) It recognizes and finds troubling the reality that the laudable use of macroeconomic policy for domestic purposes, to fight inflation or unemployment, for example, may have negative side effects for other countries. In the spring of 1981, a tight U.S. monetary policy caused problems of capital outflow for countries not suffering from inflation but seeking to stimulate lagging growth. Because of the impact of U.S. measures on their balance of payments, they could not use the more liberal monetary policy that they needed on the domestic side.

Similarly one can deduce U.S. concerns about a Pacific association from overall U.S. policy perspectives. Again, viewed largely from the strategic level, what the United States worries about somewhat with respect to the creation of a Pacific organization is as follows.

First, the United States views uneasily proposals that would involve any form of trade discrimination, such as through the creation of a common external tariff accompanied by a reduction of internal tariffs among the members. It is not so much that such proposals would contravene the General Agreement on Tariffs and Trade, because they can be made consonant with the GATT. Rather the problem is that such proposals could create the appearance of a trading bloc of countries directed against the European Community. The fear is that this might lead to the emergence of rival trading blocs, however unintentioned this consequence.

At the root of this uneasiness is the U.S. awareness that as a principal power it has global political responsibilities that constrain its tactical flexibility; and, as a Pacific and an Atlantic power in military/strategic terms, it must look in both directions. This is not to argue that a stronger set of economic affiliations in the Orient would necessarily damage the cohesiveness of NATO. Indeed, the prospect of such affiliation might do a lot for immediate NATO solidarity. But any genuine long-term commitment to an association with economic teeth, such as one employing a common external tariff, could cause tensions with Europe.

Ironically, the equanimity with which the United States viewed the Common Market in 1958 probably would not be replicated by the Europeans regarding U.S. participation in a Pacific Common Market 30 years later. Not only are economic conditions entirely different, but Europe was fragmented in 1958; the United States was not and is not. The large aggregate GNP of the European Community belies a certain lack of confidence about long-term competitiveness. Aware of the delicate quality of attitudes in Europe on this issue, the United States is likely to be very cautious about economic initiatives that the Europeans would find upsetting. Second, among the possible problems from the U.S. viewpoint is the nature of association membership. Again this can be deduced from the larger U.S. strategic perspective. For example, is Taiwan to be invited? Taiwan is certainly a legitimate candidate based on location, economic achievement, and political compatibility. On the other hand, membership for Taiwan could affect U.S. policy vis-a-vis China.(22) The option to invite Chinese participation could stage a re-enactment of the "Two China" UN debate. Conversely, China might find membership in a Pacific association composed of market-oriented democracies a bit awkward.

Similarly, the question of how to draw the line on membership on the opposite perimeter is vexing. Mexico and a number of other Latin American countries are certainly legitimate candidates. Indeed Mexican participation might almost be regarded as a prerequisite by Washington.(23) But, if Mexico is a member, the same criteria ought to be extended to include states in Central and South America who otherwise might construe the association to be inimical to their interests. On the other hand, if the association were to become prematurely large, coordination might become difficult.

From the U.S. perspective, the mix of strategic and economic interests complicates the process of developing an appropriate membership list. Yet strategic interests will not take a back seat to economic considerations, and the criterion of geographic location comes to the aid of neither strategic nor economic considerations.

Third, again reasoning from the strategic level, the United States insists upon participation by the ASEAN members but in no way wants to appear to put pressure on them to join a Pacific association.(24) The logic of this insistence is that the economic performance of a number of these countries is exemplary of what the non-Communist market economy can achieve in the developing world. Moreover, since several of the ASEAN governments have expressed reservations about the lack of participation because it might put them at a competitive disadvantage, or conversely about participation because of the fear of Japanese dominance within the association (but the same states do not hold the same positions), the United States is likely to "go slow" until these contradictions have been resolved. A unified ASEAN position may indeed emerge in favor of participation, thus easing pressures on the United States.

Fourth, the creation of a permanent secretariat for the organization is a plausible yet not entirely risk-free venture. The problem is not so much with the concept as with its operationalization. A number of the smaller states appear to be uneasy regarding the possibility of a Japanese-American condominium.(25) While the institutional cohesion and leadership supplied by such a secretariat is a plus, the tension generated by its establishment may not be worth the trouble. Other more flexible and more imaginative solutions to the issue of leadership may provide continuity without raising fears of dominance. The danger is that the degree of institutionalization may exceed that needed for the association to carry out its functions, and until those functions are more fully outlined, as far as the United States is concerned at least, the notion of the permanent secretariat should perhaps be held in abeyance.

Fifth, again seen in strategic terms, the United States is most anxious that the Pacific idea not fall victim to the North-South stalemate.(26) But the question asked in Washington is whether the regional approach is a way of escaping North-South tensions or whether that approach in fact merely encapsulates such tensions. Much depends upon how agendas are determined. If countries formulating the agenda accept the liberal international trade order as the basis for bargaining and negotiation among coalitions of countries that do not simply break down along advanced-industrial/developing country lines, the Pacific idea will have much appeal in Washington.(27) Reforms needed to increase financial aid flows and to increase access to the markets of the advanced industrial countries will meet a friendly response in such a forum. On the other hand, if the association became a platform for the disparagement of the liberal trade order without discussing such major issues as energy pricing or the sale of agricultural products, the United States would not take a very active role in the proceedings. Since to some extent one will never know the avenue the agenda will take until the association chooses one, no sure answers are likely to be forthcoming. So far the discussions with respect to a potential agenda have been quite salutory from the U.S. viewpoint.

Finally, the issue-oriented approach taken at the Canberra meetings is regarded in Washington as pragmatic and practical. But there is some concern that what is left out of such discussions is as important as what is brought in. By excluding certain issues they may become highlighted. There may be a tendency to drift toward issues on which little agreement exists. If, for example, the association has little to contribute to a resolution of energy issues, time spent on the topic might well be spent elsewhere. The concern then is to maintain the appearance of balance and scope, while focusing upon those issues where there is the greatest hope of productive exchange.

Turning now to the Canadian overall perspective as it shapes attitudes toward the Pacific idea, one notes how the emphasis on trade and commerce takes Canada in a somewhat different direction. Canadian objectives with respect to participation in a Pacific association, although not broadly discussed, are nonetheless evident.

First, Canada hopes to open up investment opportunities in South East Asia, Australia, and New Zealand. This was the explicit purpose of the 13-nation Pacific Rim Opportunities Conference, held in Vancouver during December 1980. From the Canadian viewpoint, Japan and the United States are already established investors among the ASEAN members. Canadian investors feel they must get a foothold and catch up.(28) Perhaps a Pacific association would supply such a foothold by calling attention to opportunities and by creating a proper commercial climate.

Second, Canada hopes that the Pacific idea would help diversify its trade and investment linkage.(29) More trade with Japan and more Japanese investment in Canada are primary objectives. But Canada faces a problem here that lies at the foundation of Pacific relationships. Japan is not very interested in portfolio-type investment. It also is not very interested in importing Canadian manufactured goods. Indeed, Japan is most interested in raw materials acquisition, accompanied by some semiprocessing in the host country, and the export of its own manufactured goods. Thus the Canadian desire to diversify away from the United States is frustrated not by U.S. policies but by the current structure of international trade. The United States provides far more portfolio-type investment to Canada than have other countries, and the United States accepts a far higher share of Canadian manufactured goods as a percent of total trade than either Japan or Europe. Thus, if a Pacific association were to be useful to Canada in this regard, it would have to pry open Japanese markets for more Canadian manufactures and free up a larger amount of Japanese portfolio investment.

Third, the Pacific idea looks better than a North American Accord to many Canadian analysts.(30) It looks better because Japan can perhaps be used as a counterweight to the United States. Otherwise

Canada is locked more tightly to a single large trading partner on the North American continent. Moreover, since the ASEAN group wants fewer Japanese ties and more North American ones and Canada would like to diversify its trade both toward ASEAN members and Japan, the Pacific idea might promote both of these transformations, thereby stabilizing an internal political sense of Canadian well-being.

✦ What does Canada seek to avoid from a Pacific affiliation? First, the idea of a permanent secretariat for the organization potentially dominated by Japan and the United States does not hold much appeal. From the Canadian viewpoint, the possibility of such a condominium must be discouraged. Instead leadership within any emerging Pacific association must be sufficiently flexible so that "middle powers" in the association, namly, Australia and Canada, can play a significant decision-making role and can prevent domination by either of the major states.(31) Functionalism makes a great deal of sense from the Canadian viewpoint, but it is functionalism designed to protect against encroachment by the major powers in the system.

• Second, like the United States, but for different reasons, Canada does not want to see the ASEAN group excluded from Pacific involvement. Canada looks at ASEAN participation largely in economic terms. Together, the ASEAN members offer Canada a large and growing market for manufactured goods. Canada not only wants to avoid alienating these governments by supporting an organization that has excluded them; Canada would like to encourage the association to pursue trade linkages with these countries directly.

• Third, Canada wishes to avoid a Pacific polarization along political lines either North/South or East/West. The purpose of such an association, as Canada sees it, is to facilitate trade and investment, not to attempt to resolve political grievances or to address security concerns. This narrowing of the focus of Pacific objectives still leaves plenty of room for major structural change within the international trading regime. But Canada does not want the association to become a debating forum; its purpose would be that of a functional international organization.(32)

In sum, the objectives for, and the possible objections to, a Pacific association for Canada and the United States can largely be deduced from their broader perspectives on foreign policy. That these perspectives are not identical explains in part why their attitudes toward the Pacific differ in a number of ways.

Let us now consider the second major dichotomy of perspectives that has an impact on attitudes toward the Pacific, namely, the growing disparity in ideological outlook between Canada and the United States.

As Ottawa moves further to the left, in terms of governmental intervention in the economy (intervention that goes beyond the conventional creation of Crown corporations, for example), Canada is likely to become more dependent on non-North American trading partners. As this happens, ironically, the Canadian government will become more dependent on its private sector to seek out and penetrate new markets in South and South-East Asia and elsewhere. As the United States moves further to the right, it is likely to give greater and greater latitude to the private sector and to multinational corporations to do what they have succeeded in doing so well throughout the Pacific over the last decade, namely, accelerate economic growth through investment. With its present ideological orientation and phase of economic development, Canada fears that the Pacific idea could become an association of mineral traders and little more (the area currently produces 50% of its own mineral needs).(33)

Based on its present ideological orientation and its postindustrial, capital-scarce phase of development, what the United States fears is that the Pacific concept might be used merely for purposes of making greater demands on the U.S. Treasury (the United States already provides more than 50 percent of the foreign aid to the area) in an era of declining aid budgets.

Neither of these fears may be realistic but they flow from the ideological frame of mind that each country finds itself in at present, a viewpoint that, as we have seen, is neither divorced from the respective historical phase of economic development nor a mere artifact of electoral fancy. In two-party countries, the democratic process involves a perpetual dialectic and hence future governments and administrations are likely to behave reactively to present outlooks. But this does not mean that the underlying long-term interests that shape governmental policy and set limits to policy will change very much vis-a-vis the Pacific issue. Our next task is then to assess how Canada and the United States are likely to respond to Pacific initiatives.

Canadian and American Institutional Responses

Despite different underlying foreign policy premises and outlooks, and despite very different concerns and objectives regarding the Pacific notion, Canada and the United States are not likely to diverge very much in terms of the strategy each adopts toward the Pacific concept. This is our overall conclusion. The explanation for this conclusion emerges out of the prior discussion but bears further treatment. While both Canada and the United States are intrigued by the idea of a Pacific association, both have certain reservations, as already articulated. And while the governmental ideologies of the two polities seem to be opposed in some aspects, this divergence is forcing them independently to rely on a third actor, the private sector, to establish the groundwork for such an association of trading nations.(34) For governments that are a bit uncertain about the conditions and circumstances of involvement, initiative by the private sector lowers the political risks. The political atmosphere becomes more surprise-free. In spite of Canadian reliance on governmental initiative in investment matters, the private sector grows more important in contracts with Pacific countries. In spite of emphasis by the Reagan Administration on security and strategic questions, the private sector is encouraged to pursue closer trade and investment contacts with Pacific partners. Thus each country seems to be settling on an incremental, low profile strategy vis-a-vis the Pacific that allows the private sector to establish the lead.

In the history of functional international organization this approach establishes something of a precedent.(35) It is a "bottom-up" rather than a "top-down" approach to institutionalization. Instead of relying upon governments to determine the parameters for transnational involvement, it allows the transnational firms to create an interlocking network of relationships that become so compelling as to mandate change at the intergovernmental level. Instead of trying to create incentives that firms will find appealing in investment and management terms, the approach makes use of firms to create a web of interpenetration where governmental participation becomes inescapable. To that extent, the approach follows traditional functionalist norms.

But in what way will government participation become indispensable? This is a valid question inasmuch as governments in this period are committing themselves to greater and greater amounts of regulation.(36) Surely additional governmental regulation is not what private firms are seeking. The answer is that the private sector in many ways is becoming indistinguishable from the public sector, especially regarding the stimulation of international trade and the provision of massive capital flows through loans and the establishment of new joint ventures abroad.(37) This approach is a kind of acknowledgment that the private sector needs governmental support, a favorable business climate, export and foreign investment incentives, and political cooperation in order to stimulate massive undertakings abroad, as much as the Pacific economies need a vigorous private sector.

What we are witnessing is a quantitatively new set of private sector/public sector arrangements. Often these arrangements take the form of joint ventures where the private firm has minority participation. Linking firm and government may be financing from an international lending agency such as the World Bank. These arrangements have the effect of spreading risk, giving the government a window on industry relationships, giving the firm an offset against possible nationalization (no empirical evidence exists that such arrangements reduce pressures for increased governmental participation, however), and providing the international lending agency with confidence that the venture will be efficiently managed.

These new arrangements cross North/South and East/West political lines in that private firms have worked with Communist administrations and with numerous governments in the Third World. The issue of ownership and control is frequently hedged in ambiguous directorateships which assure host government protection against internal demands by interest groups for expropriation of assets and which assure the firms sufficient authority to manage the enterprises properly.(38)

In the Pacific area, long accustomed to the activities of international trading companies, Crown corporations and other government-related firms, these new private sector/public sector arrangements are accepted with comparative ease. But what are the implications for the founding of some form of Pacific association that could facilitate and expand commercial and trade relationships among the members?

A potential problem is that by relinquishing the lead in the planning to the private sector, the governments will discover that the agenda will naturally shift toward the primary concerns of the private sector – sanctity of contract, efficient mechanisms of capital transfer, adequate sources of financing, decontrol of certain regulations that affect the operation of the firm, and capital repatriation. Less attention will be paid to such issues as the increased flow of foreign assistance, technological transfer, commodity price stabilization, management of trade imbalances, and the impact of export-led economic growth on internal income distribution.(39) To some extent the character of the association will be shaped by the issues it is called upon to address, and the issues themselves will be a product of the identity and values of the actors who define and articulate the issues.

But this brings us back to the key question raised at the beginning of this chapter. Can a Pacific association, given the comparatively minimal nature of the economic problems that exist in the area, and given the amount of authority that such an association is likely to obtain, add very much to the coordination of trade and investment relationships? Could such an association improve the "fairness" with which the system operates? These are not easy questions to answer even after an extensive examination of the Pacific idea. But one of the advantages of the private-sector-first approach that both Canada and the United States now seem to favor is that such a Pacific association as might evolve would be likely to focus on problems that affect the efficiency of the regional trading system.(40) Such an approach might give an additional stimulus to the free trade principle, with appropriate additional incentives for poor countries, at a time when this stimulus is critically important. Such an approach also might give attention to the new institutional innovations that link the various actors, thereby eliminating some of the barriers that have grown up in an energy-rich, previously rather noninflationary period.

Thus, whatever the shortcomings of the emphasis emerging out of an approach that allows firm and government to innovate jointly some form of new organizational departure for the region, this emphasis could conceivably sustain growth in GNP and trade in a way that would become something of a model for other regional associations. At least this is the pious hope of some of the founders of the Pacific idea. While the premise for this anticipation is modest enough, it is also both quite imaginative and realistic in an international political age that displays a surplus of neither quality.

NOTES

(1) Lawrence B. Krause and Hugh Patrick, eds., Mineral Resources in the Pacific Area (Papers and Proceedings of the Ninth Pacific Trade and Development Conference, Federal Reserve Bank of San Francisco, 1978).

(2) Sam A. Schurr, et al., "How Will the U.S. Economy Develop?" in Energy in America's Future: The Choices Before Us (Baltimore: Johns Hopkins University Press, 1979), pp. 106-124.

(3) J. Panglaykim, "Jakarta's Perception of the Pacific Community Idea"; Boris N. Slavinsky, "Soviet Far Eastern Perspective on the Pacific Community"; Yung Wa, "Taipei's Perspective on the Pacific Community"; Mark Borthwick, "U.S. Congressional Perspectives on the Pacific Community"; Hiroshi Kimura, "Japanese Concept to the Pacific Basin Cooperation from the Soviet Perspective"; Vladimir Ivanov, "Formation of Economic Strategy of the Developed Countries in the Asia-Pacific Economic Region." Vladimir Lukin, "Soviet Perspective on the Pacific Community"; Hak Joon Kim, "Toward an Asian Pacific Community in the Beijing-Tokyo-Washington Triangle: A South Korean Perspective"; Victor Falkenheim and Michael W. Donnelly, "Canada and the Pacific Community" (Papers presented at the International Studies Association Meeting, Philadelphia, March 18-20, 1981).

(4) Edward L. Morse and Thomas Wallin, "Introduction: Demand Management and Economic Nationalism in the Coming Decade," in Challenges to Interdependent Economics, ed. Robert S. Gordon and Jacques Pelkmans (New York: McGraw-Hill, 1979), pp. 1-26.

(5) Wassily Leontief, et al., The Future of the World Economy (New York: Oxford University Press, 1977). This study, for example, assumed two different sets of growth rates for countries in different scenarios, one in which the North and South are assumed to have the same rates and one in which the South has the faster growth rate.

(6) Peter Drysdale, "An Organization for Pacific Trade, Aid and Development: Regional Arrangements and the Resource Trade," in Krause and Patrick, Mineral Resources in the Pacific Area, pp. 611-648.

(7) For example, economic free trade within a customs union might provide the largest economic benefits for a set of polities, and for each individual polity, but politically a customs union may be among the most difficult economic relationship to achieve.

(8) Jeffrey B. Nugent, Economic Integration in Central America (Baltimore: Johns Hopkins University, 1974).

(9) Karl R. Popper, "Social Science and Social Policy," in Philosophical Problems of the Social Sciences, ed. David Braybrooke (New York: Macmillan, 1965), pp. 99-119.

(10) Bela Balassa, "Trade Creation and Trade Diversion in the European Market," Economic Journal 77, no. 305 (March 1967): 1-21.

(11) Stanley W. Black, Floating Exchange Rates and National Economic Policy (New Haven: Yale University Press, 1977).

(12) Paul Bairoch makes the interesting historical observation that none of the advanced industrial countries that industrialized early enjoyed more than a 2 percent real annual growth in GNP in the initial growth phase; a number of developing countries today anticipate population growth rates alone above 2.8 percent, suggesting the intensified demands to perform that we are placing on the various economic growth models in the contemporary system. Paul Bairoch, The Economic Development of the Third World Since 1900 (Berkeley: University of California Press, 1975), p. 204.

(13) Geza Feketekuty, "Toward an Effective International Trading System," in Changing Patterns in Foreign Trade and Payments, ed. Bela Balassa (New York: Norton, 1978), pp. 46-54.

(14) See the concept of regionalism examined empirically in Bruce M. Russett, International Regions and the International System: A Study in Political Ecology (Chicago: Rand McNally, 1967).

(15) Lawrence B. Krause and Sueo Sekiguchi, eds., Economic Interaction in the Pacific Basin (Washington: Brookings Institution, 1980).

(16) Peyton Lyon and Brian W. Tomlin, Canada as an International Actor (Toronto: Macmillan, 1979).

(17) Peter C. Dobell, "Negotiating with the United States," International Journal, The Canada-United States Relationship 36, no. 1 (Winter 1980/81): 17-38.

(18) J.L. Granatstein and R. Bothwell, " 'A Self-Evident National Duty': Canadian Foreign Policy, 1935-1939," in The In-Between Time, ed. Robert Bothwell and Norman Hillmer (Toronto: Copp Clark, 1975), pp. 213-222.

(19) A.J. Toynbee, "Canada, the Empire and the United States," in ibid., pp. 21-22.

(20) Charles F. Doran, "Left Hand, Right Hand," International Journal 36, no. 1 (Winter 1980/81): 236-240.

(21) C. Fred Bergsten, "Interdependence: Now a Cold Reality," in Toward a New International Economic Order: Selected Papers, ed. C. Fred Bergsten (New York: D.C. Heath, 1974).

(22) Donald F. Lach and Edmund S. Wehrle, International Politics in East Asia (New York: Praeger, 1975).

(23) Carlos F. Diaz-Alejando, "Latin America: Toward 2000 A.D.," in Economic and World Order, ed. Jagdish N. Bhagwati (New York: Free Press, 1972), pp. 233-256.

(24) Harold B. Malmgren, "Trade Liberalization and the Economic Development of the Pacific Basin: The Need for Cooperation," in Obstacles to Trade in the Pacific Area, Proceedings of the Fourth Pacific Trade and Development Conference, ed. H.E. English and Keith A.J. Hoy (Ottawa: Carleton University, 1972), pp. 271-284.

(25) But also consider the problems raised in Fred Green, Stresses in U.S.-Japanese Security Relations (Washington, D.C.: Brookings Institution, 1975).

(26) Roger Hansen, Beyond the North-South Stalemate (New York: McGraw-Hill, 1979).

(27) Robert E. Baldwin, et al., "Crucial Issues for Current International Trade Policy" in The New International Economic Order: A U.S. Response, ed. David B.H. Denoon (New York: New York University Press, 1979), pp. 35-77.

(28) Looking Outward, Economic Council of Canada, Ottawa, 1975.

(29) Seiji Naya and Narongchai A. Krasanee, "Thailand's International Economic Relations with Japan and the United States: A Study of Trade and Investment Interactions," in Cooperation and Development in the Asia/Pacific Region, Seventh Pacific Trade and Development Conference, ed. Leslie V. Castle and Sir Frank Holmes (Tokyo: Japanese Research Center, 1975), pp. 94-141.

(30) Ronald Reagen, "Official Announcement Speech," New York Hilton, New York, November 13, 1979, pp. 11-12.

(31) John W. Holmes, "A Diplomatic Assessment," in Canadian Foreign Policy Since 1945: Middle Power or Satellite? ed. J.L. Granatstein (Toronto: Copp Clark, 1973), pp. 35-42.

(32) Mackenzie King, "The Functional Principle of Representation," in ibid., p. 12.

(33) See N.M. Switucha, "Mineral Trade and Investment Patterns in the Pacific Area," in Krause and Patrick, Mineral Resources in the Pacific Area, pp. 69-121.

(34) John H. Dunning, "The Future of Multinational Enterprise," in Balassa, Changing Patterns in Foreign Trade and Payment, pp. 201-221.

(35) Donald J. Puchala, "The Common Market and Political Federalism in Western European Public Opinion," International Studies Quarterly 14, no. 1 (March 1970): 32-59; James A. Caporaso, "Encapsulated Integrative Patterns vs. Spillover," International Studies Quarterly 14, no. 4 (December 1970): 361-394.

(36) Stephen D. Cohen, The Making of the United States International Economic Policy (New York: Praeger, 1977), pp. 15-26.

(37) David N. Smith and Louis T. Wells, Negotiating Third-World Mineral Agreements (Cambridge, Mass.: Ballinger, 1975).

(38) Norman Girvan, Corporate Imperialism: Conflict and Expropriation: Transnational Corporations and Economic Nationalism in the Third World (New York: M.E. Sharpe, 1976), pp. 200-228.

(39) Peter T. Bauer and Basil S. Yamey, The Economics of Under-developed Countries (Cambridge: Cambridge University Press, 1957), pp. 127-148.

(40) William R. Cline, "Toward a 'NIEO' Bargain: Conclusion," in Policy Alternativs for a New International Economic Order, ed. William R. Cline (New York: Praeger, 1979), pp. 44-53.

8 Mexico's North American and Pacific Relations

Yale H. Ferguson
Sang-June Shim

On January 9, 1981, President-elect Ronald Reagan and Mexico's President Jose Lopez Portillo met and embraced on the Bridge of the Americas (Cordova bridge) linking El Pasa with Ciudad Juarez. Summit meetings between the heads of state of these two countries had been a regular occurrence for many years. What was especially notable on this occasion was that Reagan had not yet assumed presidential office and that Lopez Portillo was the first foreign head of state with whom the U.S. President-elect had felt obliged to establish a working relationship. The symbolism was deliberate and clear: oil-rich Mexico looms increasingly important in the hierarchy of U.S. foreign policy concerns. The traditional "special relationship" between the United States and Mexico is alive and reasonably well and, at least from the perspective of Washington, might be intensified.

There were different symbols implicit in other events, also carefully orchestrated, from mid-1980 through early 1981. In August 1980 Mexico announced it was following up a suggestion from a discussion in May between Lopez Portillo, Willy Brandt, and Austrian Chancellor Bruno Kreisky, after the Brandt Commission's report, that Mexico host a 1981 summit of key industrialized and developing countries to reactivate the North-South dialogue. That same month Lopez Portillo undertook a tour of six Latin American countries – Brazil, Costa Rica, Cuba, Nicaragua, Panama, and Venezuela. The tour resulted in a provocative communique with Castro and a major agreement with Venezuela to supply the imported oil needs of nine Central American and Caribbean countries on concessionary terms. Talks in October produced an agreement to double Mexico's exports of oil to Spain and to increase mutual trade and investment. In January 1981, hot on the heels of Ronald Reagan, Canada's foreign minister and Prime Minister Pierre Trudeau, as well as Japan's minister of trade and industry, journeyed to Mexico for substantive talks and negotiations.

Such events are evidence of Mexico's growing international stature and reflect that country's current policy of "diversifying dependency," using oil to help establish and strengthen an ever-broader network of international political and economic relationships.   These involve a prominent role for Mexico in the Third World, a leadership position in Latin America, a subregional sphere of influence of sorts in Central America and the Caribbean, a modest interest in Spanish King Juan Carlos's attempted revival of the concept of hispanidad, and much closer ties with Japan and Canada bilaterally and perhaps in a larger Pacific context.

All of these separate and overlapping relationships are prominent in the current Mexican world view, but in this chapter we will focus on the Pacific Basin and especially on Mexico's interactions with the United States, Japan, and Canada.   The first section of the chapter discusses Mexico's attributes as a country: its geography, history, society, economy, and political system.   The next section deals with Mexico's foreign   policy,   interdependencies   in   the   Pacific,   and   the complementarity between Mexico's goal of diversifying dependency and Japanese and Canadian interests in increasing access to the Mexican economy.   Following is an analysis of present issues in the region, their linkages, and the ways in which the issues are being addressed or avoided.   The chapter ends with an assessment of the future of Mexico's North American and Pacific relations.

MEXICO: BASIC ATTRIBUTES

Geography

Mexico's 760,000 square miles makes the country the third largest in Latin America, after Brazil and Argentina, and nearly one-fourth as large as the United States. The border with the United States extends about 2,000 miles.

The country's most prominent topographical feature is a wide range of mountains that runs north from Central America to the vicinity of Mexico City, where it divides to form the coastal Occidental (west) and Oriental (east) ranges of the Sierra Madre. Mexico City is on a broad central plateau between the two ranges, 1500 miles long and up to 500 miles wide. The plateau is about 8000 feet above sea level and is surrounded by many tall peaks, including eight above 14,000 feet. Perpetually snow-covered Orizaba (at 18,700 feet, the third highest mountain in North America), Popocatepetl (17,887 feet and an active volcano), and Ixtacihuatal (17,343 feet) have a picture-book beauty and occupy an important place in Mexican folklore. However, high elevations and rugged terrain are characteristic of most of the country.

There are lowlands and plains on the coastward sides of both great mountain ranges, and they are more extensive to the east. The portion of the eastern lowlands extending along the Gulf of Mexico, essentially west-east from central Veracruz into western Campeche, is the area where Mexico's largest rivers have their outflow. None of these rivers is particularly impressive by world standards, but the eastern lowlands are the locus of Mexico's principal oil resources. The Reforma fields, the largest producers to date, are in the states of Tabasco and Chiapas. Prior to the discovery of oil, these states were among the most remote and underdeveloped in Mexico.

Other distinct geographical zones are the Yucatan peninsula, a fairly flat region of uplifted limestone that has shores on both the Gulf of Mexico and the Caribbean; and Baja California in the northeast, a mountainous peninsula with plains and lagoons on the Pacific coast.

Although much of Mexico is in the tropics, climate is more a function of elevation and rainfall than latitude. Examples of practically every form of vegetation from tropical plants to conifers can be found, and the variations within a small area can be striking. In general, precipitation is greatest in the southeast and declines toward the northwest. The central plateau has a pronounced rainy season during the summer months; however, most of Mexico is dry. Only 12 percent of the land receives adequate rainfall, and over 50 percent is deficient. This lack of water helps account for the overall poor performance of Mexican agriculture, and the fact that so much of the driest land is in the north of the country exacerbates the migration of peasants to the United States. Farming in this area is unrewarding, and the desert-like and underpopulated character of the U.S.-Mexican border makes it relatively easy to cross.

History

When the Spanish conquerors arrived in Mexico during the first half of the sixteenth century (Cortes came in 1519), they were amazed to encounter complex Indian civilizations.(1) Between about the year 1000 and the conquest by Spain, the Aztecs had succeeded to the position of dominance in central Mexico that had previously been occupied by the Toltecs, and the Mayas had transferred their principal activities from Guatemala and Honduras to the Yucatan peninsula. Mexico today, especially in the countryside, remains one of the more Indian countries in Latin America; and since the Revolution, pride in the Indian past has been a distinctive feature of Mexican culture.(2) The Spanish, of course, left their stamp on the country, including large hacienda landholding patterns (latifundio), authoritarian government, language and architecture, a powerful church, and mines for precious metal production.

Mexico won its independence from Spain in a lengthy struggle (1810 to 1821) which produced its share of martyrs like Father Miguel Hidalgo. The country then suffered serious political instability and economic problems for over 50 years. Moreover, because its territory lay in the path of U.S. westward expansion, Mexico was the first Latin American country to come into conflict with the "Colossus of the North."(3) Mexico inadvertently courted trouble because it allowed colonists from the United States to settle in its province of Texas. The Texans revolted in 1835, gained recognition as a sovereign state from the United States in 1837, and in 1845 joined the union. U.S. citizens "remember the Alamo" and Sam Houston's victory over General (and perennial Mexican president) Antonio Lopez de Santa Anna, but Mexicans still regard Texas as a lost province.

In 1846 the Manifest Destiny ethos in the United States led President James Polk to provoke yet another war with Mexico, technically over the issue of whether the southern river boundary of Texas was the Nueces or the Rio Grande. At the end of the war in 1848, Mexico was forced to cede more than half its territory to the United States for a paltry $15 million. The ceded territory included California, some of the best land in Mexico, and stretched east into Colorado and New Mexico. In 1853 the additional Gadsden Purchase from Mexico fleshed out the present boundaries of New Mexico and Arizona.

Beginning in 1850 Mexico entered into a period known as the Reform under the leadership of a full-blooded Zapotec Indian, Benito Juarez, another hero in the country's pantheon of political history. Juarez championed the cause of the Indians, as well as the principles of liberalism and federalism, which were incorporated into the Constitution of 1857. The Juarez era was interrupted by yet another instance of foreign intervention, the imposition by the French (with the support of Mexican conservatives) of the Archduke Maximilian of Austria as emperor of Mexico from 1864 to 1867.(4) Juarez eventually defeated and executed Maximilian, but the Mexican statesman died shortly after his own reelection in 1871.

In 1876 General Porfirio Diaz seized the presidency, in which post he was to remain for 35 years. Diaz brought a measure of much-needed stability and economic prosperity to the Mexico. His national police force (rurales) brought bandits largely under control; and foreigners invested heavily in mines, railroads, and a host of other projects. Foreign investment was welcomed by the cientificos, the country's first technocrats, with whom Diaz surrounded himself. By the twentieth century the United States was the principal source of foreign investment and provided a market for three-quarters of Mexico's exports. However, critics of Diaz pointed out that foreigners had come almost to dominate the Mexican economy, that his regime was essentially a dictatorship, and that the concentration of land into fewer and fewer hands had been aggravated during his years in power. These and other resentments finally culminated in the Mexican Revolution, one of the few great revolutions of the modern world and one that predated the Bolshevik Revolution in Russia.(5)

The Revolution originated in 1910 mainly as a political revolt led by Francisco I. Madero to prevent the continuance of the Diaz dictatorship ("no reelection"). Madero succeeded in this goal and himself became president, but (apparently with the approval of U.S. Ambassador Henry Lane Wilson) was soon overthrown and murdered by General Victoriano Huerta. President Woodrow Wilson, who had adopted a policy of encouraging constitutionalism in Latin America, was outraged by

Madero's murder and shortly thereafter sent marines to occupy Veracruz.(6) Although the Huerta government did collapse, civil war in the country raged on until 1917 and gradually took on more of the character of a genuine social revolution. Emiliano Zapata in the south and Pancho Villa in the northeast espoused the cause of social justice for the landless peasant, many of whom took up arms in the struggle. Villa's attack on an Arizona border town again aroused the wrath of the United States, which dispatched an expeditionary force under General John J. Pershing into Mexico on an ultimately futile mission to capture him.

General Venustiano Carranza finally emerged the victor in the civil war and held a convention that produced the landmark Constitution of 1917. This was an innovative document that became a model for many later constitutions in Latin America and elsewhere. Article 27 denied the right of both foreigners and the Church to own land; declared that all subsoil rights belonged to the Mexican state; and laid the basis for a comprehensive program of agrarian reform. Article 3 prohibited the Church from any involvement in politics, and the clergy from any role in public education. Article 33 gave specific authorization for the Mexican president to expel foreigners from the land.   Article 123 set forth a series of workers' rights, including the right to unionize, to bargain collectively, and to receive compensation in the event of accidents.

This constitution in a very real sense established the policy agenda of the Revolution; and both the document and the revolutionary process out of which it came helped forge modern Mexican nationalism(7) and lent an extra dimension of legitimacy to subsequent political regimes. Although the claim is a bit threadbare, Mexican presidents still today invoke the ideology and symbols of the Revolution and insist that their policies are aimed at bringing it a step or two closer to its presumed eventual complete fulfillment. However, after the constitution was written, not much more than lip service was paid to many goals of the Revolution until the presidency of Lazaro Cardenas (1934-40).(8) Cardenas nationalized the country's railroads and oil industry,(9) and he carried out a sweeping land reform, distributing more land than all his predecessors combined (over 44 million acres). He also effectively institutionalized the Revolution by reorganizing the official party (the Partido de la Revolucion Mexicana, PRM) into labor, peasant, popular (including government bureaucrats, some business elements, and professionals), and armed forces sectors.

The military, supposedly depoliticized, was excluded from the official party in 1940,(10) and the name of the party was changed to the Partido Revolucionario Institucional (PRI) in 1946. Revolutionary rhetoric notwithstanding, post-World War II administrations have tended to emphasize economic development over social reform.(11) Nevertheless, the balance between the two goals has varied somewhat from administration to administration. In addition to serving as an instrument of control from above, the PRI has also been a remarkably inclusive institution that assists the regime in responding to social pressures.

Society

With 68 million people (about two-thirds mestizo and one-third Indian), Mexico is the most populous Spanish-speaking country in the world and in Latin America is second in population only to Brazil (with about 125 million). Moreover, Mexico's rate of population growth is quite high, about 2.9 percent annually, although the rate has dropped over half a percentage point in recent years. Part of the explanation for the drop is the Mexican government's encouragement of family planning since a shift in policy on this score in 1972. The present target is to reduce the rate of increase to 1 percent by the year 2000. Most of Mexico's bishops have generally supported the government's population programs, despite the Vatican's traditional position against "artificial" means of birth control and their own consistent opposition to abortion. There has been increasing recognition that rapid population growth is a problem of major proportion. Almost half of the citizens of Mexico are under 15 years of age. A burgeoning population has tended to offset gains in economic development, has generated severe unemployment and under-employment, and has placed a staggering burden on housing, health care, education, transportation, and other social services.(12)

Over half of the population lives in central Mexico, which has experienced a tremendous influx of migrants in the last few decades, mainly from the economically depressed south. Mexico City, with 14 million persons, is today the largest city in the Western Hemisphere and one of the three largest in the world. In 1960 it had only 5 million residents, so the population has nearly tripled in 20 years, and by the year 2000 estimates are that it will reach 32 million. To a lesser but still significant extent, migrants have also drifted to other urban industrial centers like Guadalajara and Monterrey and to developing communities on the U.S.-Mexican border. In addition, there has been a legal and illegal emigration across the border into the United States (more on this below).

From colonial times until the twentieth century Mexico had essentially a two-tier society made up of the landed oligarchy and the masses who worked the hacienda or the mine. However, the Revolution, the development of industry, and urbanization helped to create new intermediate social strata. These included an amorphous middle group of government bureaucrats, small businessmen, white collar employees, military officers, clerics, and others; an increasingly skilled and organized working "class" in the cities and countryside (in the more modern reformed or production-for-export sectors); and an unskilled urban labor element made up largely of peasant migrants from rural areas. The old oligarchy itself spawned a new industrial and com-mercial elite.

Despite this differentiation, a vestige of the two-tier society remains in the gap between the "haves" and "have-nots" (marginados) in Mexico today, which must be weighed against the accomplishments of the Mexican Revolution in other respects. Consider, for example, statistics on income inequality: In 1969 (and there is no reason to assume that things have gotten any better) the highest 10 percent of families received 51 percent of total national income, while the bottom 50 percent accounted for only 15 percent. Other statistics tell much the same story: Infant mortality is nearly four-times that of the United States (55 versus 15 per thousand births). Nine percent or more of the country's work force is unemployed and 47 percent is underemployed. Fully 20 percent of the people are illiterate.(13)

Since World War II the standard of living of Mexican urban dwellers has increased much more rapidly than that of their fellow citizens in the countryside. According to some estimates, per capita urban income is now twice that of rural areas. The urban middle sectors have a relatively prosperous lifestyle, but this itself has been overshadowed by the conspicuous consumption of a growing number of the very rich, mainly a business elite that enjoys one of the lowest tax rates in Latin America. However, although conditions in some city slums (especially the many ciudades perdidas or "lost cities") are indeed terrible, even the urban peasant migrant tends to be better off than the peasant in the countryside. The promise of at least a slightly better life is what induces the peasant to come to the city, and the fact that he/she usually finds it is what keeps the urban poor from being any more restive than they are. At a minimum, the migrant has the satisfaction of having made a change, or being where "the action is," and of achieving somewhat greater access to jobs, social services, and political participation.(14) To an important degree, then, migration (to town or to the United States) acts as a "safety valve" for potentially explosive discontent at the bottom of the Mexican social ladder.   Some authorities think that subsequent generations of migrant families will be a source of unrest, when the hopes of their forebears ultimately prove unrealized.(15) Meanwhile, however, the most serious social problem in Mexico continues to be the plight of the rural poor.

Economy

The Mexican economy began to change in fundamental ways with the influx of foreign capital during the Diaz years. However, the economy did not experience impressive growth until after World War II.(16) The average annual rate of growth in the Gross Domestic Product (GDP) was circa 6 percent between 1950 and 1974. In 1976, the last year of the turbulent Luis Echeverria administration, the growth rate sagged to a low of 2.1 percent, but it rebounded to 7 and 8 percent in 1978 and 1979, respectively. The growth rate for 1980 was 7.4 percent, and that projected by the government's Global Development Plan for 1981 and beyond is about 8 percent. Mexico's 1980 GDP was approximately $130 billion.

Most of Mexico's postwar economic growth has been in industry, mainly in manufacturing until the petroleum industry entered its recent boom. By the mid-1970s manufactures accounted for over one-quarter of both GDP and total exports. In 1980 manufactured exports were worth $3.4 billion, although manufacturing's share of total exports had declined to less than 20 percent because of an increase in petroleum exports. Exceptional dynamism in industry(17) has resulted primarily from the energetic efforts of a relatively small number of native entrepreneurs, supplemented by and often in direct partnership with foreign investors. As Richard S. Weinert has observed:

> Foreign investment was a potential resource that Mexico could attract for its development purposes. To attract and use this resource required a certain constellation of policies. These policies were built around rapid industrial growth, import substitution (particularly of consumer goods), capital intensive production, the use of modern sophisticated technology, and a production structure oriented to high income consumers. While this development orientation was by no means determined by foreign capital, the availability and subsequent inflow of foreign investment influenced its adoption and shaped its application.(18)

The Mexican government has stimulated private investment in industry through tax incentives and, indirectly, by keeping the progressive income tax burden light. More important, ever since 1938 when Cardenas took the controversial step of nationalizing oil and railroads and established a state-owned electrical company, the government has assumed an increasingly important ownership role. Through its participation in public utilities, transportation, communication, and irrigation – as well as its support of education, public health, and other social services – the Mexican state has provided much of the infrastructure for industrial and other economic development.(19) The government has also been involved in basic industries such as steel and petrochemicals. Today, 22 percent or so of Mexican industry is state-owned, a subject of some criticism from the private sector. Criticism mounts especially when there is talk of the government's possibly moving into yet additional industries, as there has been of late with regard to pharmaceuticals and Mexico City public transport.(20)

Prior to the oil take-off, the largest single "industry" in Mexico was tourism, and it is still of great importance. Some 4 million tourists come to the country every year, all but 10 to 15 percent from the United States. Tourism in 1979 contributed $1.4 billion to Mexico's coffers. In the last few years, partly because of concerns in the United States over some of Mexico's foreign policy positions, the heretofore rapid growth in tourism has slowed somewhat. However, the long-range picture for tourism is bright, and the Mexican government continues to build new resorts and generally gives the industry high priority. Meanwhile, Mexican tourists have been going abroad themselves in greater numbers, encouraged by the purchasing power of what most analysts consider to be an overvalued peso.

Oil, of course, is the principal element in the Mexican economy and is likely to remain so for the foreseeable future.(21) When Cardenas nationalized U.S. and British oil holdings in 1938, Petroleos Mexicanos

(Pemex) was created. This state monopoly today is struggling to cope with vastly increased production, intermittent labor disputes, and persistent charges of corruption and inefficiency. Pemex's Director-General, Jorge Diaz Serrano, is a confidant of Lopez Portillo and a former partner in U.S. Vice-President George Bush's oil firm, and is often mentioned as a possible candidate for President of Mexico.

Estimates of how much oil Mexico has vary wildly. According to official Mexican reports, proven reserves stand at about 68 billion barrels and the potential is around 250 billion barrels. If this estimate of potential is correct, Mexico would move ahead of Saudi Arabia as the country with the world's largest supply of oil.

Output in early 1981 was approximately 2.6 million barrels per day (mbpd), making Mexico the fourth largest producer in the world. Government forecasts are that production will increase to 3.5 mbpd in 1985 and to 4.1 mbpd in 1990, responding primarily to rising domestic demand. The Global Development Plan forecasts less-than-maximum development of the oil industry, in order to have adequate public funds for transport and agriculture, to allow capital goods manufacturers time to meet a greater share of the oil industry's needs, to keep windfall oil profits from exceeding absorptive capacity, to avoid depressing the world price for oil, and to encourage conservation. Conservation is a declared goal; however, the government's policy of simultaneously holding gasoline prices at "artificially" (below market value) low levels obviously works against conservation. That same policy is nevertheless politically quite expedient in convincing Mexican citizens that they are benefiting directly from their country's extraordinary good fortune in natural resources.

Petroleum accounted for 85 percent of Mexico's export earnings in 1980, as contrasted with just under 45 percent in 1979. The government has announced its decision to hold future exports to a constant 1.5 mbpd and, as a security precaution, to allow no single foreign purchaser to receive more than 50 percent of the total.(22) Since the United States had previously been receiving 77 percent, the new policy clearly provided a major opportunity for Japan, Canada, and others to increase their respective shares. As of February 1981, Mexico's petroleum clients and their bpd were as follows: United States (733,000), Spain (220,000), Japan (100,000), France (100,000), Canada (50,000), Israel (45,000), Brazil (40,000), India (30,000), Costa Rica (7,500), Nicaragua (7,500), and Yugoslavia (3,000). New contracts as of the same date included: Sweden (70,000), Jamaica (13,000), Panama (12,000), Philippines (10,000), Guatemala (7,500), El Salvador (7,500), Honduras (6,000), and Haiti (3,000).(23) There is a real question, however, as to whether or not Mexico will be able to hold exports to the projected 1.5 mbpd level, given a pattern of steadily increasing imports of capital, agricultural, and consumer goods.

Mexico also has an estimated 73 trillion cubic feet of natural gas reserves and major deposits of uranium, which may ultimately fuel the largest nuclear industry in Latin America. The new state uranium company, Uramex, as of late 1980 had discovered 147 locations of uranium in the country, including deposits in Chihuahua state that are much more accessible (in volcanic soil) than 90 percent of the world's reserves (in sedimentary soil).(24) The government expects to have 20 nuclear energy plants in operation by the end of the century. Two plants, already six years behind schedule, are being constructed at Laguna Verde and will be completed about 1983, and two more are projected for the same location by 1990.

Thus far we have sketched some of the more optimistic dimensions of the Mexican economy. Nevertheless, grave problems remain, including an annual inflation rate of about 30 percent and a large trade deficit that reached $4.2 billion in 1980. In 1980 exports rose to $15.3 billion from the 1979 level of $8.5 billion, with oil and gas accounting for $9.9 billion of the total. However, imports increased 56 percent in the same year, from $12.5 billion in 1979 to $19.5 billion in 1980.(25) According to the Banco de Mexico, the real increase in imports over the same period was 31 percent and the trade deficit was $3.26 billion, only slightly more than 1979. However, excluding oil exports that rose 150 percent in 1980, the trade deficit increased by 73 percent.(26) The oil boom (as well as the overvalued peso) has drastically increased demand for imports; agricultural shortfalls have boosted imports of foodstuffs; and Mexican manufactured goods have become greater in demand at home and decreasingly competitive in the world market. Manufacturing has suffered from the overvalued peso, but also, and more fundamentally, from inefficiency due to traditionally high protective Mexican tariffs and other barriers to foreign competition.

The "exports crisis" sparked a national "public discussion" in late 1979, which culminated in a government decision on March 18, 1980, that Mexico would not join GATT. GATT entry had been supported by the country's large private industries, represented by the Confederacion de Camaras Industriales (Concamin) that included the powerful Monterrey Alfa group, but was vehemently opposed by the Camara Nacional de la Industria (Conacintra), speaking for small and medium-size industries. Opinion in Lopez Portillo's cabinet was reportedly divided on the subject. In the end, the decision was that Mexican industry could not take the shock of less protection within GATT and that GATT rules might constrain the use of such mechanisms as subsidies, export performance requirements, and local-content requirements that are part of the government's strategy for encouraging exports and limiting imports. On the other hand, the government does plan to prod industry into greater efficiency by a gradual and more modest liberalization of import restrictions including licensing, quotas, and tariffs. Moreover, although a major devaluation of the peso (the last was in 1976) is considered too serious a blow to national pride,(27) some "creeping devaluation" has been allowed to take place and will doubtless continue. Finally, the government is attempting to stimulate domestic capital goods production. Import-substitution industrialization for consumer goods is already well under way.

Another serious problem for the economy is the burden of servicing a large foreign debt. The Banco de Mexico estimated at the end of 1980 that Mexico's public foreign debt was close to $34 billion.(28) Statistics on the private sector's external debt are hard to obtain, but most estimates place it at around $12 billion, making a total foreign debt for Mexico of about $46 billion.(29) An increase of $5 billion in the public debt is planned for 1981. Only one country in Latin America, Brazil, had a higher public foreign debt in 1980 ($59 billion), and Brazil's was much lower per capita and as a percentage of Gross National Product (GNP). With banks around the world anxious to lend to Mexico, even its total debt could soon overtake Brazil's. The debt-to-GNP ratio has dropped in Mexico, to 20 percent in 1980 compared with 30 percent in 1977.(30) However, other figures give a less positive picture of the extent of the debt burden: in 1980 Mexico spent $12 billion to service its external public debt, an amount approaching 80 percent of the country's total earnings from exports – the highest debt service-exports ratio in Latin America – and more than the $10.6 billion earned from fuel exports.(31)

Yet another problem in the economy is a transportation bottleneck. Mexico's system of roads and rails is inadequate to support rapidly expanding industrial development, a situation much aggravated by the sudden boom in oil and gas production. This not only increases the general level of economic activity but also is taking place mostly in previously remote areas of the country. Mexico has an additional critical shortage of port and shipping facilities, which would place a limit on petroleum exports even if the government had not decided to limit them for other reasons. Ports are being constructed as quickly as new resorts were starting to sprout some years ago, but it will be some time before Mexico's transportation network catches up with the increasingly heavy demands placed upon it.

All of the foregoing problems of the Mexican economy are significant, but none, perhaps, is as critical as agriculture. Production is so limited that the country in recent years has had to import almost as much food as it exports: $1.14 billion versus $1.2 billion in 1980, respectively. In that same year, food accounted for 8.2 percent of Mexico's total imports.(32) Moreover, according to the agriculture ministry, the 1979/80 crop cycle was the worst in five years, with growth at only about 5 percent or considerably less than that experienced by the economy as a whole.

Poor performance in agriculture reflects Mexico's limited rainfall, as well as landholding patterns and the lack of government assistance to agriculture in past decades. Government neglect, in turn, is a result of an emphasis upon industrial development. Finally, conditions in Mexican agriculture have not only economic but also important social and political implications.

Article 27 of the Mexican Constitution of 1917 provided for state ownership of all natural resources and restricted land ownership by foreigners and the Church. Furthermore, the Constitution declared that "necessary measures shall be taken to break up the large estates" partly as a means of "ensuring a more equitable division of public wealth"; envisaged the return of communal lands (ejidos) to peasants who had lost them prior to the Revolution; and decreed that peasant communities without enough land or water (even without historical communal title) would receive land. These provisions were largely ignored during the administrations prior to Cardenas, with the distribution of only 19 million acres of very poor and inaccessible land. However, Cardenas rejuvenated the agrarista ideal of the Revolution by distributing 45 million acres of generally excellent land, most of it in the Laguna region of north-central Mexico. In addition, he organized the ejidos into collectives and gave them active support with governmental credit, irrigation projects, and technical assistance. Ejidos involved two basic types of landholding, one in which the land was held and worked entirely on a joint basis by the peasants, and another in which the peasants held and worked their own small plots but machinery and supplies were purchased and used jointly.

On the whole, the ejido system has not been a stunning success. Part of the reason has been deficiencies built into the system itself. There were many exemptions in the relevant legislation; for example, one declaring "unaffectable" whatever land is required to support 500 head of cattle. Landowners who were not exempt were theoretically limited to 150 hectares (about 370 acres), but they were allowed to choose which parcel to keep. They naturally kept the best land and buildings on the hacienda. Also, where the land was not all needed for distribution to peasants, landowners were permitted to "sell" additional 150 hectare parcels to family or individuals (prestanombres, literally "lend-names") who assumed formal (but not effective) title. Some ejiditarios themselves frustrated both the letter and the spirit of the reform by "renting" their parcels to neighboring landowners. Even when the landowner had to give up all but 150 hectares, he was to some extent compensated and, as Judith Adler Hellman explains:

> The old landowner used his newly acquired capital resources to set himself up in a variety of agriculture-related businesses in the main cities and towns of the principal agricultural regions. In this way many of the old hacienda owners came to control the supply of credit, machinery, fertilizer, insecticides, and other products essential to the ejiditarios of the region. Hence the hacienda owners whose wealth had formerly been based on land ownership, entered into a powerful modern commercial class with strong ties to the industrialists.(33)

The ejido system also suffered from a shift in government policy away from the agrarista ideal after Cardenas. Less than 100 million acres has been distributed by subsequent administrations, and most of what has been distributed has been of relatively poor quality. Equally important has been the channeling (at least until recently) of most government credit, irrigation, and technology away from the ejidos toward private commercial agriculture. Improvements in agricultural technology in the private commercial sector have kept down the cost of production, thus making it all the harder for the less-modern ejidos to turn a profit.

Currently in Mexico, after more than six decades of real and token land reform, 85 percent of landholdings are in the form of small subsistence plots (in ejidos and outside minifundios) that together account for only about 25 percent of total crop sales. There are also still some 3 million landless peasants.

On November 19, 1976, fewer than two weeks before he was scheduled to hand over the presidency to Lopez Portillo, President Echeverria created a furor by ordering the expropriation and distribution to 9,000 peasants (633 new ejidos) of lands belonging to 73 prominent families in the northwestern states of Sonora and Sinaloa. The reaction of elite groups clearly suggests the kind of challenge that any government taking its revolutionary rhetoric seriously is likely to face in contemporary Mexico. Threatening the winter wheat crop, some 28,000 landowners promptly announced they would not work their land until Lopez Portillo assumed office. Numerous businesses in the northeast temporarily closed their doors. Mexico's wealthy also converted $300 million from pesos to dollars in a mere two days, which so rocked the economy (already shaken by a drastic devaluation of the peso) that the central bank had to put an indefinite ban on trading in foreign currencies. Not surprisingly, despite the peasants' quick occupation of some of the land, Lopez Portillo ordered most of its returned until "irregularities" could be ironed out through lengthy legal proceedings.

Although expropriation of remaining large properties does not now appear to be a high priority for the Mexican government, recent administrations have recognized the need to improve conditions in agriculture, both to boost production and to help stem the tide of urban migration. Echeverria greatly increased state investment in the countryside, for irrigation, the extension of credit to ejidos and small farmers, and the development of better seeds, fertilizers, and insecticides. In 1980 Lopez Portillo incorporated into his Global Development Plan a so-called Sistema Alimentario Mexicano (SAM) program, with a $4 billion budget and the announced goal of achieving an adequate growth rate in agriculture to assure the country's self-sufficiency in basic foodstuffs by the end of 1982. Some assistance will be given to private commercial agriculture and to other geographical areas, but the emphasis is to be on peasant farmers in the rain-fed lands in southern Mexico. The government expects to bring more land under cultivation, to increase farm prices generally, to subsidize fertilizer and other supplies, and to set up a chain of government retail shops. In addition, an effort is being made to restructure the ejido system into larger units, by collectivizing and merging some existing ejidos and by luring in some small private landowners. It remains to be seen how successful the SAM program will be. Outside observers tend to regard its production goals as overly ambitious, and alterations in the ejido system have been opposed within the PRI by the Confederacion Trabajadores Mexicanos (CTM) and Confederacion Nacional de Campesinos (CNC).

Politics

The Mexican President, even more than his U.S. counterpart, stands at the center of his country's political system.(34) He has vast powers of appointment; rules an increasingly large government bureaucracy; and is the leading figure in the dominant party, the PRI. Although the national government also has a two-house legislature and a judicial branch, these are clearly subordinate to the president in all important areas of policy. Likewise, although Mexico theoretically has a "federal" political system, the states have extremely limited powers and their independence is further undermined by the nationwide PRI structure.

The president is "elected" by direct popular vote and serves a six-year term, with no reelection allowed. In fact, the incumbent president names his successor after a lengthy process of consultation with his closest advisers and many prominent persons and interests in the ruling political elite. The leading candidates (tapados) usually become known informally during the fifth year of a president's term, but to preserve his influence, the president normally waits as long as possible before revealing his final choice (destapado). Presidents have customarily served in a cabinet or other major post in their predecessor's administration and have not been too closely identified either with any specific sector of the PRI or an ideological extreme. On the other hand, part of the genius of PRI rule has been an apparent tendency to alternate more liberal presidencies with moderate or more conservative ones. For example, the law-and-order Gustavo Diaz Ordaz was followed by Echeverria's at least rhetorical emphasis on socioeconomic change and tercermundismo foreign policy; and Echeverria, by Lopez Portillo, who has proved much more acceptable both to the domestic business community and to the United States.

Many analysts over the years, recognizing the numerous unique aspects of Mexican politics, have spoken simply of "the Mexican system" or "the Mexican model" (model for what not specified). A more satisfactory general label is that of an "inclusionary corporatist" regime, which highlights the broad network of paternalistic relationships radiating, hierarchically, from the political system and linking it with much of Mexican society. In contrast to "exclusionary corporatist" regimes like those in Argentina, Brazil, or Chile, which have sought to keep "unacceptable" interests from political participation, Mexican political elites have attempted to incorporate as many diverse groups as possible. It was helpful to them in this task that they initiated it prior to the onset of major industrialization. New social groups spawned by economic development were integrated into the bosom of the state before they became substantially organized on an autonomous basis.(35) The success of the inclusionary corporatist system has drastically limited the utility of open electoral competition and probably exacerbated the corruption that has always been rampant in Mexican politics. However, it has also reduced the need for government repression of dissident elements and has even allowed many of these to play the role of a token opposition. Merilee Serrill Grindle has expressed it:

The patron-client linkage is pervasive in Mexico and is instrumental in integrating the society. Present in the interaction of local cacique and peasant, of national politicians and their camarillas, of the economic elite and the bureaucratic leadership, of union bosses and their syndicalized followers, it is a mechanism which permits the accommodation of diverse and often conflicting interests within the political arena. In perhaps the most corporately organized political system in Latin America, these bonds between individuals tie Mexican society together and enable the governmental regime to survive and regulate the flow of demands made upon it.(36)

As Grindle's description suggests, there are several distinct, but intertwined, sets of corporatist relationships in Mexico. The president derives a great deal of his influence from the first of these, his power of patronage. Each president has about 15,000 appointments to make, thus ensuring that he can put his personal stamp on his administration. At the same time, many of the appointments are at the direct disposition of lesser political figures, linking them, in turn, with the president above and the recipients of posts below. Patronage and civil service positions together comprise the extensive bureaucracies of the Mexican government, and each bureaucracy has its own cluster of clientele groups.

The PRI is the major pillar of the corporatist system in Mexico. The Party of the Institutionalized Revolution for the past three decades has had three main sectors: the officially sanctioned labor movement (CTM); the approved peasant confederation (CNC); and the popular sector (CNOP — Confederacion Nacional de Organismos Populares) that represents bureaucrats, professions, and small (and some larger) business interests. The popular sector has been growing increasingly powerful and currently is the most prominent in the PRI. As we have mentioned, when the party was founded in the 1920s and 1930s, the military comprised a fourth sector, but this sector was dissolved in 1940.

Mexico is one of the few countries in Latin America that succeeded in edging its military establishment out of politics as the military gradually became more professional. Those officers who have wished to continue in politics have done so via the popular sector. On the whole, however, the military has largely limited itself to the status of a prominent pressure group, dedicating most of its efforts to defending the interests of the armed forces as an institution.   As David E. Ronfeldt has noted, the military also has a "residual" political role in helping to maintain order in the face of challenges like riots, demonstrations, and guerrilla violence.(37) Most observers agree that the military's taking over the government is highly unlikely unless Mexico is ultimately plunged into serious political instability by insuperable economic problems and social strains. For the first time in the modern era, there were rumors of a possible coup at the close of the Echeverria administration in 1976. Nevertheless, it was never entirely clear whether the coup would have been in support of Echeverria and his reforms, or in support of conservative efforts to defeat them. In any event, no coup was attempted, and the military in subsequent years has limited its rumblings to an occasional comment by a general that there is no real reason why the next "civilian" president could not be a military man.

A final element in the corporatist system are the camarillas, which range all the way down from the presidency and the upper echelons of the bureaucracy through the PRI and its organized interests on both national and state and local levels. Camarillas are political brotherhoods or "families" that emanate from a boss (jefe) and his inner circle, extending their influence with ties to "persons of responsibility among the syndicates, the professional associations, and within the ranks of formal party organs that belong to or depend upon the PRI." Surrounding camarillas are "anomic and diverse groups. . . . aspirant satellite groups which seek to become cliques" with membership as "fluid as is the changing pattern of their ideologies."(38) Much of Mexican politics might be writ as a struggle for power between various camarillas, and successful governing involves aggregating support from the requisite camarillas as much or more than it does utilizing the formal institutions of government and party.

How "authoritarian" is the Mexican political system? As Lawrence E. Koslow and Stephen P. Mumme have demonstrated in a careful survey of the relevant literature, the answer to the question lies largely in the eye of the beholder.(39) One pole of interpretation regards the system as strictly authoritarian, emphasizing the very real power of the political elite, their intolerance of any serious opposition, and their occasional blatant repression of dissident elements. At the other pole is the view that the system is actually more in the nature of a one-party "reconciliation system" with genuine pluralist dimensions. Perhaps the middle-ground description, "limited authoritarian," is the most accurate overall. In any event, it is important to recognize not only that the role of the state and the behavior of the political elite is far from that associated with "democratic" systems; but also that within and without the framework of official corporatist institutions, there exist numerous competing interests and factions that must be co-opted, accommodated, isolated, or suppressed if the system is to continue to function.

According to the leading student of the subject, Peter H. Smith, Mexico does not have a "unified power elite," rather "a fragmented power structure that is dominated, at the uppermost levels, by two distinct and competitive elites." These two elites are politicians and entrepreneurs. They come from somewhat different social backgrounds, go to different schools, follow separate careers, and maintain "a sense of social distance plus an admixture of mutual disdain." Smith acknowledges that both elites "have specific common interests, most notably in the continuing subordination and manipulation of the popular masses and in the promotion of capital accumulation." However, they are "at the same time struggling for control of the country's development process – and for supremacy over each other, as illustrated by the public-private tensions of the Echeverra years." There is thus "constant interplay between a relatively coherent state interest and a somewhat less coherent set of business interests":

> What has been good for the state has been good for the country's capitalists. But this concurrence is a result of governmental policy, rather than the guiding motive for it. In principle this relationship could change at any time. . . . In recent decades the political and economic elites have maintained an implicit alliance, although an uneasy one, in part because of a lack of perceived plausible alternatives. It is entirely possible that the active pursuit of state interests will increase the level of conflict in the future.(40)

Additional perspectives on Mexico's "limited" authoritarianism concern the roles of the opposition, elections, and the media. Opposition political parties are allowed to exist and may be officially recognized if they can demonstrate that they have at least 65,000 supporters among the nation's eligible voters, including 2,000 or more in each of two-thirds of the 31 states. Recognized parties are even guaranteed a certain minimum representation in the national Chamber of Deputies. The oldest and still most significant of the opposition parties is one to the right of the PRI, the Partido de Accion Nacional (PAN), which was founded in 1939 to counter the Revolution's anti-Catholicism and "socialistic" course. Currently, with the Church no longer persecuted, PAN still has strong support among the Monterrey business elite and in relatively conservative circles nationwide. The most prominent party on the left is the Partido Popular Socialista (PPS), but this party today – like the much smaller Partido Socialista de los Trabajadores (PST) and the slightly right-of-center Partido Autentico de la Revolucion (PARM) – are often seen as little more than appendages of the PRI. The Partido Comunista Mexicano (PCM), often suffering from internal schisms, has of late attempted to pull itself together and to organize an alliance with other left-wing parties like the Partido Mexicano de los Trabajadores (PMT). There is talk of running a joint leftist slate in the 1982 presidential election. PAN has also declared its intention of challenging the PRI in 1982, which it failed to do in 1976.

Elections have been held at every level of the Mexican system for decades. Nevertheless, the PRI has never lost a single election for president, governor, or national senator. Elections for deputy or local government are somewhat less restrictive; for example, in late 1980 and early 1981 the PCM was allowed to gain control of some municipalities in the states of Guerrero and Oaxaca. Why the unbroken pattern of PRI victories at other levels? Part of the explanation, of course, is the PRI's genuine popularity as the traditional party of the Revolution. It is obvious that the PRI could easily win most important contests even if the electoral process were entirely honest. In fact, however, Mexican elections are anything but honest. Fraud and intimidation are widespread, and results unacceptable to the PRI are customarily nullified for "technical" reasons.   For instance, PAN remains convinced that only fraud explains its loss of the governorship in 1976 in its stronghold state of Nuevo Leon.

Yet another barrier to an effective opposition, during and between elections, is the lack of a truly free media. Television, radio, and the press are all allowed to disseminate information critical of the regime, but there are limits beyond which the media cannot go without incurring the government's wrath. Journalists and publishers are occasionally jailed. Newspapers that get too far out of line find themselves the target of government-instigated "strikes" and/or unable to obtain an adequate amount of paper from the government newsprint monopoly. President Echeverria imposed tight controls on television; closed the left-wing weekly, Porque; and went so far as to take over Excelsior, Mexico's most prestigious newspaper and one of the leading dailies in Latin America.

A more fundamental explanation of the PRI's continued success at the polls – distinct from popularity or tradition – is its sheer power in the Mexican political system and its consequent co-optation of the opposition. As Hellman notes, the officially recognized opposition parties have often been seen as a "kept" opposition, financed directly by the government or at least playing the game with full awareness that they are adding to the legitimacy of the political status quo. She observes: "At election time the opposition parties either throw their support to the official party candidate from the outset, or they provisionally oppose PRI candidates as a means of bargaining with the government for patronage positions, loans, contracts, and other favors for the most prominent opposition party members."(41) This process of co-optation is not limited to opposition parties but also extends to intellectuals and the numerous labor and peasant organizations that have formed outside of the PRI. All find that

> there is only one way to get things done in Mexico. Whether one is a functionary of the PRI, a government bureaucrat, or the leader of an "independent" peasant or labor union, one is forced to go to the center, to the government offices in Mexico City to get action. There is no alternative source of authority. Bureaucratic institutions exist at the local, regional, and state levels, but decision making of all kinds takes place in Mexico City and nearly all policy directives emanate from government offices in the capital. . . . For intellectuals who choose to live in Mexico, some direct or indirect association with the government is almost impossible to avoid. . . . Although the experience can be deeply frustrating, a large proportion of self-defined leftists end up working either in the government or in the PRI bureaucracy.(42)

Independent labor and peasant groups discover that their capacity to obtain concessions from the government diminishes in direct proportion to their militancy.(43)

Finally, the political elite has never hesitated to maintain its supremacy, if necessary, through the use of force. Again quoting Hellman, "It would be no exaggeration to say that probably every day in some part of Mexico, a dissident peasant, a radical labor leader, or a militant student is killed either by the army, the police, or by political opponents on the local scene."(44) However, the most publicized instance of government repression in recent history was on October 2, 1968, when the armed forces attacked a large group of students and others who were assembled for a demonstration – timed to embarrass the regime during the Olympic Games – in the Plaza of Three Cultures. Some 50 persons were killed, 500 wounded, and 1,500 arrested. A similar "massacre" occurred in conjunction with a student march on Corpus Christi day, June 10, 1971, although on that occasion there was speculation that the attack by a paramilitary organization (the balcones) had been ordered by Echeverria's enemies to shame his administration. In any event, there was some irony in the situation since Echeverria, as Gobernacion secretary under President Diaz Ordaz, had been officially responsible for the 1968 episode. In addition, the Echeverria presidency was marred by the surfacing of a variety of guerrilla groups that operated both in the countryside and the city. These groups staged several spectacular kidnappings, including that of the president's father-in-law, but they were effectively hunted down by the government and at present do not constitute any significant threat.

How stable, then, is the Mexican political system? In the immediate future the regime need not worry seriously about predictable criticism either from the right or the left, nor are guerrillas nearly as much of a nuisance as they were some years ago. A more important concern is abstentionism in the electoral process, which might be expected when the outcome is usually a foregone conclusion but nevertheless is often seen (no doubt correctly) as evidencing some "softness" in the PRI's base of support. For example, turnout in the 1979 congressional elections was only 49.2 percent. Yet this figure compares favorably with turnout in non-presidential-year congressional elections in the United States. Looking toward the future, some analysts have suggested that the oil boom could widen the already lamentable gap between rich and poor in Mexico, raise the masses' expectations, and increase social tensions to politically destabilizing proportions.(45) More probably, however, trickle-down from oil-generated growth will buy considerable additional time for the regime.(46)

MEXICO'S FOREIGN POLICY AND THE PACIFIC CONTEXT

In Mexico, foreign policy is almost exclusively the province of the president, even more than it is in countries like the United States that have a strong legislature. The president, of course, picks his own closest advisers, and his patronage power also extends into key posts in the foreign ministry as well as into other national bureacracies with more limited international involvement. Smith's study indicates that most top-level careers last no longer than a single presidential term and there is fully a 90 percent turnover in national political elites every three presidential terms. This adds to the president's control of policy and helps account for the liberal-to-conservative swings that have tended to characterize successive administrations.(47) On the other hand, shifts in foreign policy have been constrained because of the existence of a traditional foreign policy consensus that dictates, for example, militantly nationalistic positions on many international issues. Nor was there much shift between Echeverria and Lopez Portillo, because both sought the advice and assistance of ideologically left-of-center (not extreme left) intellectuals in the formulation and adminis-tration of foreign policy. The current foreign minister, Jorge Castaneda, is a former professor at the renowned Colegio de Mexico.(48) As Mexico's role in international affairs has become in-creasingly important, its foreign policy bureaucracy has grown larger and more professional. Although Mexico has yet to match the high standard of professionalism in foreign policy set by Brazil, it is well ahead of its sometime rival, Venezuela.

Mexico's fundamental external orientation has obviously been toward the United States, its geographic neighbor, main source of investment, and leading trading partner. The two economies have become integrated in significant ways, and diplomatic relations between the two countries have generally been cordial despite friction over some specific issues. Nevertheless, the persistent thread of militant nationalism in Mexican policy has customarily been directed against the United States. Mexican decision makers seize virtually every opportunity to demonstrate their "independence" from the United States and have fashioned "radical" policies. Washington has come to consider this behavior on Mexico's part, although often irritating, to be entirely "normal" and designed largely for domestic consumption. Other analysts and critics of the Mexican system agree: a "radical" foreign policy serves the function of to some extent "distracting" the Mexican public (and the rest of the world) from the regime's overwhelming "dependency" on the United States and the country's grave social problems.(49) Put another way, foreign policy is about the only aspect of Mexican policy that is "revolutionary" and much of this is strictly rhetorical.

For the last two decades or so, Mexico's "independent" foreign policy has offered consistent support for the inter-American norm of nonintervention and consequent opposition to U.S. security policies aimed at curbing the establishment of "Communist" or "leftist" regimes in the Western Hemisphere. Mexico was the only Latin American country to refuse to abide by the Organization of American States' decision that member states should sever diplomatic and economic ties with Castro's Cuba. Arguing that it could be used as a pretext for an armed attack on Cuba, Mexico also abstained from the OAS resolution endorsing the "quarantine" at the time of the Cuban Missile Crisis. Later, Mexico was an outspoken critic of the U.S./OAS military intervention in the 1965 Dominican Republic civil war and of the U.S. role in undermining the Allende government in Chile.(50) After Allende's overthrow, Mexico became a haven for refugees from Chile. At the height of the Sandinista offensive against Somoza, Mexico joined other key Latin American governments in successfully opposing the Carter administration proposal to send an OAS peacekeeping force to Nicaragua. The joint communique with Castro that Lopez Portillo issued upon the occasion of his visit to Cuba in August 1980 expressed support for the revolutionary government of Nicaragua and condemned all "hegemonies," nefarious activities of transnational enterprises, U.S. continued economic sanctions against Cuba, the Guantanamo naval base, and human rights violations by the U.S.-backed junta in El Salvador. Subsequent agreements between the two countries provided for Mexican importation of Cuban sugar, Pemex assistance in exploring Cuba's continental shelf for possible oil deposits, and Cuban purchase of a small amount of Mexican oil. In addition, Mexico gave public encouragement and some material assistance to leftist rebels in El Salvador and repeatedly expressed its concern as the Reagan adminis- tration sent military advisers to that country and stepped up criticism of both Cuba and Nicaragua for allegedly channeling arms to the rebels.

A measure of independence from the United States and support for governments and groups advocating structural change in Latin America is quite consistent with Mexico's ambition, which has emerged mainly since Echeverria,(51) to be an important middle power on the world scene. This ambition has had four basic components: First, through a series of highly publicized state visits around the world, the aim has been to gain significant international recognition for the Mexican president. Echeverria during his tenure was the most-traveled Latin American head of state, and Lopez Portillo has kept up only a slightly less frenetic schedule of trips to foreign capitals.

A second component of Mexico's ambition has been to cultivate closer ties with the Third World and the Non-Aligned Movement, which policy under Echeverria acquired the label of tercermundismo. Critics of this policy have suggested that it, too, has served to distract attention from problems at home(52) and has, as well, provided a useful smokescreen for Mexico's part in raising world oil prices (counter to the interests of many resource-poor developing countries). Mexico has never joined OPEC, primarily because of the denial of U.S. trade preferences that cartel membership would entail but has regularly praised the organization and has carefully avoided undercutting the OPEC-established price for crude oil. Echeverria and President Carlos Andres Perez of Venezuela were among the architects of the proposed New International Economic Order (NIEO) and certainly two of its most eloquent spokesmen. NIEO goals were partially embodied in the Echeverria-sponsored 1974 UN General Assembly resolution setting forth a Charter of the Economic Rights and Duties of States. Mexico has also edged (with Brazil) toward a more pro-Arab position in the Arab-Israeli conflict, which included voting for the extremely con- troversial 1974 UN General Assembly resolution equating "Zionism" with "racism." (Echeverria was somewhat embarrassed by the resulting precipitous, albeit temporary, decline in tourism from U.S. Jewish groups and individuals.) Lastly, Echeverria made no secret of the fact that he wanted to become Secretary-General of the United Nations upon his retirement from the presidency. His desire to do so was so obvious that, for a time, it was difficult to distinguish where his personal campaign for UN office left off and a genuine commitment to tercermundismo began. Lopez Portillo has demonstrated his continued commitment to tercermundismo and divergence from Washington by his administration's refusal to support the boycott of the 1980 Moscow Olympics, unwillingness to renew the visa of the Shah of Iran, and offer to host a major North-South conference in mid-1981.

A third component of Mexico's ambition to improve its international status has been at least a modest attempt to assert leadership in Latin America as a region. In 1974 President Echeverria proposed the establishment of an organization to be known as the Latin American Economic System (SELA), which concept attracted the prompt endorsement of Venezuela's President Perez. SELA was inaugurated with the declared mission of (1) developing and advancing common Latin American positions on issues of international economic relations, (2) increasing the production and supply of basic commodities (especially food), and (3) promoting the creation of Latin American multinational enterprises. Brazil was initially unhappy about Cuba's participation in SELA but eventually came around to giving the organization its official blessing. Argentina was always enthusiastic and has remained so. Little, in fact, has come of SELA, partly because it was vaguely conceived from the outset and partly because successor administrations in Mexico and Venezuela have not assigned it a very high priority. Mexico and Venezuela together were also instrumental in founding OLADE, a Latin American organization concerned with regional energy problems. However, both countries eventually gave less attention to OLADE than to their own bilateral arrangement for supply of Central American and Caribbean countries.

A fourth and more successful component of Mexico's policy has been an effort to create its own "mini" sphere of influence in Central American and the Caribbean. Venezuela's similar interest in this area has led the two countries into a situation of, thus far, reasonably friendly rivalry and even active cooperation. In the cooperation category, as we have noted, Venezuela and Mexico have jointly agreed to supply the oil needs of Central American and Caribbean countries at concessionary prices. Nevertheless, Mexico and Venezuela have recently been somewhat at odds over Cuba and El Salvador. Caracas has remained critical of Castro's dictatorship at home and subversive activities abroad and has tended to be uneasy over the influence of the far left in the opposition Frente Democratico Revolucionario (FDR) in El Salvador.

Yet another major aspect of Mexican foreign policy, more associated with Lopez Portillo than Echeverria, has been an attempt to "diversify dependency" through an intensified relationship with certain developed countries other than the United States. Mexico's 1980 oil-for-trade-and-investment pact with Spain was a notable initiative along these lines. More significant for the present essay is Mexico's growing interest in closer links with Japan and Canada, which interest happened to arise at a time when it was mutual and therefore all the more likely to bear important fruit.

Mexico signed a treaty of commerce and navigation with Japan as early as 1889.(53) This was most significant from the Japanese point of view because the treaty assumed the equality of both parties, unlike the unequal treaties that Japan was then having to conclude with many other foreign powers. Small-scale Japanese emigration to Mexico began in 1907, when an organization called Tairku Shokumin Gaisha (Continental Colonialization Company) was established to facilitate it. The total number of emigrants did not approach the much larger scale of Japanese emigration to Brazil, some 190,000 persons from 1918 through 1941 alone. In 1960 there were only about 6,000 to 8,000 individuals with Japanese background in Mexico.

Mexico's relations with Japan became more intensive beginning in the 1960s. Mexican presidents journeyed to Japan in 1962, 1972, and 1978; and the Japanese prime minister came to Mexico in 1959, 1974, and 1980. Exchange visits of foreign ministers and other high-level officials, as well as private businessmen, kept the diplomatic and commercial dialogue alive between summits. After a visit by the Japanese foreign minister in 1967, a Joint Mexico-Japan Economic Commission was established, which met in 1968 and again in late 1977 to discuss trade and investment. A Mexico-Japan Businessman's Committee was also created. On January 30, 1969 the two countries signed a major trade agreement granting each other most-favored-nation status. The Mexican Foreign Trade Institute (IMCE) sent trade missions to Japan in 1971 and 1975, organized Mexican participation in the Yokohama and Tokyo international import fairs in 1975, and in 1974 conducted a seminar in Japan on "Do Business with Mexico." IMCE maintains an office in Tokyo, as do Nacional Financiera (Nafinsa) and Pemex.(54)

Despite all this activity, however, until very recently Brazil, rather than Mexico, was by far the major center of Japanese interest in Latin America. Brazil's attraction has been, to a large extent, its substantial population of Japanese ancestry and also, of course, the "Brazilian miracle" of industrial development that was most impressive in the late 1960s and early 1970s. As of 1978 Brazil's share of Japan's exports and imports was double that of Mexico's, and Venezuela provided a slightly larger market for Japanese exports (though was not a larger supplier). Nevertheless, from other standpoints, Mexico and Japan have hardly been inconsequential to one another. Mexico has long occupied the position of the second most important trading partner for Japan in Latin America, and Japan has usually been the second or third most important country in Mexican trade (with the trade balance decidedly in Japan's favor). Japan's share of foreign investment has only been around 4 percent, but this is second in importance only to the U.S. share.

Moreover, Japan's involvement in Mexico may very well be growing as a result of a desire to shift away from dependence on Middle Eastern oil, in line with the Pacific Basin cooperation concept proposed by the late Japanese prime minister, Masayoshi Ohira.(55) As Ohira advanced the concept in January 1980, it would include both Mexico and Canada: in the energy field, Japanese access to Mexican oil and whatever oil may be extracted commercially from Canadian sand tar; as a supplement to Australian coal and uranium, and Chinese coal and oil. As we shall see, Mexico has conditioned greater access to its oil upon an increased influx of Japanese investment capital.

Canada's concern for Latin America, including Mexico, was minimal until the advent of Prime Minister Trudeau in 1968. Canada established diplomatic relations with the major Latin American countries after World War II, sent trade missions to several of them, acquired membership in the UN Economic Commission for Latin America (ECLA) and the Pan American Institute of Geography and History (PAIGH), refused to join the inter-American trade boycott of Castro's Cuba, and contributed to a small "soft loan" program of the Inter-American Development Bank (IDB).(56) There matters stood until Trudeau(57) sent a study mission to Latin America in 1968 and his administration in 1970 issued an important policy review book entitled Foreign Policy for Canadians. This volume articulated what was known as a "Third Position" for Canada, the notion that Canada should cultivate closer ties with Europe, Latin America, and the western Pacific as an alternative to complete political and economic domination by the United States.(58) This prescription accorded with Mexico's later concept of diversifying dependency and the Japanese proposal of expanding Pacific Basin cooperation.

A number of significant developments involving Canada's role in Latin America followed the publication of the policy review book.(59) Canada promptly sought and obtained Permanent Observer status at the OAS and membership in additional inter-American bodies like the IDB and the Pan American Health Organization. The Trudeau government publically criticized Washington's use of the IDB and other international financial institutions as tools to pressure the Allende regime in Chile. Canada, meanwhile, undertook a modest increase in its bilateral and multilateral development assistance to Latin America. A spin-off of the Canadian mission's trip to Mexico in 1968 was the creation of a Joint-Ministerial Committee, which met for the first time in 1971 to explore possible bases for future cooperation. That same year a Canada-Mexico Businessman's Committee was also established, which has subsequently met each year. Mexico sent a major trade mission to Canada in 1972, President Echeverria in 1973, and Lopez Portillo in 1980. The Ministers met again in 1974, 1977, and 1980. Trudeau visited Mexico in 1976 and 1981.

Canada's current trade with Mexico remains only about 4 percent of total Canadian trade, and Venezuelan oil accounts for over 60 percent of Canada's imports from the region. Trade with Mexico has been at a level of about $200 million each way, with the balance a bit in Canada's favor, but this is more trade than Canada has with any other Latin American country except Venezuela and Brazil. Also, the future appears to promise considerably more interaction between the two countries. Canada is keenly interested in Mexican oil and markets. Mexico wants greater access to Canadian markets, agricultural goods, investment, and nuclear power technology.

ISSUES

Issues in Mexico's relations with the key Pacific countries of the United States, Japan, and Canada may be grouped under several headings: (1) security in Central America and the Caribbean, (2) trade, (3) immigration, (4) investment, (5) fishing rights, and (6) water resources. We will examine these in sequence, although as Lopez Portillo himself has observed, "everything is part of everything else."(60)

We will not review in detail several additional "issues" that for some time now have appeared to be either resolved or relatively quiescent:(61) stolen Mexican archeological properties (resolved by a 1971 treaty), boundary problems (the "last" resolved by a 1970 treaty),(62) animal health, and illegal drug traffic from Mexico. The drug issue came to a head with President Nixon's "Operation Intercept" that slowed regular border tourist crossings and commercial transactions to a snail's pace in 1969. Soon, however, the United States was publicly expressing its general satisfaction with stepped-up Mexican control measures. Today, although Mexico remains the main source of illegal drugs entering the United States, the Mexican government strives to keep production and traffic down to a level "acceptable" to the United States. However, Mexicans do tend to see the fundamental problem as a drug-sick U.S. society that tempts both Mexican growers and law-enforcement officials into immoral behavior.

Security in Central America and the Caribbean

We have already discussed Mexico's customary at least lip-service alignment with the political forces favoring structural change in Latin America and its vehement opposition to United States "intervention" in the region. Little more need be said, except to stress that this posture may come under increasing strain as a result of the Reagan administration's preoccupation with the alleged advances of "Communism" in Central America and the Caribbean. Prevailing attitudes regarding this issue in U.S. decision-making circles are more ideologically right wing than any administration since Eisenhower. Secretary of State Alexander Haig has told Congress that he sees a Moscow "hit list" at work in Central America which has already largely succeeded in subjugating Nicaragua, seeks to do the same to El Salvador, and has the longer-range objective of capturing Guatemala and Honduras. The administration has also expressed its objection to arms shipments from Cuba and

Nicaragua to Salvadoran leftists; Cuba's continued military involvement in Africa; and the pro-Cuban orientation of the present regime in Grenada. U.S. military advisers have been sent to El Salvador to assist the junta in repressing the opposition.

At this writing, both the potential strength of the Salvadoran leftists and the lengths to which the Reagan administration might prove willing to go to insure that they will not come to power are impossible to predict. However, Mexico has strongly indicated to the United States (much as the United States warned the Soviets with regard to Poland) that it is deeply distressed with present U.S. meddling in El Salvador and that any eventual Dominican-style intervention would have a disastrous impact on the broad spectrum of U.S.-Mexican relations. Meanwhile, Mexico and Venezuela were attempting to hammer out a continuing joint position on El Salvador beyond simple opposition to growing U.S. involvement. At the outset both had supported the FDR leftist coalition, but Venezuela gradually backed away from this stance, apparently fearing both the extent of far-left influence in the FDR and the prospect of angering the Reagan administration. Of late Venezuela has been emphasizing that it could never countenance the establishment of a dictatorship of the left in El Salvador.

Trade

The United States has traditionally been Mexico's leading trading partner, providing a market for some 70 percent of Mexico's exports and supplying about 65 percent of Mexico's imports. Mexico is the United States' leading trading partner in Latin America but from the perspective of either imports or exports represents only about 3 to 4 percent of U.S. total trade. Historically, about half of Mexico's large trade deficit has come from trade with the United States, and this has been only partially offset by Mexico's gain from tourism and special border transactions. However, two-way trade with the United States has recently been expanding rapidly and, with this, the U.S. share of the trade deficit. For example, U.S.-Mexico trade grew by more than 60 percent in 1980, and the U.S. share of the trade deficit was 72.8 percent in the first nine months of that year.(63) At present the two countries' trade in agricultural goods is roughly equal. The bulk of U.S. exports to Mexico are, of course, manufactured goods. In 1980 oil exports to the United States from Mexico were worth about three-times more than Mexico's exports of manufactured goods.

Some of the Mexican manufactured goods that are exported to the United States come under the Generalized System of Preferences (GSP). This is one important reason why Mexico has not formally joined OPEC; the U.S. Trade Act of 1974 denies GSP benefits to countries that are members of commodity cartels. Many other Mexican manufactures are covered by sections 806.30 and 807.00 of the United States Tariff Schedule, which imposes a duty only on the foreign value added when components are supplied from the United States. This provision is a cornerstone of the Border Industrialization Plan that has been in effect between the two countries for many years. For its part, Mexico waives its duties and other restrictions on imports of U.S. goods and capital to be used by assembly plants (maquiladoras) within the border zone, on the condition that all goods produced will be exported. Mexico extended the same arrangement to similar assembly plants throughout the country in 1972. Robert S. Tancer states, "As a practical matter, the maquiladora plant in Mexico is often the subsidiary of a U.S. multinational, frequently operating as a 'twin plant,' with the American parent locating all or part of its operation on the U.S. side of the border."(64)

Oil is now plainly the central concern in Mexico's U.S. trade relations. As noted, it has limited total oil exports to 1.5 mbpd and has indicated that it wishes no country to receive more than 50 percent of its total exports. Mexico views the latter policy as a security precaution, and the United States appears to be resigned to it. Washington no doubt recognizes that little, except perhaps a continued sharply growing deficit for Mexico in trade with the United States, could induce the Mexicans to increase the targeted U.S. share; also, that is possibly unwise for the United States itself to become too dependent on Mexico as a source of supply. The Mexican government has thus far carefully avoided making any threat to withhold delivery on the oil allocated to the United States or to reduce the U.S. share still further. Nevertheless, it is clear that oil gives Mexico substantial extra bargaining leverage on a host of other matters – access for its exports, immigration, Central America, and so forth.(65) Less certain is whether or not Mexico can hold its exports to 1.5 mbpd, given the problems being experienced by other domestic economic sectors and the rising demand for imports.

The first serious U.S.-Mexico confrontation over energy since the Cardenas administration occurred over natural gas.(66) Early in the Carter administration several U.S. private companies negotiated an arrangement for the importation of large quantities of Mexican gas to flow through a new pipeline (gasoducto), at a price somewhat above that then being paid for natural gas imported from Canada. This arrangement was vetoed in a very undiplomatic fashion by Carter's then-Secretary of Energy James Schlesinger, who insisted that the deal would drive up the overall price of natural gas and undercut Carter's general energy program. The companies were outraged, and the Mexican government highly insulted. Although a compromise was finally reached in 1979, providing for a slightly lower price, many observers questioned whether this small concession had been worth all the "flap."

The United States and Mexican economies are already so interdependent, one line of thinking goes, that they should be even more formally integrated. A proposal of this order is that of a North American Common Market, with the United States at its center and embracing both Mexico and Canada.(67) This concept has been advanced from diverse quarters since the mid-1970s, including, among others, the Trilateral Commission, the U.S. Congress, California Governor Jerry

Brown, and candidate Ronald Reagan. Congress included a provision in the 1979 Trade Agreements Act directing the executive branch to study the idea and report back on its feasibility by July 21, 1981. Henry Kissinger and David Rockefeller traveled to Mexico on their own initiative while Carter was in the White House, trying to interest Lopez Portillo's government and Mexican businessmen in the proposal. All of these efforts have been largely unavailing. Both Lopez Portillo and Trudeau have consistently opposed a North American Common Market, most recently at their summit conference in Mexico City in January 1981. Mexico fears any scheme that might institutionalize dependency: give the United States preferential access to Mexican oil and gas reserves, while at the same time restrict the range of Mexican options with regard to protecting domestic industry, promoting exports, and regulating foreign capital. Improved access to the U.S. economy for Mexican exports, the Mexicans tend to assume, would be vigorously opposed in the U.S. by affected business and labor interests or might be negotiated on a case-by-case basis even without a general common market. Other less ambitious and therefore perhaps more feasible measures might be bilateral sectoral agreements covering such areas as agriculture, automobiles, or petrochemicals; a large free trade zone along the border; an extension of the list of items falling under the GSP; and/or an increase in the U.S. quotas for imports of specific products like textiles, shoes, or steel. Nevertheless, opposition from affected groups in the United States would also be anticipated for some or all of these measures.

Although the concept of extensive formal integration with the United States economy generates little enthusiasm in Mexico, improved access to the U.S. market for Mexican exports remains an important goal. Improved access is now somewhat harder to achieve because Mexico has decided not to enter GATT. Anticipating that Mexico probably would enter GATT, the United States had negotiated and was ready to implement tariff reductions on a number of goods. These reductions now will not go into effect. Moreover, Mexican trade practices continue to be to some extent contrary to U.S. (and GATT's) notions of "fair trade."(68) The Trade Agreements Act set up mandatory procedures for the investigation of "unfair" practices alleged by private parties, including a provision for review by the courts of intermediate and "final" decisions made by the Commerce Department and the International Trade Commission. In the event that unfair practices are found, penalties must be imposed unless waived by the President "in the national interest."

Mexico seeks greater access to the U.S. market but nevertheless hopes to reduce the U.S. share of Mexican exports from the present level of about 70 percent to closer to 60 percent, by opening up additional markets and sources of supply. Japan and Canada, in the Mexican view, are two countries where there are important opportunities for expanding trade, and their respective governments are increasingly interested in doing so.

In 1978 the developing countries accounted for 46.4 percent of Japan's exports and 53.5 percent of Japan's imports. Within the developing-countries category, trade with Latin America amounted to 6.8 percent of Japan's exports and 3.8 percent of imports. Brazil contributed 1.3 percent to the Latin American share of Japan's exports and 1 percent to imports, compared with Mexico's respective contributions of .7 percent and .4 percent. Mexico's overall trade with Japan was of the same magnitude as Argentina, Panama (often a conduit for goods enroute to other final destinations), Peru, and Venezuela. In 1978 Japan exported $639 million in goods to Mexico and imported some $356 million.(69) Important exports to Mexico included hot- and cold-rolled iron and steel sheet, power-generating machinery, chemicals, scientific and optical instruments, watches and clocks, and office equipment. Imports from Mexico included mainly raw cotton and frozen shrimp; also some concentrated manganese, unrefined copper, salt, meat, and coffee; and (circa 5% of the total) machinery and chemicals.(70)

At least until very recently, there has been a large and growing trade deficit in favor of Japan. Some Mexican analysts have attributed this partly to the highly protected nature of the Japanese economy — quotas, tariffs, and nontariff barriers like health requirements — and partly to the failure of many Mexican entrepreneurs to share the IMCE's interest in promoting exports to Japan. As a result of the latter, the Japanese have heretofore been inadequately pressured to make new concessions and even such opportunities as might already be available under Japan's existing system of preferences have not been fully explored.(71)

Currently, the Mexico-Japan trading relationship is undergoing basic change as a result of Japan's purchase of Mexican oil. Japan is receiving 100,000 bpd (compared, for example, to Spain's 220,000) but is strongly urging the Mexicans to step up the contract to 300,000 bpd. Mexico, in exchange, is demanding (among other things) increased access to the Japanese market to a point where Mexico's total exports to Japan will triple in value. Should such an arrangement come about, even assuming increased imports from Japan, it should be more than sufficient to wipe out the traditional deficit.

As we have seen, Canada's trade with Latin America in 1980 and 1981 is still only about 4 percent of that country's total trade, and about 60 percent of Canada's imports from Latin America consist of Venezuelan oil. Trade with Mexico has been limited to only about $200 million each way, with the balance normally tilted slightly in Canada's favor. This trade is nevertheless more than Canada has with any other Latin American country except for Venezuela and Brazil.

Canada's relationship with Mexico, as is the case of Japan's, seems to be intensifying — perhaps with a shade less urgency because Canada is not nearly as dependent on shaky Middle Eastern oil. However, Canada definitely is interested in Mexican oil and in finding markets in Mexico for Canadian goods and technology. When Lopez Portillo visited Trudeau in Canada in May 1980, Mexico agreed to supply Canada with 50,000 bpd, and the two countries pledged increased cooperation (trade in goods and/or technology, more investment) in such fields as mining, timber processing, transport, agroindustry, petrochemicals, communications, and long-distance high voltage electricity transmission.   When Trudeau came to Mexico in January 1981, Mexico apparently agreed to increase oil shipments in the near future to 75,000 in exchange for a Canadian promise to meet Mexico's grain needs for 1981 and 1982. That same month the Canadian Atomic Energy Commission opened an office in Mexico City, with the aim of promoting Canada's bid to supply Candu reactor technology to Mexico's nuclear energy program. This technology is particularly suitable for Mexico because it calls for unenriched uranium. On the other hand, Sweden and France have also been competing for a role in the program, both stressing (like Canada) that they offer an alternative to dependency on the United States. France reportedly has been holding out the additional inducement that technology might be supplied sans controls against its use in military weaponry.(72) Since Mexico was the initiator of the Tlatelolco Treaty for the Prohibition of Nuclear Weapons in Latin America, the latter inducement might not be persuasive, but Mexico might wish to keep its options open in this regard.

Immigration

One of the thorniest and seemingly intractable bilateral problems in U.S.-Mexican relations is illegal immigration to the United States. The movement of Mexican migrants north to the United States started in the mid-1880s and has never ceased, although some periods have been heavier than others. The flow was increased by the bracero program initiated between the two governments during World War II, under which agricultural workers from Mexico were admitted with seasonal contracts. Although this program was officially terminated in 1964, some 30,000 Mexican workers have continued to be admitted on a temporary basis each year.(73)

Congress in 1976 set a limit of 20,000 legal immigrants per year from each country in the Western Hemisphere, and 50,000 Mexicans are also granted "green card" permanent resident alien status. However, responsible estimates place the number of illegal immigrants (variously known as "illegals," "undocumented aliens," or "wetbacks") from Mexico at a maximum of 800,000 to 1 million a year.(74) A serious difficulty in making an accurate estimate of the net population gain for the U.S. is evidence that up to 70 percent of those entering in a given year have done so at least once before. Another estimate is that about 15 percent of Mexico's total labor force is now in the United States.   Smith maintains that the actual number of Mexican illegals resident in the U.S. is about 3 million or less, with 2 or 2.5 million holding some form of job.(75)

Most of the migration is to the U.S. Southwest and to Midwestern industrial cities like Chicago and Detroit. Migrants are "pushed" by the lack of employment in Mexico and "pulled" by their own ambition, the

U.S.-Mexico wage differential of 7-to-1 for unskilled jobs and 13-to-1 in agriculture,(76) and family connections. A recent survey(77) suggests that the migrants tend to come from defined regions in Mexico: 70 percent from the central plateau states and 11 percent from the northern border counties. As Wayne A. Cornelius explains:

> Numerous field studies conducted during the past five years have demonstrated the existence of communities and regions which seem to "specialize" in migrating to the United States in search of employment opportunities. . . . A century of migration from these places has led to the development of many thousands of binational kinship-employer networks that directly link potential migrants in Mexico to their United States-based relatives and United States employers. . . . The migrant's choice of destination is influenced primarily by the location of job opportunities, which in turn is influenced mainly by the presence of relatives and friends in those places.(78)

From the Mexican perspective, some 21 percent of Mexico's population is to some extent dependent on income from a family member in the United States.(79)

Certainly one of the leading factors arguing for a relatively liberal U.S. policy on migration is the Mexican government's urgent need to have this additional safety valve for the unemployed and discontented. Those making the trek to the United States are doubtless many of the very same individuals who might be making revolution if they were forced to stay at home with no other perceived way out of a dead-end situation. Consequently, although the Mexican government is naturally somewhat embarrassed to address publicly the issue of U.S. policy regarding migrants (or its own policy, for that matter),(80) it has on occasion done so and has repeatedly stressed in quiet communications the gravity of any substantial and/or sudden U.S. cutback. Mexico would prefer to keep the steady exodus of its citizens from reaching the proportions of a stampede, but ending the flow almost entirely would pose virtually insurmountable economic and political challenges. A second source of support for a relatively open border are the U.S. agricultural and industrial employers who are utilizing cheap migrant labor. Most of them insist that migrant labor is good for profits and, in fact, is absolutely essential because migrants do "stoop" and other unpleasant work that U.S. workers are unwilling to do. Moreover, demographic projections indicate that the native U.S. labor pool is steadily growing smaller in relation to demand. Finally, a large Hispanic minority in the United States – about 13 million in 1981 and by 1990 probably the largest single U.S. minority group – is concerned about any policy that might be "insulting" to Hispanics. Mexican-Americans (Chicanos), who account for well over half of the total, also worry about the severing of family ties and generally favor the United States maintaining good relations with the "mother country" of Mexico. Some Chicanos, of course, find their own jobs and wages threatened by new arrivals.(81)

Objections to a liberal policy also come from several main quarters: First, some organized labor groups complain, contrary to the stated view of employers, that migrants are filling jobs that otherwise would be filled by U.S. citizens working for a decent wage. A second group of complainers focuses on the migrants' burden on social services – health, education (to make matters worse, the federal courts have tended to mandate bilingual programs), and welfare. A third line of objection, often voiced with some caution because it has obvious racist overtones, is that Hispanics are indeed becoming too powerful a socioeconomic and political force.

Yet another body of opinion, which might be seen as offering support to proponents of either a liberal or a more restrictive policy, concerns itself with the human and civil rights of migrants. Numerous commentators deplore the conditions under which many migrants have to live and work, as well as the alleged brutal treatment of illegals during and after their arrest by law-enforcement officers and agencies.

Responding to criticism of the existing situation, President Carter on August 4, 1977, submitted a proposal for a sweeping Alien Adjustment and Employment Act. His proposal would have granted permanent resident status to those illegals who had been in the United States continuously since before 1970, given only a five-year additional temporary resident status to illegals who had arrived between 1970 and 1977, stepped up border security, improved the administration of labor standards, imposed civil penalties for the employment of illegals, and increased the annual limitation on Mexican and Canadian immigration from 20,000 each to a combined total of 50,000. With immigration from Canada declining, the last provision would surely have meant a boost for Mexico.

Carter's proposal immediately proved to be so controversial both domestically and in Mexico that it never received more than a single formal hearing in Congress (before the Senate Judiciary Committee in May 1978). The next step was the creation of a Select Commission on Immigration and Refugee Policy, headed by Father Theodore Hesburgh of Notre Dame, to study the issue further and report early in 1981. Meanwhile, proposals in circulation ranged all the way from cutting back even on legal immigration and building a 2000-mile electrified fence (the "Tortilla Wall"), to legalizing much of what is now an illegal flow of migrants. During the presidential campaign, Ronald Reagan argued for more stringent controls on illegal migration coupled with an expanded "guest worker" program, which would allow more Mexican workers to enter the United States for periods of several months to take specific types of jobs.

The Hesburgh commission's report in February 1981 estimated that the total number of illegal residents in the United States in any given recent year has been less than 6 million and perhaps as few as 3.5 to 5 million, of which probably less than half came from Mexico. The commission recommended granting a one-time amnesty to illegal aliens already in the country, a "modest increase" in the ceiling for legal immigration, and a possible "slight expansion" in arrangements for temporary workers. In addition, for the first time, U.S. employers who knowingly hire illegal workers would be subjected to civil and criminal penalties. By a narrow majority, the commission also voted to recommend the adoption of a more secure form of identification for workers.

Investment

Foreign investment has played a significant role in Mexican economic development since the Diaz administration, but it has shifted its sector emphasis over the years. This has been mainly a matter of choice on the part of foreign investors, although Mexican government policies have to some extent limited the choices. In the early years, foreign capital went primarily into the generatino of electrical power, transportation, communications, and mining. After World War II the new emphasis was industry, and investment in the traditional sectors declined. Foreign investment in Mexico increased fivefold between 1950 and 1970, from $566 million to $2.8 billion. In 1970, 74 percent of the total was in industry, 16 percent in commerce, and 6 percent in mining; there was practically none in electrical power generation, transportation, or communications.(82)

At the end of 1979 total foreign investment stood at $6.9 billion. The U.S. share of this total was about $4.7 billion or 69 percent, down only slightly from the historical level of 80 percent.(83) Estimated new U.S. investment in 1980 alone was around $1 billion.(84) According to the 2,800-member American Chamber of Commerce in Mexico City, there are about 4000 U.S. companies doing business in Mexico either directly or through correspondents and there are some 500 U.S. banks (most important: Citibank, Chase Manhattan, Bank of America, Manufacturers Hanover Trust, Chemical Bank, and Morgan Guaranty Trust). Although Canadian investment in Mexico to date has been very limited, Japan's share at the end of 1979 was second in importance to that of the United States. Nevertheless, Japan's share was only 5.3 percent(85) or some $366 million, hardly as yet a close second to the United States. As of 1977 there were at least 58 companies in Mexico with a significant amount of Japanese capital, primarily in the basic metal industries, chemicals, and in electrical and electronic manufacturing.(86) The Japanese were also involved in the automobile industry and in the manufacture of a wide variety of consumer products ranging from pianos to whiskey.

Is the Mexican economy, as some critics of Mexican government policies maintain, <u>dominated</u> by foreign capital and multinational corporations? This is a difficult question to answer precisely, because the concept of "domination" is itself somewhat vague and also because available statistics could lend themselves to more than one interpretation. Certainly one should not dismiss the roles of domestic entrepreneurs and the Mexican state. For example, one estimate for the year 1975 placed foreign investment at only about 2.5 percent of total investment in Mexico.(87) That same year, even adding foreign debts to foreign ownership of enterprises, the share of GNP produced by foreign capital was just 27 percent. Moreover, not one of the 20 largest companies in present-day Mexico have any noteworthy share of foreign capital.(88) On the other hand, it is possible to argue that, while foreign firms do not dominate all sectors of the economy, they do substantially control the most dynamic sector, which is manufacturing. A study which Richard S. Newfarmer and Willard F. Mueller did for the Senate Foreign Relations Committee's Subcommittee on Multinational Corporations reported that over 86 percent of the U.S. firms in Mexico that the authors surveyed rated themselves among the four leaders in their main product lines and 44 percent ranked themselves first.(89) However, Weinert takes issue with this and other studies that define "foreign firm" as one that is as little as 25 percent foreign-owned. In fact, as he demonstrates, when one makes the key distinction between majority and minority ownership, a rather different perspective emerges. He points to an analysis by Bernardo Sepulveda and Antonio Chumacero of foreign investment in Mexican industry in 1969(90) that showed only 17 percent of total industrial production came from firms with majority foreign ownership, 43 percent from firms with minority foreign ownership, and 40 percent from firms with no foreign owner-ship. Furthermore, Newfarmer's and Mueller's own data suggest that, among U.S. affiliates, market concentration is greater when Mexican capital is in the majority.(91)

That there are so many joint ventures in Mexico is partially a testament to a longstanding government policy of attempting to control foreign investment for the purposes of protecting sovereignty and channeling investment into preferred areas.(92) The Mexican Constitu-tion forbade foreigners from owning land in certain "prohibited zones," 50 kilometers from the coast and 100 kilometers from the land frontiers; and they could own interior land or obtain mining concessions only by permission from the Secretariat of Foreign Relations and with their advance acceptance of the Calvo Clause (giving Mexican law and courts exclusive jursidiction over any claims that might arise). A policy of "Mexicanization" of other forms of investment is generally dated from the Cardenas nationalizations of the 1930s. This gathered momentum following World War II and became quite determined in the 1960s. The government itself assumed a more prominent ownership role and also used its purchasing power, taxes, and tariffs as a means of favoring enterprises with participation of private Mexican capital. Eventually, at the close of the Diaz Ordaz administration, in July 1970, a decree was issued that consolidated and extended past practice. New foreign investment was prohibited in five sectors of the economy that were reserved for the state and in eight others that were reserved for wholly owned Mexican enterprises. Reserved sectors included electricity, banks, insurance, communications, transportation, and fishing. In addition, 51 percent Mexican ownership was required in steel, cement, glass, fertilizers, cellulose, aluminum mining, chemicals, and rubber.(93) Under Echeverria there was a further evolution of Mexican laws relating to foreign investment. In 1971 the basic petrochemical industry was reserved for the state; 60 percent Mexican ownership was mandated for companies processing petrochemicals; and a 66 percent Mexican share was required for mining. More encouraging for foreign investors, that same year the government authorized Mexican banks to serve as trustees of real estate located in prohibited zones for periods of 30 years when it could be used for industry or tourism, under which provision foreigners could own beneficial interests without violating the Constitution.   Then, in 1972, 60 percent Mexican ownership was required for companies manufacturing auto parts.(94) In each instance the provisions were not made retroactive, but they did apply both to new companies and to the expansion of existing enterprises. The decrees did much to alter the situation of foreign capital in the country, yet serious control problems remained. These included the efforts of some foreign interests to disguise the true extent of their ownership through such devices as pyramiding corporations and shares owned by Mexican nationals who acted as prestanombres. Also, from the vantagepoint of the foreign investor, the Mexican standards were often ambiguous and their application required lengthy negotiations with numerous government agencies often having overlapping jurisdiction.(95)

Finally, in February 1973, the government promulgated a comprehensive Law to Promote Mexican Investment and Regulate Foreign Investment. The law incorporated previous provisions regarding various sectors of the economy and added the key restriction that all new enterprises would have to be 51 percent Mexican-owned. The restriction also applied to new investment in old enterprises, and it exempted maquiladoras, which could continue to be 100 percent foreign-owned. A National Commission on Foreign Investment (NCFI) was established to pass on new foreign investment in the light of the fundamental law and 17 additional criteria. For example, investments that would occupy a monopolistic position or have an adverse effect on the balance of payments were to be discouraged, while those were to be encouraged which would train Mexican technicians or help invigorate   under-developed areas of the country. The law also forbade such time-honored circumvention techniques as prestanombres and pyramiding corporations, as well as the possession by foreigners of bearer shares in a corporation (owner not revealed). A complementary Law to Regulate Transfer of Technology created a separate Registry of Technology to review all royalty and licensing arrangements, applying several additional restrictions. These include the provisions that technology already available in Mexico may not be imported; and that no arrangement can provide for reversion of technology to the grantor, attempt to curb research and development, place any limitation on exports, or be for a period of more than ten years.(96)

The foreign investment community was chagrined by the 1973 provisions, but it has largely learned to live with them. Drawn in part by the oil boom, foreign capital has continued to flow into Mexico at an impressive rate, and Lopez Portillo has tried to create a somewhat more receptive climate for it than his predecessor. In early 1981 the Mexican government launched the Fondo Mexico, an investment fund to be listed on stock exchanges in New York, Japan, and Europe. Nafinsa will buy a portfolio of stocks on the Mexican exchange and issue certificates of equal value which will then be sold to foreign investors. Foreigners can thus invest in Mexican corporations without exercising any direct ownership role.

In accord with the policy of diversifying dependency, the Lopez Portillo administration has also made an effort to attract increased capital from elsewhere than the United States. More investment from Canada may be forthcoming under the recent plans for greater industrial cooperation. However, a particular target in the Mexican diversification campaign has been Japan. Mexico has been talking of making an increase in oil shipments to the 300,000-bpd level desired by Japan, contingent not only on the trade concessions already mentioned, but also on a tenfold increase in Japanese investment beyond the average $100 million per year provided in the late 1970s (prior to 1979). The projected $1 billion per year would be equal to the total 1980 U.S. investment in Mexico and would preferably take the form of joint ventures to promote Mexican exports and improve internal transportation networks, ports, and shipping.

In fact, Japanese investment has already begun to increase. In 1979 Mexico received $516 million, compared with $694 million for the rest of the entire decade of the 1970s. This was 42 percent of Japan's total 1979 investment in Latin America, compared with Mexico's historical share of 4 to 5 percent.(97)

It remains to be seen whether the hard-bargaining Japanese will eventually maintain this level, cut back, or increase investment to the full extent that Mexico wishes. Much depends upon Mexico's genuine capacity and willingness to meet more of Japan's oil needs, the outcome of other trade negotiations, and the exact conditions likely to be attached to specific investment projects.(98) Whatever the long-term outlook, the tables have obviously turned from not many years ago when it was the Japanese who were doing almost all of the arm-twisting. For example, Japan secured Nissan Motor's terms of entry into Mexico's domestic auto production market by threatening to curb Japanese purchases of Mexican cotton and other products.(99)

Fishing Rights

The fishing rights issue has come to the fore only since July 31, 1976, when the Lopez Portillo administration – in the context of trends in the general international law of the sea – proclaimed a 200-mile Exclusive Economic Zone (EEZ) off the coasts of Mexico and set forth the rules governing fishing within the EEZ by foreign vessels. The next year the Mexican government began an ambitious $1.3 billion program to develop the Mexican fishing industry into one of the most important in the Western Hemisphere, with a projected annual catch by 1982 five times the half-million tons harvested in 1976. Frictions have arisen over what the experts term "cross-border" species: those species of fish and shellfish that are of present or possible future economic importance to both the United States and Mexico, that exist on both sides of the border, or that migrate across the border at some stage in their life cycle. These species include tuna, shrimp, anchovy, lobster, red crab, abalone, and various sport fish.(100)

The most friction to date has involved tuna and has been sufficiently serious for some observers to have dubbed it a "tuna war." In the past, fishing for Pacific yellowfin tuna has been regulated by a multinational organization, the Inter-American Tropical Tuna Commission (IATCC). The charge of the IATCC has been to guard against overfishing and to guarantee each country a fair share of the catch. Complicating the task of regulation is the fact that the tuna is a migratory fish. Mexico has withdrawn from the IATCC, accepting its annual quota for the catch but insisting on the exclusive right to harvest all the tuna in the Mexican EEZ. The United States protested, and when Mexico began seizing U.S. tuna boats, retaliated both by embargoing all Mexican tuna exports to the United States (usually one-third of Mexico's total tuna exports) and "reserving" (temporarily suspending) quotas for the importation of Mexican squid and other fish. All this was done under authority of the U.S. Fisheries and Management Conservation Act of 1976 (FMCA). Mexico responded by attempting, with some success, to find alternative markets in Europe for the U.S. share of tuna exports and then, in December 1980, by terminating all fishing agreements with the United States.

Problems with other species are only somewhat less acute. Mexico announced in 1979 that foreigners could no longer fish for shrimp in Mexican waters in the Gulf of Mexico except through joint ventures. Thus far, U.S. fishermen have not been willing to enter into such ventures and Mexico is seeking to interest Cuba and other fishing countries in them. Meanwhile, Mexico is trying to exapdn markets outside of the United States for its shrimp, reducing its dependence on the United States and thereby its vulnerability to possible U.S. punitive measures. There is also considerable concern in the United States that alleged Mexican overfishing of the anchovy in coastal Pacific waters will drastically reduce the U.S. catch or even cause a precipitous decline in the species, which, in turn, would impact on many types of marine life in the area generally. Mexico denies that overfishing is occurring and claims that the United States concern is less than compelling, because the U.S. catch is consumed as a "luxury" item or used as bait for sport fishermen while the Mexican catch goes to fishmeal for animal food. Difficulties with other species include Mexico's objections to poaching by U.S. citizens catching lobster, abalone, and red crab off the Baja California coast; and the decline in various sport fish that could lead to a ban on U.S. sport boats in Mexican waters.

In addition to controlling imports from Mexico, the United States has some leverage in fishing conflicts through its capacity to regulate

Mexican fishing in U.S. waters. Indeed, it appears that a U.S. refusal to assign Mexico a quota for squid fishing off the New England coast may have been the last straw in convincing the Mexican government to terminate all fishing agreements with the United States. As Patrick H. Heffernan emphasizes, one of the complexities of the entire issue of fishing rights is the fact that, in contrast to the centralized decision-making system of Mexico, U.S. decision-making with regard to fishing under the FMCA is quite decentralized. Regional fisheries management councils establish a Total Allowable Level of Foreign Fishing (TALF) for each species within its region. This has the disadvantage of making decision making possibly overresponsive to pressures from local fishing interests and the advantage of removing the U.S. Government from complete responsibility for the decisions reached.(101) The challenge, of course, is persuading the Mexican government not to hold Washington responsible.

Water Resources

By far the most acrimonious dispute concerning water resources in recent years has been the question of the salinity of the Colorado River. Irrigation projects and increased water use for other purposes has greatly raised the saline content of the lower Colorado, part of the waters of which were allocated to Mexico under the 1944 United States-Mexico Treaty for the Utilization of Waters of the Colorado, Tijuana, and Rio Grande Rivers. When Mexico formally complained about the situation in 1961, the Kennedy administration agreed to negotiate, but substantive bilateral talks did not get under way until 1972. At that time the Nixon administration pledged the United States to build a costly desalinization plant. Mexico has been impatient with the slow construction of this plant and also increasingly disturbed about rising salinity in the Gulf of California, to which the Colorado River is one tributary.

As surveyed by C. Richard Bath, other rivers and groundwater may also be a source of conflict in the bilateral relationship.(102) The rivers include one (Rio Grande) that forms the international boundary, one that flows into Mexico from the United States (Tijuana), and two that flow in the reverse direction (New River, San Pedro). The Lower Rio Grande receives dangerous municipal and agricultural wastes from the U.S. side. The New River is polluted by human wastes in Maxicali and later by agriculture in California. The San Pedro River is laden with waste from Sonora copper mines before it gets to Arizona. The Tijuana poses a periodic threat of floods, and the United States has failed to build its share of flood control projects contemplated by a 1966 agreement between the two countries. Groundwater problems that sooner or later will necessitate international agreement have emerged in two geographical areas, the Yuha Valley between Calexico and San Diego, and the region of El Paso-Ciudad Juarez.

Yet another problem, pollution from petroleum spills in the Gulf of Mexico, was highlighted by the 1978 blowout of Ixtoc I well that menaced Texas beaches, wildlife, and fishing. Although favorable winds carried much of the pollution away from the coast, there were demands in the United States for damages from Mexico, which Mexico heatedly rejected. Mexico's position was that the blowout was an unforeseen accident caused not by negligence but an "act of God," and that the United States was arrogant in discussing damages in this case when none had ever been paid for Colorado River salinity. An interesting subplot in this drama was the statesmanlike stance of Texas Governor William P. Clements, who urged the United States to make no claim as a gesture to improve U.S.-Mexican relations. He appeared a little less magnanimous when it was revealed some days later that Sedco, the company he had founded and which was then headed by his son, had supplied the oil rig used for Ixtoc I. In any event, to avert another controversy, the United States and Mexico in June 1980 concluded an agreement on the subject of responsibility for <u>future</u> spills.

THE FUTURE

Over the next few decades, Mexico's international stature, nationalism, and desire for more independence from the United States will doubtless be increased by the further development of the country's oil industry. On the other hand, the economies of the United States and Mexico are so closely linked and interdependent – an interdependence that is now more mutual because of Mexican oil – that the bilateral relationship is almost inevitably going to continue to take precedence for Mexico over Pacific, Central American and Caribbean, or any other external ties.

Decision makers on both sides of the U.S.-Mexico border have proved adept over the years at keeping conflicts over particular issues from souring the total relationship. Even if political tensions were suddenly to escalate well beyond the limits of the past over Central America, fishing rights, or some other issue, the bedrock realities of trade and investment would tend to act as a stabilizing factor over the longer haul. The Mexican government might seek to punish the United States by cutting its share of oil exports still further or by temporarily withholding all oil shipments from the United States, and there surely would be no difficulty in finding buyers for the "excess" oil. However, Mexico can hardly afford seriously to jeopardize a relationship that (as we have seen) currently provides a market for two-thirds of Mexican exports, supplies two-thirds of Mexican imports, offers circa $1 billion annually in new investment, and accounts for 69 percent of existing foreign investment.

The foregoing said, one should neither overestimate nor under-estimate the possible significance of Mexico's present effort to diversify dependency, coupled as it is with the lure of oil, a relatively stable political system, and a growing domestic market. Japan is obviously the key country in this regard. If allowed, Japan could conceivably rival the United States as a purchaser of Mexican oil. But Japan is not likely to offer Mexico a comparable market for nonoil exports (though it is expanding), nor a comparable source of goods, technology, and services. The Japanese market is traditionally even more protected than the United States, and Mexico's economy is far too dependent on U.S. multinationals. Many of Mexico's manufactured exports derive essentially from transfers within and among large U.S. companies; these same companies tend to look to their own parent or to other U.S. enterprises for technology; and so on. Nevertheless, if (a "big" if) Japanese investment continues at its present level – and especially if it increases to the target set by the Mexicans – Japan will rival the United States as a source of new capital. Given Mexico's long history almost entirely in the shadow of the Colossus of the North, as well as Japan's traditional emphasis on Brazil, that in itself would be a remarkable development.

NOTES

(1) Several good histories of Mexico are: Michael C. Meyer and William L. Sherman, The Course of Mexican History (New York: Oxford University Press, 1979); Peter Calvert, Mexico (New York: Praeger, 1973); Charles C. Cumberland, Mexico: The Struggle for Modernity (New York: Oxford University Press, 1968); Robert E. Quirk, Mexico (Englewood Cliffs, N.J.: Prentice-Hall, 1971); and Justo Sierra, The Political Evolution of the Mexican People (Austin: University of Texas Press, 1969).

(2) On the Indian legacy and other aspects of Mexican culture, see especially two books by Octavio Paz: The Other Mexico: A Critique of the Pyramid (New York: Grove Press, 1972); and The Labyrinth of Solitude: Life and Thought in Mexico (New York: Grove Press, 1962); and Victor Alba, The Mexicans: The Making of a Nation (New York: Praeger, 1967).

(3) Useful historical surveys of U.S.-Mexican relations are: Karl M. Schmitt, Mexico and the United States, 1921-1973: Conflict and Coexistence (New York: Wiley, 1974), and Howard F. Cline, The United States and Mexico, rev. ed. (New York: Atheneum, 1963).

(4) An interesting article on the early efforts of U.S. speculators to gain concessions and investment opportunities in Mexico prior to the major increase in foreign investment under Diaz is: Thomas Schoonover, "Dollars over Dominion: United States Economic Interests in Mexico, 1861-1867," Pacific Historical Review 45, no. 1 (February 1976): 23-45.

(5) On the Mexican Revolution, see especially: Frank Tannenbaum, Mexico: The Struggle for Peace and Bread (New York: Knopf, 1950); Leslie Byrd Simpson, Many Mexicos, 4th rev. ed. (Berkeley: University

of California Press, 1967); two works by Charles C. Cumberland: Mexican Revolution: Genesis under Madero (Austin: University of Texas Press, 1952), and Mexican Revolution: The Constitutionalist Years (Austin: University of Texas Press, 1972); John Womack, Jr., Zapata and the Mexican Revolution (New York: Knopf, 1968); and Robert E. Quirk, The Mexican Revolution, 1914-1915 (Bloomington, Ind.: Indiana University Press, 1960).

(6) On U.S.-Mexico relations during and after the Revolution (prior to World War II), see especially Robert Freeman Smith, The United States and Revolutionary Nationalism in Mexico, 1916-1932 (Chicago: University of Chicago Press, 1972); and Cole Blasier, The Hovering Giant: U.S. Responses to Revolutionary Change in Latin America (Pittsburgh: University of Pittsburgh Press, 1976), chap. 5. On the Veracruz incident, see Robert E. Quirk, An Affair of Honor (New York: Norton, 1967).

(7) On the evolution of nationalism as an ideology, see Frederick C. Turner, The Dynamics of Mexican Nationalism (Chapel Hill, N.C.: UNiversity of North Carolina Press, 1968).

(8) See John W.F. Dulles, Yesterday in Mexico: A Chronicle of the Revolution, 1919-1936 (Austin: University of Texas Press, 1961).

(9) See Lorenzo Meyer, Mexico and the United States in the Oil Controversy, 1917-1942 (Austin: University of Texas Press, 1977); and Bryce Wood, The Making of the Good Neighbor Policy (New York: Columbia University Press, 1961), chaps. 8-9.

(10) See Dwin Lieuwen, Mexican Militarism: The Political Rise and Fall of the Revolutionary Army, 1910-1940 (Albuquerque: University of New Mexico Press, 1968).

(11) See Howard F. Cline, Mexico: Revolution to Evolution, 1940-1960 (New York: Oxford University Press, 1963); James W. Wilkie, The Mexican Revolution: Federal Expenditures and Social Change Since 1910 (Berkeley: University of California Press, 1967); and Stanley R. Ross, ed., Is the Mexican Revolution Dead? rev. ed. (Philadelphia: Temple University Press, 1975).

(12) See two articles in Lawrence E. Koslow, ed., The Future of Mexico (Tempe, Ariz.: Center for Latin American Studies, Arizona State University, 1977): R. Kenneth Godwin, "Mexican Population Policy: Problems Posed by Participatory Demography in a Paternalistic Political System," pp. 145-168; and Luis Lenero Otero, "Mexican Population Policies from a Sociocultural Perspective: Past, Present, and Future," pp. 169-186.

(13) Statistics in this paragraph (except those on unemployment) from Peter H. Smith, Mexico: The Quest for a U.S. Policy (New York: Foreign Policy Association, 1980), p. 5.

(14) See especially Wayne A. Cornelius, Politics and the Migrant Poor in Mexico (Stanford, Calif.: Stanford University Press, 1975); Susan Eckstein, The Poverty of Revolution: The State and the Urban Poor in Mexico (Princeton, N.J.: Princeton University Press, 1977); and Susan Eckstein, "The State and the Urban Poor," in Authoritarianism in Mexico, ed. Jose Luis Reyna and Richard S. Weinert (Philadelphia: ISHI Press, 1977), pp. 23-46.

(15) Wayne A. Cornelius comments:

> Eventually, as the nation's population becomes increasingly con-centrated in the larger cities, opposition to the existing political system – electoral or otherwise – will almost certainly increase. But this will have little to do with the presence of large numbers of recent migrants in the cities. Of far greater poten-tial importance as a source of opposition to the regime are the more highly educated, city-born, offspring of migrants and native-born city dwellers in general, who may even find them-selves at a disadvantage vis-a-vis recent migrants in competition for certain kinds of jobs. (Politics and the Migrant Poor in Mexico, p. 228)

(16) See Clark W. Reynolds, The Mexican Economy: Twentieth Century Structure and Growth (New Haven, Conn.: Yale University Press, 1970); and John B. Ross, The Economic System of Mexico (Stanford, Calif.: California Institute of International Studies, 1971).

(17) There were some signs in 1980 that the dynamism in manufacturing was starting to slow somewhat. Manufacturing output increased only 5.6%, much less than the 10%-per-year target in the government's Global Development Plan.

(18) Richard S. Weinert, "Foreign Capital in Mexico," in Mexico-United States Relations, ed. Susan Kaufman Purcell, published as Proceedings of The Academy of Political Science 34, no. 1 (1981): 116.

(19) Total government spending amounted to nearly 37% of GNP in 1980. (Latin America Weekly Report, March 30, 1981, p. 8.)

(20) Because of private-sector resistance, the Mexican government has apparently made at least a temporary decision not to take over private buses in Mexico City.

(21) See especially George W. Grayson, The Politics of Mexican Oil (Pittsburgh, Pa.: University of Pittsburgh Press, 1981); Edward J. Williams, The Rebirth of the Mexican Petroleum Industry (Lexington, Mass.: D.C. Health, 1979); David Ronfeldt, Richard Nehring, and Arturo Gandara, Mexico's Petroleum and U.S. Policy: Implications for the 1980s, prepared for the U.S. Department of Energy, Rand publication R-2510-DOE (June 1980); United States, Library of Congress, Congressional Research Service, Mexico's Oil and Gas Policy: An Analysis (Washington: GPO, 1979); George W. Grayson, "The Mexican Oil Boom," in Purcell, ed., Mexico-United States Relations, pp. 146-157; and George Philip, "Mexican Oil and Gas: The Politics of a New Resource," International Affairs, Summer 1980, pp. 474-483.

(22) For background, see Edward J. Williams, "Mexican Hydrocarbon Export Policy: Ambition and Reality," in International Energy Policy, ed. Robert M. Lawrence and Martin O. Heisler (Lexington, Mass.: Lexington Books, 1980), pp. 65-79.

(23) Latin America Regional Reports: Mexico & Central America, March 20, 1981, p. 8.

(24) Latin America Weekly Report, November 21, 1980, p. 7.

(25) According to planning and budget ministry, reported in Latin America Weekly Report, February 27, 1981, p. 1.

(26) Latin America Regional Reports: Mexico & Central America, March 20, 1981, p. 8.

(27) On the 1976 experience, see Norris Clement and Louis Green, "The Political Economy of Devaluation in Mexico," Inter-American Economic Affairs 32, no. 3 (Winter 1978): 47-75; and J. Wilson Mixon, Barry W. Poulson, and Myles S. Wallace, "The Political Economy of Devaluation in Mexico: Some New Evidence," Inter-American Economic Affairs 33, no. 2 (Autumn 1979): 71-85.

(28) Latin America Weekly Report, January 30, 1981, p. 5.

(29) Ibid.

(30) Latin America Weekly Report, December 5, 1980, p. 5.

(31) Latin America Weekly Report, March 6, 1981, p. 9.

(32) Latin America Regional Reports: Mexico & the Caribbean, January 9, 1981, p. 8.

(33) Judith Adler Hellman, Mexico in Crisis (New York: Holmes & Meier, 1978), p. 73. In our discussion of the ejido system, we have drawn heavily upon chapter 3.

(34) On the Mexican political system, see especially Kenneth F. Johnson, Mexican Democracy: A Critical View, rev. ed. (New York: Praeger, 1978); Reyna and Weinert, eds., Authoritarianism in Mexico; L. Vincent Padgett, The Mexican Political System, 2nd ed. (Boston: Houghton Mifflin, 1976); Roger D. Hansen, The Politics of Mexican Development (Baltimore: Johns Hopkins Press, 1971); Martin C. Needler, Politics and Society in Mexico (Albuquerque: University of New Mexico Press, 1971); Pablo Gonzalez Casanova, Democracy in Mexico, trans. Danielle Salti, rev. ed. (New York: Oxford University Press, 1970); Frank Brandenburg, The Making of Modern Mexico (Englewood Cliffs, N.J.: Prentice-Hall, 1964); and Robert E. Scott, Mexican Government in Transition (Urbana: University of Illinois Press, 1959).

(35) See especially two items by Robert R. Kaufman: "Mexico and Latin American Authoritarianism" in Authoritarianism in Mexico, ed. Reyna and Weinert, pp. 193-232; and "Industrial Change and Authoritarian Rule in Latin America: A Concrete Review of the Bureaucratic-Authoritarian Model," in The New Authoritarianism in Latin America, ed. David Collier, (Princeton, N.J.: Princeton University Press, 1979), pp. 165-253.

(36) Merilee Serrill Grindle, Bureaucrats, Politicians, and Peasants in Mexico (Berkeley, Calif.: University of California Press, 1977), p. 174.

(37) David F. Ronfeldt, "The Mexican Army and Political Order Since 1940," in Armies and Politics in Latin America, ed. Abraham F. Lowenthal, (New York: Holmes & Meier, 1976), pp. 291-312.

(38) Johnson, Mexican Democracy, pp. 83-84.

(39) Lawrence E. Koslow and Stephen P. Mumme, "The Evolution of the Mexican Political System: A Paradigmatic Analysis," in The Future of Mexico, ed. Koslow, pp. 47-98.

(40) Peter H. Smith, Labyrinths of Power: Political Recruitment in Twentieth-Century Mexico (Princeton, N.J.: Princeton University Press, 1979), pp. 214-215. See also Peter H. Smith, "Does Mexico Have a Power Elite?" in Authoritarianism in Mexico, ed. Reyna and Weinert, pp. 129-151.

(41) Hellman, Mexico in Crisis, pp. 99-100.

(42) Ibid., pp. 100-103.

(43) Ibid., pp. 107-108.

(44) Ibid., pp. 124. See also Evelyn P. Stevens, Protest and Response in Mexico (Cambridge, Mass.: M.I.T. Press, 1974).

(45) See, for example, Susan Kaufman Purcell, "The Future of the Mexican System," in Authoritarianism in Mexico, ed. Reyna and Weinert, pp. 173-191.

(46) See, for example, Edward J. Williams, "Petroleum Policy and Mexican Domestic Politics: Left Opposition, Regional Dissidence, and Official Apostasy," The Energy Journal 1, no. 3: 75-96.

(47) Smith, Labyrinths of Power, p. 166.

(48) Two good collections of essays from the Colegio de Mexico on Mexican foreign policy (and related matters) are: Lecturas de politica exterior mexicana (Mexico, D.F.: El Colegio de Mexico, 1979); and Vision del Mexico contemporaneo (Mexico, D.F.: El Colegio de Mexico, 1979). both include Castaneda's essay on "En busca de una posicion frente a Estados Unidos."

(49) On this point see, for example, Carlos A. Astiz, "Mexico's Foreign Policy: Disguised Dependency," Current History 66, no. 393 (May 1974): 220-223, 225; Lynn Darrell Bender, "Contained Nationalism: The Mexican Foreign Policy Example," Revista Interamericana 5, no. 1 (Spring 1975): 1-4; Wolf Grabendorff, "Mexico's Foreign Policy Indeed a Foreign Policy? Journal of Interamerican Studies and World Affairs 20, no. 1 (February 1978): 85-92; and Richard R. Fagen, "The Realities of U.S.-Mexican Relations," Foreign Affairs 55, no. 4 (July 1977): 685-700. An overview of current trends and issues in the bilateral relationship can be gleaned from the excellent collection: Purcell, ed., Mexico-United States Relations. See also Stanley R. Ross, ed., Views Across the Border: The United States and Mexico (Albuquerque: University of New Mexico Press, 1978); and Richard D. Erb and Stanley R. Ross, U.S. Policies Toward Mexico: Perceptions and Perspectives (Washington, D.C.: American Enterprise Institute for Public Policy Research, 1979).

(50) See Errol D. Jones and David Lafrance, "Mexico's Foreign Affairs under President Echeverria: The Special Case of Chile," Inter-American Economic Affairs 30, no. 1 (Summer 1976): 45-78.

(51) For background and perspective on the Echeverria policies, see Olga Pellicer de Brody, "Mexico in the 1970s and Its Relations with the United States," in Latin America and the United States, ed. Julio Cotler and Richard R. Fagen (Stanford, Calif.: Stanford University Press, 1974), pp. 314-333; Guy E. Poitras, "Mexico's 'New' Foreign Policy," Inter-American Economic Affairs 28, no. 3 (Winter 1974): 59-77; William H. Hamilton, "Mexico's 'New' Foreign Policy: A Reexamination," Inter-American Economic Affairs 29, no. 3 (Winter 1975): 51-58; Harvey J. Kaye, "How 'New' Is Mexico's Foreign Policy?" Inter-American Economic Affairs 28, no. 1 (Spring 1975): 87-92; and Edith B. Couturier, "Mexico," in Latin American Foreign Policies: An Analysis, ed. Harold Eugene Davis and Larman C. Wilson (Baltimore: Johns Hopkins Press, 1975), pp. 117-135.

(52) See Olga Pellicer de Brody, "Las relaciones comerciales de Mexico: una prueba para la nueva politica exterior," Foro Internacional 17, no. 1 (julio/septiembre 1976): 37-50.

(53) Mexico's relations with Japan through 1976 are discussed in detail in Sang-Juner Shim, Japan and Latin America: A Changing Relationship (Ph.D. thesis, Rutgers University, New Brunswick, N.J., October 1978). On the relationship in the nineteenth century, see also Mexico, Secretaria de Relaciones Exteriores, Coleccion del Archivo Historico Diplomatico Mexicano, Mexico y Japon en el siglo XIX: la politica exterior de Mexico y la consolidacion de la soberania Japonesa (Mexico, D.F.: Secretaria de Relaciones Exteriores, 1976).

(54) Much of the information in this paragraph was derived from Department of Economic Studies, "Mexican-Japanese Trade Relations," Comercio Exterior de Mexico, February 1979, pp. 77-78.

(55) See, for example, Lawrence B. Krause and Sueo Sekiguchi, eds., Economic Interaction in the Pacific Basin (Washington, D.C.: Brookings Institution, 1980); and Hara Yasushi, "How to Make a Concept Real – The Idea of Pacific Basin Cooperation," Japan Quarterly 27, no. 4 (October/December 1980): 471-478.

(56) James Guy, "The Growing Relationship of Canada and the Americas," International Perspectives, July/August 1977, pp. 3-6.

(57) See J.C.M. Ogelsby, "A Trudeau Decade: Canadian-Latin American Relations 1968-1978," Journal of Interamerican Studies and World Affairs 21, no. 2 (May 1979): 187-208. Ogelsby notes that Trudeau had been editor of a leading Quebec journal, Cite Libre, where he established his position on political involvement in the inter-American system. Moreover, one of Trudeau's closest friends and a member of his Cabinet was Gerard Pelletier, who had considerable familiarity with Latin America and a longstanding interest in improving Canadian-Latin American relations (pp. 187-189).

(58) See David C. Story, "Foreign Policy for Canadians and the Third Option Paper: Assessments," International Journal 33, no. 2 (Spring 1978): 379-414; and Jean-Emile Denis and Emmanuel Lindekens, "Third Option Never Given a Fair Chance," The Canadian Business Review 7, no. 1 (Spring 1980): 5-7.

(59) See Ogelsby, "A Trudeau Decade"; and Guy, "The Growing Relationship."

(60) Quoted by Viron P. Vaky in his "Hemispheric Relations: 'Everything Is Part of Everything Else,'" Foreign Affairs (issue on "America and the World 1980") 59, no. 3: 616-647.

(61) For good background on these issues, see Lyle C. Brown, "The Politics of United States-Mexican Relations: Problems of the 1970s in Historical Perspective," in International Congress of Mexican History, IV, Santa Monica, Cal., 1973, Contemporary Mexico (Los Angeles: University of California, Latin American Center, 1976), pp. 471-493.

(62) See Sheldon B. Liss, A Century of Disagreement: The Chamizal Conflict (Washington, D.C.: University Press of Washington, D.C., 1965).

(63) Latin America Weekly Report, January 9, 1981, p. 5.

(64) Robert S. Tancer, "Regulating Foreign Investment in the Seventies: The Mexican Approach," in The Future of Mexico, ed. Koslow, p. 203.

(65) See, for example, Edward J. Williams, "Oil in Mexican-U.S. Relations: Analysis and Bargaining Scenario," Orbis 22, no. 1 (Spring 1978): 201-216; George W. Grayson, "Mexico's Opportunity: The Oil Boom," Foreign Policy, no. 29, Winter 1977/78, pp. 65-89; and Congressional Research Service, Mexico's Oil and Gas Policy. For a warning, on the contrary, that the oil era could be one of increased dependency for Mexico, see Olga Pellicer de Brody: "Relaciones exteriores: interdependencia con Estados Unidos o proyecto nacional," in Mexico hoy, ed. Jose Ayala et al., (Mexico, D.F.: Siglo Veintiuno Editores, 1979), pp. 372-384; and "La crisis mexicana: hacia una nueva dependencia," Cuadernos Politicos 14 (octubre/diciembre 1977): 45-55.

(66) See Richard R. Fagen and Henry R. Nau, "Mexican Gas: The Northern Connection," in Capitalism and the State in U.S.-Latin American Relations, ed. Richard R. Fagen (Stanford, Calif.: Stanford University Press, 1979), pp. 382-427; George W. Grayson, "Mexico and the United States: The Natural Gas Controversy," Inter-American Economic Affairs 32, no. 3 (Winter 1978): 3-27; and Jesus Puente Leyva, "The Natural Gas Controversy," in Mexico-United States Relations, ed. Purcell, pp. 158-167.

(67) For a discussion of this and other alternatives, as well as the Mexican reaction thereto, see Gary Clyde Hufbauer, W.N. Harrell Smith IV, and Frank G. Vukmanic, "Bilateral Trade Relations," in Mexico-United States Relations, ed. Purcell, pp. 136-145. We have drawn heavily on this essay. See also Dale B. Truett and Lila Flory Truett, "Mexico and GSP: Problems and Prospects," Inter-American Economic Affairs 34, no. 2 (Autumn 1980): 67-85.

(68) This is a point stressed in Hufbauer et al., "Bilateral Trade Relations."

(69) Japan, Economic and Foreign Affairs Research Association, Statistical Survey of Japan's Economy, 1979 (Tokyo: Economic and Foreign Affairs Research Association, 1980), pp. 37, 44, 57.

(70) Japan, Prime Minister's Office, Statistics Bureau, Japan Statistical Yearbook, 1980 (Tokyo: Statistics Bureau, 1980), pp. 304-308.

(71) Department of Economic Studies, "Mexican-Japanese Trade Relations," p. 79.

(72) Latin America Weekly Report, March 6, 1981, p. 7.

(73) See Richard B. Craig, The Bracero Program: Interest Groups and Foreign Policy (Austin: University of Texas Press, 1974). The literature on the migrant issue is voluminous. See, for example, Loy Bilderback, Paul Erlich, and Anne Erlich, The Golden Door: International Migration, Mexico, and the United States (New York: Ballantine, 1979); Michael S. Teitelbaum, "Right Versus Right: Immigration and Refugee Policy in the United States," Foreign Affairs 59, no. 1 (Fall 1980): 21-59; Walter Fogel, "United States Immigration Policy and Unsanctioned Migrants," Industrial and Labor Relations Review 33, no. 3 (April 1980): 295-314; and Wayne A. Cornelius, "Mexican Migration to the United States," in Mexico-United States Relations, ed. Purcell, 67-77.

(74) Smith, Mexico, p. 24.

(75) Ibid.

(76) Cornelius, "Mexican Migration to the United States," p. 70.

(77) By Carlos H. Zazuyeta and Fernando Mercado, cited by Cornelius, "Mexican Migration to the United States," p. 69.

(78) Cornelius, "Mexican Migration to the United States," p. 69.

(79) Michael Redclift and Nanneke Redclift, "Unholy Alliance," Foreign Policy, no. 41, Winter 1980/81, p. 121.

(80) See Stephen P. Mumme, "Mexican Politics and the Prospects for Emigration Policy: A Policy Perspective," Inter-American Economic Affairs 32, no. 1 (Summer 1978): 67-94.

(81) See Rodolfo O. de la Garza, "Demythologizing Chicano-Mexican Relations," in Mexico-United States Relations, ed. Purcell, pp. 88-96.

(82) Weinert, "Foreign Capital in Mexico, p. 117.

(83) Olga Pellicer de Brody, "A Mexican Perspective," in Mexico-United States Relations, ed. Purcell, pp. 6-7.

(84) Latin America Weekly Report, August 29, 1980, p. 7.

(85) Olga Pellicer de Brody, "A Mexican Perspective," p. 7.

(86) Department of Economic Studies, "Mexican-Japanese Trade Relations," p. 78.

(87) Tancer, "Regulating Foreign Investment in the Seventies," p. 209.

(88) Smith, Mexico, p. 14.

(89) Richard S. Newfarmer and Willard F. Mueller, Multinational Corporations in Brazil and Mexico: Structural Sources of Economic and Noneconomic Power, Report to the Subcommittee on Multinational Corporations of U.S. Senate Committee on Foreign Relations, 94th Congress (August 1975). Cited and discussed in Richard S. Weinert, "The State and Foreign Capital," in Authoritarianism in Mexico, ed. Reyna and Weinert, pp. 109-128.

(90) Bernardo Sepulveda and Antonio Chumacero, La inversion extranjera en Mexico (Mexico, D.F.: Fondo de Cultura Economica, 1973).

(91) Weinert, "The State and Foreign Capital," pp. 117-118.

(92) See especially two essays by Weinert: "The State and Foreign Capital" and "Foreign Capital in Mexico"; Tancer, "Regulating Foreign Investment in the Seventies"; and Douglas Bennett, Morris J. Blachman, and Kenneth Sharpe, "Mexico and Multinational Corporations: An Explanation of State Action," in Latin America and World Economy: A Changing International Order, ed. Joseph Grunwald (Beverly Hills, Calif.: Sage, 1978), pp. 257-282.

(93) Weinert, "The State and Foreign Capital," pp. 119-120.

(94) Ibid.

(95) Tancer, "Regulating Foreign Investment in the Seventies," p. 195.

(96) There is a careful analysis of all the major legislation regulating foreign investment in Tancer, "Regulating Foreign Investment in the Seventies," and Weinert, "The State and Foreign Capital." On technology transfer, see also Miguel S. Wionczek, Gerardo M. Bueno, and Jorge Eduardo Navarrete, La transferencia internacional de tecnologia: el caso de Mexico (Mexico, D.F.: Fondo de Cultura Economica, 1974).

(97) Latin America Weekly Report, January 9, 1981, p. 4.

(98) Although we have not mentioned it in any other context, Mexico is also asking that Japan increase its tourism to Mexico fourfold.

(99) See Douglas C. Bennett and Kenneth E. Sharpe, "Agenda Setting and Bargaining Power: The Mexican State Versus Transnational Automobile Corporations," World Politics 32, no. 1 (October 1979): 81.

(100) Patrick H. Heffernan, "Conflict over Marine Resources," in Mexico-United States Relations, ed. Purcell, p. 169. Our analysis is drawn almost entirely from Heffernan's excellent essay.

(101) Ibid., pp. 177, 179.

(102) C. Richard Bath, "Resolving Water Disputes," in Mexico-United States Relations, ed. Purcell, pp. 180-188. See also Stephen R. Mumme, "U.S.-Mexican Groundwater Problems: Bilateral Prospects and Implications," Journal of Interamerican Studies and World Affairs 22, no. 1 (February 1980): 31-55; and John Boslough, "Rationing a River," Science 81 2, no. 5 (June 1981): 26-37. We have relied mainly on Bath.

9 Pacific Region Building

Gavin Boyd

The magnitude of the values allocated and negotiated by enterprises and governments in the Pacific is as great as that in the West European pattern, which extends into Africa. Within the European Community, however, a relatively well-developed collective decision-making apparatus is functioning, and its orderly processes produce substantial benefits that are distributed in a fairly equitable manner and that sustain integrative behavior by the participating states. This Community is making slow although uneven progress toward more extensive policy coordination, largely in response to problems of the international political economy that have affected its members since the first energy crisis of the 1970s.

The absence of a collective decision-making system to manage the interdependencies and dependencies of the Pacific is a problem of world order, and regional order. For the European Community it is a source of competitive pressures and uncertainties, although there are advantages to be derived from the economic rivalry between the United States and Japan. For the less-developed states, including those in the Pacific, it means, among other things, that joint decision making by two powerful industrialized democracies on issues affecting the proposed New International Economic Order will remain difficult for the foreseeable future.

Political economists studying the Pacific have advocated the establishment of consultative institutions to promote broad cooperation between the open advanced and developing states of East Asia and North America. Most of the policy proposals put forward have advocated an incremental approach and have suggested that cultural dissimilarities across the Pacific would prevent the building up of an institutional framework like that in the European Community. Yet it is clear that wide-ranging policy coordination across the Pacific is becoming more and more imperative, because of the expansion of complex links between its political economies, and that endeavors to

234

promote collaboration, if successful, will tend to produce a sense of community, bridging cultural and political differences. The European experience, then, should be studied closely, and the problem of relating it to the requirements of Pacific cooperation must be approached in an imaginative fashion.

The establishment of the European Community resulted mainly from the emergence of a strong transnational elite consensus for community formation, with emphasis on market integration. In East Asia and North America, at present, there is only a small transnational elite consensus in favor of Pacific community building, and it is a significant influence on foreign policy only in Japan and Australia. A consensus in support of wide-ranging Pacific cooperation can be promoted if vigorous leadership is given, however, and this may well come from East Asian and North American elites that see the need for decisive collective choices that will provide comprehensive allocations of values, for growth and equity across the Japan-centered and U.S.-centered patterns of Pacific relations.

Transnational consensus building for broad regional cooperation in the Pacific is imperative because the vast links between political economies in this area are expanding rapidly, especially because of high growth rates in several East Asian states, particularly Japan, and because over the past decade there has been a general shift toward less cooperative and more competitive management of Pacific foreign economic policies. This has been evident most of all in Japan-U.S. relations, which have been strained by Japan's extraordinary successes in export promotion.

A consensus for Pacific cooperation must have elements of forecasting, theory, and design. This can be argued from the West European experience, in which community formation was seen as a remedy for historic antagonisms, and in which neofunctional logic was utilized for market integration, with a vision of self-sustaining integrative activity that would lead to regional political unity. In the Pacific context, forecasting has to be based on political and strategic as well as economic factors, especially because of the vulnerabilities of several East Asian states to Soviet pressures and penetration. Neofunctional logic, concerning the activation of integrative policies through the rewards of cooperation, has to be related more to the guidance of transnational production expansion than to trade liberalization, because of the great increases in foreign direct investment and intrafirm trade by international companies since the establishment of the European Community. Political designing, then, has to be directed towards institutionalizing interactive processes through which the spread of transnational production processes will be initially guided.

FORECASTING

The degrees of probability with which projections can be made in a regional context depend on the levels of continuity and coherence, and the functional qualities of the interacting forms of foreign policy behavior. Continuity and coherence in such behavior result if there are relatively uniform elite socialization processes, especially within well-developed institutions, and are made more probable by steady achievements in statecraft that sustain a public policy consensus, and by fairly constant configurations of inputs from the bureaucracy and interest groups. Predicting the outputs of highly pluralistic foreign policy processes is very difficult, and, if the polity is authoritarian and underdeveloped, the leadership's scope for arbitrary and idiosyncratic decision making and issue avoidance will be very wide.

Fairly high probability predictions can be made about Japan's foreign policy behavior because of the relatively uniform and constant value orientations of its economic and political elites, which are sustained by potent socialization processes that operate with high degrees of continuity in strong party, interest group, and bureaucratic structures. Major achievements in managing the political economy contribute to the maintenance of a policy consensus, although this is subject to stresses because of threatening displays of Soviet military power and uncertainties about the security of fuel and raw material supplies. Depending on the effects of these external problems, Japanese external policy over the next decade is likely to continue its neo-mercantilist quest for a powerful position in the international political economy, through highly competitive management of trade, investment, and monetary relations with the United States and the European Community, as well as through the expansion of overseas production bases and the export of technology to secure raw materials. The political component of this policy is likely to remain small, to minimize the risks of access to foreign markets, but can be expected to maintain the established alignment with the United States, especially for security against the Soviet threat, although with accommodative gestures toward Moscow in response to any perceived weakening of the U.S. role in the global strategic balance.(1)

The United States will almost certainly remain a highly pluralistic international actor over the next decade under shifting idiosyncratic executive direction that may vary greatly in potency and coherence. The congressional assertiveness that developed in the 1970s will continue to impose constraints on external security policy, while adding to the complexities and uncertainties of decision making on foreign economic issues. Domestic strains associated with slow economic growth, inflation, and balance of payments problems are likely to add to the difficulties of aggregating and ordering demands relating to foreign economic policy. Tensions between protectionist pressures and commitments to a relatively liberal international economic order will continue to cause ambivalence on trade and foreign investment issues, while tending to weaken the goodwill and trust of other industrialized democracies that are also alliance partners. In external security affairs, the acceptance of a somewhat inferior position in the global strategic balance, in the hope of preserving detente, is likely to be accompanied by toleration of limited Soviet direct and indirect gains in Third World areas, which in turn will affect Chinese as well as Japanese attitudes towards the USSR. Nevertheless, the U.S. positions in the international political economy and in the global strategic system will remain much stronger than those of any other industrialized democracy, and it will continue to have unequalled capabilities for wide-ranging engagement with issues across the world system.(2)

Canada's foreign policy behavior, while quite restricted in scope, will probably exhibit more overall continuity, because of the influence of more uniform elite socialization processes, and a well-established pattern of executive dependence on the permanent bureaucracy. Internal tensions associated with the Quebec problem and slow economic growth will affect management of the principal external endeavor, which will be the implementation of a more competitive foreign economic policy, especially through engagement with the problems of highly asymmetric interdependence with the United States.

Mexico, Malaysia, and Singapore, relatively open polities dominated by well-established single parties with patronage and clientelist features, but with fairly powerful leaderships, are likely to remain stable. Mexico's external policy will probably continue to emphasize aggressive engagement with the issues of heavy dependence on the United States and the assertion of a leadership role in Latin American affairs. The need to diversify external trade will probably be felt more and more strongly by Mexican decision makers, but the development of commerce with East Asian states will probably be slow. Malaysia and Singapore, institutionally more advanced than Mexico and more diversified in their foreign economic relations, but directly exposed to pressure generated by Soviet and Chinese policies, will probably tend to support trade liberalization and moves towards policy integration within the ASEAN group, while remaining politically aligned with the United States but committed, with reservations, to a concept of neutralization in Southeast Asia.(3)

Of the three authoritarian ASEAN members, Indonesia and Thailand are likely to remain bourgeois praetorian systems, with neopatrimonial features and some of the aspects of bureaucratic polities. Societal support for the military leaderships in these states will continue to be low because of the alienating effects of widespread administrative corruption, heavy repression, and toleration of gross inequities in the distribution of wealth. To cope with problems posed by Soviet and Chinese activities in Southeast Asia, the Indonesian and Thai ruling elites will continue to look to the United States for support, but the Thai policy of collaborating with China in support of anti-Vietnamese guerrillas in Cambodia will probably receive further Indonesian opposition. Meanwhile the more heavily centralized authoritarian regime in the Philippines, which is likely to retain its neopatrimonial qualities, will tend to maintain its close economic ties with the United States in a strained dependency relationship, in part because of moderate sensitivities to the Soviet presence in Indochina. Philippine economic links with the other ASEAN members will remain weak, and politically the Philippine regime will probably continue to be somewhat isolated from them. The highly protectionist trade policies of the Philippine, Thai, and Indonesian administrations, which would be difficult to liberalize, will of course hinder initiatives for market integration within the ASEAN group.

Forecasting continuity and change in the authoritarian ASEAN members is highly problematic because of the effects of neo-patrimonial, clientelist, and factional behavior on their elite socialization processes, their lack of institutional development, the inhibiting effects of insecurity on their bureaucrats, and the degrees to which the dynamics of their power struggles tend to force highly authoritarian personalities to the top, and then in effect give them wide scope for policy making at will. Basically similar interplays of political and social forces occur in China and Vietnam, but the resulting uncertainties tend to be more difficult to assess because of information problems caused by the closure of those regimes and because their intraelite conflicts tend to be more intense, due to the kind of isolation within which their leaderships operate while asserting authority on the basis of claimed ideological wisdom.

In China the relatively pragmatic group of technocrats and military figures that has been led by Deng Xiao-ping may consolidate its control, or it may be destabilized by internal divisions and opposition from leadership figures determined to prevent deradicalization. If the present ruling group does consolidate its control some institutional development may result, and an ideological consensus in support of pragmatic modernization may become established. External policy will then continue to emphasize alignment with the USA as an adversary of the USSR and as a source of technology. A shift of power to elements influenced by the Maoist tradition, however, could be followed by strong expressions of ideological hostility to the United States, as well as to the USSR, and vigorous encouragement of revolutionary violence in the Third World. With this foreign policy shift, ideology would again impose constraints on the application of a technocratic approach to modernization. Intraelite divisions, affecting the presently dominant technocratic group or a leftist successor faction, may well be increased by frustrations and fears resulting from the growth of the Soviet presence in Southeast Asia, and the USSR's acquisition of a stronger position in the central balance.(4)

Vietnam, although under a more strongly centralized and less collective leadership than that in the late Ho Chi Minh period, will probably experience more intraelite stability than China. The established high-level consensus on ideology, nationalist values, and strategy for modernization, however, may be weakened by high-level divisions over the long term because of issues in the relationship with the USSR. The ethos of the Vietnamese regime is strongly independent, and it is fairly probable that the routinized management of Soviet policy towards Vietnam will become both insensitive and demanding. Vietnamese policy, while stressing the retention of Soviet military and economic support, will probably give priority to the building up of an affinitive revolutionary movement in Thailand because of antagonism towards the Thai military elite's collaboration with Chinese-supported guerillas in Cambodia. An important secondary endeavor is likely to be the cultivation of ties with Indonesia and Malaysia, in part to reduce the political isolation that makes Vietnam heavily dependent on its connection with the USSR.

The Soviet Union will remain a strongly unified conflictual international actor, very much dependent on the projection of its military power for political purposes, because deradicalization has weakened its symbolic capabilities, and, thus, its influence on affinitive revolutionary states and movements. Serious intraelite strains will probably be experienced because of the difficulties of resolving the large succession problem, which affects the Political Bureau and the Central Committee of the Communist Party. Settlement of this issue is hindered by inadequate institutional development in the higher levels of the party, the absence of agreed rules for high-level decision making, and the intense factional contests for power that tend to be generated by the regime's high-level dynamics. Some incoherence in external policy may result from intraelite conflicts, but a high degree of continuity seems likely, because the utility of present lines of strategy has been demonstrated by the improvement of the regime's position in the global balance and its gains in Third World areas through the combination of detente diplomacy at the superpower level and engagement with affinitive and client states and movements. Major opportunities for more extensive engagement of that kind have been opened up in East Asia through the provision of military support to Vietnam and through the virtual imposition of constraints on China's use of military pressures against Vietnam. China's military weakness has thus become more evident to other Asian states, yet, largely on this account, the U.S. administration has become more cautious on matters of security cooperation with China.

A stronger Soviet naval and air presence has to be expected in Southeast Asia and in the area around Japan. Major Soviet objectives are likely to be the imposition of disruptive stress on the Chinese leadership, through hostile demonstrations of that presence, the development of greater Japanese sensitivities to the proximity of Soviet power, and the gradual removal of the U.S. presence from Southeast Asia, possibly through a forceful political campaign for neutralization of the area, on terms unfavorable to the United States and China.(5)

ALTERNATIVE REGIONAL FUTURES

The projections that can be made regarding foreign policy behavior by East Asian and North American states suggest alternative futures for the Pacific. These will be shaped by the evolution of established patterns of economic interaction and by trends in the complex interplays between Soviet conflictual behavior, the activities of revolutionary movements, and the dynamics of Pacific states that are vulnerable to Soviet penetration and pressures.

The patterns of largely constructive Pacific interaction, concerning mainly trade and investment, comprise the Japan-U.S. relationship, the Japan-centered East Asian interchanges, and the U.S.-centered North American interconnections. The Japan-U.S. relationship bridges the other two patterns, on the basis of high interdependencies, but there are asymmetries because the United States is a major intrusive actor in the Japan-centered East Asian pattern, while Japan has few interchanges with Canada and Mexico. At the transnational level there are further asymmetries because Japan-based international firms, active in East Asia and North America, operate in close partnership with their national administrations and implement vigorous expansionist strategies, while U.S.-based international firms operate in highly individualistic ways and have few active links with the U.S. government.

The productivity of all the state-to-state interactions and their degrees of concord or strain determine the degrees to which they reinforce or weaken the motivations of the participating governments, depending of course on the effects of national processes of change that may alter the policies of those governments. The most productive interactions are those in the Japan-U.S. relationship, but they are affected by serious strains, and their utility is only medium in terms of the requirements for managing the vast interdependencies in this connection.

In the Japan-U.S. relationship, trade and production interdependencies will continue to grow substantially, especially because of Japanese entrepreneurial vigor and high labor productivity, but the cultural and political factors that limit foreign penetration of the Japanese economy will remain quite effective. Each state's policy toward the other will tend to become more actively competitive, while the levels of mutual goodwill and trust will be generally moderate to low. The strongly neomercantilist ethos of the Japanese political and economic elites will be given further expression in a highly functional foreign economic policy through export promotion and rapidly expanding foreign investment. The lack of coherence and the basically liberal spirit of U.S. foreign economic policy will continue to be advantageous for Japan, yet the United States will retain strong leverage because of its great size, its capacity to resort to protectionist measures, and its importance as Japan's source of military protection against the USSR. U.S. pressures will tend to shift Japan toward a somewhat more liberal foreign economic policy, but will probably not induce the Japanese administration to adopt more expansionist monetary and fiscal policies.

The economic interaction between the two major Pacific states will probably remain basically an interplay between U.S. disjointed incrementalism, with shifting sectoral bias, and coherent Japanese execution of a large design for controlled industrial internationalization and trade. The long social distances between the two states will tend to hinder the development of cooperative approaches to the problems of harmonizing their policies, and, on the Japanese side, recognition of the difficulties of decision making in U.S. foreign economic policy will tend to motivate more vigorous implementation of the established neo-mercantilist design, for risk reduction from a position of increasing strength. The need for comprehensive joint management of the expanding interdependencies between Japan and the United States will continue to grow, however, and this will challenge the U.S. manufacturing, trading, and banking organizations to build up a national association that will express their foreign trade and investment concerns coherently.(6)

Strains in the relationship between the two major Pacific economic powers will affect their dealings with the smaller East Asian and North American states that are linked with their economies. U.S. pressures against Japan's neomercantilist policies will tend to stimulate the already vigorous application of those policies in East Asia, somewhat more so than in other parts of the Third World. The ASEAN members, South Korea, and Taiwan, because of their high-growth rates and geographic proximity, will tend to draw much Japanese investment and will assume great significance in Japan's foreign commerce. Because of the lack of cohesion between these modernizing states, however, the growing magnitude of their dependencies on Japan will entail relative declines in each one's modest bargaining power. The authoritarian administrations in some of the ASEAN governments, moreover, will tend to become more susceptible to manipulation by Japanese inter-national firms, and, especially on this account, elite and popular resentment at the Japanese economic presence will tend to increase in those states, despite the very substantial contributions that Japanese enterprises will make to economic growth.

The ASEAN group, together with South Korea and Taiwan, will continue to work for the diversification of their external economic relations, especially through increasing ties with the United States, but are likely to encounter further selective U.S. protectionism that will hinder expansion of their exports of manufactured goods. The volume of U.S. investment that is attracted, moreover, will probably remain smaller than the inflow from Japan, and its effects will not match the broad impact of the industrial complexes established by multigroup Japanese technology exports.

The lack of cooperation between the ASEAN members will continue to be advantageous for Japan, as that country's bargaining power will be maximized in separate dealings with them, and it will have more control over the expansion of its industrial establishment into their economies through bilateral dealings than it would if this spreading of its production processes had to be negotiated with the ASEAN members as a group. Of course it will be more and more imperative for the ASEAN nations to cooperate with each other for the purpose of managing their common interests in dealings with Japan, but this will continue to be difficult. The evolution of integrative behavior within the ASEAN group will be hindered by the cultural and political differences between its members, their divisions over policy towards Vietnam, and the unwillingness of the highly protectionist authoritarian members of the group to support trade liberalization, which is ac-ceptable to Malaysia and Singapore.(7)

The ASEAN group's economic interaction with the United States will probably be at a low level because of Washingto 's preoccupation with policy toward China and Japan and the difficulties of forming a common ASEAN negotiating position on issues in the relationship with the United States. Security cooperation with the United States, however, will remain highly important for Thailand, and quite significant for Indonesia and the Philippines, although U.S. military support for these ASEAN members is likely to be modest and cautious, especially because of concerns to avoid strengthening the coercive state apparatus in each of these countries and to minimize the dangers of being drawn into conflictual indirect encounters with the USSR on unfavorable terms. Yet the United States will continue to be capable of undertaking initiatives for the expansion of its ties with all the ASEAN members, and their interest in the development of these ties will tend to grow as the diversification of their foreign economic relations becomes more imperative.

In the U.S.-centered North American pattern of relations, which is not significantly penetrated by Japan at the official and transnational levels, the moderate-to-low levels of understanding and goodwill in Mexico's interactions with the United States are not likely to rise as U.S. foreign trade policy will tend to remain strongly protectionist, in the Mexican view, and Mexico will continue to be at a disadvantage because of heavy dependence on access to the U.S. market. Mexico's need to diversify its exports will increase, and the most significant opportunities for this will be offered by Japan rather than by other Latin American states, but the openness of the Japanese market during the next few years will not substantially reduce the major asymmetries in the Mexican-U.S. relationship.

Canada will have a greater need than Mexico for strong associations outside the North American context in order to diversify its foreign economic relations, but will have to contend with slow growth and with more intractable problems of economic sovereignty. The available options for Canada will be quite restricted by comparison with Mexico, as that state will retain scope for more active involvement in Latin American affairs. Little cooperation is likely to develop between Mexico and Canada, and the United States, on present indications, will probably not be inclined to foster joint decision making with those states on North American issues because the bilateral relationships with each of them can be managed more effectively than the multilateral interactions which would have to be envisaged in the North American context. In such a context, of course, Mexico and Canada would tend to have diverging perceptions of their identities of interest and of what would constitute regional as distinct from bilateral issues.

Increasing strains in U.S. relations with the European Community may well cause U.S. policy toward Canada and Mexico to become more strongly self-interested. Rising protectionist demands, it must be stressed, will tend to find expression in Washington's strongly pluralistic policy processes, reducing the normally limited attention that is given to long-term and larger issues. The North American patterns of foreign policy behavior, however, will remain basically constructive because of the strength of established U.S., Canadian, and Mexican elite commitments to cooperative interaction, with restraints on the use of leverage. In the Japan-centered East Asian pattern also, foreign policy behavior will probably continue to be collaborative, although with lower levels of trust, understanding, and goodwill, especially between the authoritarian ASEAN governments and Japan.

Both the North American and East Asian interactive patterns will be affected by conflictual and cooperative elements in the behavior of the Communist regimes, especially the USSR, and the consequences are likely to be greater in East Asia than in North America. Japan will have to contend with a stronger Soviet military presence in the immediate environment, and Thailand may well be a major object of Soviet strategy in East Asia. The evolution of the Chinese system, moreover, which will be affected by the growing projections of Soviet power, will influence the results of Soviet interactions with Japan and the ASEAN group, perhaps dramatically if there is a shift toward accommodation in Peking's behavior toward the USSR.(8)

Relatively constructive behavior, based on perceived current identities of interest, is likely to continue in China's relations with Japan and the United States, unless the Peking leadership is seriously affected by stresses deriving from Soviet gains in East Asia or is inclined to shift its policy toward the left because of those gains, and in order to acquire new influence over Asian revolutionary movements. A leftward policy shift of course would be expressed in hostility toward the ASEAN group and to any development of ASEAN ties with Japan and the United States. The effects, especially within the ASEAN group, would be inhibiting, and it would be extremely difficult for the Japanese administration to choose between the pursuit of a new detente with China and the strengthening of ASEAN ties. Meanwhile U.S. policy would be disoriented, because of established tendencies to attach high value to the China connection and failures to establish close bonds with alliance partners for the management of relations with Peking.

While China's presently constructive behavior continues, it will not significantly hinder or give impetus to the development of cooperation in the Japan-centered East Asian pattern of relations. Peking's official approval of cooperation within the ASEAN group is not likely to change, but this approval, even if expressed more positively, will probably not give any integrative motivation to the ASEAN members: their attitudes toward each other are likely to remain distrustful and only moderately cooperative. China, moreover, will have very little scope for initiative within its established network of relatively constructive interactions. Ideology, of course will continue to have restrictive effects on Peking's external communications, and, more fundamentally, on the perceptions of interest and opportunity that influence those communications.

China's interaction with the United States will continue to rank higher, for each side, than any other interchanges, except those with the USSR. The values affected will be strategic and political, rather than economic, but, despite their magnitude, levels of understanding and trust in this relationship will probably remain moderate to low, and the presently cautious forms of cooperation are unlikely to become more substantial. For the United States, choices regarding the possible expansion of this cooperation will be difficult to make because of communication problems with the Chinese, and because of uncertainties regarding Peking's behavior and the likely effects of Sino-American interchanges on Soviet policy.

The way in which China relates to the United States will largely determine the course of Chinese behavior toward Japan, since that country's strategic significance for Peking derives mainly from its military association with the United States, and Japan's commitment to support China's industrialization with large-scale technology exports is based in a large measure on an identity of interests with the United States, as well as on tacit concerns with developing a close connection with Peking that will have utility for dealings with both the United States and the USSR. For Peking, the main benefits of the connection with Japan will continue to be economic; that country's military development will be gradual and modest and thus will not significantly affect the evolution of the regional strategic balance.(9)

Soviet interaction with the United States, China, and Japan will continue to be largely conflictual. Projections of Soviet military and naval power on an increasing scale are likely to be accompanied by more aggressive use of that power for political objectives.(10) Interchanges with the United States relating to East Asia will be managed with care to prevent tensions escalating to crisis levels, but also with determination to establish a stronger presence in the region through firm assertions of influence on governments and active support for "progressive" and revolutionary movements. U.S. responses are likely to be cautious, because of higher priority concerns with the central balance and the security of Western Europe and uncertainties regarding Chinese intentions. Japanese responses, on this account, are also likely to be cautious, because of a perceived need to avoid excessive identification with U.S. security policy in East Asia and to maintain policy positions that will be relatively accommodative to the USSR by comparison with those of the United States. Chinese responses, while featuring much verbal hostility, can be expected to exhort more determined U.S. opposition to the Soviet Union, but without forms of behavior that risk provoking greater Soviet hostility. In the Sino-Soviet relationship, the imposition of disruptive stress on the Peking leadership will evidently continue to be a prime Soviet objective, to be furthered through the acquisition of a very strong presence in China's immediate environment and the weakening of Peking's bonds with both the United States and Japan.

Soviet interaction with the ASEAN members, while limited because of their interests in avoiding such engagement, will seek to increase their awareness of Vietnam as a revolutionary base in Southeast Asia, and, thus, their willingness to work toward a basis for coexistence, with renunciation of their U.S. and Chinese connections. The ASEAN members will remain too disunited to deal collectively with the USSR, and, if Thailand has to contend with a potent mix of Soviet pressures and inducements, the remaining states in the association will probably not be able to evolve a common counter strategy. This, moreover, will be all the more likely if the levels of understanding, trust, and cooperation in ASEAN relations with the United States and Japan remain low.

The USSR's opportunities for involvement in North American affairs will probably be very small; it will not be able to offer significant inducements to Mexico or Canada, in order to influence their behavior towards the United States. Nevertheless, if new leftist regimes emerge in Latin America and align with the USSR, their presence will tend to cause some changes in Mexico's foreign policy orientation. Association with these regimes may be sought by the Mexican administration, on a basis of limited ideological affinity, and to acquire stronger leverage in the relationship with the United States. Soviet opportunities for collaboration with radical groups in Latin America of course will continue to be quite extensive, as the repressive policies of this region's numerous authoritarian governments tend to generate widespread social discontent.

An important advantage for the USSR's overall strategy, especially with reference to East Asia and Latin America, is the lack of cooperation between governments whose common interests are threatened by the expansion of Soviet power and by Soviet involvement with revolutionary and "progressive" movements. On present indications, the absence of solidarity between the various non-Communist administrations will continue to benefit the USSR, while of course the oppressive character of some of those governments will entail vulnerabilities to Soviet-supported political violence. From the U.S. point of view, these vulnerabilities, particularly those visible in Indonesia, the Philippines, Thailand, and South Korea, discourage close identification with the insufficiently legitimized administrations and will continue to do so unless there is a basic U.S. policy shift toward vigorous engagement with the problems of imposing accountability on those governments.

The general lack of security cooperation has dangerous implications for East Asia, and especially for the ASEAN group. Soviet advances in their area, through the support of revolutionary warfare and the development of influence over endangered governments, will tend to lower the morale and weaken the strength of those ASEAN governments that fail to respond in solidarity, and the disarray in that association will tend to discourage U.S. initiatives for improved security in Southeast Asia. The United States, it must be stressed, will be the only power whose resources and communication capabilities will be sufficient to support large-scale diplomacy for the promotion of defense collaboration in East Asia, but the evolution of a will to do so may be difficult because of the diverging approaches to external security issues among the major participants in the U.S. policy process.

Altogether, then, on present indications the security and economic interdependencies of the East Asian and North American states will not

be adequately managed. Interactions relating to both forms of interdependence will remain confined to bilateral dealings that largely
exclude regional interests, and engagement with the issues in those
bilateral contexts will tend to be excessively influenced by concepts of
national and even sectoral advantage and will be limited in scope
because of common orientations toward incremental and disjointed
decision making, except in Japan. Over time, substantial and partial
issue avoidance will result in an accumulation of unresolved problems,
and these will be added to as the economic interdependencies assume
larger dimensions and greater complexity. In addition, increasing strains
between Pacific states on account of failures in interdependence
management will tend to hinder the growth of a sense of community,
thus indirectly affecting the possibilities for broad security cooperation.

POLICY PLANNING: IMPERATIVES AND PROBLEMS

The futures that have to be envisaged for East Asia and North America
raise questions about the possibilities for policy planning, especially by
the United States and Japan. Well-developed policy-planning functions
can infuse holistic perspectives into decision processes that tend to be
dominated by preoccupations with the comparative political advantages
of alternative incremental options. The extent to which policy planners
can promote broad and long-range concerns, however, will depend on
the importance they acquire in the managerial, exchange, symbolic and
other dimensions of the policy process.

Japan has highly developed capabilities for foreign policy planning,
and such planning is a constant and potent factor in the policy process.
Its focus, however, is on foreign economic relations, and its strongly
neomercantilist value orientation, which derives from intense awareness of dependence on external resources and fuels, is somewhat
insensitive to East Asian and Pacific interests. In terms of endowments
and external associations, Japan is seriously disadvantaged by
comparison with the members of the European Community and the
United States, and accordingly has very strong incentives to gain a
powerful independent position in the global political economy and to
minimize the risks of inconsiderate treatment by other industrialized
democracies in joint decision making on global and regional issues.

The scope for Japanese economic diplomacy in the Pacific, moreover, is limited, as has been stressed, because of cultural differences
and the extent to which the expansion of the Japanese economy into
East Asia is seen as an intrusive process rather than as one open to
collaboration and partnership. This is not to deny that the regional
spread of the Japanese economy brings very substantial benefits, but it
does mean that Japan would have difficulty in providing leadership for
the collective management of Pacific interdependencies.

In the U.S. foreign policy process, planning functions tend to be
subordinated to current operational tasks, especially because planning

officials have incentives to advance their careers through such operational involvement and because those tasks tend to receive all the attention of the high decision makers.   As political appointees with short tenure, relatively unacquainted with the experience and wisdom of the permanent staffs and very sensitive to the political interests of the chief executive, the high decision makers tend to be engrossed in the problems of managing foreign relations through incremental choices on immediate issues. These choices are made under pressure, due to overload and bureaucratic rivalries, as well as the complications of congressional involvement, and accordingly there is little openness to the thinking of planners on long-term and larger issues.(11)

For the implementation of a major design, therefore, strong leadership and a broad consensus are necessary, but these requirements are difficult to meet in the US system . Leadership energies tend to be diverted into the politics of building coalitions for the support of legislative programs, and any consensus that develops within Congress on external policy tends to be fragile because the commitments of its participants tend to be subordinated to their domestic interests. A bureaucratic consensus is very difficult to promote because of the diverging perspectives of the political appointees at the higher levels and their limited receptivity to inputs from the permanent staffs. Within the business elite, moreover, the growth of a policy consensus as extensive as that in Japan is greatly hindered by the proliferation of interest groups and by the degree to which the policy process draws them into close interaction with legislators and bureaucrats on very specific issues.

In the U.S. polity there is an acute need for strong aggregating structures that will order the preferences of the highly diversified industrial, commercial, banking, and service interests. Such structures are necessary for the making of coherent and functional policies, and, if they can be established, they will help the growth of a basic policy consensus. Tensions between economic groups in the United States, because of slow growth, inflation, and balance of payments deficits, are making the need for effective aggregating structures more urgent. If such structures can be established, they will have a special responsibility for evolving holistically functional orientations on issues of foreign economic policy, to be articulated to Congress and the bureaucratic agencies shaping such policy. Initiatives for building up vigorous national economic associations with the necessary broad concerns could be taken very appropriately by groups with a Pacific focus, because the most significant opportunities for innovation in U.S. foreign economic policy are being presented in relationships with Japan, the ASEAN group, Australia, Canada, and Mexico.

Policy-planning capabilities in the Mexican, Canadian, Australian, and ASEAN foreign affairs establishments are quite small, narrowly focused, and somewhat isolated from the major economic interest groups. In most cases the planners tend to be firmly subordinated to executive direction and accordingly are often pressed into operational responsibilities. Opportunities for engagement with the larger and long-term questions of foreign economic policy are thus quite limited, and of course perceptions of those questions are influenced by awareness of the relatively confined scope within which each of these states functions in Pacific affairs.

The opportunities for transnational activities by nongovernmental Pacific groups, especially in the United States and Japan, must therefore assume great importance for private individuals and officials who see the vast potential for cooperation between East Asian and North American states. While strong national economic associations in the United States assist the development of more coherent and functional policies, hopefully they will interact very productively with similar organizations in Japan. In collaboration with those Japanese associations, the major U.S. economic organizations should be able to encourage business associations in the smaller Pacific states to join in consultations for the development of coordinated approaches to Pacific trade and investment issues and for the articulation of these approaches to Pacific governments.

Private regional policy planning, for the coordination if not integration of national economic policies on a Pacific basis, could extend to the promotion of industrial complementarity, on a broad regional scale, with emphasis on rationalizing the spread of transnational production processes. This second type of planning could indeed have far-reaching effects and could well take priority, because commitments to Pacific cooperation at the governmental level in most of the East Asian and North American states are likely to develop slowly in response to proposals from private groups advocating such a policy.

At present the most active transnational organization that is seeking to promote Pacific collaboration at the official and nongovernmental levels is the Pacific Basin Economic Council, a network of industrial, banking, and commercial organizations in the United States, Japan, Australia, Canada, New Zealand, Mexico, and the Philippines.(12) The National Committee of this Council in the United States is not yet widely linked with the business communities in the United States, but it is providing significant degrees of leadership for the regional association.

REGIONAL DESIGNING

The advocates of Pacific economic cooperation are mostly Japanese, U.S., and Australian scholars and businessmen. Many of them are active in the Pacific Basin Economic Council, and their principal objective is to promote regular multilateral consultations between Pacific states with open market economies, so that more collaborative if not integrative foreign economic policies will result. Such consultations, they hope, will increase trust between the participating governments and make those administrations more sensitive to each other's interests, while imposing restraints on each one's pursuit of its own advantage. The need for cooperation is stressed with reference to the sequences of narrowly conceived unilateral measures by Pacific states that harmed each other's interests during the 1970s and to the expanding dimensions of their production, trade, and policy interdependencies. Recognizing that several Pacific governments are not yet willing to engage in regional consultations, however, some of the concerned individuals and groups are attempting to draw officials from Pacific administrations into private forums for discussions of policy issues affecting the common interests of East Asian and North American states. For the present, the development of such forums is hindered by the reluctance of several ASEAN governments to participate in broadly regional consultations that would be joined by the United States and Japan, and by the strong orientation of U.S. business elites, bureaucrats, and scholars toward the preservation of a liberal international economic order, rather than toward involvement in trade blocs.

The sponsorship of private forums on Pacific cooperation, with some involvement by officials from the East Asian and North American administrations, may well introduce some significant new governmental inputs into the foreign economic policies of those administrations. In most cases, however, the strength of these inputs will depend on the personal influence and competence of the concerned officials, the perceived status of the private forums, and the domestic political forces shaping each state's external relations. Representatives from the foreign affairs establishments of Pacific states that are sent to such forums will normally have high rank but will not be drawn from the top decision-making groups unless the private forums begin to articulate demands from powerful regional economic associations. Policy inputs from these officials will interact with those of numerous other bureaucrats who will not have been influenced by the private regional forums and will also interact with the demands of legislators and interest groups whose outlooks, in many of the Pacific states, will be narrowly focused. The multilateral consultations between officials from Pacific states at private regional forums, moreover, are likely to be short, lacking in continuity, and exploratory rather than substantive; hence they are not likely to lead to sustained informal intergovern-mental exchanges. Progress towards the frequent substantive consulta-tions desired by most advocates of Pacific cooperation is thus likely to be difficult if the mechanisms used are private forums.

Privately sponsored consultations involving Pacific officials and nongovernmental representatives are proposed by several advocates of regional cooperation in the United States and Japan, not only because of hopes that considerable policy coordination will result, but also because of beliefs that more ambitious attempts to promote Pacific integration will fail. The cultural differences between Pacific states, the sharp contrasts between their levels of economic development, and the long distances separating many of them are considered to be insuperable barriers to the formation of an economic union like the European Community. Such a union, it is felt, would be possible only between states with strong societal affinities and similar levels of modernization, in geographic proximity. In the United States, scholarly literature on the management of this nation's interdependencies with neighboring states and with Japan gives little attention to the European Community's achievements in policy integration, and that subject is largely ignored in Japanese studies of the possibilities for Pacific collaboration.

Nevertheless, the experience of the European Community can provide a basis for political designing to establish a Pacific economic union, and, for the open market political economies of North America and East Asia, the strong position of the European Community in the international political economy is a <u>challenge</u> to move toward comprehensive regional economic cooperation. The logic of this choice is quite potent in terms of U.S. and Japanese interests, and it adds to the significance of the lessons that can be drawn from the European Community's history for the promotion of integrative activity in the Pacific.

The first lesson of the European Community is that the development of a common market results in substantial trade <u>creation</u>, not merely trade diversion, thereby giving impetus to economic growth, especially by stimulating the spread of transnational enterprises within the integrated market.(13) In the European Community the trade creation occurred despite the persistence of deep antagonisms toward Germany among the states that had been recent victims of its aggression and despite a rapid growth of trade between most of the members and the United States, the largest and most vigorous political economy outside the Community. If a common market began to emerge in the Pacific there would be no intense antagonisms to hinder the growth of trade and no dynamic economies outside the grouping would exert attractions or assume intrusive roles that would hinder the development of inter-dependencies between the members. The long distances between many Pacific countries would not be significant hindrances to commerce and would certainly pose few problems in trade between the United States and Japan; the communication problems that would persist because of those distances, moreover, could be gradually overcome through intensive use of currently available technologies for the transmission of data, the holding of consultations, and the conclusion of contracts.

The second lesson of the European Community is that the expansion of transnational production, relative to trade flows, which is an established trend in the international political economy, tends to be increased by market integration.   Trade liberalization increases opportunities for transnational enterprises and generates pressures for the liberalization of investment flows. Transnational enterprises based <u>outside</u> the integrated market benefit as well as those based within its member states, depending on the policies of those states regarding the interests of national firms, and the common policies of the grouping toward foreign direct investment. Administrations in the member states tend to favor transnational enterprises based in their own territories, but with restraints imposed by interdependencies with other member states and with outside countries.(14) Disparities in the distribution of gains from trade liberalization cause member governments in both the advantaged and disadvantaged states to increase their emphasis on the protection and support of locally based international firms and to resort to moderately discriminatory measures against transnational enterprises based in other members and in outside states; but the likely costs of provoking retaliatory measures necessitate caution, and the scope for such measures tends to be reduced by the growth of collective decision mechanisms for the management of the common market.

With the expansion of transnational production, increasing shares of the commerce between the interdependent states become intrafirm trade, which is less hindered by tariff and nontariff barriers. At the same time, pressures for the reduction of such barriers tend to increase within the interest groups of the states in the preferential trade grouping unless strong currents of economic nationalism are generated by disparities in the distribution of gains from trade liberalization.

For the Pacific context, in which the development of a common political will to liberalize trade would be difficult, the spread of transnational production that has occurred in the European Community is especially significant insofar as it has increased cross-national functional links between industrial establishments, raised the levels of policy interdependence, and generated pressures for the removal of outstanding barriers to trade. If, in the Pacific, impetus could be given to a more extensive expansion of transnational production than is presently occurring, and if this expansion could be guided according to a coherent plan for complementary industrial growth, the Pacific economies would become more closely integrated, the imperatives to coordinate national policies would become stronger, and measures to liberalize trade would become politically more feasible. Political designing for a Pacific economic union, then, will have to emphasize the encouragement, support, and guidance of expansion in the area by transnational enterprises. This, however, will have to be part of a larger plan that will draw on the total experience of the European Community.

The market integration within the European Community has had a laissez-faire basis, and the principal consequence has been a very uneven distribution of the benefits from trade liberalization.(15) This is the third lesson of the Community's experience, and its importance is very great because the differences in levels of industrial development between the Pacific nations are much larger than those in Western Europe. Trade liberalization would be much more difficult politically in the Pacific, and, if it began, the problems of redistributing the benefits of such liberalization on an equitable basis would be of greater dimensions. But this does not mean that trade liberalization should not be sought. The conclusions to be drawn are that trade liberalization in the Pacific will have to be selective and graduated and that the promoters of economic union in that area must seek to generate a strong common will to regulate the liberalization of trade and to redistribute the gains from freer trade in the interests of the weaker economies.

Trade liberalization between the United States, Japan, Canada, Australia, and New Zealand could be substantial and immediate, but as it proceeded major problems would be confronted. Japan would benefit greatly from wider access to the other markets, while its own would remain relatively protected by cultural factors and by the well-established neomercantilist orientation of the business-government partnership. The unfavorable balance in U.S. trade with Japan would grow, but U.S. exports to Canada, Australia, and New Zealand would increase. Unless protected, moreover, efficient moderately sized industries in those smaller economies would be absorbed or eliminated by U.S. and Japanese firms. The articulation of Canadian, Australian, and New Zealand interests in Pacific trade negotiations of course would not be supported by strong bargaining power, and equitable consideration of those interests would be ensured only through the building up of structures and norms that would institutionalize Pacific economic interactions. Trade liberalization promoted through informal consultations, it should be observed, would not alter the uneven distribution of bargaining power in the Pacific context: equitable terms of participation in Pacific economic interactions would <u>necessitate</u> appropriate institutional arrangements, and these would have to be supported by a common political will, based on feelings of regional identity and obligation.

Within the ASEAN group the very slow process of trade liberalization that began in the late 1970s cannot move faster unless there are drastic changes in the policies of the highly protectionist authoritarian regimes that constitute a majority in this grouping. The necessary shifts away from protectionism, moreover, will have to be accompanied by measures to enhance the positions of national firms in these countries and to orient those firms more toward trade <u>within</u> the association, as excessive proportions of their foreign commerce are handled by externally based transnational enterprises, and the potential for commodity exchanges within the association is utilized only to a small degree. Meanwhile slow trade liberalization within the ASEAN group will restrict the possibilities for reducing trade barriers between ASEAN members and the other Pacific states, and those possibilities will also remain limited because of the pressures from interest groups in the advanced Pacific states that sustain discriminatory tariffs and nontariff restrictions against the primary exports and low technology manufactures of developing countries. A solution to the problems of trade liberalization and expansion between the ASEAN members and the industrialized Pacific states, however, can be envisaged on the basis of an improved version of the Lome II Agreement between the European Community and its associated African, Caribbean, and Pacific states. This would give the ASEAN members substantially better access to the U.S., Japanese, Canadian, Australian, and New Zealand markets for manufactured goods and primary products and would provide compensation for export losses by ASEAN members in such trade, while pledging developmental aid, at significant levels, that would help to improve the export capabilities of the ASEAN group.

A further point to be drawn from the experience of the European Community is that an economic union in the Pacific would be affected by problems resulting from uneven growth. The uneven distribution of trade gains would be accompanied by the emergence of greater disparities between the larger and more dynamic industrial centers and the more backward areas. This would require corrective action, especially through the ordering of investment flows, and, as with the problems of redistributing the gains from trade, structural arrangements would be required in order to institutionalize appropriate terms of participation in a collective decision-making mechanism for the Pacific. The alternative course would be policy coordination between the concerned states through consultations, but, as has been suggested with reference to the gains from trade, the consultative framework would not entail any alteration in the distribution of bargaining resources that places the smaller states at a disadvantage. In the European Community, a Development Fund is utilized for allocations to increase growth in backward areas, but such forms of aid do not meet all the requirements for promoting balanced growth. The volume of assistance is limited to what is feasible under the Community's unanimity rules, and the utility of that assistance depends very much on the quality of each receiving state's industrial policies.

A fifth lesson that can be seen in the European Community's experience is that the expansion of activities by transnational enterprises operating within the integrated market increases the need for collective regulation of these firms. Because of the spread of their activities, such firms can evade taxes, especially through transfer pricing; they can establish monopolistic or oligopolistic market positions; and they can avoid or limit cooperation with the overall developmental policies of host governments. The centralized controls, financial resources, management skills, and technology of transnational enterprises enable them to contribute very actively to the growth, diversification, and integration of national economies. Their managements, however, have to cope with heavy taxation in states whose governments are inclined toward expansionist monetary and fiscal policies and with regulatory measures that can be burdensome and discriminatory. Accordingly, there are incentives to circumvent or compensate for the controls of home and host governments, particularly through transfer pricing and the exploitation of market advantages, as well as through the extraction of concessions from governments soliciting direct investments. Multiple uncertainties posed by the behavior of home and host governments as well as by market instabilities increase the incentives to evade regulation. In the European Community little has been done to meet the need for collective regulation of the transnational enterprises, but national administrations, especially those in West Germany and France, have sought to develop very close working relations with international firms based in their territories.(16) In a Pacific economic union, transnational enterprises operating within the Southeast Asian members would continue to have extensive opportunities to exploit the weaknesses of their host administrations and would tend to utilize these opportunities in order to reduce the risks of loss through political strife or arbitrary changes in official policy. In addition, the outstanding problems of regulating the transnational enterprises active in the advanced Pacific states would require collective attention. An important implication, then, is that considerable institutional development would be needed in a Pacific economic union in order to ensure appropriate collective engagement with the problems of evolving and implementing common policies on international firms.

The requirement for institutional development can also be stressed with reference to the sixth conclusion to be drawn from the European Community's record, namely, that the beginnings of cooperation, for the harmonizing or integration of policies, increase policy interdependence as well as production and trade interdependencies. Once policy coordination starts on trade, industrial, and monetary issues, each participating state has incentives to continue sharing in the benefits of that collaboration, unless these are seen to be distributed inequitably or are outweighed by heavy costs. Of course each member of the grouping will have an interest in improving its bargaining position by resorting to threats of noncooperation if its essential demands are not met, but constraints on the expression of such threats will be imposed by the increased interdependence that will have been accepted with the initial ventures in cooperation. Meanwhile, depending on the nature of the coordinated policies, they will tend to increase and diversify the links between the economic processes of the participating states through commerce and the spread of transnational production. These increased interdependencies and the policy interdependencies will require management, through more extensive cooperation, but whether this will develop will depend very much on cost/benefit perceptions by the participating governments and on the level of institutional development in the structures within which those governments interact.(17)

In a Pacific grouping, policy coordination that begins with measures to promote industrial complementarity and liberalize trade will increase policy interdependence, but with much greater asymmetries than in the European Community because of differences in size and levels of development between the Pacific states. The commitments of those states to policy integration, moreover, would probably be weaker than those of the European Community members at their current phase of evolution, and the Pacific regional institutions would no doubt be less developed. Hence the growth of production and trade interdependencies, if it occurs through transnational cooperative private planning, will assume great importance as a source of pressures for wider policy coordination and, hopefully, as a source of guidance for the development of regional institutions to promote policy cooperation. This, it should be stressed, will depend on the degree to which the promoters of regional private planning become committed to the building of an international community, with concerns for questions of equity affecting the interests of smaller and less developed states.

The seventh conclusion that can be derived from the evolution of the European Community concerns the bargaining that develops on policy, production, trade, and monetary issues. This bargaining involves coalition behavior, the linking of issues, the use of pressures and inducements, the maintenance of restraints on the development of common institutions, and general reliance on confederal decision making supported by intergovernmental consultations.(18) In the European Community most of the impetus for continued policy collaboration comes from the Franco-German coalition, which is based on a complex and extensive identity of interests and which maintains issue linkages that are most visible in the Common Agricultural Policy. France is the main source of restraints on the development of common institutions, and in this regard Britain's behavior is in effect supportive of French policy.

In a Pacific economic union there would be a considerable basis for ASEAN fears that a U.S.-Japan coalition would use its great bargaining power to dominate the grouping. Such fears could be overcome by the development of greater cohesion within the ASEAN group, the promotion of strong bonds between that association and the smaller advanced Pacific states, the assumption of Lome II-type obligations to the ASEAN group by the industrialized members of the grouping, and the building up of strong institutions that would ensure appropriate scope for participation in collective decision making for the smaller and weaker Pacific states. During the formation of a Pacific economic union the apprehensions of the ASEAN governments would have to be relieved by firm assurances from the transnational promoting groups that the evolving community would be based on commitments by the advanced members to foster and support integration among the ASEAN members, to assist the modernization of the ASEAN group, and to give it a strong voice in the regional structures.

Institutional development, it must be stressed, would assume very great importance in an emerging Pacific economic community, especially to compensate for the lack of societal bonds between participating states, the long social distances between them, and their differences in levels of industrialization, as well as to aggregate, order, and give thrust to proposals for policy integration while maintaining patterns of multiple accountability that would cause each participating government to be sensitive to the interests of the others. In the European Community, institutional development has lacked coherence and has been insufficiently functional, for reasons that have significance in the Pacific context. The intentions of the founders of the Community were that there would be orderly progress toward institutional integration, with the Commission assuming more and more powers as the common will to integrate policies became stronger, and with the emergence of a regional executive responsible to an elected European Parliament. The policies of the members, however, became rather narrowly self-interested after the late 1950s; very assertive nationalism, roused by de Gaulle, was expressed in French behavior, and the other members, obliged to be more concerned with their own advantage, were influenced by the uneven distribution of benefits from trade liberalization. With the decline of confidence in collective goodwill, there was general opposition to the development of the Commission's roles. The continuing expansion of interdependencies, however, and the emergence of serious external challenges, including the 1973 oil crisis, obligated the setting up of consultative arrangements to facilitate policy coordination without enhancing the position of the Commission. The main result was the establishment of a system entitled Political Cooperation, which expressed both needs to consult and desires to avoid institutional development that would limit the freedom of national governments.

In a Pacific community, national administrations would tend to be strongly oriented toward the pursuit of self-interest, with restrictive implications for the development of regional institutions, and levels of mutual trust and understanding would be medium to low. Meeting the great need for regional structures with advanced aggregating, processing, and output capabilities would thus require vigorous promotional activity by Pacific associations of political and economic groups and the development of collective private planning, under the sponsorship of those associations, on a scale that would activate pressures within the member governments for broad policy coordination, and, then, for the structuring of such collaboration on a permanent basis.

For the political designing of a Pacific community it will be imperative to aim at comprehensive and orderly institutional development, so that the structural and functional problems of the European Community will not be encountered. Needs for the wider management of interdependencies cannot be met within the European Community's present pattern of institutions, and advancement from that basically confederal system of decision making to the establishment of a federal type executive will be extremely difficult because the growth of transnational bonds between societies in this grouping has not led to a substantial regionalization of their major political movements and interest groups. In the Pacific context, then, the energetic private diplomacy that is clearly necessary will have to be directed toward the building of regional institutions with substantial powers at a fairly rapid pace, before there is any slackening of the enthusiasms that will have been roused for such an economic union and before major issues of redistribution and allocation are posed in trade and investment policies. An incremental approach, promoting policy coordination through informal consultations, is not likely to have much influence on national decision making, and any policy harmonization that does result will probably not be sufficiently rewarding to generate commitments to wider collaboration.

TRANSNATIONAL COLLABORATION

Transnational enterprises tend to be more rational international actors than their home and host governments, whose decision making is more cybernetic, that is, more a matter of disjointed and sectorally biased incrementalism. This is not to deny that high order values are mostly excluded from the decision processes of managements in international firms and that their relations with governments are instrumental and manipulative. In the pursuit of their own interests, however, and especially when collaborating with other international firms, these transnational enterprises do extend, contract, and diversify their operations coherently, and the functional links they establish between their operations in different countries tend to increase the interdependencies of those countries in an orderly fashion. Large and growing shares of international trade are managed by these firms, moreover, and their deliveries to the markets of host countries through transnational production are becoming larger than total trade volumes.(19)

In an emerging Pacific economic union, transnational enterprises would assume vital roles. For the promotion of industrial complementarity between the participating states, the progressive integration of their production processes, cross-nationally, the articulation and aggregation of interests extending across the region, and the support of governmental efforts to develop common policies, international firms could perform very significant functions, especially if given strong leadership through a Pacific association of business and political groups. A special responsibility of such leadership would be to promote cooperation and restrain competition between international firms based in Pacific countries, so as to rationalize the spread of their production processes and the expansion of their commerce and promote operating codes that would be in harmony with the basic interests of national governments.

Pacific associations of economic and political groups can encourage and support collective planning of investment and trade activities by international firms based in North America and East Asia. Coherent large-scale results would require general and constructive participation by Pacific transnational enterprises, and of course this would be difficult to achieve, as many of those firms would engage in or work against the planning endeavor as members of rival coalitions and under the influence of diverse relationships with their home governments, and with interests that would be affected by extensive private planning as well as by resulting forms of governmental regulation.

The principal appeal that can be made to the managements of international firms based in North America and East Asia is that through broad collaboration for rationalized expansion and trading they can share in large-scale collective benefits, moderate their competition, and increase their capacities to cope with any onerous regulation by governments. To individual managements, of course, the advantages to be gained from noncooperative, obstructive, and collusive strategies may well seem larger and more certain, and it may appear to be imperative to oppose regionalized private planning because of fears that the process would be dominated by unfriendly groups. Nevertheless, the case for accepting and participating in such planning can be made very persuasive through educational and promotional work by private groups, especially those associated with the Pacific Basin Economic Council. These groups, moreover, may well be able to exert influence on both governments and international firms so as to pose incentives that will make the planning process a more and more attractive venture for transnational enterprises.

The specific incentives to which international firms will respond, in the initial stages of promotional activity by advocates of private regional planning, will depend on the organizational strength and general orientation of the sponsoring associations and on the interactions that develop between interested transnational enterprises and governments. The greater the strength, unity, and firmness of purpose demonstrated by the sponsoring associations, the more potent will be their capacities to enlist cooperation from international firms based in the Pacific.

The building of a strong Pacific network of groups working for regional cooperation, it must be stressed, will require vigorous and sustained promotional and educational activity by private associations, especially in the United States. But, before such activity becomes extensive, the concerned associations may well be able to sponsor collaborative planning by a number of transnational enterprises in the Pacific for orderly marketing and for complementarity in the spread of production processes, with emphasis on ventures offering substantial and stable returns. The planning process, then, would tend to draw in other firms, especially in related areas of specialization.

The managements of most transnational enterprises seek to expand through the acquisition of more and more extensive controls over foreign markets, especially through the spread and diversification of manufacturing and sales, although impulses to diversify tend to be moderated by concerns with exploiting the advantages of specialization and by desires to preserve strong central direction. Competitive relationships between international firms discourage collaboration, but collaboration sponsored by independent groups may succeed through the encouragement of arrangements for market division and specialization. Such arrangements will offer benefits that will depend on host government policies, and these will be influenced in varying degrees by the concerns of national firms, but of course the collaborating international enterprises will have incentives to seek understandings with the host administrations.

The objectives and strategies of the managements of international firms express economic imperatives and the value orientations of business subcultures that are mostly related to national cultures. The principal economic imperative is to secure steady modest returns while strengthening market controls and reducing risks through expansion and diversification, but of course perceptions of the practical implications of this imperative are affected by the behavior of other firms and of host and home governments. Managers of Japanese international firms are always conscious of their ties with their national administration and of their actual or potential links with other Japanese transnational enterprises, and relate to managers of West European and North American international firms in a highly competitive fashion. Managers of U.S. transnational enterprises exhibit a competitiveness that derives from intense awareness of the need for self-reliance, in the absence of government support, and would be less willing than their Japanese counterparts to pursue their interests within production sharing and market division agreements based on regional private planning.(20) Restraints imposed by U.S. antitrust laws, moreover, would tend to discourage U.S. managers from participation in the large-scale collaborative arrangements that could result from private planning on a Pacific basis. Nevertheless, the administrations of U.S. international firms are being challenged to respond to the vast expansion of Japanese transnational enterprises and to related large-scale exports of Japanese technology in the Pacific, and the interests of these U.S. firms will be best served if their responses are collaborative.   But the fears of smaller Pacific states about the dangers of U.S.-Japanese collaboration will have to be relieved, and the promoters of regional private planning will have to insist on understandings regarding the interests of national firms and the public policy concerns of national governments. These latter concerns, and the scale of the regional private planning, will tend to draw official representatives of the Pacific states into the planning process, and this indeed should be encouraged by the advocates of such planning.

The main reason why the promoters of regional private planning should seek to draw in governmental representatives is that the promoters themselves will tend to <u>lose control</u> of the collaborative processes that they initiate between transnational enterprises, as these firms develop enthusiasm for joint and multilateral arrangements that begin to cartelize the Pacific. With interests being pursued autonomously, such enterprises will lack sensitivity to the concerns of host governments and national firms, unless obliged to interact, at least on a consultative basis, with official representatives of the Pacific states.   The sponsors of the planning process, however, must exert themselves to ensure that governmental efforts to influence if not regulate the growth of cooperation between international firms will be collective rather than unilateral, so that a Pacific economic <u>community</u> will become established.

The tasks of the private planning promoters can be presented more specifically and with more emphasis on their growth and equity aspects if there is some reference to the operation of international firms in the European Community. In that community there has been no regional political force working to promote collaboration for regional specialization and orderly marketing: governments have been pursuing their own interests rather independently, and transnational enterprises have been seeking profit on a basis of all round competitiveness. In particular, the West European international firms have been adapting to each national administration's protectionist/neomercantilist practices, taking measures to preserve divisions between national markets for oligopolistic advantages while utilizing nontariff barriers that separate those markets, and responding to government subsidies designed to attract foreign investment and, in effect, to limit foreign market penetration through trade. Restrictive business practices implemented by these firms, in excess of or in conflict with the policies of host governments, offset the contributions these transnational enterprises make to West European integration. In East Asia basically similar behavior is evident among the international firms operating within the ASEAN group and would have to be anticipated within a Pacific economic union. The promoters of private regional planning thus must utilize their influence and leverage to ensure, as far as possible, that the governmental involvement in the planning and regulation of transnational production processes and trade will become regionally integrative rather than discriminatory and protective.

If the influence of national administrations and of the planning promoters is not sufficient to guide the development of production and trade arrangements between international firms operating in the Pacific, the outcome of the planning venture may be an assortment of cooperating and conflicting cartels in various stages of development. These could present such formidable challenges to the regulatory concerns of national administrations that the evolution of common policies would be very difficult, and each government would thus be inclined to rely on unilateral measures, instead of adopting a more integrative orientation. The rational choice of regional governmental collaboration would tend to be more feasible for each participating administration if the planning effort had been vigorous enough to produce a coherent process of cartelization that was already susceptible to the influence of concerned governments.

STRUCTURES AND FUNCTIONS

As Pacific governments attempt to guide the development of activities by transnational enterprises in East Asia and North America, the sponsors of private regional planning must endeavor to promote cooperation between those administrations and must seek to institutionalize such collaboration at a significant pace, while promoting regional solidarity. Initially it would be appropriate to aim at policy integration through a Pacific Council of Ministers, comprising representatives from participating governments, and through the aggregating and planning functions that would be assumed by a Pacific Commission similar to the Commission of the European Community. This Commission would be a bureaucratic organization capable of autonomously eliciting proposals from political and economic groups within the member states and of interacting vigorously with their administrations and with the Pacific Council of Ministers.

In the planning of institutions for Pacific cooperation, emphasis must be placed on the generation of support for the intended structures, through the promotion of a transnational consensus for community formation. The support that will be forthcoming after the institutions are set up will depend on general satisfaction with the terms of involvement in the collective decision making and on the benefits of that decision making, as well as on the capacities of the regional institutions to communicate meaning and commitment to participating national elites.

The political and economic groups sponsoring collective private planning in the Pacific will have to become the promoters of a consensus for community formation. This will require organizational and publicity work on a much larger scale than will be necessary for the development of regional private planning, and of course it will be difficult because of the absence of affinities between major political parties in the Pacific states and the cultural dissimilarities between most of those states. The principal task will be the building of a consensus within the United States, with emphasis on the nation's need for strong economic bonds with Japan and with the immediate neighbors – Canada and Mexico – and on the growth of the European Community as a powerful force in the international political economy that is in effect challenging the United States to strengthen its own bargaining position in that economy.

The United States is the principal center of a vast process of internationalization that is integrating knowledge in the humanities and the social sciences, through wide-ranging intellectual exchanges aided by modern technology. In addition, the United States is at the center of vast international flows of information within and between trans-national enterprises, governments, national firms, research institutes, and political groups relating to trade, investment, technological development, and monetary affairs that influence private and official decision making throughout the global political economy. Of the other major centers in these two globalizing processes, Japan is the most dynamic, although culturally the most isolated, and therefore a focus on interchanges with Japan is likely to become an increasingly prominent feature of the U.S. role in each vast pattern of cultural, scientific, and operational interactions. Leadership by academic, economic, and political groups within the United States could strengthen that focus on Japan, and thus could provide the main element that would be needed for a consensus in favor of a Pacific Community. Such leadership could stress the promotion of private efforts to integrate, on a regional scale, the economic, technological, scientific, and political information flows of the Pacific, for increasingly comprehensive private and public planning.

A transnational integrative consensus, linking especially elites in the United States and Japan on the basis of partnership at the center of global information flows and cultural interactions, will support structures for Pacific cooperation. This support, hopefully, will help to counteract any tendencies by participating governments to restrict the competence of the regional structures they establish. Such tendencies are serious hindrances to integrative advances by the European Community, and they result from the self-interested efforts of governmental leaders to maximize the benefits of cooperation through incremental confederal decision making, within limitations set by cybernetic rather than rational methods of policy management – disjointed, sectorally biased, and narrowly focused on disaggregated short-term issues.

A Pacific Council of Ministers, comprising representatives of each national executive, will be essential for continuing policy coordination by the participating governments and for the development of common policies to be implemented by a Pacific Commission. Occasional meetings of Pacific government representatives, it must be stressed, would not lead to substantial ongoing policy collaboration and could well cause much frustration, disenchantment, and issue avoidance. Frequent and regular meetings would be necessary, and these could begin on the basis of general understandings regarding the need for policy harmonization on trade, investment, monetary, and industrial issues and for the drafting of a treaty to define areas of competence for the Council. As in the European Community, unanimity would be necessary for decision making, since without such an understanding the participation of the smaller Pacific states would be doubtful, but impetus towards achievement through collective choices would be provided by the intergovernmental interactions that would develop across national boundaries between matching bureaucratic agencies and by the common technocratic structure, the Pacific Commission. This Commission, hopefully, would have considerable autonomy to draft policy proposals, on the basis of independent research and efforts to aggregate demands elicited from interest groups in the participating states. These inputs into common policy would be supported by expertise and informal bargaining strength deriving from the implementation of decisions made by the Council of Ministers; that would be the Commission's primary responsibility, but it would be fulfilled on the basis of a substantial grant of authority rather than under restrictive subordination to that Council. The staff of the Commission would be international civil servants with secure tenure and broad irrevocable powers.

Over time, tensions will no doubt develop between the Council of Ministers and the Commission. Members of the Council of Ministers will be identified with the concerns of their national administrations, which will be influenced more by the demands of groups pressing for protectionist measures than by the interests articulated by export-oriented groups, except in the case of Japan. The senior staff of the Pacific Commission, unless appointed under severely restrictive terms, will tend to develop an integrative task orientation, directed toward trade and investment liberalization within the region and the promotion of more and more extensive policy coordination, especially in the industrial issue area. After substantial collaboration begins, for collective guidance of industrial development and progress toward trade liberalization, pressures from threatened or affected interest groups will tend to have increasing influence on the attitudes of participating governments and thus may well cause them to be more assertive and demanding as they negotiate over issues of future cooperation. The Commission's aggregating functions and its initiatives for policy co-ordination are thus likely to be viewed as obstacles to the full utilization of each government's bargaining power, in conditions that call for maximum use of that power, to compensate for disparities in the benefits resulting from market integration and trade liberalization, and to cope with difficulties resulting from the unanimity rule in the Council's decision making.   While the unanimity rule will express a common commitment to consensual decision making, it will tend to incline each national administration, especially the disadvantaged, toward negotiating tactics designed to extract high prices for cooperation.

The promoters of institutional development in the Pacific regional system will thus have to aim at the replacement of the Council of Ministers, after the initial stage of policy coordination, by an executive that will answer to a representative regional legislative body. This Pacific parliament would include directly elected and functional representatives from the member countries, and, unlike the weak parliament in the European Community, would have significant powers, to be exercized through its executive, and would share a permanent location with the Pacific Commission.

The powers of the Pacific parliament would have to be substantial enough to enable its executive to manage the regional economic community, but not too large to preclude national support for the necessary grants of authority to this regional organization. An appropriate collective choice would be difficult to negotiate, but it would certainly be desirable to give the parliament exclusive rights to control and raise revenue from the use of ocean resources in the Pacific beyond the 200-mile offshore zones; to regulate Pacific shipping and air traffic; to establish and support Pacific research institutes and universities; to sponsore collaborative planning for industrial complementarity; to institute common environmental regulations; to set external tariffs for the community, and to sponsor negotiations between member states for the eventual elimination of tariffs within the grouping.

The implementation of measures under the Pacific parliament's grant of authority would be the responsibility of the Commission, but of course it would require extensive cooperation from each member government, especially for adjustments and the further development of common policies. Some strains would be inevitable between the regional authority and most of the participating administrations, particularly because of the uneven distribution of benefits from community formation; but hopefully the leaders of the regional executive body would be able to draw increasing support from within the member states as their achievements in the promotion of common policies and the building up of the economic union became evident.

The Pacific parliament, it goes without saying, would have to be constituted in ways that would ensure workable majorities. The probability of these emerging and enduring would depend very much on the vigor of the regional economic and political groups that would be promoting collective private planning, since these groups would provide the functional representatives in the Pacific parliament, and would endeavor to build up ties between political parties in the Pacific states. Institutional arrangements to foster caucusing by the smaller Pacific states would also assist the emergence of workable majorities, although an equitable distribution of voting strength would not enable these states to dominate the assembly, if they were sufficiently united, except in cooperation with Japan or the United States. The executive would function with majority support in the parliament and hopefully would not be removable before the end of that assembly's term except through a "constructive vote of no confidence," which would place a new executive in office without delay. A provision of this kind, based on part of the West German constitution, would be a significant check on irresponsible behavior by the elected members of the parliament.

POLICY ISSUES

The major policy issues to be anticipated within a Pacific economic community will concern direct investment, trade, monetary affairs, technology transfers, and resources. The sponsors of collective private planning will have to promote a consensus on approaches to the management of these issues, and hopefully the main principles of this consensus will be written into a charter for Pacific cooperation. Many of the policy questions to be decided will be posed in ways that will oblige participating governments to distinguish between sectoral, national, and regional interests, in short- and longer-term perspectives.

The main source of issues concerning direct foreign investment is the expansionist compulsion of international firms. Their managements are impelled to spread their activities globally, and, in many cases, to diversify in order to minimize economic and political risks, gain stronger market positions, secure stable rising returns, impede actual and potential competitors, evade onerous home and host government regulation and taxes, and cover the costs of new technology that is necessary to continually increase competitive advantages. In general, expansion augments each firm's managerial, financial, information, technological, and market strengths and facilitates more efficient exploitation of new location endowments, but at some social costs. Home and host governments, as has been stressed, experience losses of economic sovereignty as national political economies are affected to increasing degrees by the production and trading decisions of international firms. Excess profits are made by such firms after acquiring monopolistic or oligopolistic market positions. Major uncertainties concerning the behavior of these firms affect government policies and the options of national firms. Severe dislocations can be caused in the industries of open economies by the trade and investment ventures of international firms seeking to penetrate new markets. Finally, the spread of direct foreign investment can so restrict the scope for local firms that serious considerations of equity are raised, in conjunction with questions of social efficiency.(21)

Many Pacific governments, with the exception of Japan, lack policy instruments for effective unilateral regulation of international firms. They resort to neomercantilist and protectionist devices that are inadequate for that purpose, but that of course impede trade and investment liberalization. A basic issue in an emerging Pacific economic union is thus likely to be the scope for sectoral penetration of the economies of the participating states by international firms based in those members, and linked with this will be the question of common regulation of the activities of such firms within their agreed areas of operation. Because of uncertainties about the effects of common measures, governments will tend to rely mainly on their own policy instruments, as has been evident in the European Community, but for the regulation and guidance of large-scale transnational production processes and trade flows that affect their economies they will need the collaboration of other Pacific states. This point has to be reiterated, so that the urgency of a comprehensive consensus on the issue will be appreciated, especially in order to forestall the proliferation of nontariff devices and neomercantilist practices in response to the uncertainties and to the intensified activities of international firms during the formative stages of a Pacific economic community.

The desired consensus would strike a functional and equitable balance between national concerns, with economic sovereignty and growth, and regional interests in the collective management of interdependencies, and, thus, in the development of conditions in which there will be orderly growth and diversification of those interdependencies. For the evolution of this consensus it would be appropriate to distinguish between research-intensive industries, service industries, and non-research-intensive industries.

In research-intensive industries, large-scale international operations are necessary to finance the development and use of new technology. These industries comprise principally machinery, precision goods, transport equipment, chemicals, rubber, and petroleum. Most of the international enterprises in these categories are specialized rather than diversified, are not oriented toward vertical integration, and are closely linked with their home governments, receiving official favors in the form of grants, loans, subsidies, and contract preferences. In a Pacific economic union all participating states will have benefits to gain if investment terms throughout the region are sufficiently liberalized to allow extensive scope for these enterprises, but of course national administrations will seek to sponsor and support their own public and private sector firms in most of these areas of industry, while limiting opportunities for foreign firms. A regional design that will represent a compromise between the two major concerns will be desirable, but its feasibility will depend on the levels of understanding and trust between Pacific governments and on their confidence in the institutions for regional cooperation. This design could be worked out on the basis of the Pacific Commission's guidance of private planning by the research-intensive industries, with emphasis on phased guidance and support of emerging firms within the smaller Pacific states and on their later exposure to competition from established firms in the larger states.

In the service industries, notably banking, insurance, construction, and engineering, very liberalized terms of investment throughout the

Pacific region seem desirable in the interests of competitiveness. Diversified firms whose activities spread across these categories and into nonservice industries outside the high technology fields, however, can establish high barriers to entry because of monopolistic or oligopolistic market positions and therefore should be subjected to restraints that would allow national firms extensive scope in non-research-intensive areas – food, primary metals, textiles and apparel, wood, paper, and furniture. To ensure that these areas will be largely reserved for national firms in each Pacific country, moreover, un-diversified international firms operating within these industries should be given only limited scope for market penetration, mergers, and acquisitions but more than that permitted for diversified international firms, especially those approaching conglomerate dimensions.

A consensus on commercial policy could be based on general acceptance of the principle of differential industrial growth, that is, with non-research-intensive industries reserved largely for national firms, service industries quite open to international firms, and research-intensive industries under mixed regimes designed to foster national firms while utilizing the capabilities of international firms. Trade liberalization in the Pacific should be substantial for research-intensive products, but moderate protectionism in non-research-intensive products should be accepted. The long-term costs of such protectionism, in terms of social efficiency, would probably be small, and it would help the smaller Pacific states to maintain acceptable levels of economic sovereignty while accepting increased inter-dependencies within the regional economic union.

Since the present patterns of foreign direct investment and external trade in the Pacific have evolved as consequences of unrelated decisions by national and international firms and governments, the resulting interdependencies lack coherence and would require extensive and gradual adjustment to fit the basic design for differential treat-ment of commercial and investment activities according to research-intensive criteria and considerations affecting the service industries. The development of a consensus about the desired degrees of openness and specialization will have to be striven for within the political and economic groups sponsoring private collective planning, but of course this consensus will need the support of national governments, and its substance will have to be adopted by the Pacific Commission.

For a consensus on monetary affairs it will be necessary to reconcile the expansionary tendencies in U.S. policy with the restraint in Japanese policy and to agree on measures for a higher U.S. growth rate, since Japan's faster pace of development must be accepted as a model if the United States is to avoid inflationary measures that are intended to compensate for or overcome slower growth. A consensus along these lines will be very difficult to promote and would have to spread very widely within the United States in order to take effect. Evasion of the problem, however, will be a fundamental source of difficulties within a Pacific economic union, as the inflationary pressures on the U.S. dollar will continue to contribute to deterioration in U.S. terms of trade, while facilitating major Japanese gains from trade and direct foreign investment.

Technology transfers to benefit the ASEAn group will be a major element in the regional policy consensus. It will be desirable to foster agreement concerning the scale, character, and financing of these transfers, and understandings on these matters will have to be linked with shared views regarding the social consequences of external aid to authoritarian modernizing regimes and the basic question of imposing forms of transnational accountability on the administrations in such states. The scale of transfers should be above the 1 percent of donor GNPs envisaged in Third World proposals for a New International Economic Order, because of the economic and strategic importance of giving the ASEAN governments inducements to accept and support the Pacific community concept and of enabling them to transform themselves rapidly into modernized members of the economic union. Most of the transfers should go into public sector infrastructure development, so as to improve the local environments for private sector growth. Direct grants by the industrialized Pacific states should be the principal method of financing the technology flows, but after the governing structure of the Pacific Community begins to receive its own revenue, especially through its controls over common ocean resources, it could become the main source of financial aid for technology imports by the ASEAN group.

Finally, agreement on national and regional resource issues, relating especially to control of the exploitation of the Pacific ocean commons by national and international firms and by regional organizations should be fostered within the general consensus. If no common understandings are reached on this area of regional policy, in line with the interests of all the participating states, the monopoly power of international firms in extractive and agricultural products will tend to become stronger, to the detriment of national firms, especially in the ASEAN group and Mexico. In addition, the larger international firms in the extractive industries will virtually dominate the use of the Pacific ocean's resources, especially through seabed mining outside areas of national jursidiction.

The types of regional issues that arise, and their magnitude, urgency, and susceptibility to resolution, will depend very much on the character and phasing of the integrative process. If this process begins with extensive collective private planning, for rationalized expansion of transnational production, research-intensive and non-research-intensive industries will be affected, as will the interests of national firms of all kinds in the smaller and less-developed Pacific states. International firms will be drawn into the initial planning on the basis of perceptions of interest within the uncertainties of incipient cartel formation and in response to regional interests only as articulated by the sponsors of the planning endeavor. There will be strong incentives for the larger firms to initiate production and market-sharing arrangements in advance of the planning process if their managements perceive that this process has some impetus and that common understandings of this kind will be advantageous in future negotiations with governments. The groups sponsoring private planning, then, may not be able to argue very persuasively for respect of the interests of national firms in the non-research-intensive industries. Hence protection of the interests of those firms and of others that are encouraged to develop in those industries may be possible only with governmental involvement, and it must be stressed that the activation of such involvement should be a major element in the integrative consensus.

Within the three highly protectionist ASEAN members, major increases in import-substituting manufacturing by international firms seem likely as consumer demand expands in these states, and would probably be stimulated by collective private planning, although the promoters of this planning would hopefully restrain this process in order to encourage export-oriented growth in those ASEAN members and preserve scope for the development of national firms in all the non-research-intensive industries. With the spread of import-substituting and export-oriented manufacturing by international firms, expansion in the service industries by other transnational enterprises is likely to follow. This, as has been suggested, should be encouraged by the regional private planners, especially because of the potential benefits to national firms in non-research-intensive industries.

The regional private planning that is envisaged would of course give impetus to the expansion of international firms into the non-research-intensive industries and the service industries of the smaller advanced Pacific states, notably Canada and Australia. The controls and guidance imposed by governments of those states would be more responsible and effective than those of the authoritarian ASEAN group, but the integrative consensus that hopefully will inspire the planning will help to strike a balance that will aid diversification in these smaller economies, while resolving issues of penetration by international firms in accordance with a coherent design for specialization.

If private cooperative planning for industrial complementarity does not evoke sufficient support, a consensus for limited and experimental trade liberalization might develop among Pacific states, as a consequence of initiatives by political and economic groups working for community formation. The most difficult issues to be resolved would concern Japan's nontariff barriers, the strong protectionism of the authoritarian ASEAN members, and the tendencies toward imbalance in U.S. foreign commerce.

Balanced reductions of nontariff barriers require extraordinary efforts in multilateral trade negotiations, and some of the barriers that ensure high rates of effective protection are societal preferences that are not negotiable.   Others, moreover, derive from interlocking interests in relationships between governments and national industries and are also not negotiable in most cases. The assortment of nontariff barriers is very formidable in Japan, as has been stressed, and it tends to limit the significance of any tariff reductions that may be accepted. The most seriously affected trading partner is the United States, and it must be emphasized that the evolution of a Japan-U.S. partnership will be essential for the operation of a Pacific economic union and will be aided by multiple accountabilities to the other members. Among these members, meanwhile, the authoritarian ASEAN members will have to be induced to lower their high protectionist barriers, in their own interests.

Private initiatives to promote trade liberalization may lead to mediatory involvement in the resolution of differences between governments. Alternatively, there may be involvement through bargaining, that is, in collaboration with interested firms and governments, in varying degrees of opposition to the preferences of other firms and governments. In either case, much will depend on the status governments accord to the private groups advocating market integration and on the capacities of those groups to aggregate the interests of administrations and enterprises, and, thus, to mediate and negotiate for the removal of trade barriers. In order to gain status and influence, the private groups may be strongly inclined toward the building of coalitions with national economic associations, firms, and governments at the cost of losing some of the credibility of professed commitments to regional concerns. Over time, this could become a serious problem. The organizational strength and bargaining power acquired by the private groups, moreover, may be difficult to preserve, as national administrations seek to increase the effectiveness of their economic policy instruments in order to cope with the effects of regional trade liberalization.

Over the long term, accordingly, the private groups should work for the establishment of a Pacific technocratic structure, sponsored by the participating governments, to contribute to the regional collaboration that will be necessary for the management of an integrated market and to provide impetus for the necessary trade liberalization. The basic need for such an organization has been indicated with reference to the role proposed for the Pacific Commission. Such an international body could develop very substantial capabilities for the promotion, support, and guidance of multilateral negotiations, with influence extending into the political processes of the member states, through informal political networks. Without the key external inputs that a common institution can provide, an ongoing multilateral negotiating process will not actualize the potential for collaboration that is evident in the orientations of participating governments toward collective choice. For reasonably productive issue processing, in integrative contexts set by planning for industrial complementarity or by trade liberalization, a regional structure with appropriate expertise, organizational strength, and capacities for socialization and interaction can draw national executives into greater rapport, wider informal accountability, and more trustful as well as broader cooperation. Of course governments will tend to assert perceived immediate and short-term interests more actively in response to inequalities in the spread of benefits from regional cooperation, but it must be stressed that their shifts away from integrative behavior can be restrained by a common institution and that a substantial grant of authority to such a body at the beginning of a scheme for regional collaboration will ensure that it has the capabilities for guiding the multilateral interaction along constructive lines after difficult redistributive issues have been posed by the initial collective choices to integrate.

REGIONAL AND WORLD ORDER

The establishment of a Pacific economic union would bring together the industrialized democracies outside the West European regional system and would link them closely with some of the more rapidly growing Third World political economies, that is, the ASEAN group and South Korea. To the extent that a sense of community developed, that equitable terms of participation were arranged, and that the increased interdependencies and dependencies were collectively managed in the general interest, a new regional order would emerge. This order would be an advance toward world order and would probably stimulate increased integrative activity within the European Community, together with a strengthening of that Community's bonds with the African states. Together, moreover, the West European and Pacific groupings would be able to interact more constructively with Third World states for the building of a New International Economic Order.

The configuration of the Pacific regional system would have certain permanent and slowly changing features. The United States and Japan would be the core members, and no other state or group of states would rival their economies in size or in volumes of trade and foreign investment. Overall, the disparities between these two economies and the others in the Pacific system would remain greater than those between the core members of the European Community and the other participants in that system. The global economic involvement of the United States and Japan, moreover, would remain greater than that of the core members of the European Community. Partly on this account, but, more important, because of cultural dissimilarities, the level of cohesion within the Pacific system would be lower than that in the European Community. Overall rates of growth in the Pacific system, however, would be higher, especially because of the dynamism of the Japanese economy and the spread of its overseas production bases.

The more changeable features of the Pacific system would be determined by competitive and integrative activity in the behavior of the member states. The economic rivalry between Japan and the United States could be moderated, and their areas of cooperation could be widened, or their competition could become more active and less restrained. Strong regional institutions, it must be stressed, would contribute to a continual growth of cooperation in this vital relationship. The dynamics of the U.S. polity, however, would be a source of uncertainty at each stage of the Pacific system's evolution. The smaller Pacific states would have incentives to strengthen their cooperation with each other, to advance common interests, if the U.S.-Japan relationship became highly collaborative, but because of a general lack of rapport most of them could be drawn individually into increasingly asymmetrical economic ties with either or both of the core members. This could also happen if the Japan-U.S. relationship became more strongly competitive, in which case the choices of those smaller states would be responses to more salient uncertainties than those that would be seen if Japan and the United States were cooperating quite actively. These alternatives, of course, strengthen the logic of incorporating into the region-building design some provisions for uniting the smaller Pacific states in a permanent coalition.

After an initial phase of general collaboration, it must be stressed, the Pacific system's evolution could be halted by protectionist and neomercantilist shifts in U.S. policy, stimulated by Japanese gains through trade and investment in the emerging economic union. While the grouping remained in a state of arrested integration, its configuration would be affected by a general lowering of levels of understanding, trust, and goodwill, and by reorientations of foreign economic policies toward the development of ties with outside states. If the Pacific system became more cohesive and produced more common benefits, however, this change in its configuration would be followed by others, including probably institutional development in the regional structures and the attraction of new members, especially from Latin America.

If the Pacific system does become sufficiently cohesive to produce substantial negotiated allocations of values, it will be in a strong position to bargain with the European Community on issues affecting their interdependencies. The member states in the European Community would probably respond by coordinating their policies more closely and might well advance toward a higher level of structural integration in order to relate more effectively to the Pacific states. In addition, the European Community members would no doubt tend to expand their links with the numerous African states that are associated with the Community under the second Lome agreement. This likely trend would be accelerated if a number of Latin American states followed Mexico's example by joining the Pacific system.

During the formative stages of the Pacific economic union, relations between its leading members and the European Community would continue to exhibit the current mix of competitive and cooperative behavior. The extensive U.S. economic interests in Western Europe and U.S. strategic concerns relating to the central balance would impose much restraint on the use of the Pacific system's bargaining power, however, and the West Europeans would have strong incentives to avoid measures that would seriously antagonize the United States or Japan. The United States, because of the breadth of its ties with Western Europe, would be well placed to promote cooperation between the two economic unions for more effective management of their vast interdependencies, as well as the dependencies linking them with the Third World.

The most urgent issues to be resolved between the Pacific and West European states concern monetary, energy, and industrial policies. The interests of the entire Trilateral grouping call for the imposition of controls on the Eurodollar market, as unrestricted lending within that market is a major source of inflationary pressures in the industrialized democracies. More fundamentally, there is a need to coordinate monetary policies across the Atlantic and the Pacific, and this need will increase as the European Monetary System becomes established. The development of a common energy policy by the West European and Pacific states, meanwhile, will be necessary to reduce inflation problems caused by high oil prices, and, over the long term, to cope with the bargaining strength of the OPEC members. The harmonizing of Pacific and West European industrial policies will be a much larger and even more basic task. With the expansion of their complex interdependencies, the economies of all the industrialized democracies have become vulnerable to the transmission of disturbances from their trading and investment partners, and the prosperity of many of their national firms has been exposed to risk by large, although not necessarily more efficient, international enterprises. The problems of industrial and related commercial and investment policy that have been identified within the Pacific context are also posed in the larger setting of Pacific-West European relations and will be more open to resolution in that broader context if there is effective engagement with them in the Pacific economic union.

Third World dependencies on the industrial states could be managed more effectively by those advanced polities as members of cooperating West European and Pacific systems for several reasons. The present lack of unity between the industrialized democracies is a source of uncertainties that oblige caution in their dealings with the modernizing states, and of course it prevents collective use of their bargaining assets to negotiate comprehensive settlements of the issues posed by Third World demands for a New International Economic Order. Cohesion within and between the West European and Pacific systems would facilitate progress toward the long-term objective of a global economic order that would fulfill Third World aspirations and over the short and middle terms would make it possible to build up expanding regional orders that would draw in developing states, on understandings concerning trade and investment according with virtually all the demands that have been voiced for a New International Economic Order. Within the Pacific economic union, trade and investment provisions of benefit to the Association of Southeast Asian Nations could be a model for the establishment of a future global economic system.

The Pacific industrialized democracies are currently operating within an international trading system that has critical weaknesses, evidenced in the widespread evasion and circumvention of GATT rules and in the cumbersome negotiations of the Tokyo Round. Overall, there is not sufficient trust and goodwill to make possible improvements in the system, but the West European states, within their economic union, are somewhat insulated against the stresses of the international trading regime and are able to cope with those stresses through collective action. Moreover, their voting strength in GATT is sufficient to block changes seen to be against their interests, although it cannot be used effectively to promote reform in the international trading regime. The United States and Japan, then, tend to further their interests through side agreements outside the GATT system but endeavor to operate principally within that system. Accordingly, the development of a regional trading order within a Pacific economic union could be viewed by the United States and Japan not only as a major advance toward the resolution of their problems as GATT members but also as a necessary step toward reconstruction of the entire international trading system and, thus, toward the removal of uncertainties and of obstruction to commerce that affect the diversification of interdependencies, and the management of interdependencies.

The international investment regime within which the Pacific industrialized democracies operate is more primitive than the GATT system. There is an assortment of uncoordinated national policies on direct foreign investment, shaped with varying degrees of reciprocity between the industrialized democracies and devised with mixes of permissiveness and regulatory intent by Third World states. Regionally, the confederal decision-making structure of the European Community is beginning to evolve a common policy for the regulation of transnational enterprises based on or operating within its member states. A detailed policy of that nature was formulated by the Andean Common Market, but has not taken effect because of disarray in that organization. At the global level, OECD is attempting to introduce a voluntary code to guide operations by multinational enterprises, and the United Nations is seeking to evolve an authoritative code of conduct for such organizations through its Commission on Transnational Corporations, which is especially sensitive to the interests of the developing countries. Because of conflicts between the aspirations of the Third World states and the wishes of the industrialized democracies, the negotiation of a UN code is very difficult, and the result is likely to be a relatively vague and nonbinding agreement.

The evolution of a regional direct foreign investment regime in the Pacific would be possible within the framework of the economic union that is being proposed in this volume and would appropriately complement the Pacific trade regime. The regional direct foreign investment regime would define the scope for expansion in the Pacific by international firms in a way that would encourage innovative collective private planning and the development of coordinated national policies. By settling most of the basic foreign investment issues of concern to national administrations and international firms, it would establish a basis for eventual world order planning on transnational enterprises. Its immediate effect, however, would be to provide a stable and dynamic context for growth within the Pacific area, and that would attract investment from outside East Asia and North America.

Altogether, the contributions which the Pacific economic union would make to world order would be very substantial. Moreover, they would not be simply economic and political: in part they would be strategic, for Japan-U.S. cooperation would be strengthened at all levels; the prospects for political as well as economic development in the ASEAN group would be enhanced, thus improving their security; and China's social and political evolution would be influenced, perhaps decisively.

The security problems of the Pacific are very great. The Soviet Union is steadily increasing its already powerful military presence in East Asia, with the cooperation of Vietnam, and is projecting its armed strength in ways that are intended to evoke accommodative tendencies in Japan and similar tendencies in China, possibly after the imposition of disruptive stress on the Peking leadership. In addition, the USSR is attempting to utilize social tensions in the authoritarian ASEAN members for the promotion of revolutionary change and is also seeking to draw the administrations of those states into favorably neutral policies that will close them to Western influences and developmental aid. For the Soviet Union, the risks attached to direct or proxy uses of limited force in Southeast Asia would be considerably lower than in areas closer to the European theatre, as this part of the Third World has only modest significance in the U.S. strategic perspective and is overshadowed by uncertainties relating to China. The feasible gains for the USSR in Southeast Asia, moreover, through the acquisition of compliant dependent states, the cultivation of friendly neutrals, and the promotion of revolutionary change, must have high salience for Moscow, because of the urgency of preempting China's opportunities in this area and of increasing the pressures on the Chinese regime from its immediate external environment.

The United States has accepted heavy responsibilities for security in the Pacific but has not built up a sufficiently extensive alliance system and has not yet developed adequate forms of economic and political cooperation to support its network of military ties. The principal remedies for this situation will have to be initiatives undertaken by the United States itself, because of its unique scope for constructive statecraft in East Asia; and the most functional approach, in the short and long terms, will be to make a large contribution to the development of the social and economic foundations of a regional community in which common policies will increasingly engage with external and internal security concerns in the context of managing interdependencies and producing vast collective benefits. Japan's vital security needs will be fulfilled in such a Pacific community, and for the members of that community Japan will be a model of economic dynamism, social cohesion, and administrative achievement, a model that hopefully will be reflected in the development of structures and of policy integration within the Pacific Community.

NOTES

(1) See T.J. Pempel, "Japanese Foreign Economic Policy: The Domestic Bases for International Behavior," in Between Power and Plenty: Foreign Economic Policies of Advanced Industrial States, ed. Peter J. Katzenstein (Madison: University of Wisconsin Press, 1978), pp. 139-

190; Taketsuguru Tsurutani, "Japan as a Postindustrial Society," in Politics and the Future of Industrial Society, ed. Leon N. Lindberg (New York: David McKay, 1976), pp. 100-125; and Robert A. Scalapino, ed., The Foreign Policy of Modern Japan (Berkeley: University of California Press, 1977).

(2) See Stephen D. Krasner, "The Tokyo Round: Particularistic Interests and Prospects for Stability in the Global Trading System," International Studies Quarterly 23, no. 4 (December 1979): 491-531; Richard H. Solomon, ed., Asian Security in the 1980s (Santa Monica: Rand Corporation, 1979); and Christopher Bertram, ed., Prospects of Soviet Power in the 1980s (London: International Institute for Strategic Studies and Mac Millan, 1980).

(3) See Charles E. Morrison and Astri Suhre, Strategies of Survival: The Foreign Policy Dilemmas of Smaller Asian States (New York: St. Martin's Press, 1978).

(4) See Herbert S. Yee, "Demaoization and Foreign Policy," The World Today 37, no. 3 (March 1981): 93-101.

(5) See Solomon, Asian Security in the 1980s; and Seweryn Bialer ed., The Domestic Context of Soviet Foreign Policy (Boulder, Colo.: Westview Press, 1981).

(6) See Lawrence B. Krause and Sueo Sekiguchi, eds., Economic Interaction in the Pacific Basin (Washington: Brookings Institution, 1980); and Leon Hollerman ed., Japan and the United States: Economic and Political Adversaries (Boulder, Colo.: Westview Press, 1980).

(7) See H.W. Arndt and Ross Garnaut, "ASEAN and the Industrialization of East Asia," Journal of Common Market Studies 17, no. 3 (March 1979): 191-212.

(8) See Solomon, Asian Security in the 1980s; and Yee, "Demaoization and Foreign Policy."

(9) See Shinkichi Eto, "Recent Developments in Sino-Japanese Relations," Asian Survey 20, no. 7 (July 1980): 726-743.

(10) See Solomon, Asian Security in the 1980s; and David D. Finley, "Conventional Arms in Soviet Foreign Policy," World Politics 33, no. 1 (October 1980): 1-35.

(11) See Lincoln P. Bloomfield, "Planning Foreign Policy: Can It Be Done?" Political Science Quarterly 93, no. 3 (Fall 1978): 369-91.

(12) See Sir John Crawford, ed., Pacific Economic Cooperation: Suggestions for Action (Singapore: Heinemann, 1981).

(13) See Bela Balassa, "Trade Creation and Diversion in the European Common Market," in European Economic Integration, ed. Bela Balassa (New York: American Elsevier, 1975), pp. 79-120.

(14) Ibid. and pp. 225-274.

(15) Ibid.

(16) Ibid; and see Don Wallace, International Regulation of Multinational Corporations (New York: Praeger, 1976); Thomas G. Parry, The Multinational Enterprise (Greenwich, Conn.: JAI Press, 1980); and Gerard Curzon and Victoria Curzon, eds. The Multinational Enterprise in a Hostile World (London: Macmillan, 1977).

(17) See Paul Taylor, "Confederalism: The Case of the European Communities," in International Organization: A Conceptual Approach, (London: Frances Pinter, 1978); and "Interdependence and Autonomy in the European Communities: The Case of the European Monetary System," Journal of Common Market Studies 18, no. 4 (June 1980): 370-387.

(18) See Helen Wallace et al., Policy Making in the European Communities (New York: Wiley, 1977).

(19) See Jack N. Behrman, "Multinational Enterprises as a New Form of International Industrial Integration," in The New Economic Nationalism, ed. Otto Hieronymi (New York: Praeger, 1980), pp. 185-200; Bernard Mennis and Karl P. Sauvant, Emerging Forms of Transnational Community (Lexington, Mass.: D.C. Heath, 1976); and Bertil Ohlin, Per-Ove Hesselborn, and Per Magnus Wijkman, eds., The International Allocation of Economic Activity (New York: Holmes and Meier, 1977).

(20) Anant R. Negandhi, ed., Functioning of the Multinational Corporation: A Global Comparative Study (Elmsford, N.Y.: Pergamon Press, 1980).

(21) Ibid.; see also Sauvant, Emerging Forms of Transnational Community; and Curzon and Curzon, The Multinational Enterprise in a Hostile World.

Index

ASEAN, 3-5, 7-9, 11-14, 36,
    40, 44, 47-50, 53,
    79-100, 245
  communications, 95
  decision making, 92-95
  industrial comple-
      mentarity, 96
  institutions, 92
  political economies,
      80-83
  prospects, 98
  regional policies, 86-95
  relations with Japan,
      86, 96, 241, 255
  relations with USA, 97,
      242, 255
  societies, 79, 84
Asian Development Bank, 67
Australia, 5, 53, 64, 68,
    107, 109, 113, 135,
    247

Burma, 20

Canada, 5, 8, 131, 145-147,
    151, 163-183, 237,
    247
  Pacific trade, 175, 242
China, 7, 9, 17, 19-27,
    32-36, 39-49, 105
  foreign trade, 36
  political economy, 32

China (Cont.)
  prospects, 238
  regional diplomacy, 44
  relations with Japan, 44
  relations with USA, 45,
      243

East Asia, 17-52
European Community, 1, 2,
    5, 6, 250, 251, 259,
    271

GATT, 155, 272

Indonesia, 7, 23, 24
  foreign investment, 34
  foreign trade, 33, 34,
      80, 91
  political economy, 28, 80,
      81
  prospects, 237
  regional diplomacy, 40,
      84, 88
  relations with Japan, 88
  security issues, 47
  society, 81
Interdependencies, 103-142,
    153-156, 254
International firms, 20, 24,
    41, 144, 146, 250, 251,
    256-259
  regulation, 253, 264

Japan, 1-14, 17-27, 33,
        37-50
    business groups, 64
    culture, 56
    foreign aid, 68
    foreign trade, 48, 60-63,
        116-127
    Komeito, 26
    Liberal Democratic Party,
        26, 38, 55, 64
    Ministry of International
        Trade and Industry,
        59, 64
    policy planning, 246
    political economy, 25, 54,
        55
    prospects, 236
    regional diplomacy, 38, 57,
        63, 66-71
    relations
        with ASEAN, 59, 60, 65,
            67, 241
        with China, 58
        with East Asia, 19, 20,
            38, 48, 50, 53-74
        with USA, 19, 20, 37,
            49, 70, 72, 74,
            116-127, 240,
            266, 270
        with USSR, 58, 70, 133
    security issues, 71
    Socialist Party, 26

Malaysia, 22, 23
    foreign trade, 34
    political economy, 27, 83
    prospects, 237
    regional diplomacy, 41,
        84, 85, 87
    security issues, 47
Mexico, 5, 8, 129-131, 146,
        148, 149, 152
    agriculture, 194-196
    fishing rights, 219-221
    foreign debt, 193, 194
    foreign investment,
        216-219
    foreign policy, 202-208
    foreign trade, 193, 209

Mexico (Cont.)
    history, 186-189
    immigration issue,
        213-216
    inflation, 193
    oil industry, 191, 210
    policy planning, 247
    political economy,
        190-202
    prospects, 222, 237
    relations
        with Canada, 207, 212
        with Cuba, 208
        with Japan, 206, 212
        with Latin America,
            205, 208
        with Third World, 204
        with USA, 203, 204,
            209-211, 242
    society, 189, 190
    water resources, 221, 222

New International Economic
        Order, 7, 204, 270-274
North America, 8, 143-161
    configuration, 144-147
    political economies,
        149-153
    prospects, 159, 160
    regional interaction,
        153-159
    societies, 147-149
North Korea, 24, 32

OPEC, 7, 204

Pacific Basin Economic Coun-
        cil, 64, 248
Pacific Commission, 260
Pacific Community concept,
        68, 110-115, 164-167,
        248, 256, 261, 264, 270
Pacific Council of Ministers,
        262
Pacific interdependencies,
        4-6, 103-136
Pacific investments, 3, 127-129,
        264, 273
Pacific parliament, 263

Pacific security issues, 274
Pacific trade, 2, 3, 115, 116
Philippines, 23, 24
    foreign trade, 80, 91
    political economy, 29, 81,
        82
    prospects, 237
    regional diplomacy, 41, 84,
        88
    security issues, 30, 47

Regional cooperation, 3-6,
    11-15
Research intensive industries,
    265
Resource issues, 267

Service industries, 265
Singapore, 24
    political economy, 27
    prospects, 237
    regional diplomacy, 87
South Korea, 5, 22, 40
    foreign trade, 35
    political economy, 31

Taiwan, 20, 22
    foreign trade, 35
    political economy, 31
Technology transfers, 267
Thailand, 22, 24
    foreign trade, 34, 80, 91
    political economy, 28,
        80, 81
    prospects, 237

Thailand (Cont.)
    regional diplomacy, 40, 84,
        85, 88
    security issues, 46, 89
    society
Trade creation, 250
Trade liberalization, 251, 252

United States, 1-5, 143-161
    policy planning, 246
    political economy, 145, 147,
        149
    prospects, 236
    relations
        with Canada, 144, 152-156,
            159, 168-172
        with China, 10, 45, 243
        with East Asia, 18, 19,
            42-44, 90, 107, 173
        with European Community,
            6, 165, 173, 271
        with Japan, 19, 20, 37,
            49, 70, 72, 74,
            116-127, 240, 266,
            270
        with Mexico, 144, 156-159,
            203, 204, 209-211,
            242
        with USSR, 11, 42, 45, 46,
            49, 244
USSR, 7, 11, 19, 36, 45, 131-134,
    239, 244

Vietnam, 24, 90, 94, 98, 238

About the Contributors

GAVIN BOYD is Professor of Political Science at Saint Mary's University, Halifax, Nova Scotia, Canada, and a consultant to the Canadian Defense Department. In 1980-81 he was a visiting research professor at the Center for Asian Studies, Arizona State University, Tempe, Arizona. He edited, with Charles Pentland, Issues in Global Politics (1981), with Werner Feld, Comparative Regional Systems (1980), with James N. Rosenau and Kenneth Thompson, World Politics (1976), and with the late Wayne Wilcox and Leo Rose, Asia and the International System (1972). He authored Communist China's Foreign Policy (1962) and has contributed chapters to several recent works on international relations.

CHARLES F. DORAN is Chairman, Canadian Studies Program, School of Advanced International Studies, The Johns Hopkins University, Washington, D.C. He authored The Politics of Assimilation: Hegemony and its Aftermath (1971) and Myth, Oil and Politics (1977) and has published numerous articles on international politics.

YALE FERGUSON is Professor of Political Science, Neward College of Arts and Sciences, Rutgers, The State University of New Jersey, Newark. He was a contributing editor of the State Department Handbook on Latin American Studies (1980), co-authored The Web of World Politics: Nonstate Actors in the Global System (1976) and edited, with Walter F. Weiker, Continuing Issues in International Politics (1972). He also edited Contemporary Inter-American Relations (1971).

SUEO SEKIGUCHI is Professor of Economics at Osaka University, Japan, and an Associate of the Japan Economic Research Center. He edited, with Lawrence B. Krause, Economic Interaction in the Pacific Basin (1980) and has written numerous papers on Japan's foreign economic relations.

281

MARTIN H. SOURS is Professor of International Studies, American Graduate School of International Management, Glendale, Arizona. He has authored numerous articles on Asia and the Pacific.